Positive Reviews from R[...]
The Way of The Mile High Maverick

"If you want insight into what the top 1% are doing and thinking, get the book. It represents the 'cutting edge' of successful martial arts business systems along with the various perspectives, attitudes and techniques that support those systems. The information applies to ALL styles of martial art.

"I personally enjoy and agree with Mr. Oliver's perspectives concerning the huge negative influence that modern sport MMA can have on proper martial art training (and the success of your school). MMA instructors should heed his advice, but for many it will require a significant paradigm shift toward doing what is best for your students, your competition team, and your community. That is the 'gateless gate' that many MMA instructors will fail to pass, resulting in failure to achieve the full potential of proper MMA training for your students and community. Get the book, avoid these common mistakes, and reach your full potential!"

MASTER INSTRUCTOR DAVID ARNEBECK
OVER 40 YEARS MIXED MARTIAL ARTS
EXPERIENCE; OVER 30 YEARS TEACHING
EXPERIENCE; FOUNDER: WARRIOR'S COVE
MARTIAL ART CENTERS; FOUNDER &
MASTER INSTRUCTOR: SHINBUDO MMA
SYSTEM; RICKSON GRACIE BLACK BELT:
BRAZILIAN JIU JITSU; OFFICIAL RICKSON
GRACIE INSTRUCTOR: BRAZILIAN JIU JITSU

"As someone who grew up in Mile High Karate and had the opportunity to know Stephen Oliver as both an instructor, employer, business owner, and mentor I can tell you first hand he knows what he is talking about. In my 25 years as a part of the Mile High Karate organization, I have experienced first hand the dramatic affects of what Stephen Oliver's business models can do

for new schools, and established schools alike. I have seen him walk into schools with 20 students and within weeks have the school flooded with hundreds of new students.

One of the things I appreciate most about Grandmaster Oliver, is his fresh but historical perspective on the martial arts industry as a whole. He has captured that perspective, along with a blast of sometimes brutal honesty in his new book *The Way Of The Mile High Maverick*. Every chapter has insights and benefits that will help both novice and experienced school owners alike. I would highly recommend this book to anyone and everyone in the martial arts industry looking to move to the next level.

KOREY AND SARA STITES
PERSONAL ACHIEVEMENT
MARTIAL ARTS
WHEAT RIDGE, CO

"The strategies that Stephen shares and at times 'pounds in' will resonate well for both martial arts school owners and entrepreneurs alike. *The Way of Mile High Maverick* is a playbook for those not only looking to improve not only their bottom line, but the concepts he stresses will successfully take any business to the next level."

DON SOUTHERTON, CEO
BRIDGING CULTURE WORLDWIDE
AND AUTHOR

"Stephen Oliver is the hidden genius behind some of the largest MMA, Traditional Martial Arts Schools, even transported after-school care schools in the world. He's become the 'go-to' consultant for the very top tier to take them to the next level of profitability while showing them how to improve their life-style in the process. I've known him for over 10 years and have seen him in action. He's the 'Real Deal' — straightforward, at times even brutally so.

I'd highly recommend his latest book: *The Way of The Mile High Maverick* as a rare peak behind the curtain to help you jump your school into the top 10% or, even 1% of the Martial Arts Industry. I promise you this book will shave years off your learning curve!"

Lee Milteer
Author of *Success Is An Inside Job*;
Millionaire Smarts Coach
www.milteer.com

"I HATE, HATE, HATE it … when one of my competitors produces an incredible resource. I read Master Oliver's *The Way of the Mile High Maverick* and was blown away by his content, insight and 'just tell it how it is' style, complete with facts and figures. This is an absolute MUST read for EVERY Martial Arts School owner out there. I hate to admit it but it is GREAT! Get and read this book NOW!

Congratulations to Master Oliver on a great job very well done!"

Leigh Childs
The MA Success Guy

"I just read Stephen's new book, *The Way of The Mile High Maverick*. Great book! It is written for Martial Artists, but it is a great resource for anyone.

For Martial Artists, I especially liked the sections talking about ethics and "walking the walk." For everyone, I liked the chapter "The 10 Secrets of Leadership."

There are tons of valuable strategies for the old timers and for those who are new to Martial Arts. If you are thinking about opening a Martial Arts school or if you have been around for years, this is a must for you. As it mentions in "Mile High Maverick," NEVER stop learning.

One last point: 'Why reinvent the wheel?' Get the book and take advantage of those who have years of experience in business and are willing to share it with others."

Pat Worley
USA Karate, Inc.
Minneapolis-St. Paul

"I've known Stephen Oliver for over 40 years. It's amazing to have watched his growth in our industry. He's now the 'Go To' expert for all of the veterans like myself who would have thought there might not be anything left to learn as well as the 'Young Guns' who are in the top 1%, or top 5% of school owners. He's the guy who stays at the 'Leading Edge' of what's REALLY working today — and, I guarantee you he'll be the first to use and share each of the new tools that come available.

If you are successful in our industry you're probably already working with him, if not you should be. If you are planning on 'making your mark' in Martial Arts, Stephen's the only Business Consultant to get you into the very top rungs!

Grandmaster Jeff Smith

"When people ask me how to advance, I always give the same suggestion: 'Find someone who has mastered what you want to do, and then find a way to learn their secrets.' You believe you have the ability to teach good martial arts well, and you believe you have the duty to prosper to where you live with dignity and the financial power to permit your family to follow their dreams too? Find a master who has done what you dream of doing and learn the tested secrets.

"My friend Stephen Oliver is one such master who has invested years to build and test his program for creating martial arts school success. Get his book and study it, and pay attention to any ideas that cause you to balk or resist; that is where you need to upgrade your thinking to get bigger better results. Stephen Oliver shares lots of good secrets and guides you through the confusion to help you build success."

STEPHEN K. HAYES
BLACK BELT HALL OF FAME
FOUNDER, TO-SHIN DO NINJA
MARTIAL ARTS
AUTHOR OF 20 BOOKS ON MARTIAL AND
MEDITATION TRADITIONS OF JAPAN
WWW.STEPHENKHAYES.COM

"OK, I am blown away with the content of your book. There is so much. I need to study all of it! God Bless You and Thank You. I do not think there is another publication out there that can come close to your book!"

KEITH JOSEPH BENNETT

"Just finished Steve's new book. Must read for everyone in the martial arts biz. Jump to the chapter on leadership first then go back and read the rest. Fast read worth the time spent. Many hidden ideas inside. Take notes while you read."

MASTER BILL CLARK

"Stephen Oliver is the 'Maverick of Martial Arts'. His book is inspirational!"

JOHN CHUNG

"If you play a professional martial arts instructor and are fed up with playing and you are ready to take your school to the next level, there is no other choice but the one. If you do not know who the one is that's OK. Read his book *The Way of The Mile High Maverick* and you too will be the 1.... The top 1% that is. I have lingered in the lower 90% for six years thinking I knew the answer; After all, I am a great instructor. Thanks to Master Stephen Oliver I learned that you can be the best instructor in the world but that does not mean you will be a great school owner. Bottom line: With this man's expertise and help, along with this amazing book, I know I am we'll on my way to joining him in the top 1%. Will you join me? Worth it's weight in gold!

ADAM DISTEFANO

"Stephen Oliver has set the standard in true Martial Artist professionalism. I have known Mr. Oliver for three decades and he had my attention when he produced a national tournament, the Mile High NASKA event, but it was behind the scenes that really impress me. His organizational skills are the standards for some in the industry, he is my friend and fellow martial artist who will be continually be in the eyes of the martial arts community for progressive progress in the business world of martial arts. He is what we say at the Museum: 'a Professional Maximizer.'"

PROFESSOR GARY LEE, 9TH-DAN
FOUNDER, NATIONAL SPORT KARATE
MUSEUM

"History allows us to take a step back and evaluate the impact of those before us. It opens our eyes to disappointments but it also reveals pathways to success. The martial arts has a unique history going back to its Asian roots and extending itself to the rest of the world. As it spread across the country, it has changed, recreated itself many times and continues to evolve; and such is the case for today's martial arts schools.

Gone are the days of just putting a flier on a car window, today we have the Internet, social media and a variety of ways to bring awareness to our location. Stephen Oliver is not only a man who has had his share of battles, but has proven to overcome all obstacles and establish one of the most successful martial arts industries today.

In an effort to share his methodology of building a more successful martial arts school environment, he has created a more comprehensive approach at bringing the modern day school owner into this new era of social media. In this new book, he provides a unique way of examining our own history and taking our passion into a more rewarding and even profitable industry. Training has changed and so should operating a school. I found this book to be very encouraging.

It is not a how-to book, but a book on philosophy and reshaping our mindset to make a successful living on something we love. Stephen doesn't hold back, he says it like it is, and if you can keep an open mind and not get offended, he provides a series of concepts that will have an immediate and direct effect on school enrollment, a more improved working environment and a pathway to running a more successful school.

> MICHAEL MATSUDA
> PRESIDENT,
> MARTIAL ARTS HISTORY MUSEUM

"Thank you for allowing me an advance look at your latest book. I simply couldn't put it down, and although I have followed the teachings of the "Mile High Maverick" for 8 years now, this book will be read and re-read as are your other publications. Your absolute clarity and clear road map to success have seen the quality of our students ,the standard of our Martial Arts and my families financial security take massive leaps forward.

Having previously been at the top of the industry in New Zealand, I traveled to the USA in 2006 looking for the next step as a Martial Artist and as a businessman.

With my oldest daughter in my school and three more about to start I knew I had to find the best I could for them. Attending a NAPMA Extreme Success event, I learned more about teaching and running a school in two days than I had in the previous twenty years — and I had tried many avenues.

Sneaking into a presentation with you and Grandmaster Smith on the Mile High Karate system during a lunch break, I found you were taking schools outside of TKD and outside the USA. I was the first hand up in the room. I couldn't believe here was the opportunity to go straight to the top of the Industry.

I have since brought my own Instructor into MHK in what is the true full circle we often speak of in the arts. Any Martial Artist who wants to improve their impact in their community — dramatically improve the quality of their instruction to create a prosperous and secure financial future for themselves and their families — must get connected with you either via your books, NAPMA or though Mile High Karate.

Your knowledge is universal as evidenced by our success in New Zealand, obviously a long way from the States. Again thank you for your contribution to Martial Arts.

No one know where a teachers influence ends."

> SIFU GRANT BUCHANAN
> 6TH-DEGREE BLACK BELT KEMPO
> MILE HIGH KARATE TAURANGA
> NEW ZEALAND

"Master Stephen Oliver is without a doubt one of the martial arts industry leaders in combining martial arts training with tried and true business skills. This book is a must in recommended reading for anyone considering opening up a martial arts school!"

> MASTER KAREN EDEN

"Ignorance is not bliss, it's torture. I didn't know what I didn't know, once I read this book — *The Way of the Mile High Maverick* — I realized how deep the rabbit hole goes. This book is the tipping point from mediocrity to excellence in Martial Arts business management, comprehensive, thorough and to the point. Beware, a read through means you can no longer use the excuse, 'I didn't know.'"

> PETER JOHNSON
> NAPMA PEAK PERFORMER
> ELITE BILLY BLANKS TAEBO INSTRUCTOR
> ULTIMATE BLACK BELT GRADUATE TEAM

The Way of the Mile High Maverick

By Stephen Oliver
8th-Degree Black Belt, MBA

About the Author

Stephen Oliver
8th-Degree Black Belt
CEO, NAPMA

Stephen Oliver began martial arts training in 1969 in Tulsa, Oklahoma, at a branch school of the Jhoon Rhee Institute. He opened his first school in 1975. He later moved to Washington, D.C. to work for the Jhoon Rhee Institute, first as an instructor, and later as their youngest-ever branch manager, while earning an honor's degree in Economics at Georgetown University.

In 1983, he moved to the Denver metropolitan area, and opened five schools in 18 months with only $10,000 in capital. He went on to promote the Mile High Karate Classic NASKA World tour event and serve on NASKA's Board of Directors from 1989-1999, and on EFC's Board of Directors from inception until 2002.

In 1992 he earned his Master's in Business Administration (MBA) from the University of Denver, and went on to serve on their Venture and Entrepreneurship Advisory Board. He has also written several other books including: *How to Market Your Martial Arts School Using the Internet* and *Direct Response Marketing for Martial Arts Schools.* He has been actively involved in NAPMA since before its inception, and has been an on-going and active contributor and speaker.

Currently, he is CEO of the National Association of Professional Martial Artists (NAPMA), and Martial Arts Professional Magazine (www.MartialArtsProfessional.com). He continues to focus on his Mile High Karate schools, which has "Regional Developers" in place throughout the world, and is the leading, and fastest-growing, professional Martial Arts School Franchise system (www.MileHighFranchise.com), with locations worldwide. In the Denver area, he has nine locations, and continues to speak to and write for martial arts school operators throughout the world, as well as consult for a very select team of school owners.

He is currently an 8th-Degree Black Belt in American Tae Kwon Do, and oversees an organization that teaches a diverse range of martial arts styles.

"The Way of the Mile High Maverick"
By Stephen Oliver, MBA
8th-Degree Black Belt
CEO, National Association of Professional Martial Artists
CEO, Martial Arts Professional Magazine
CEO/Founder, Mile High Karate
1767 Denver West Blvd., Suite A, Golden, CO 80401

ISBN ISBN-13: 978-1492357360 | ISBN-10: 1492357367

© Copyright 2009-2013 Stephen Oliver. All Rights Reserved. May not be distributed through any means without explicit permission from the copyright holder.

Contents

Preface

Many of the chapters of this book are from confidential high-level letters to my Inner Circle coaching members, or from newsletters sent only to "Maximum Impact" members, or rarely, internal correspondence to my Mile High Karate franchise owners or staff. Therefore some will have dated references or references to events happening at the time that the memo, letter or newsletter was written. They have been included because the philosophy behind the conversation is "evergreen" and important for you as a school owner.

September 2013

Stephen Oliver, Evergreen, Colorado.

I know what you may be thinking:

Who Is Stephen Oliver and Why Should I Listen To Him?

Stephen Oliver
8th-Degree Black Belt
CEO, NAPMA

Gee, in our industry it seems like everyone has popped up to offer advice. How do you tell fact from fantasy? Value from fraud? Unfortunately in the Martial Arts School industry most of the really successful people are spending their time growing their staff, students, martial arts schools, and especially their net profit not sharing their secrets with you. I am different from most of those sharing information in a variety of VERY important ways that are important to you and will help you dramatically grow your school and, your income!

Many of the "gurus" in our industry fall into one of the following categories:

1. Never been there — never done that.

That's right, there's a BUNCH of people trying to sell you advice who have never sat where you sit and dealt with the problems and opportunities that you face every day in your karate school. They often are excellent speakers and persuasive purveyors of their own products, programs or subscriptions, but really never did it themselves. Their ideas are unproven. Their perspective limited to that of an outsider.

How am I different?

Well, I opened my first school in 1975. And, I have been continuously operating my Mile High Karate schools in Denver since 1983. I currently have successful locations throughout North America, Australia, New Zealand , United Kingdom and the world. I've operated a large

multi-martial arts school operation. Have taught thousands of martial arts students and run every aspect of a school.

2. Not even a martial artist!

Believe it or not, there are "experts" in the martial arts business who aren't even a martial artist. They don't understand the training, mindset, and love for the martial arts that we share—then dare to tell real martial artists how to run a school teaching real martial arts skills and curriculum.

How am I different?

I began studying martial arts in 1969. Trained in Tae Kwon Do with the Jhoon Rhee Institute along side the likes of World Champions Jeff Smith, John Chung, Charlie Lee, and the most awesome stable of kickboxers ever assembled. More recently, I was promoted to 8th-Degree Black Belt by Grandmaster Jeff Smith.

3. Have only run a school in their memory.

Some of those who consult or give expert opinions only run a martial arts school in their memory — in some case distant memory. Some of those recollections seem more like a distant dream (or, in some cases vivid nightmare!). Many of these people operated in very different circumstances and times.

How am I different.

I am still totally immersed in the daily operations of martial arts schools — up to doing 527 enrollment conferences in the past three years

---

personally — nose-to-nose, belly-to-belly. Every Monday and Friday I meet with and train our school managers and instructors — and, solve the everyday problems that you face in the real world (albeit at possibly a higher volume).

4. Never ran a successful school.

Even those advice givers who really are Black Belts and run, or have run schools — usually never ran a particularly successful operation. Many got into offering advice about running a school since they really couldn't figure out how to make much of a living running schools.

How am I different?

Right now, many Mile High Karate schools will do well over $500,000.00 in gross revenues (in some cases much more). I broke the $1,000,000.00 a year barrier way back in 1985, and continue to operate a hugely successful operation. I've made a six-figure-plus personal income for over 30 years strictly from schools.

5. "Flash in the Pan"

Often this comes in the guise of "gee, I just started figuring this stuff out and had a great year last year. What if you pay me to tell you about my short-term successes. I did $ (pick a number $100,000 net, $400,000 gross, etc., etc.), will do more this year, and would love to show you how I did it."

How I am different?

Well, I've already covered this for you, but let's just say that there are many people who have a good year of two. Let's see if they can weather the ups and downs of our industry, and, boom years and recession. I only trust those who have weathered some internal and/or external crisis and gotten back or stayed on top. Don't trust the unproven, untested enthusiastic newcomer.

6. Personality driven: NOT Duplicate-able.

I think we'd both be able to draw upon a few examples of Magnetic Personalities whose per-

sonal success is exciting, but really not something that could EVER be replicated in your operation.

How am I different?

I've run a large school operation since 1983. In that time nearly 100% of our teaching, marketing, and sales were accomplished by employees (or now, partners) who had to implement my systems. They are not dependent upon charisma or unstoppable energy. I have spent years studying operations and marketing, including formally achieving a Master's in Business Administration, that included having a literal bevy of MBA's and Ph.D.'s analyze the martial arts school business to help me create powerful duplicatable systems for school operations.

7. Have lost touch with what works in the 21st century.

Unfortunately the industry is full of dinosaurs and leaders of the past, whose time has long since passed, but whose friends and associates are unwilling to say "the emperor has no clothes." Systems that may have been revolutionary in 1970 or 1980 (even 1990 and beyond) may be out of date or just plain insufficient in the current environment.

How am I different?

In a variety of ways I continue to explore the "leading edge" of new technologies, teaching techniques, marketing strategies, and technological enhancements. I explore the latest approaches not only through my own school implementation but through an unmatched "master-mind" team of industry leaders that I network with and share ideas with constantly.

I will only share with you ideas and system that have been PROVEN to work through extensive testing in the real world of daily school operations. And, no short-term "fixes," only long-term success strategies. No ideas that look interesting, but really have never been tried. I may occasionally offend, but will promise to tell you the way it is — no editing or ulterior motives.

Stephen Oliver, MBA
8th-Degree Black Belt
CEO NAPMA (National Association of Professional Martial Artists)

Consultation Certificate

**This Certificate Entitles the Bearer to a Personal
1-on-1 Martial Arts School Business Analysis
With a NAPMA-Certified Business Analyst.
This Individual Consultation is Valued at $495.00.**

Certificate expires 12 months from the date of purchase.
To schedule your personal business analysis, complete this form and fax to NAPMA at
1-800-795-0853; mail to 1767 Denver West Blvd., Suite A, Golden, CO 80401;
or visit www.PrivateCoachingSession.com

PLEASE FILL OUT COMPLETELY AND WRITE LEGIBLY

Name _____

School Name _____

Address _____

City _____ State/Province _____

Zip _____ Country _____

Phone _____ Fax _____

E-Mail _____

_____
Authorized by Toby Milroy
Chief Operating Officer, NAPMA

3 FREE GIFTS FOR SERIOUS SCHOOL OWNERS

FREE Personal School Evaluation	**FREE Two 90-Minute Seminars**	**FREE CD-DVD Package and Report**
Two 30-minute Sessions A sure-fire way action plan to double your results or better.	with **"The Millionaire Maker Grandmaster Stephen Oliver** "The 5 Stupid Mistakes All Too Many School Owners Make that Kill Their Growth" and "The Key Step-by-Step Blueprint for Being a Big Winner"	**"How Hundreds of Smart School Owners Like You Doubled Their Revenue in the Last 12 Months** Even in the Midst of the Greatest Recession since the Great Depresson, and How You Can, Too!"

It's Your Choice: Abundance or Lack of Abundance

Once again, I talked to 10 school owners this week from throughout the United States. Several lamented the economy, stated that they just aren't great businesspeople and how it's impossible to convince parents or adult students to pay or commit in the current economy. I remember one conversation, scheduled for 20 minutes, but the first 10 minutes were spent listening to a very articulate explanation of why it is just impossible for anyone — "but someone like me" — to make a living in the current economic climate.

During the same day, several others told me about how they are hitting all-time records. It's interesting how that works.

One school owner said that during November and December, he was in the middle of an emotional meltdown — in a panic about a cratering school and numbers. Blaming the economy! That same school owner did $45,000 during April, which, for him, is in record territory — and he is making continuing improvements.

Tony Robbins, on a few of his CDs and during his appearances, talks about "my delusion." What he means is that, in many cases, you can choose a belief system about a set of circumstances that either supports your success or your failure. Objectively, it's possible that neither is true. If you had the choice of a helpful belief or one that harms you ... then, which would you choose?

For instance:

You can believe that we are in a marvelously recession-proof industry. You can think it's exciting that people look to fitness and exercise as an opportunity to feel better and learn confidence and focus, when there's an overall downturn. There's plenty of empirical evidence to support that belief, by the way. During a recession, the movie industry thrives (distraction/entertainment) as well as fitness centers (and liquor stores for that matter). Alternately, you can believe that no one is willing to pay for martial arts lessons and it's a great time to "throw in the towel" or just accept a downturn in your income.

Let me ask you a question — which belief is more likely to lead to YOUR success: Abundance or lack of abundance?

I'll tell you factually that LOTS of schools are thriving this year. School owners and staff members may be working harder. They certainly are working smarter; but their incomes are improving and their enrollments are up.

One of our Mile High Karate schools enrolled 15 new students during the first week and a half of May. Another did 17 during the first two weeks. Another generated 200 leads and 65 appointments for introductory conferences from just one event during the first week of May, while another generated 25 intros during the first week of May.

There's plenty of opportunity in the current economy. Possibly more opportunity than ever. Anyway, I'll guarantee that you'll get what you expect and see what you believe.

I'm Looking Over Your Shoulder

Now, before I move on, I'll remind you of a few recommendations that I gave you during January — have you taken action yet?

First Priority: ALL possible Internal Activities and Events to create REFERRALS and Family Add-Ons

These include all of the many internal promotional campaigns and materials (including customizable artwork) that NAPMA.com provides you each month. You've received a wealth of information in recent Tool Kits to hold many summer lead-generating and retention events.

So, REFOCUS on and MASTER Referrals:

1. READ one of the books I recommended (Bob Burg's, for instance).
2. SCHEDULE many Birthday Parties.
3. SEND invitations to all friends of students for EVERY Belt Graduation.
4. SCHEDULE crazy internal events, regularly — pump it up now. For example, July is Anti-Boredom Month and includes Cousins Day, while the third week of August is Friendship Week. There are many Web sites with more choices and information. All designed to pull more prospects into your school.

Second Priority: Hit ALL of the Grassroots Opportunities

1. Elementary schools (Show & Tell, Foreign Heritage Day, Career Day, Street Safe Class, summer/fall carnivals/fairs, silent auctions, etc.)
2. Every church, recreation center, community group and day care.
3. Every Boy Scout and Girl Scout function.
4. Every mall show.
5. Every kids' fair, fitness fair, etc.
6. Every community Expo, fair, carnival, flea market, etc.

Third Priority: A Starting Point to MASTER Referrals

The following books about creating referrals are listed at Amazon.com.

1. *Endless Referrals*, *Third Edition* by Bob Burg

(Paperback; Oct. 25, 2005).
2. *Get More Referrals Now!* by Bill Cates (Paperback; Mar 19, 2004).
3. *The Go-Giver: A Little Story About a Powerful Business Idea* by Bob Burg and John David Mann (Hardcover; Dec. 27, 2007).
4. *The Referral of a Lifetime: The Networking System That Produces Bottom-Line Results Every Day* (The Ken Blanchard Series) by Tim Templeton, Ken Blanchard, and Lynda Rutledge Stephenson (Paperback; Jan. 1, 2005).
5. *Don't Keep Me A Secret: Proven Tactics to Get Referrals and Introductions* by Bill Cates (Paperback; Aug. 27, 2007).

Another Reminder: Back to Basics

What gets measured gets done. Are you keeping accurate stats of your school's performance? Are you focusing on exactly what's happening and benchmarking with other successful school owners? Peak Performers and Inner Circle members benchmark with each other, constantly.

The NAPMA members' Web site includes complete Statistics Reports for your use. Make sure you are keeping accurate numbers. Toby Milroy and I have spoken to several schools, hoping to help them, only to find that they had no idea what was happening at their schools. You must have accurate accounting records (Profit and Loss Statements, Balance Sheets, etc.) and accurate operating stats every week, month, quarter and year to know exactly how your school and staff are performing.

1. Set Goals.
2. Know your Numbers.
3. Start with the Right People.
4. Develop a proper Staff Structure.
5. Create a Work-Hard, High-Energy Culture.
6. Ultimately, it's about marketing and selling every day.

7. Keep your "Mission" in mind and what you are trying to accomplish.
8. No whiners. "Winners Remember Results, Losers Remember Reasons."

#1: You must have a high target or goal for a mid-range objective, i.e., what are the Gross Revenue, Active Count and Net Profit levels you want to achieve by the end of the year? What must you accomplish TODAY, this week and this month to be on track to reach those goals? Every month, set high, but achievable, targets for Enrollments, Renewals, New Monthly Payments and Cash-at-School. Make sure everyone knows what they must accomplish EVERY Day to be on track.

DAILY TARGET =
TARGET ENROLLMENTS DIVIDED BY BUSINESS DAYS

#2: Measure and Track Everything. Keep several key measures in your head (and in all of your staff members' heads) every day. Focus regularly on improving service, decreasing your dropout rate, improving renewals and expanding your student body. If you don't track your numbers and your ratios, then it's impossible to make an informed judgment of how to fix your results.

#3: Start with the right people. "You can't teach a pig to sing; it wastes your time and irritates the pig." It's important to hire the HIGHEST quality people that you can find and create an environment where they can equal or exceed their other career/income opportunities. Choose staff members, not based on athletic talent, but on intelligence, drive, charisma and the ability to accomplish your and their goals. If you must supervise full-time people too much, then you have the wrong people. For part-timers and leadership volunteers, it's okay to supervise (and you must) every 15 minutes.

EVERYONE on your staff must look, act and be the role model that we are looking to develop in our students. The reason for enforcing hairstyles, cleanliness, proper uniforms, etc. is to control and help to manage this Product-of-the-Product necessity.

#4: The right staff structure. It's imperative to have two high quality people at any school. One of them is the owner-operator, if the owner-operator is 100% focused on the results of the business. Neither of them can be a full-time college student or high school student nor working a second job. It's imperative to have a full-time quality person focused on teaching classes effectively (and 75% of students renewing on time, 3% or less monthly dropouts, family add-ons, referrals AND external community marketing events). It's also important to have a full-time person focused on student service, intros, enrollments, renewals AND internal and external marketing activities. Neither of these people can be teenagers. Neither can have an additional career. Neither can be college nor high school students.

#5: Don't create a culture of clock-watchers. If someone starts complaining about working Saturday, or working too hard … then they are the wrong person for the job. It's important that the day be segmented, with time for external promotional activities (gym teacher/day, after-school programs, church group activities, fairs, carnivals, business-to-business marketing, day-care demos, community center programs, etc.) and prime-time classes, renewals, enrollments and family add-ons.

Set a tone of No Excuses and focused goal setting. Involve everyone in making things happen each and every week.

#6: There is a saying making the rounds of emails, which is something to the effect of "Every day, the antelope wakes knowing it must run faster than the fastest lion to survive. Every day, the lion wakes knowing it must run faster than the slowest antelope to survive."

Your version of that thought, for you and your school, is MARKETING. Every day, you must wake knowing that you must have 20-plus new students this month (and every month for the rest of your life) to thrive. NAPMA provides you with plenty of marketing systems, ideas and information; however, you must start the day with your blank pad and ask, "What additional will I do today, this week and this month to make sure I hit my enrollment numbers?" At one end of the spectrum, you can hit the mall with a clipboard and guest passes, host big internal events or have a successful school program.

The question is "Are you running faster than the fastest lion?"

#7: Keep in mind what you are trying to accomplish. Create your school mission. Refer to it daily. Stay on track.

ANY obstacles or unnecessary distractions from your primary student mission are potentially destructive.

#8: You can't develop winners if you aren't one. Ultimately, regardless of all of the stuff you can provide your students, they will model you and your staff. You can't develop "no-excuses" students, if you are full of excuses. You can't develop confident students, if you lack it yourself. Make sure that you are a product of the product, every day, in every way. Ultimately, your success is up to you. You work hard, pay attention and follow the system — or not. There's nothing to blame, if you fail to thrive. Every tool you need is available. Every support system is in place. The question is "Will YOU choose to be a winner or not?"

Are You a Soldier in the "Alarm-Clock Army?"

I've had in-depth conversations with approximately 15 martial arts school owners during the past week. Some are grossing $50,000 to $70,000 a month. Two of them are down from $400,000 to $450,000 per year to now $250,000 to $300,000 a year. A few others are in the $6,000 to $10,000 range.

After talking with these school owners and discussing the opportunities and problems of another 30 or so schools, I've arrived at several conclusions about what factors limit business owners of all sorts — including martial arts school owners.

Let me start with a quote from an interview with Ted Nugent that I stumbled across. (When I was 17 watching him perform "Cat Scratch Fever" in Tulsa, I never expected to use him for success quotes! By the way, at that concert RUSH was his warm-up act!)

Ted Nugent talks a lot about discipline. Speaking on the phone from his ranch outside Waco, Texas, the Detroit-born guitarist comes back to it again and again. His life of clean living is the way to go, he says, living another way is nothing less than insane.

Nugent, who comes to Phoenix Sunday not to perform, but to speak at the National Rifle Association's annual conference, is an old-school conservative. As a member of the NRA's board of directors, he's a gun nut, to be sure, but he's also a bow nut, a family nut, an organic food nut and an alarm clock nut.

"I like to call it the 'alarm clock army.' Those of us that still set our alarm clocks because we have a responsibility to perform, to produce, to be punctual and attentive, and professional and pursue excellence. We come in every shape and form, we come from every walk of life."

I thought it was an interesting quote. "Alarm-Clock Army?"

I think back to another friend (former CEO of this company) who gave me a great quote one time. "One of my objectives is never to have to wake up to an alarm clock ever again." I had observed, first-hand, this retiring on the job without telling anyone. The culture evolved to emulate that behavior.

Well, many of the school owners I have talked to during the last week echo that sentiment in one way or another. They have mentally "checked out." They have hit numbers that put them beyond their "comfort zone," and then semi-retired on the job. The number doesn't matter. I've seen a range of breaking even to more typically $50,000 to $70,000 a year, and, in some cases, the low $100,000s. Then, rather than hoping for more and building a better business, a stronger school and a more robust student environment … instead, they go into semi-retirement.

Immediately the numbers slip.

Guess what most of them do next?

They complain about the economy. They complain that their students have no money. They complain that the economy has negatively impacted their school. All the while, they forgot the "Alarm Clock." They became lazy and, instead of taking action, they looked for a good excuse.

How else is this exemplified? Well, in many cases, it's by hiring staff, and then "abdicating responsibility for their results." I can't tell you how many times I've talked with an owner who just doesn't know what his program director does on a minute-by-minute or hour-by-hour basis. They don't know the scripts that have been created for use in enrollments, intros or renewal conferences.

This certainly isn't a problem that only happens in martial arts schools. It's not even a small-company problem.

A great story I remember hearing is about when Frank Wells and Michael Eisner took the helm of Disney. Eisner brought Jeffery Katzenberg (now of DreamWorks SGK [Spielberg, Geffen, Katzenberg]) with him from Paramount. According to the story, they inherited a 9-to-5 culture, and by Friday early afternoon all of the executives were gone … many to the golf course. Immediately, Katzenberg started scheduling movie production meetings (upcoming script reviews, marketing planning, etc.) for the Disney movie studios on Sunday morning.

Obviously, many of those executives who had become lazy left in a huff. However, soon to follow was a string of the studios biggest hits since Walt died, as well as the launch of Touchstone Pictures, with the release of *Good Morning Vietnam* and *Down and Out in Beverly Hills.*

Three Deadly Mistakes (and a Bonus Fourth)

Another BIG problem that I've seen relates to staffing.

I've been banging this drum for as long as I can remember, but many haven't heard it or "gotten it." School owners tend to do three things that are deadly.

First, they hire LOW QUALITY people. They hire only from within. They hire the man or woman who will work cheap, or who's been the most "loyal" for many years. Then, school owners experience low results. They suffer from what I like to call, "You can't teach a pig to sing; it wastes your time and irritates the pig."

One of my chief trainers at Mile High Karate said it recently this way, "You can't have mules selling to thoroughbreds." It's an interesting thought. What does that mean really? Well, your staff has to be a "product of the product." Ask yourself, if you were the mom on the bench, then would you pay $15,000 or $20,000, so your child could emulate or develop a character similar to the instructor, assistant instructor or program director at you school?

Second, school owners have too much "head count." In other words, they have several part-timers, including high school students trying to do the work that should be handled by one quality full-time person. For a school to perform well, it needs TWO high quality full-time people. One of these may be the owner-operator. A school also needs a full-time program director (typically the owner, in my opinion) and a full-time head instructor. Three part-time instructors (20 to 30 hours a week) does not equal one full-time person who's really focused on results and building his income as well as career.

Third, when school owners find a quality person, they tend to underpay him or her. If someone will work for $7 to $10 an hour, or $1,200 to $1,700 a month, then that should be a good indication that it's the wrong person. I typically start full-timers at $30,000 to $40,000 a year in base salary or 10% of the gross, or whichever is greater. Frankly, if they only earn the base salary more than one or two months in a row, then I'm looking for their replacements. You want people capable of earning $50,000-plus per year and willing to be focused and work hard to accomplish it.

Another deadly mistake of school owners is a failure to recognize the hourly value of their time.

I was talking with a coaching client a couple of years ago. His school was on the lowest rung of what I typically accepted ($12,000 a month gross).

He made two statements back to back that immediately struck me as silly.

First, he said that he was frustrated at not

being able to break the $12,000-per-month barrier at his school. He had been stuck on a plateau, prior to working with me, and urgently wanted to achieve larger numbers.

Second, he said that he was very pleased that he had been enrolling many personal training clients at $80 an hour.

I paused for a minute before commenting, and then asked if he had a calculator.

Then, I asked him to divide $12,000 a month by 4.2 (weeks in a month).

Then, I asked him to divide that number by 40.

When I asked him the total, he said it was a little less than $80.

I pointed out that obviously he had valued his time at $80 an hour and that's approximately the level the school was performing.

Next, I asked, "Where would you like to be within the next 90 days? His response was $30,000 a month. Well, working backwards, I explained that everything he touched had to be worth $180 an hour, if his school was to earn $30,000 a month during a 40-hour workweek. To move to $50,000 a month meant each hour must be worth $300.

Another school owner, doing a little more than $10,000 a month on average, explained that he had taken a $35,000-a-year "day job" to supplement his income. Well, that translates to $17 per hour. There are MANY things you can do to make $80, $100, $120, or even $300 or more per hour, if you are working on your school effectively, with maximum energy.

Another Quick MHK Update

There are approximately 50 regions in the United States for Regional Developers and we've already had to reject repeatedly school owners and regional developer prospects because their areas having already been taken. I recommend that if you want to develop a substantial business with few staff members, then take a look at our Regional Developer structure. This is only for successful and adequately capitalized school owners ready for the "next step." To take the guesswork from developing your school and to be a "well-oiled machine," with all systems in place overnight, consider our franchise opportunity, and visit www.MileHighWebinar.com for more information.

An Embarrassment of Riches

For the first time in recent memory … I'm so embarrassed!

I recently returned from the Martial Arts SuperShow in Las Vegas. I must admit that I was treated like a king: Front-row seat for a luncheon with Dana White, a special "Platinum" award from Century at Studio 54 and "red-carpet treatment" start to finish. Of course, Century spent a virtual fortune on the show, including a private jet for Tony Robbins to travel to the show.

OK, so why am I embarrassed? Well, for the first time, I've noticed the "tipping point" among the martial arts crowd and, unfortunately, it's back to the 1960s.

The martial arts that I love is exemplified in *Karate-Do: My Way of Life* by Gichin Funakoshi or *The Karate Dojo: Traditions and Tales of a Martial Art* by Peter Urban, and not, alas, in *Iceman: My Fighting Life* by Chuck Liddell and *Chad Millman, Blood in the Cage: Mixed Martial Arts* by Pat Miletich, *Furious Rise of the UFC* by L. Jon Wertheim, *This Is Gonna Hurt: The Life of a Mixed Martial Arts Champion* by Tito Ortiz, or the many other books that have hit the best-seller lists recently.

Now, don't misunderstand me. We've been studying "Mixed Martial Arts" long before UFC. I studied Judo during the 1960s, as did Bill Wallace, Chuck Norris and many others. Jeff Smith fought in one of the earlier MMA championships during the 1970s in Hawaii. The concept of MMA is not new. Go watch *Enter the Dragon* to see Bruce Lee leading the charge during the 1960s and 1970s.

Frankly, the other thing that's not new is having people of low character or, at the least those who represent the baser instincts, in martial arts.

Again, back to the early days. The reason Texas and Oklahoma point fighting was called "blood & guts" was that it was mostly without rules and about, well, blood and guts. Again, nothing new.

Once, when Grandmaster Jhoon Rhee was a guest of mine at a big event with several thousand Mile High Karate students in attendance, I asked him, "Master Rhee, why don't you present a background and history of Tae Kwon Do? We've never done that and with you it would truly be historical." He answered, "All those guys were thugs and criminals. My father forbade me to study with them, so I had to do it behind his back. I don't want to talk about that!"

I'm embarrassed because I went to Vegas, where conservatively 60–70% of the audience was there for an UFC-fighter autograph, only to learn the next way to choke someone out. I went to the offensive movie *Bruno* in which a cage-fighting scene makes the character in the movie seem "normal" compared to IQ-deficit MMA fans (plus, a scene on how to protect yourself from a gay by an instructor who hopefully knew it was a gag).

I saw an article about the scene in *Bruno*.

Sacha Baron Cohen, the 37-year-old British actor, said the scene involved his gay character, Bruno, hosting a real cage fight in Arkansas.

"There were 2,000 drunk, good-old boys baying for blood," he said, while appearing as himself on *The Late Show with David Letterman*.

"I was told not to worry, it would take someone two minutes to climb in the cage. The audience booed me and I challenged them to a fight, thinking I was safe.

"Then a 6 ft. 8 in. guy on steroids catapulted over the fence in two seconds and stood in front of me as the crowd cheered, 'Kill him, kill him'."

Next, Monday morning I picked up *The Wall Street Journal*, which actually had a review of UFC 100. The review was embarrassing as well.

It ranged from Brock Lesnar and his opponent rolling with each other in a hug (I was expecting them to "spoon" next and watch Animal Planet) to Lesnar flipping off the crowd and boasting that he was going home and drink Coors Light® (good for Colorado, bad for the UFC sponsor Bud Light®) to what he would do to his wife that night (i.e., "animal planet"). This spectacle was seen by 1,000,000 households, which were probably 4,000,000 to 5,000,000 people.

Unfortunately, the positive image of martial arts, as a clean-cut activity for kids and families, that was portrayed in *The Karate Kid* movies and since, is being progressively eliminated by this image of MMA as "Martial Arts."

Now, again, let me be clear. I certainly don't blame Dana White. He seems a VERY intelligent guy who has done everything right to build UFC into a billion-dollar company and its fights into one of the most popular spectator sports anywhere. I also don't blame him for the bimbos in bikinis, tattoos, foul language and beer sponsors. He was TARGETING the lucrative (for TV advertising) 18- to 30-year-old male crowd.

That's a great crowd for spectator sports, but, frankly, a horrible audience for school owners looking to develop quality students.

Really, I blame us. It's the old statement, "We Have Seen the Enemy and It Is Us," from the cartoon, Pogo. Why have so many martial artists been swayed by the popular trends and destroyed what we do? Many schools really have become "Mixed-Up Martial Arts."

It's become so crazy that even some of these foul-mouthed guys think they are running kids and family programs. I don't know about you, but my 7-year-old won't be anywhere near any of this crap. What must we do?

RUN, do not walk in the opposite direction. If you want to attract students who are educated, can pay a reasonable tuition, and will stay for several years rather than several months, then you MUST not be associated with the expanding MMA image. It's impossible to run the highest quality family program, if you are also offering the other stuff.

That doesn't mean that you don't integrate various styles. There are many OUTSTANDING BJJ instructors and clean-cut schools. There are many instructors who combine fighting styles. Personally, I've had this conversation with Bill Wallace, Joe Lewis, Jeff Smith, Carlos Machado and many other stars of the industry. All of them agree with my perspective. Clearly, most highly successful school owners, such as Bill Clark, Keith Hafner and others, have run in the opposite direction. Some have embraced the MMA trend, but, frankly, I think it's a bad idea.

Finally, don't miss the point that you will soon be competing with UFC gyms, LA Boxing and many others that are opening, as national franchises or corporate locations.

On a lighter note, I actually made time for what I truly mean to do on an ongoing basis. What is that? Well, I've been touching base again with some dear old friends and sharing their honest and divergent opinions about our relationships.

Is Your Biggest Challenge Your Attitude and Energy?

I've talked with many school owners during the last month, and I've discovered two common issues that limit their success and those are their attitudes about their lives and businesses — and the energy they expend for their schools.

My objective is to reveal common denominators that cause school owners to struggle with the way they see and react to the world around them.

The title of Wayne Dwyer's book, *You'll See It When You Believe It*, speaks volumes, and could turn around many lives, if its meaning is really understood.

When events in your life create negative feelings or when people with whom you interact everyday leave you frustrated, then it's time to evaluate your belief system. After all, the world around you is just a reflection of your thinking.

Although the term, "people management" may be inappropriate, it is a good place to start. As one smart author once wrote, "You manage things; you lead people." During the years, I've adopted some meaningful metaphors for feeling frustrated when "managing people."

Accomplishing anything in one's life (or business) is like "pushing rope."

Managing people is like "herding cats."

These metaphors may reflect the way you've felt many times, they indicate an attempt "to manage" instead of "to lead."

Pushing people to accomplish tasks, be responsible or excel is really worse than "pushing rope," since people will "push back" or resist your attempts to manage them. In either case, pushing people or herding cats are both highly unproductive.

Like me, I am sure you have struggled with the same unproductive mental cycle — irritation, frustration, anger, and then finally, realization that the only way to lead your organization is by example.

If you want your instructor to teach better, then teach a class yourself, and then help them to improve their teaching methods from your example.

If you want to improve your sales efforts, then model success and teach by example.

The old adage, "do as I tell you, not as I do it," neither leads nor inspires. Too many school owners find themselves trapped when they "lead from the front" for martial arts training, but "push" their staffs to improve business performance, while ignoring it themselves.

It just doesn't work.

Tweaking your systems, writing manuals or implementing rewards and punishments programs will never fix a failure to lead from the front. Assigning staff members the responsibility of managing systems or accomplishing tasks you don't understand yourself is a similar failure to lead.

As a school owner, you must master each of the core processes — marketing, sales and teaching — before you hire a new employee or involve a current employee in the management of these processes, regardless of how well those employees may be able to do the job.

Sales is a particularly misunderstood and mismanaged process in most schools. Instructors feel that selling is beneath them, while never realizing that their most important job as a teacher is to sell the students on becoming Black Belts and developing their maximum potential.

Any high school teacher should understand that a key mission of their teaching role is to encourage students to graduate and aspire to higher education. Few of those students (or their parents) would respect a teacher who refused to "sell" students to stay in school and graduate.

Never Stop Learning

No matter how much you know, there's always more to learn.

Are you an AGGRESSIVE student?

How many non-fiction books have you read this year?

Do you take notes when you read?

Do you write in the books and jot ideas and implementation strategies?

Do you ever re-read a book 2, 3, 5 or 10 times?

Do you LOVE Amazon.com or your local Barnes & Noble bookstore?

How many biographies have you read?

How many audio CDs have you purchased, and then listened to their contents, repeatedly?

Are you on the Nightingale-Conant preferred-customers list?

Do you obtain ANY industry-specific information available?

Do you subscribe to all of our industry's school materials?

How many DVDs have your purchased and watched?

Do you own the Kovar series?

How many curriculum-oriented DVDs do you have?

Do you have materials from Zig Ziglar, Jay Abraham, Tony Robbins or Denis Waitley?

Do you go to many seminars?

Do you go to every industry-specific seminar?

How much would you spend for a seminar? Would $2,000, $3,000, $5,000 or $10,000 be too much? Why?

What types of seminars would you and have you attended? Is it time to "learn outside the box" and explore other subjects?

Have you thought about returning to college?

Would a BA, BS, MA, MS or MBA be helpful?

Do you have any MENTORS?

How often do you talk to them?

Do you know their strengths and weaknesses?

How's your peer networking?

Do you talk with at least three people per week who are doing something better than you?

Do you share and obtain ideas regularly?

Do you talk to successful people outside your "normal" circle of acquaintances?

The most successful people I know do several things religiously:

1. Read biographies of successful people.
2. Read often.
3. Keep a dictionary on their desks and search for words that they don't know or use consistently.
4. Break from their "paradigm" to look at things in new ways.
5. Talk to people who are more successful than they.
6. Listen more than they talk.

As soon as you stop being a student, you stop growing. Look for new information AND apply it to your business and life. Avoid learning just for it's own sake, but apply that information quickly.

The Economy Sucks? Really?

I've had the interesting and annoying experience of "car shopping" recently.

A couple of months ago I was running errands — trying to find copies of *The E-Myth* at various bookstores around Denver, since I had waited until the last minute to decide to use that book for our Regional Developer Training. While we waited to turn left into a Barnes & Noble parking lot, an otherwise nice 18-year-old, recent high school graduate gunned his SUV while looking for songs on his iPod. He failed to notice my car's blinking turn signal and rammed into my Mercedes at probably 35 mph and accelerating.

His SUV looked like it had been in a war. His "deer catcher's" front end was torn off. Smoke was coming from the engine. His front bumper was gone, hood crumpled. His SUV wasn't drivable. In my case, my Mercedes had a dent in the rear quarter panel. The bumper was unharmed, except the plastic cover, which snapped back into position. Rob and I and the young man waited for the police. I consoled the young man, proceeded to purchase a couple more copies of the book and drove to our next errand.

Well, the insurance company also "totaled" my car, giving us approximately $10,000 more than the repair estimate. Apparently, Mercedes parts can cost more than expected, and some of the electronics can really increase the price.

Now, I'm looking for a replacement.

It's interesting because I know that car companies, dealerships and salespeople have been whining for a year now about how bad their industry has become.

Anyway, on to my point.

We've been visiting many BMW, Mercedes, and Lexus dealerships, looking for a mid-size, 4-door sedan with all-wheel drive. That narrows the choices to a Lexus GS 350 AWD, BMW 5-Series (BMW 535ix) and another Mercedes E Series (E500 4-Matic).

Now, after visiting a bunch of dealerships, you would think that these guys are semi-retired and really would prefer to collect the cars rather than sell them.

What do I mean?

Well, Jodi (my new ex), seems determined to get the BMW 535ix. (The totaled Mercedes was really her car. I primarily drive the Porsche Turbo.) We went to a HUGE, new dealership in south Denver. It has a HUGE inventory and a multi-million dollar facility in a location between Cherry Creek and Highlands Ranch (a RICH area of town).

We've been to that dealership three times now. EACH time, we've dealt with salespeople who did the following:

1. Kept us waiting for what seemed like hours (probably 15-20 minutes before being helped).
2. Had no idea what inventory they had.
3. Had no idea how the features and functions of the cars they were selling worked.
4. Spent one to three hours with us, including test-drives in at least one car.

After all of the above, none of the three salesmen asked for my name, address, phone number or email. None asked any "background questions," i.e., what I do for a living or why we were shopping now. None asked SPECIFICALLY what car we wanted, so they could find it for us. None followed up, and obviously had no system/method to do so.

Now, this dealership must have MILLIONS of dollars invested in its facility, a huge overhead and PLENTY of inventory.

Most of the time, its salespeople were hanging out in the dealership (several of them played with my daughter's new puppy during one trip). I'm sure they are bitching about the recession. The owner is worried by the downturn.

I'm betting he spent 100 times on the facility compared to service and sales training for the staff.

Stupid, VERY stupid on his part. We needed a new car and we walked into the dealership with a check in my pocket ready to buy. Clearly, we were as "live" a prospect as exists.

Anyway, we visited another dealership. The salesperson was a retired chief from the Air Force. He asked background questions. He did his best to determine exactly what Jodi wanted. (Not that I could recognize the difference of the three she hadn't liked. The wood trim on the door was the wrong color or orientation, or some such thing.)

This salesperson has followed up.

He researched new and used inventory that was on its way to the dealership. He called whenever a new car was headed for prep. He generally built rapport, followed up and has done his job.

I'll tell you sincerely that even if it's not exactly the car we wanted, then I want to buy it from him. If the other dealership has exactly the right car at the right price, then I'll be disappointed and frustrated to buy it from there.

How does this apply to you?

Well, your students are more persuaded by your follow-up, sincerity, competence and care for them than your technical proficiency — certainly more than price. At the first dealership, I'd haggle for every penny. At the second, I'd want to be quoted a reasonable price, but wouldn't be pushing for every penny.

Oh, at the second dealer, the salesperson has had several cars arrive just this week, and they were sold before we had time to look at them. Recession, what recession?

Several Illuminating Lessons

Allow me to share an email I received from one of my Mile High Karate school owner/operators. He operates one of our schools.

"I did two renewals today that went well; and one Saturday that went to HELL. The wife was infuriated with our agreements and us, and wished to terminate. She apparently did some research about your martial arts coaching and you, and was rather irritated that we would like to make money for a living. She was rather upset that her child had gained confidence in the program! How in the hell do you respond to that statement? She was ignorant about the martial arts and our program, and just frustrated the living hell out of me. Sorry, I just thought I would vent a little."

I want to share this message with you because it provides several illuminating lessons.

First, and, most importantly: You can't please everyone all the time.

If you try to please everyone, then the results are inevitable: You mean nothing to anyone. It's important to recognize that most personal success stories are "polarizing."

The successful people tend to be at one end of a spectrum or another, such as Rush Limbaugh and Howard Stern on radio, Donald Trump on TV or even Bruce Lee.

Anyone who is very successful gains both a loyal following and an opposing group that loathes his or her success. Successful people must realize that offending a segment of the population goes with the territory.

Second: Be immune to criticism.

Never, I repeat, never, take rejection personally or worry about what the critics say. My school operator was obviously frustrated; and his report to me was full of his raw emotions because he was reacting to the woman's criticisms, personally.

I immediately recognized his "personal" reaction; however, I also realized that if his feedback about this dissatisfied mom was even 30% accurate, then we didn't want her at the school. Part of the definition of a professional is the ability to reduce the intrusion of emotions or personal reactions into the decision-making process and operation of your profession.

If movie stars and celebrities did not have this ability (and not all of them do), then they would be emotional wrecks. You must be immune to criticism to be successful, and the more successful you become, the more critics you will attract!

Third: Be extremely satisfied with "two steps forward and one step back."

You read the email: "I did two renewals today that went well; and one Saturday that went to HELL." Naturally, the owner/operator was allowing his frustration and disappointment about the one renewal to make it seem more important than the two that went well.

Those were easy; full of pleasantries and no spikes of emotion to register sharply on the memory. While the one "that went to HELL" sent emotions off the scale, which is the one most remembered.

The trick is to re-direct your emotions to your successes. Revel in those and forget the rejection. After all, one renewal per business day equals 20 to 25 per month — and I'd be happy with that any month. There's no value to becoming frustrated by one dysfunctional human being, except to learn that there will be more!

Fourth: The solution is often "supply & demand."

Supply and demand is one of the oldest theories, or laws, of economics, and it applies to your martial arts school in much the same way as the largest global corporation. Understanding supply and demand and using it advantageously will solve MANY problems operating a martial arts school.

In simplest terms, you win when what you supply is limited, but there is great demand for it. If you have a huge surge of new enrollments and current students begging to join your Black Belt Club, Master Club, Leadership program or whatever your highest level "upgrade program" happens to be, then a number of positive results occur.

First, fewer people complain. Second, you are less concerned about students who "don't fit" with your school's culture. Third, you reduce the need to "sell" because the trust and credibility of your "social proof" begins to dominate prospects' decision-making, which makes them want to be involved with your school.

Consultation Certificate

This Certificate Entitles the Bearer to a Personal 1-on-1 Martial Arts School Business Analysis With a NAPMA-Certified Business Analyst. This Individual Consultation is Valued at $495.00.

Certificate expires 12 months from the date of purchase.

To schedule your personal business analysis, complete this form and fax to NAPMA at 1-800-795-0853; mail to 1767 Denver West Blvd., Suite A, Golden, CO 80401; or visit www.PrivateCoachingSession.com

PLEASE FILL OUT COMPLETELY AND WRITE LEGIBLY

Name _____

School Name _____

Address _____

City _____ State/Province _____

Zip _____ Country _____

Phone _____ Fax _____

E-Mail _____

_____
Authorized by Toby Milroy
Chief Operating Officer, NAPMA

3 FREE GIFTS FOR SERIOUS SCHOOL OWNERS

FREE Personal School Evaluation

Two 30-minute Sessions A sure-fire way action plan to double your results or better.

FREE Two 90-Minute Seminars

with **"The Millionaire Maker Grandmaster Stephen Oliver** "The 5 Stupid Mistakes All Too Many School Owners Make that Kill Their Growth" and "The Key Step-by-Step Blueprint for Being a Big Winner"

FREE CD-DVD Package and Report

"How Hundreds of Smart School Owners Like You Doubled Their Revenue in the Last 12 Months Even in the Midst of the Greatest Recession since the Great Depresson, and How You Can, Too!"

Multiple Schools, Licensing and Partnerships

I've been inundated recently with questions from Coaching and Mastermind members and others about opening multiple schools through license agreements, partnerships or various other "business agreement" scenarios. There was also an article in an industry magazine that addressed this topic, and I believe the author was partially right, but suggested dangerously wrong conclusions.

Those who have been asking me about how to expand to multiple schools are contemplating what amounts to a franchise business without complying with franchise law. That is a risky, and frankly, unwise move.

This is a subject in which I've become an expert during the last four or five years. I'm an American Bar Association member, a member of the ABA's forum on franchising and an International Franchise Association member.

I've also provided the means for the law firm that represents my interests to live in opulent style for the past several years helping me to register as a legitimate franchise business.

The International Franchise Association recently estimated that $250,000 to $500,000 is required for a new franchisor to open the doors, and the franchisor failure rate is approximately 70%. Having been through the process from A to Z, I don't question either number.

The rationale for an entrepreneur to become a franchise business owner is undeniable, as the following excerpt from a recent article confirms.

"A good way to reduce your risk of failure is to purchase a franchise because franchises typically have a higher success rate than other types of small businesses. Conventional wisdom holds that franchises have a failure rate of about 5 percent, compared to the 50 percent failure rate of independent entrepreneurs. Successful franchisors have developed 'formulas' for starting a new business. The good franchisors want your new business to succeed. If you fail, they fail."

I receive enough returned mailings and general correspondence to know that the failure rate of independent martial arts schools far exceeds 20% per year, which is 100% in 5 years; and, that doesn't include what I call the "Walking Dead."

Another article excerpt will reinforce my point.

"This is the franchise duck test: If you act like a duck, look like a duck and talk like a duck-then, YOU ARE A DUCK!!! Even if the duck advisor, i.e., your attorney, says you are a COW. You can't do business legally as a COW, if you are really a DUCK. More importantly, you don't get to vote! Franchising is regulated by law.

"The general test of whether or not a business opportunity is a franchise, can be summarized as follows:

If you sell a business opportunity to any person and you.

Allow the buyer to use your company name or logo.

Charge a fee to the buyer (inside or outside of product or service).

Provide any significant assistance or maintain any significant control over any part of the business."

I strongly urge that you talk to me first, if you are contemplating multi-school expansion. I remain convinced that the best expansion process involves on-site ownership with "residual income" for your efforts as trainer and chief instructor. If you are searching for a solution to this issue, then e-mail me at StephenOliver@MileHighKarate.com or www.MileHiighFranchise.com.

Further Thoughts on "Mixed-Up Martial Arts"

I just spent a couple of days here in Evergreen, Colorado with my old and dear friend, Tim Kovar. As you may know, for many years, he was the business backbone of Kovar's, that he ran with his brother Dave, who's a consummate martial artist.

Tim has been out of the business for a while now (about two years). He left Satori as they added outside management and as the company grew by leaps and bounds, bringing in several million in outside venture capital.

If was fun and exciting to catch up with my old friend. It was also interesting to hear his take on the current state of the martial arts industry and a few private thoughts on his business development inside and outside the industry.

He and his brother may join us at the Extreme Success Academy. If Tim joins us, then it will be to share ideas about alternative income sources as a martial arts school owner. In his case, he has become very experienced in real estate development as well as complementary businesses to martial arts schools.

Now, to follow up on my comments last month in this newsletter about "Mixed-Up Martial Arts," I'll relate a conversation that I had with Tim many years ago. During the first iteration of UFC®, when it was still dominated by the Gracie family, Tim and I had talked about the future of the martial arts industry.

He told me that his brother was concerned that UFC would be the death of traditional schools. When asked what Dave meant, Tim explained that as people watched UFC and recognized the effectiveness of grappling and various MMA movements they would no longer be interested in learning Tae Kwon Do, Kenpo or whatever style in favor of a preference for MMA-type training.

At the time, as you may imagine, I told Tim I thought that was crazy.

I explained my thoughts in part by relating this observation. One of the top boxing matches in recent memory (then) was Evander Holyfield-Mike Tyson 1. As I recall, it was one of the most anticipated matches (having been cancelled or rescheduled several times), and had one of the biggest pay-per-view audiences to that point. Given the *huge* spectator appeal of that fight, by the UFC/ MMA logic, there obviously was a *huge* outpouring of interest in taking up boxing in the weeks and months following the fight, right? Boxing gyms' phones were ringing off the hook? I'm guessing that didn't happen.

See, we confuse the popularity of a *spectator sport* with *participant activity*. In the United States, soccer is one of the biggest participant sports for kids; however, for years, soccer has had a very difficult time obtaining TV coverage, much less popularity as a spectator sport. During recent years, NASCAR has been incredibly popular as a spectator sport; however, I doubt that most NASCAR fans have bought a racing suit and driving shoes and enrolled in driving classes at their local tracks.

Anyway, I digress. I told Tim at the time that if he and his brother thought that was true (UFC killing traditional lessons because of "effectiveness"), then he should run a simple test. I suggested taking an edited highlights video of recent UFC fights and playing it during their introductory classes during the next couple of months. I commented that if their conversion rates improved (more people enrolled), then they were right. If they declined, then, perhaps, I was right.

In retrospect, that conversation missed a few key points.

First, unfortunately, UFC has become so popular that the general public now confuses it as "Martial Arts," and, therefore, the assumption about "killing traditional training" is correct for the wrong reasons.

Second, clearly, in one way, Dave was right.

There is a market (albeit small) for people looking for realistic training. Krav Maga, BJJ, MMA, etc., have all attracted an audience with that in mind.

Finally, the whole discussion misses the mark by failing to recognize market segments. The Kovar's typical students (and Mile High Karate's and Keith Hafner's, etc.) are kids, or the family market, and adults who are not primarily looking to become "fighters." That having been said, the appeal of a spectator sport does not translate into a solid "grassroots" participant activity.

What Is Your Professional Education Worth?

Recently, I've received several comments about the cost of professional education products. Most of their messages can be encapsulated into:

"Gee, all of this stuff is really expensive. I can't afford to spend so much."

I even had one old friend who said:

"I'm doing 10 enrollments a month and grossing $30,000 a month. I need to reach 20 enrollments a month and I've been told you are the best in the martial arts industry at marketing … tell me what I need and I'll get it."

The conversation came completely undone when my first suggestion received the following response:

"That's too much."

Keep in mind, that in his case, increasing enrollments from 10 to 20 per month generates $30,000 a month or $360,000 per year in added revenues. An even more important consideration is that $360,000 in added revenue per year probably increases his net from $70,000 per year to approximately $400,000 per year — a 500% to 600% INCREASE.

The conversation finally ended when my least expensive suggestion, costing approximately $1,200, was countered by his willingness to invest no more than $600.

If you know me at all, then you're able to guess my attitude.

I'm still driving my Porsche and he's still enrolling 10 new students a month. It's "no skin off my nose." It's his loss, and it makes no difference whatsoever to my lifestyle or outlook. I am only able to help those school owners who want the help, and are willing to invest in their professional education.

How much are you investing on your professional education?

I recommend two strategies:

First, you must be willing to invest one dollar, if it returns two or more dollars. I often rail on this subject, but I do believe in the Benjamin Franklin quote: "Empty your purse into your mind and your mind will fill your purse."

Second, YOU SHOULD HAVE A CONTINUOUS STUDY PROJECT.

There is much to choose, but my past course of study may help you:

Educational Psychology
The Psychology of Motivational Teaching
Direct Response Marketing
Internet Marketing
Effective Personal Selling
Rapport Building in Communications
NLP — Applied to Teaching
NLP — Applied to Persuasive Copywriting
NLP — Applied to Effective Personal Selling
Direct Mail
Leadership
Employee Management and Supervision

Let me help you focus the decision-making process.

We'll assume you are already furthering the mastery of your martial arts skill.

Therefore, your business skills probably require the most attention. I propose that there are three primary skills you must develop to succeed in the martial arts industry.

Teaching

Selling

Marketing

Once you begin mastering those subjects, you then must move to staffing and master subjects, such as recruiting, hiring, training, supervision and motivation.

If you have decided to really grow your career, then where do you start?

First, acquire, read and study the information available from all the great industry sources, including reviewing and re-reading the NAPMA monthly packages you received during the last two to three years; and ask about my Extraordinary Marketing and Coaching programs, which have a wealth of marketing and selling information.

As an aside, when I joined Jonathan Mizel's Internet Marketing Coaching Program and Dan Kennedy's Coaching Program, the first thing I did was to print EVERYTHING available on their Web sites (more than 2,000 pages each). I then organized that material in notebooks and read everything and took notes.

These professional education suggestions only scratch the surface of what's available in our industry. Dave Kovar offers great content on teaching; Tommy Lee on selling; Jeff Smith on developing great Black Belts; and so much more.

Once you've exhausted all of the industry sources, then start with generic topics, such as selling, marketing and teaching. I recommend:

Selling: Tom Hopkins, Zig Ziglar, Robert Cialdini and Dan Kennedy.

Marketing: Dan Kennedy and his Magnetic Marketing & Copywriting Programs (visit www. KennedyCopy.com.), Joe Sugarman, John Caples, Claude Hopkins and others.

Teaching: I recommend that you read what your local elementary and middle school teachers are required to read for their teaching certification. Lorenzo Trujillo, who has a Ph.D. in Psychology and a doctor of education degree, guided me through all of the teacher resources. It would be a good exercise for you as well.

Your head may hurt, but great knowledge doesn't come easy. Take your time, organize and one step at a time.

The mastermind effect that you'll experience as a Peak Performers or Inner Circle member will move you to the next level by dramatically accelerating your learning curve. My coaching experience with Dan Kennedy, Lorenzo Trujillo, Jonathan Mizel and others has definitely paid huge dividends.

Success Is Never a Straight Line

40 years in martial arts.

37 years in the martial arts business.

26 years since the founding of Mile High Karate.

Geez, I feel old!

In my day-to-day conversations with school owners generating as little as $6,000 a month and as much as $1,000,000-plus per year, I'm continually reminded of both my own "arbitrary line" to the target and the typically tumultuous line to the top for most successful business people.

I have always been a huge fan of reading biographies, autobiographies, interviews with, and profiles of, successful people — as well as books that analyze and describe the route to success for millionaires, billionaires and successful politicians and scientists.

It's obvious when you read about just about any successful person — from Howard Hughes and Walt Disney to Ray Kroc to Steve Jobs and Bill Gates — that no one had an uninterrupted "straight line" to success.

Many now forget that Steve Jobs, just a few years ago, as Apple's co-founder, was fired by the board of directors and universally reviled inside and outside the company. Now? He's the genius behind Pixar, the largest single shareholder of Disney, the genius behind "Apple's return," including iTunes, the iPod, the return of the Macs, and now the iPhones.

How about Donald Trump?

A favorite quote: The Donald to Marla, "Marla, see that bum on the grate — he's $300,000,000 richer than I am." Marla, "How can that be — he doesn't have anything?" The Donald, "That's right, he has nothing — I'm $300,000,000 in the hole."

Now? Obviously, he's WAYYYY back on top.

It's important to remember that success is not a straight line.

During the last year to 15 months, many schools have closed their doors, while others have learned that the economy has changed so much that they must implement a different set of business systems and rules, which has led to huge growth, despite the recession.

Those who have stumbled have received the same universally, repetitive speech from me:

- It's not as bad as it looks;
- It's not nearly as bad as it feels;
- Stay focused on 2-, 3-, 5-, and 10-year objectives;
- Decide where you want to go and start to work.

Those who have had success have typically received common feedback:

Now, it's time to expand your thinking to the next level. Decide how you want your life to unfold and create your business to fully support that direction.

In some cases — a school owner, making $30,000 net a year ago, is making that much in a quarter — in some cases in a month — now. That's a big change in lifestyle. Now, it's time for an expansion of thinking to move to the "Next Level" of success.

I'd like to suggest that you pick a "Success Study Project." One that might be useful is to read some biographies or to read one of the books that will help you understanding the success personality.

Some suggestions:

Profiles of Power and *Success: Fourteen Geniuses Who Broke the Rules* by Gene N. Landrum

Profiles of Genius: Thirteen Creative Men Who Changed the World by Gene N. Landrum

Great Business Biographies:

Pizza Tiger by Thomas Monaghan

McDonald's: Behind The Arches by John F. Love

Hard Drive: Bill Gates and the Making of the Microsoft Empire by James Wallace and Jim Erickson

iCon Steve Jobs: The Greatest Second Act in the History of Business by Jeffrey S. Young and William L. Simon

Accidental Millionaire: The Rise and Fall of Steve Jobs at Apple Computer by Lee Butcher

Citizen Hughes: The Power, the Money and the Madness by Michael Drosnin

Pour Your Heart into It: How Starbucks Build a Company One Cup at a Time by Howard Schultz

Walt Disney: The Triumph of the American Imagination by Neal Gabler

I'll leave you with a "Goals Statement," written by Bruce Lee in 1969.

"My Definite Chief Aim:

I, Bruce Lee, will be the highest paid Oriental superstar in the United States. In return I will give the most exciting performances and render the best of quality in the capacity of an actor. Starting in 1970, I will achieve world fame and from then onward till the end of 1980, I will have in my possession $10,000,000. Then, I will live the way I please and achieve inner harmony and peace."

Bruce Lee, January 1969.

Business Knowledge Aggressively Implemented Produces Awesome Results

We just returned from the NAPMA Extreme Success Academy in beautiful San Antonio, Texas. Now, I'm prepping for a long weekend of staff, school owner and Black Belt training in Breckenridge, Colorado this weekend.

The Extreme Success Academy in San Antonio was incredible from start to finish. Clearly, Toby Milroy, Jeff Smith, Bill Clark, Dave Kovar, Terry Bryan and Keith Hafner are *always* fantastic. A relatively last-minute addition was Karl Mecklenburg, former Denver Bronco NFL player, who was a six-time All-Pro and played in three Super Bowls. I must say, for me, at least, he was the surprise highlight of the weekend.

I've spoken with many of the participants, both during the event and since. There's been universal agreement that this event was much better than last year's Extreme Success Academy — and, the best NAPMA event ever, in terms of focused content and a real action plan for success to implement.

Samuel Scott, one of our more successful members (and Inner Circle member) sent me this email about the event:

"I just wanted to thank you again for another highly enriched business seminar. This session was much smoother and much more focused than last year's. The blatant truth about the mindset of the so-called "Old-School" mentality is a pill we all need to swallow if we truly want to be living examples of success for our students.

"My team was on fire, and immediately began implementing a number of ideas — with awesome results — that they received from the training sessions. The bottom line for us is simple: acquire the knowledge, IMPLEMENT what was taught and stay CONSISTENT — period! Thanks for raising the bar ... for the few, the disciplined, the martial artist!"

SAMUEL SCOTT
FULL CIRCLE MARTIAL ARTS ACADEMY
GLENN DALE, MD

Gee, I wish it were that easy! On another, similar subject, I received this email (edited for space) today.

"I've had a school for more than 16 years. The last five have been very unproductive. I have been a NAPMA member for most of 14 years. My biggest problem to overcome is causing the phone to ring. I used NAPMA's marketing material in the past, with little to no results. The ads are awesome, but interest in them is not. I am interested in trying anything, but the after-school busing program.

"Bottom line: I want my school to grow. You provide the resources to make it happen. Let's test the system. Give me an ad with the offer that was very successful at another school; I'll duplicate the process, and then let's see my results.

"I am aware that it isn't all about new student enrollments; but this is number one on my hit list. If I can't cause the phone to ring or drive prospects to my Web site to schedule an appointment, then the rest of your marketing

ideas for retention are irrelevant."
MASTER JEFFREY WHITNEY
WHITNEY'S KARATE AMERICA
WHITNEYSKARATEAMERICA.COM

Well, I must say it's a shame that Master Whitney didn't attend Extreme Success Academy. He would have heard Keith Hafner's spectacular presentation on generating new students a few years ago. He explained about community outreach rather than one letter or "ad slick." Master Whitney would have heard Bill Clark, Dave Kovar, Jeff Smith and me discuss how the market has changed and what you must do to be successful.

Several of my schools have generated 50 to 100 new introductory students during the last 30 days through community outreach activities, *not* paid advertising or using a one-off ad slick. During the 1980s and 1990s, I could just pour money into newspaper and "saturation-bombing" direct mail, and do fine. Those times have passed.

During my presentation, interpreted by some as the "Prophet of Doom," I presented four factors dooming many in our industry to failure and, in a real way, contributing to more than 4,500 schools closing their doors during the past 12 months.

One of those factors is the general unresponsiveness of the market to the standard "come-take-karate message." I believe that UFC®, Tapout® and others have poisoned the market, in addition to a general economic downturn. That doesn't mean you cannot be *very* successful, but it takes more learning and less of just taking an ad slick to FedexOffice™ to reproduce it and distribute it to the media.

Learn the Skill of Scanning

The first "secret" of the skill of scanning is that it's unnecessary to read, study, understand and master every topic. Instead, find the ONE good idea that will enhance your operations every month in one of the three key areas: enrollments, retention and renewals.

I know I've increased the discussion from ONE good idea to THREE key operational areas of your school, but I am confident you're still able to follow. When you scan the materials, you only need to look for that ONE good idea that will improve any ONE of these THREE key operational areas. You don't need ONE good idea for each.

I recommend that you try the following steps to scan and absorb the latest Maximum Impact package material easily and quickly.

Make copies of the written materials.

Scan each document and use a highlighter to note anything that catches your attention as a potential ONE good idea to improve enrollments, retention and renewals. It may be a subhead of a section of text, a statement in the opening paragraph and/or points in the review section. Information presented as bullet points, numbered lists or in boxes is often where that ONE good idea resides.

It will only take you a few minutes of your time to scan even the longest document because you are only looking for the high points to highlight. You'll notice that suddenly you've carved a few words and phrases from documents of thousands of words.

Listen to the audio CD next and note how the high points you marked on transcript are presented and discussed by the contributors. Pause the CD to take notes if the contributors provide additional information that will help you understand and implement any of the ONE good ideas you highlighted on the written materials.

Watch the DVD, and use the same procedure above to find those ONE good ideas.

Return to the written material and read and study just those sections, paragraphs, phrases, etc. that you highlighted. You may have to read some text before and after your highlighted text to understand it fully, but you DON'T have to read the entire document to find ONE good idea or even two!

Listen to the teleconference and learn how other school owners are implementing the ONE good idea they found in previous months' lessons and concepts.

Try this scanning method a few times, and you'll quickly discover how little time you need to invest in large amounts of materials.

Remember, however, you want to avoid EMPTY knowledge, that is, knowledge you gain simply to be able state you possess it. Instead, you want to find and absorb a few key concepts that will help move your school to the next level.

What is also truly remarkable about this scanning method is that the documents you scanned so quickly can be read and studied further in the future to extract other good ideas. It's like having a gold mine you can visit whenever you want to mine another nugget!

This is what I call the "circling-back" experience. As you use this scanning method more and more, you'll find yourself circling back to key knowledge areas to add to your understanding. Every time you do so you're adding another layer of knowledge and continuing to strengthen your foundation for greater growth.

In my case, I started with technical martial arts skills, and then moved to martial arts instructional skills. Prior to opening my first school, I worked to master direct-response marketing and selling. From there, I moved to higher levels of skills training, and then extensive educational psychology. I then "circled back" to sales and sales processes, developing my knowledge further. I circled again to direct-response marketing for even more knowledge about that topic.

This is also a strategy you should use with your Maximum Impact package. If you continue to circle back to increase your knowledge of the three key operational areas above, then you'll learn more, intensify your level of understanding and mastery of the various subjects and grow more as a person and professional.

Don't be stressed about reading, or even understanding, every Maximum Impact package; it's unnecessary.

I do want you to be stressed about adding ONE good idea or strategy from each package that will make an immediate and positive impact on your school. Of course, that's hardly stressful at all, considering I've shown you how quick and easy it is.

How Would You Know If You "Lost Your Mind?"

ast week was interesting. I returned from our annual Black Belt Retreat in Breckenridge, Colorado, where approximately 200 Black Belts tested, with more than 500 in attendance. It was uplifting, as several new Mile High Karate schools joined us (Mission, TX and Erie, PA, among others). There were many tremendous success stories; instructors from throughout North America in attendance; and Jeff Smith, our Regional Developers and myself conducted operations training all weekend. Truly an uplifting experience (and all at 9,000-foot elevation)!

A couple of days later, we had approximately 10 school owners in training for the week, and then Denver was hit by a massive blizzard. Next thing I know I'm headed home after being stuck on I-70 in our new BMW just as an ambulance pulls into my driveway, with EMTs looking for the "baby who's not breathing."

Well, the next couple of hours were hair-raising. My 18-month-old son is transported in the ambulance to the hospital in a blizzard. Mom is in the ambulance; I'm following in our SUV (Volvo XC-90 "Soccer Mom Mobile"). Anyway, I didn't know how scary it really was until I arrived at the hospital. Apparently, Chase did stop breathing in the ambulance. I walked into the emergency room with what looked like the entire hospital staff hovering over my screaming and terrified son. Anyway, two days in the hospital and numerous visits from doctors and he was fine, but undiagnosed. Apparently, some combination of asthma and allergies caused him to have difficulty breathing and to stop breathing on the way to the hospital.

Now, I've had tough days, months and weeks before, but nothing tops following an ambulance with your 18-month-old in it in a blizzard. I'm trying not to slide into the ambulance or become stuck on the way. I then walked into a scene from the television show *ER*, with my screaming baby. Personally, I've always been great at handling crisis, so the effect really didn't hit me until Friday or Saturday (Wednesday was the ambulance run).

Well, in the meantime, during some downtime at the hospital, I made the mistake of checking my email. I now discover that a little war of words is actively in progress for a couple of days: an old friend of mine who seems to have finally lost his mind.

Toby sent an email, sharing a couple of ideas that Master Bill Clark presented at the Extreme Success Academy in San Antonio. Tom Callos apparently had a meltdown from Hilo (HI) that resulted in blog posts, emails and a raft of back and forth between him and Toby. Now, I always hate to "swing at pitches in the dirt," but the whole thing became ridiculous. Tom apparently starts calling NAPMA, Toby, Bill Clark and I and everyone involved, saying we were unethical, underhanded and teaching concepts (remember this was a shorthand explanation of Master Clark's idea, and not a NAPMA idea directly) that are "Beneath the Dignity of a Martial Artist."

Well, it's a terrible thing when you lose your mind.

For obvious reasons, I didn't intervene other than to send Tom a short note that he really should (and does) know me better after 20 years and that he might think before "flaming." He did, after flooding the Internet with this crap, apologize.

Anyway. What's beneath the "dignity" of a martial artist? Well, certainly I believe that being broke is beneath the dignity of any martial artist. I certainly believe you should do nothing that creates exposure, but hurts your image. (*The Jerry Springer Show*, guests passes distributed at a strip club or liquor store, etc.,…it's a long list.) However, *most* school owners in our industry sit on their asses and do nothing. Rather than risk going too far, they do nothing.

Personally, I'd like all quality teachers to be "raging thunder lizard evangelists" for the value of martial arts training. The marketing concepts that I've typically taught include everything from Web sites and search engine optimization to direct mail, television infomercials and community outreach ideas; anything to be in front of 300 to 3,000 people at once. I prefer "high-leverage" activities to one or two at a time. *However*, rather than sit in your school and bemoan your lack of results, it would be better to go door-to-door, stand in the school car line and talk to parents one at a time, or distribute guest passes at the shopping mall.

Tom, in his misplaced indignity, misses the point that the vast majority of school owners in our industry just do nothing. Those who are growing rich have one thing in common: "Massive Action." They also share another common trait: "taking credit or the blame for their results," rather than looking for someone or something to blame.

Unfortunately, too many giving advice in our industry aren't running profitable martial arts schools. Some never have. For others, it's been a LONGGGGGG time. Trust me when I say that my objective for you is success in the easiest and most efficient way possible, but it's not "magic pixie dust"; you must wake every morning and go to work.

Winners Remember Results ... Losers Remember Reasons. Which Are You?

I was in Atlanta a few weeks ago for an event with Dan Kennedy, Bill Glazer, Lee Milteer, George Foreman and others. Several NAPMA members have taken my advice to pay attention to what Bill and Dan have to say, and were also there. (A couple of them foolishly missed the NAPMA Extreme Success Academy, and that probably would have done them *much* more good — for those who were at both, congratulations for bettering yourselves.)

Anyway, one speaker was my friend Lloyd Irvin. It was interesting to hear Lloyd speak. Throughout his presentation, he continued to talk about a Genius Martial Artist who started him on the path to becoming a "Martial Arts Millionaire."

He spoke of provocative emails received, and about comments made, such as "any idiot can run a school doing $30,000 or more per month," and advice he had been given when he was running a $7,000-a-month school that propelled him to $1,000,000-plus.

Interestingly, I was the "Genius" he meant. Frankly, in my state of mind at that event, my reaction was erroneously, "Gee, sounds like I used to be pretty smart." Obviously, not great self-talk; however, it was incredibly interesting to hear my advice filtered through Lloyd to the crowd (and to several staff members and me in attendance).

He explained how he had spent $397 for a "password" that was my digital Extraordinary Marketing Book and how that book, while he was in Brazil training, pushed his gross from $7,000 to $20,000-plus. (It's available free at your NAPMA member site.)

He then described paying $2,750 for the first Ultimate Martial Arts Marketing Boot Camp, and then $5,000 for a "Box of Marketing Stuff" that I was selling at the event. Each time he made an investment, his return was 100 times or more in financial results.

That was his first step to create a $1,000,000 school and, frankly, a $10,000,000-plus "Marketing Empire" that includes training various UFC fighters, running his school and marketing a variety of "stuff" online.

He reminded me that I told him that unfortunately 97% of people, who attend a seminar, read a book or learn some material, would do nothing with that knowledge. Another piece of advice that he shared was when I asked him, "What are your goals for the next 12 months, 3 years and 5 years?" When he answered that he hadn't thought of his goals, I apparently responded with a sarcastic, "That's OK, 97% of the people haven't thought about them either — those that won't do anything."

He called what I had taught him the "secret room." In other words, others would think that you went to a seminar or event (think Extreme Success Academy), and a few attendees were taken to a "secret room" and given the "real secrets." Obviously, at the events he attended, and that made him a millionaire, *there was no secret room*. He heard the same message from me as others did. It's just that he VIOLENTLY EXECUTED.

His metaphor, taken from a conversation on a tape that I gave him (sold him) called *The Go To Guy* by John Carlton and Gary Halbert, is a "gun to the head." Implement as if someone has a gun to your child's head, and if you don't do it during the time allotted, then your child will be shot.

Clearly, most of us take action as if tomorrow is as good as today. Big winners take action that absolutely *must* happen this minute — as if there were a gun to their heads or their children's heads — and will implement *right* now.

It's what used to frustrate me the most about the bottom one-third of my coaching clients. We'd have the same conversation every month. I'd give them a list of tasks, and then 30 days later they would still not have implemented them.

A couple of years ago I just chose not to accept coaching clients that I thought would be like that, and fired those coaching clients with whom I ever had the conversation the third time or if I had many conversations a second time.

What's a takeaway? Implement as if your life depended on it. Wake every morning and knock off your top 5 or 6 items on your to-do list. Do them and move forward — *quick*!

Consultation Certificate

This Certificate Entitles the Bearer to a Personal 1-on-1 Martial Arts School Business Analysis With a NAPMA-Certified Business Analyst. This Individual Consultation is Valued at $495.00.

Certificate expires 12 months from the date of purchase.
To schedule your personal business analysis, complete this form and fax to NAPMA at 1-800-795-0853; mail to 1767 Denver West Blvd., Suite A, Golden, CO 80401; or visit www.PrivateCoachingSession.com

PLEASE FILL OUT COMPLETELY AND WRITE LEGIBLY

Name _____

School Name _____

Address _____

City _____ State/Province _____

Zip _____ Country _____

Phone _____ Fax _____

E-Mail _____

_____
Authorized by Toby Milroy
Chief Operating Officer, NAPMA

3 FREE GIFTS FOR SERIOUS SCHOOL OWNERS

FREE Personal School Evaluation

Two 30-minute Sessions A sure-fire way action plan to double your results or better.

FREE Two 90-Minute Seminars

with **"The Millionaire Maker Grandmaster Stephen Oliver** "The 5 Stupid Mistakes All Too Many School Owners Make that Kill Their Growth" and "The Key Step-by-Step Blueprint for Being a Big Winner"

FREE CD-DVD Package and Report

"How Hundreds of Smart School Owners Like You Doubled Their Revenue in the Last 12 Months Even in the Midst of the Greatest Recession since the Great Depresson, and How You Can, Too!"

The 10 "Secrets" of Leadership

There are many effective styles of leadership, probably, as many as there are different personality types of employees and bosses.

That having been said, I do believe that there are several "secrets" to leadership in any organization.

Vision

You must have a clear and compelling VISION for the future of your organization. These are not benchmarks, targeted gross revenue or active student count, but something much more powerful.

Your vision is a picture of where you want the organization to progress. It's the big picture of how your business should look, in as much sensory-rich detail as possible.

Leadership starts from within. If you have a clear picture of the future of your organization, then your conversation, actions and goals will tend to fall in line with this vision, and, ultimately, manifest it.

Communication

Having a clear vision of the future is valueless unless you become exceedingly effective at communicating that vision to others. That does NOT mean that you must be a gifted public speaker. Many great leaders (including Thomas Jefferson, among others) were not gifted speakers. You may communicate your vision through pictures, public speeches, written communications or ANY media, but your message must be received by its intended recipients in as compelling a way as possible.

Emotional Commitment

You must lead people from their heart and not their head. Daily commitment comes from an emotional attachment to the leader, mission, vision or the target feelings conveyed by your vision of the future. All leadership is based upon the emotional commitment of the followers much more than an abstract intellectual understanding of goals and objectives.

Values-Based

Although financial rewards help motivate or maintain motivation, ultimately, people will wake early and work late with the highest levels of intensity to contribute to others and the community. If financial rewards are directly tied to personal contribution to others, then motivation will remain high. Long-term motivation in any win-lose environment is nearly impossible. Be clear about your overriding values, and operate daily within those espoused values.

Congruence

Your words and actions must be congruent. You cannot motivate people to contribute and encourage them to a higher purpose if, ultimately, your integrity is questionable. Although business owners and managers — and politicians — have attained high levels with questionable integrity, I maintain that long-term leadership must be based upon honesty and the highest integrity. If your manager co-opts your help to hide his extramarital affairs, then how much trust will you give him? If your boss has a different persona in public than in private, will you trust that his or her communications with you is sincere?

Team Orientation

Someone once said: You can accomplish anything if you don't care who receives credit for it. In the martial arts, this attitude is exceptionally rare. Many "master" instructors have started to believe their own press, and act as if anything good that happens to them was their idea. Give credit. Involve the entire team. Work as much as possible to accomplish new directions through consensus. It's better, as the leader, to play a supporting role in many discussions and let the team members find the "means" to accomplish the "ends" in your vision.

Results Orientation

Focus on results, NOT process. Create accountability from every team member and student for the end result, not the activity. Many ideas are good, if implemented effectively. The greatest idea will fail if implemented poorly. Allow people, within limits, to choose their own means to achieve your agreed-upon end. Manage, based upon results, not activity.

Goals

Once you've implemented all the other "secrets," establish daily, weekly, monthly, quarterly and yearly goals. Make sure that they are all congruent with your mission, values and vision. Peter Drucker once said: "What gets measured gets done." Keep records and statistics on everything in your business, but focus on two, three or four key numbers, and then watch them like a hawk. Graph them. Post them in your office, at the reception desk, in the employee break room, or even on the front door of the school. Nothing motivates action like a huge graph of your targeted active student count in plain view. Look at your key numbers daily or even hourly to maintain focus.

Walk Your Talk

I know this is redundant, but nothing fails to motivate employees or students more than hypocrisy. Make a decision to live by your values and to be who you say you are 24 hours per day, 7 days per week.

Fairness

Ultimately, everyone must benefit from success and suffer from failure. In compensation, reward people greatly for successes, and make sure there are consequences for failure. If you delegate authority, then focus on the team and allow its members to be 100% responsible for their outcomes. Be supportive, but not paternalistic. If you never allow anyone to fail, then you've never allowed him or her to achieve much either.

Are you a "Raging Thunder Lizard" Evangelist?

t's fascinating to me the number of martial artists who live for their arts, but are bashful about sharing the value of those arts with others. Hopefully, that's not you.

Frankly, if what you do has an incredibly positive, life-changing impact on your students, then don't you owe it to *everyone* in your community to show them, in a convincing way, what it is you teach and the value of your product for them?

Marketing, or publicity, is just communications with the people in your community. You can purchase advertising (print, broadcast, direct mail, etc.) Or you can communicate for free (publicity). You can be a speaker or teacher to "affinity" groups (academic schools, day cares and churches, etc.) and introduce your school to large numbers at once or you can be a telemarketer or door-to-door salesperson and introduce your school to individuals one at a time.

You must have a great product, however, AND be a true believer (so must your staff). You must be passionate about sharing the value of your program with everyone who's willing to listen.

How do you convince people in your community that martial arts training at your school is REALLY valuable?

Rule Number 1: "Long-form" communication is better than "short-form," which means a one-hour live presentation is better than a 30-second live presentation. On television, 30 minutes (or 27:30) is better than 30 seconds. By mail, a 20-page letter or big package of information, with a DVD or CD, is better than a postcard. At an elementary school, a series of presentations is better than one presentation. The more information you can convey and the longer you keep your audience, leads or prospects engaged, the more opportunity you have to "make your case."

Rule Number 2: In-person communication always "trumps" broadcast communications. For instance, if you have a choice of a prospect visiting your Web site or talking to you in person (by phone or at your school), then in person is almost always *much* better. If you have a choice of prospects receiving an email or you calling them, then the call will be much more effective. If you have a choice of talking to them live or them receiving a "Robo-Call," then in person is always better.

Rule Number 3: A "class" or "participation" is *always* better than a "demonstration," with prospects as "spectators." In all cases, convincing them to participate and keeping them engaged will always trump passive observation. In a practical sense, compare a "Mall Demo" in front of several hundred to a class taught at center court to 20 or 30. The class will always work better to move prospects into ongoing participation.

Rule Number 4: Even if a prospect is not interested *today*, it doesn't mean he or she won't be interested next month, quarter or year. You always want to obtain contact information from all "spectators," "participants" and "interested parties," and then you must constantly and repetitiously follow-up. Email your lead list weekly or daily. Mail information to your prospects monthly, or more often. Call them quarterly, or more often. Send them invitations to events or activities. Without contact information, you will enroll a *very* small portion of whom you could, potentially.

Rule Number 5: "Farm your community." Remember, your community is always changing. Individuals are being married and divorced. They are moving to and from your community. Couples are having kids and their kids are growing, developing and evolving. Adults and families are sometimes rich and sometimes broke (and typically someplace in between). Sometimes, they are bored, sometimes overwhelmed. During some months, certain members of the community will experience trauma that moves them to explore new activities. Others will experience trauma that moves them to withdraw from activities. You must be constantly in front of as many people as possible and often as possible. While you may need to expose them to your message seven or nine times before they pay attention…you must also place your message in front of them when *they are receptive.* That means you must constantly and repetitiously generate leads, mail them and call them, and constantly be returning to the same community of people.

Rule Number 6: You must "Do Enough Stuff." For some schools, it's as simple as do more stuff. Most school owners underestimate the effort and expense to enroll a new student. If you are enrolling 5 students a month and need 20, then it may be as simple as doing four times as much stuff (time and energy or spending). Never discount that fact that you just may not be doing "Enough Stuff" to generate the results you need. There is no "Magic Pill." You may just need to work harder or invest more money in your business, or both.

Get Off Your Ass!

In a special report for all members in January, I outlined the 10 things you must do to thrive this year. It was a very valuable and important outline of the steps that are necessary in today's environment in order to grow your school and have a dramatic impact on your students and your community.

> *Hello Stephen,*
>
> *The "10 Things You Must Do to Thrive" was spot on! I couldn't agree with you more and I wanted to tell you. If only more school owners would really understand number one!*
>
> *Anyway, I wish you every success and all the best to Jodi, Jaeda and Chase.*
> BUZZ DURKIN

Now, if you don't know Buzz, in addition to being one of my oldest and dearest friends, he is one of the top school owners in the United States. He runs one of the most solid, highest quality schools that I've ever seen. In a small community he maintains a large enrollment with the strongest student retention that I've ever seen. He embodies true concern for his students and a deep reach into his community.

As a reminder the 10 points were (see the complete report at www.NAPMA.com in your members section:)

Number 1: Premium Pricing is the Quickest Route to a High Net.

Know your value and price your tuition accordingly. We are not in an industry where low price buys market share. In almost all cases all low price does is limit your revenue per student and convince your students of your limited value. "Absent other Criteria, Price Determines Percep-

tion of Value." It's my belief that you should be in the range of $200 a month for a new student's lessons in your school. I'd recommend two to three months "down payment" to initiate a minimum of a six months and preferably a 12—18 month initial contract for lessons.

Number 2: Focus "Internally First."

Take out a blank legal pad and focus on what you can do to improve student perception of value. Value starts with Rapport. Hire only sincere and honest people who truly care about their student's achievement more than their own.

Number 3: Have a Strong Sales Process in Place.

Have a *strong* introductory, Enrollment, Orientation, and Upgrade Process in place. Implement a focused *system* to support that process. Vigorously train all staff on that system, continuously. NAPMA provides extensive training on all sales and marketing processes as well as comprehensive programs

Number 4: "What gets measured gets done."

Keep complete operations statistics on your school and always have an up to date Profit and Loss statement. Learn how to read your numbers. Learn what your benchmarks should be for each area.

Number 5: Upgrade your staff.

The most important thing you can do once you have employees is to run regular (weekly or twice weekly training.) An employee either does or does not have the aptitude to perform the role that you need filled. They bring their own motivation to the job.

Number 6: "Martial Arts Without Philosophy is Just Street Fighting."

The move towards mixed martial arts has allowed

many to abandon the underlying personal development aspects of martial arts training. Certainly, simple things like having a student creed make a huge difference. Teaching weekly "character development lessons," having a "leadership team," and sharing positive "life skills" are essential.

Number 7: Focus on Retention.

The least expensive sale you ever make is the second or third sale to the same student. Unfortunately, in most every case, it's expensive, either in time or money to enroll a new student. You may spend $500 to $1,000 or more in paid advertising to get a new student.

Number 8: The Marketing Parthenon.

Relying on only one or two methods for generating new students is not only lazy but inherently dangerous. You must develop a wide range of systems and methods for creating introductory traffic consistently.

Number 9: Separate Your Hobby from Your Business.

The vast majority of school owners confuse their interests as a "hobbyist" with their role as a professional educator. You must not forget that your interests and needs as a Black Belt are different than the interest and needs of most of those who are interested in taking lessons from you.

Number 10: Eliminate Self-Defeating Thinking and Elevate your Expectations.

Just like in the recent phenomenon "The Secret," ultimately you get what you expect and attract what you focus on intently. It's important to look for references that support your goals and objectives and to ignore the naysayers. Be very careful that you pay attention to the top 10% of our industry and ignore the opinions, pricing, results of the rest.

Now, I hope you will review this list. Take a blank legal pad and on the top of each page make a note of one of these points. "Brainstorm with yourself" about how to effectively implement each point. Write down questions on each item and email them to me at StephenOliver@NAPMA.com for discussion on our next "Maximum Impact" Teleconference or for inclusion into an upcoming NAPMA now as I answer member questions.

In reviewing the list I recognize that there are perhaps a few things missing. I'm reading a book that Don Warrener wrote and was kind enough to send me a signed limited edition of *The Kata of Business*. Now, I haven't gotten very far, but it's got some great material in it. That having been said, I doubt if I'll agree with everything, but a couple of comments in the book stuck out as especially appropriate. One was his note that the difference between a failing school owner and a successful one is 20 hours per week.

Well, I should have made that number 11 on the list. Frankly, most school owners just really don't work very hard. They show up at the school at 4 or 5 p.m. and leave at 8 or 9 p.m. and think that they've done a full day. Honestly, most of the "Big Success Stories" that I know of start their day early and put in regular 10 to 12 hour days. They're putting in 60 to 80 hour weeks pretty regularly. In the case of our staff I expect them spend daytime hours on marketing activities (7 a.m.—3 p.m.) and evening hours focusing on retention, renewals, and enrollments.

This quarter I'm running all of my staff and school operators back through Tom Hopkin's great book, *Master the Art of Selling*," and, a key point in the book is that you must "see 20 people belly to belly every day." January's "Millionaire Skills" call (for Peak Performers and Inner Circle) included Brian Tracy making the same point. He said that most business owners spend precious few minutes actually face to face with prospective customers in a sales effort.

If you are not talking to prospective students

(or existing ones about upgrades or referrals) then you just aren't doing what's most important for your business. You've got to have that extra 20 hours per week out seeing live human beings how can enroll in your school or who have an audience of likely suspects for your school. All the time spent on Facebook, Twitter, surfing the net, or on unnecessary paperwork, or other social activity during the day just keeps you from getting out and talking to school principles, church leaders, and others in your community who can help your school grow.

Back to Don's book. He spends a lot of time breaking down what I have in my "10 Things" list as point number three. And, he's right. Although we cover an awful lot of high level material in Maximum Impact, Peak Performers and Inner Circle, it's always essential to circle back to the basics of how to answer your phone (Info Calls), Proper Introductory Lesson processes, the all important enrollment conference, and the renewal process. At the Extreme Success Academy that was covered by Toby Milroy in the A-Z day. NAPMA's "Way of the Phone," and "Way of the Enrollment" cover those basics in depth (and, we've just spent several months updating several of these programs. The rule of thumb that I learned from Nick Cokinos is always circle back and retrain your staff (and yourself), every 13 weeks. Always go back to basics and drill, practice, and rehearse on all of the basics.

To close on this reminder of the "10 Things You Must Do to Thrive," I'll remind you to pull the NAPMA Stats reports off of www.NAPMA.com and really track your numbers. It's amazing what happens when you really pay attention to what's happening in all aspects of your school how rapidly you can make huge improvements.

Beware of the Gurus

To help dispel some recently developed myths or just plain bad information, I'll give you the short version; however, at times, I will read a little like a college professor, who says, "Well, it all depends."

Cash versus Billing?

Here's a big "Well, it depends."

First, there are state laws, especially in California, Maryland, New York and other states and local municipalities, which you must follow. First, you should make sure that you are bonded or otherwise legal, depending on your local regulations.

Second, if the majority of revenue, on average, is routed through your monthly billing, then you will be "leaving money on the table," and will not earn as much income as otherwise possible.

Third, if you "push too hard" for 100% cash, then you will likely lose some students and create a less favorable environment for your school.

Fourth, if you receive cash for short programs (four to 12 months), then it won't make much of a positive impact on your revenue; however, if you receive cash for two, three, four or more years, then you will, on average, receive more money.

Fifth, people rarely ask for refunds, and you rarely need to give them (unless you have a regulatory issue that requires refunds). Taking cash payments, therefore, does not put you generally at risk of reimbursements.

Sixth, how good is your school? The better your student retention, the less it is important to ask for cash early.

Finally, there are two additional BIG considerations:

Are you a good or bad money manager? Martial arts instructors/school owners are notorious for bad money management, and often spend un-

earned revenues. You must manage your money wisely before you take large amounts of cash that you haven't really earned because you haven't provided the lessons yet.

How hard are you willing to work? If your billing check does not cover your monthly expenses, then you must be willing to "make it happen" every month. Going to China, Brazil or wherever for a month will kill your school if you do not have a track record for healthy monthly revenues.

You start each month new anyway, and you must HUSTLE every month to keep your school steady or growing.

Does Advertising Work?

I'm willing to accept the moniker of our industry's "marketing guru" and tell you two accurate bits of advice:

First, given the choice of an enrollment that didn't cost anything and one that cost $500, $750 or $1,000, in just about every case, I'll take the one for free.

Second, every school owner must put MUCH time and energy into all phases of marketing his or her school and should budget 12-15% of the target gross revenue on that effort. Yes, when done properly there are many effective television, radio, direct mail and print media opportunities that work consistently.

The gurus who tell you that advertising doesn't work just don't know how to make it work. A strong school, however, should be able to generate 50% or more of its enrollments from internal and "grass-roots" efforts, and shouldn't have to rely totally on paid advertising for new enrollments.

What this argument doesn't address is the following REALITY:

You should realize that your marketing efforts flow through a grid that includes:

LABOR INTENSIVE and RELATIVELY INEXPENSIVE.

EXPENSIVE and RELATIVELY LITTLE EFFORT REQUIRED.

If you have a small school, then you must concentrate, first and foremost, on the marketing methods that require effort, but relatively little money. As you grow, you will find that an increasing emphasis on "buying intros" makes more and more sense.

This explains why it is so difficult to "grow your school" while working a "day job," with the hope of making a transition one day. In almost all cases, it just never happens because the marketing efforts require either TIME or MONEY, and without both you are left with few options or opportunities.

Are You Worried about Student Retention?

I'll give you an easy and short answer. Do you want to like what you see in the mirror each day? If so, then work on excellent student service and rapport building.

Can you fix student dropouts? No, we all have them.

Harvard has a 98% graduation rate. That means 2% of those who are accepted do not successfully complete the four-year program, which is the equivalent of a 0.04% dropout rate per month.

As an industry, we have a long way to go. While 7% may be an industry average (and it may even be 10% dropping out PER MONTH) that's not a given. I've personally seen highly successful schools with less than a 2% rate per month. Not great by Harvard's standards, but the difference between 7% and 2% makes a HUGE difference in your student count, word-of-month reputation and, ultimately, your revenue.

FOCUS on QUALITY service, as perceived by your students, and all other elements of your business will take care of themselves (that is, if you become a expert MARKETER, master of SALES skills and manage your business effectively).

Why don't we "Walk our Talk?"

When talking with many school operators during the last few months, I had a "Blinding Flash of the Obvious." I've always loved that reference (I borrowed it from Tom Peters).

What's the "Blinding Flash of the Obvious?"

All martial arts instructors say that we teach focus, discipline and confidence. Many of us also claim to teach success skills, such as goal setting, self-esteem and self-image.

I see a total lack of those same attributes or a failure to translate lessons learned physically to the operation of their martial arts schools. This is the #1 problem of school owner/operators.

We should all be a "product of the product," and NO, I'm not talking about a walking, talking, killing machine. What I'm talking about is becoming goal-oriented, focused on results and having HIGH EXPECTATIONS of our schools and ourselves.

How Much Can You Spend to Generate an Enrollment?

Last month, I presented some ideas about how much you can afford to generate a new enrollment. Now let me lead you deeper into a couple more layers of complexity of this topic.

First, to keep your average marketing budget at approximately 10% of your gross, there's one other factor to keep in mind. How many free enrollments do you generate? How many referrals do you obtain? How many walk-ins? How many family add-ons? How many from demos? How many from birthday parties?

If you obtain half of your enrollments from sources such as these, then you could double how much you pay per new enrollment and still be within your target percentage of 10% of your total gross committed to advertising.

Example (based on example #2 of last month): Let's assume the school has an average lifetime student value of $4,000-plus. The owner spent $800 on paid advertising for each enrollment, but half of all enrollments were from free sources. The owner would still average 10%, or $400, per enrollment — even if his/her student acquisition cost was $800 for paid advertising-generated traffic.

Second, let's compare costs "At the Margin" with "The Average." If you spent $5,000 a month for advertising, then the next marginal expenditure is one more dollar, or $5,001. Often, in marketing, you may encounter "declining marginal return." In other words, for each additional dollar you spend, you receive less and less return per dollar.

A school spends $0 on marketing and advertising in any given month. For that month, it obtains five new students as referrals and three as walk-ins. Thus, it has acquired eight new students at $0 direct costs. If it then spends $1,000 in advertising and obtains two additional students, then it now has two more students at a marginal cost of $500 each. Its marginal cost per new student acquisition jumped from $0 to $500 immediately. Its average cost jumped from $0 to $200 per enrollment (10 new students, divided by the total cost of $1,000).

How much are you willing to pay at the margin? Ultimately, look at that question like this one: What is the most you would be willing to pay today to receive $4,000 during the next 33 months? Ultimately, at the margin, you should be willing to pay a relatively huge amount of money for one additional student.

All the information above depends upon the lifetime value of your students. This number includes all monies that students will pay your school, including down payments, exam fees, gross profit on retail items, monthly tuition payments and prepaid tuition.

Use the following formula to calculate easily an approximation of this number for your school. Divide your year's gross by the number of enrollments. For example, $500,000 gross divided by 250 enrollments equals $2,000 average value per student. If your numbers have been changing rapidly (especially if you are growing rapidly), then look at the totals of the last three years' numbers from that longer-term perspective.

Jeff Smith, Mile High Karate director of instruction, says you must take into account the total potential value of a student:

initial enrollment

plus Black Belt Club

plus 2nd-Degree

plus 3rd-Degree

plus 4th-Degree

plus retail

plus exam fees.

Then he compares that total to the total average in his student body and continually works to move the average closer to the potential.

You accomplish that with greater retention and cash enrollments and renewals. You increase your lifetime student value with greater retention, higher tuition rate, retail sales and products, services to sell to your students.

Winners and Losers on the West Coast

It's been interesting over the last couple of weeks. We had a *fabulous* NAPMA Maximum Impact Coaching call to kick-off March, with Toby Milroy and I extensively covering the new promotion, and the A-Z of back to basics on the new student introductory process.

Next, I made quick stops in San Diego, Los Angeles, and San Francisco doing small "Mini-Bootcamps" with members and non-members alike. If you live in California and missed these, you missed what became a very valuable small group learning opportunity. Each participant left with a comprehensive marketing plan for targeting 20 or more new students in March.

The participants represented quite a range. The most successful school represented (in San Diego) was (no surprise here) a Peak Performers Group member who's had tremendous growth and the strongest highest average student value of anyone I met in the three cities. It became obvious right away in San Diego, then again in Los Angeles, that I could spot the Big Winners from the losers, or those who have just been "sliding along laterally," right away. No, it wasn't if they were wearing a suit or wearing a Rolex. The difference that was evident right away was one of *focus*. Just about everyone who attended was an accomplished martial artist. Many had 20, 30, or more years in operations.

"Losers" in the group tended to have two evident traits: First, their primary focus in talking to other participants prior to the "Martial Arts Business & Marketing Mini-Bootcamp" was predominantly on martial arts style, or on various ways they were modifying, developing, enhancing or expanding their curriculum. They talked about the "technical aspects" of their style, and then planned to expand their small school by adding a different "style" or curriculum.

In contrast the "Winners" focused on new marketing ideas, better student service processes, and how to maximize their revenue per student and retention. They talked about their school objectives, not from the standpoint of technical curriculum, but from an orientation of "target market" success in attracting that market and their goals for growing their school.

Another sign of the "losers," and this is mostly of the "sliding along laterally" or losing 10-20% this year, was in their lack of active participation in personal education. The lowest performing schools that had been open for a while had formerly been members of NAPMA, and perhaps other training sources as well. They had gradually stopping paying attention to the materials they were receiving. Possibly let their membership lapse. Usually stopped going to events like Quantum Leap and Extreme Success Academy. Ultimately, they had "reverted to the familiar" and spent most of their time with "martial arts peers" who had similar low expectations.

Fortunately, I believe for both groups, I opened their eyes. School owners who believe that 50-100 students and charging $50-$125 a month for lessons is doing pretty good were awakened to a much broader world with much bigger opportunities. Really, it should be easy with all the resources that I give you in Maximum Impact (and especially through Peak Performers, Inner Circle, and Coaching) to run a school grossing $30,000 to $50,000 or more per month.

There are lots of examples of schools doing *very* well just because they pay attention and continue to expand their education (moving from Maximum Impact to Peak Performers, for instance). One success example we used at the last live event was of a school that moved from $17,000 a month to well over $110,000 a month in the last 18 months. I work with them monthly on coaching calls. They've only implemented a few of the strategies that I've taught them, but they *do* implement and have a positive belief system that it is *possible*.

Oh, and before I forget, the schools that are struggling have one other thing in common. They are surrounded by peers in the same situation. The best way to improve your results is through "Peer Pressure" to validate the potential for double, triple, or quadruple the results that you are having currently. That's why there really is no substitute for live events like Extreme Success Academy and Quantum Leap and for Peer Coaching Environments like Peak Performers and Inner Circle. I can tell you all day long what's possible. But to see others who are no smarter than you are achieving much better results is the ultimate proof that you can do it yourself.

For those who think that right now it's tough. We had my first Mile High Karate school (same location 30 years) enroll 36 new students ($397 down, $197 a month, 12 month enrollment) last month. One of our newest Mile High Karate schools generated 79 intros from a wide variety of mostly non-paid community outreach systems. Another generated 210 intros in February from one community outreach activity.

That having been said, I sincerely believe that with the exclusive arrangements we've lined up with distribution companies for "*The Karate Kid*" and "*The Last Airbender*," that this year may be a return to the absolute peak of our industry. Add to that what should be a steadily improving econom-

ic climate and the year is going to be HUGE for those who keep learning, who implement what we coach them on, and who really get things in gear.

This month I completed an interview with Cliff Lenderman for MAIA's version of "Sounds of Success." We discussed NAPMA, MAIA, Century, and the SuperShow's ongoing excellent working relationship. We also discussed the trend towards implementing MMA curriculum in professional schools. Clearly, NAPMA's live events are *very* different from the SuperShow. The SuperShow is a great event similar to the old NAPMA World Conferences. Our efforts (which to date have been very successful) are to bring a smaller team of very focused school owners together to be trained extensively in "Best Practices." A Martial Arts trade show with a variety of "Break-Out" sessions is very useful and we support those efforts. For our part we want a 9 a.m.–midnight "roll up the sleeves and immediately go back and implement." Therefore, we have lots of stories now of leaving Quantum Leap or Extreme Success Academy and jumping from $17,000 a month to over $100,000, or jumping from part-time to $200,000 a year-plus *net* personal income. Designed to immediately improve your income. Our events are not designed for meeting the newest UFC stars or for focusing on your personal technical competency but on learning immediately implementable business and marketing practices and processes.

In the Los Angeles event we discussed the MMA/UFC boom pretty extensively. Several schools (grossing less than $100,000 a year) were teaching several different MMA-type curriculum and focusing on that trend. To see the complete discussion see the partial recording at www.NAPMABlog.com or at your NAPMA member Web site.

"Mixed-Up Martial Arts" Draws a Reaction

First…more on "Mixed Up Martial Arts," the recent cover story of *Martial Arts Professional* magazine that has generated lots of controversy — as was obviously intended. I'd love to have you share with me your feedback — in support, opposition or any other position relative to the basic premise. If you haven't read the article go to www.Martial-ArtsProfessional.com and let me know what you think about my opinions on the subject.

I received this today from Joe Lewis:

This (below) just came in on my Facebook page about the same article in Martial Arts Professional. I do not get the magazine and nor have I seen this controversial article you called me about today. Again, everything is taken out of context; no one in martial arts knows what I had to go through with the way the media was treating martial artists (especially the fighters) when I arrived back here from Okinawa in 1965. Many interviewers, both print and TV reporters, tried their best to hose me about this violence issue, but I was ready to fire back and point out their ignorance (none of them could give me an appropriate definition of violence), and also their lack of doing their homework any good reporter should always do in advance. The famous psychologist, Dr. Nathaniel Branden, was my Godfather and mentor — and we kicked ass!

Anyway, I am NOT the "moral conscience of the martial arts" — to run the show and dictate everything to the rest of us (proper tradition, ethics codes, character development values, etc, etc.).

I'll remain a spectator and stick to the real fighting science and taking care of my family of black belts. Remember my leadership motto: "Real leaders are not followed, they are accompanied."

Here's a good one for this surfacing issue:

"A winner knows how much he still has to learn, even when considered an expert by others.

A loser wants to be considered an expert by others before he has learned enough to know how little he knows."

— Sydney Harris

JOE LEWIS, FORMER WORLD KARATE/KICKBOX CHAMPION, USMC

Hi Joe,

I just got done reading a story from Martial Arts Professional magazine, "Let's restore the dignity of a Black Belt." I can't agree more. When you and I served, we said "no" to violence. Now the news media is all over this MMA stuff. I have been in the martial arts since I was nine years old. I come from a good "blood line," where a Black Belt is earned, not given. Now this crap, I have students in my dojo who want to leave to do MMA. I'm a 2nd-Degree Black Belt with Shihan Funakoshi and Sensei Sevvatasi, and a 3rd-Dan with the JKF. I've seen so many bad schools, and now good schools, changing the standards of excellence and the quality of a black belt rank. How sad.

GRAYDON LEWIS

It's in reference to a quote from one of his previous emails that was included in a sidebar to the article (with his knowledge). Personally, I love the Sydney Harris quote. It goes right along with another disturbing trend in our industry … more about that later.

And, Robert Blum commented and shared a video:

> *I couldn't agree with the article more — this is what is taking place in higher income areas like mine because of MMA: http://www.youtube.com/watch?v=W8Cto9vIrt8 (take a look for yourself, it's either scary or comical depending upon how you look at it).*

Actually, I'm surprised that many martial arts school owners find the subject controversial. However, I was shocked and concerned to find out how many school owners seem to find it necessary to jump on this very unproductive bandwagon. In my experience with coaching school owners, I've over and over taken schools from $12,000 to $17,000 a month to $35,000 to $50,000-plus Some in as little as 90 days; others over 9 to 15 months. Either way, the hidden truth of most of these quick turnarounds was the need to "deprogram" them of convoluted systems and processes, as well as simplify their operation. Many suffered the delusion that the way to success was to keep laying on additional curriculum and classes.

This leads me to my next topic. While talking a few months ago to one of my early students (participant in the first "Ultimate Martial Arts Marketing Bootcamp), Lloyd Irvin, who at the time had a $7,000 a month school, and is now a $1,000,000-plus school, plus several other unrelated multi-million dollar businesses. He reminded me of several pieces of advice that I gave him when we first met.

The first…however blunt and brutal was:

"Any brain-dead idiot can run a $20,000-plus per month school."

Now, fortunately or otherwise, I might say it in a more polite way now. However, that sentiment is more true now than ever. In the late 1970s and early 1980s, the Jhoon Rhee Institute had nine, then 12 schools averaging more than that amount (30 years ago!) For many years — as early as 1983 — my schools as employee-owned schools all averaged more than that number. I remember one year (1991, I believe) that was $1,680,000, with five schools, all absentee owner-employee operated. To do that math for you: that's an average of $28,000 a month across five locations for the year. That was not an unusual year.

Now. There's lots of school owners doing way less than that number. My question is why?

I'm convinced that there are several main reason.

First. Inappropriately low expectations.

Several school owners that I met in California just legitimately didn't know that it was possible to *net* $100,000 or more running a single martial arts school. Once your eyes are opened and you believe it's possible then, opportunities open up for you.

Second. Lack of personal education.

Many school owners think that their years of martial arts study entitle them to success. The unfortunate reality for them is that success in running a martial arts school is dependent more on knowledge of marketing, sales, service, and teaching methodology than it is on technical mastery. Some of the best champions in the martial arts would never be able to run a profitable martial arts school. Many of those same individuals are mediocre at best teachers.

That's something that's special about my teachers Jhoon Rhee and Jeff Smith. Take Grandmaster Smith. He was the #1 Ranked Point Fighter in the World, the first PKA Light-Heavy Weight Kickboxing Champion. He won one of the early MMA competitions and fought and won the Heavy-Weight Title on the most watched kickboxing match in history (50,000,000-plus.) However, he's also been the Head Instructor and General Manager of the multi-million-dollar Jhoon Rhee Institute chain, then run his own multi-million dollar school chain, including individual branches grossing as much as $750,000 a year. He's learned to move from athlete to Master Teacher to Master Salesman, and then to Master Business Owner. Are you willing to put in the same "pain and suffering" on educating yourself as an educator, school administrator, and business owner as you were on your own physical training?

Third. False "Gurus."

Unfortunately many of those running around the martial arts industry giving advice haven't truly been very successful themselves running schools. Some last ran schools many years ago in a much different environment. Others run personality-based schools with some success, and then try to teach their methods to you.

I was having a conversation with several associates recently about this phenomenon. The comment was that I was responsible for most of the guys running around right now that fit the above description. I think a more appropriate, although simplistic, observation was that many came out of the Jhoon Rhee/EFC circle in the 1980s and early 1990s. More recently, as I started coaching and offering exclusive bootcamps, a series of former clients had some success from my teaching (i.e.: $12,000 to $30,000 in a few months), then made the unfortunate conclusion that they had "arrived." They then started running around sharing their "wisdom" with the industry.

Remember the above quote?

"A winner knows how much he still has

to learn, even when considered an expert by others.

A loser wants to be considered an expert by others, before he has learned enough to know how little he knows."
— SYDNEY HARRIS

It's unfortunate for many in the industry who don't know who's real from who's not.

Here's a few questions for you to ask.

1. Where did this "Guru" get his or her knowledge, and do they openly and freely acknowledge their debt of gratitude?
2. Do they currently operate successful Martial Arts Schools? I say "schools" rather than "school," due to the fact that many who run a successful single school are relying on their own "force of personality" more so than a system that works.
3. If not, how long has it been and what was their track record then?
4. Is their advice sufficient to take you to the highest levels of the industry, or are they limited in their own "scope and capability."
5. How's their ROI? I've always promised high-end coaching clients a minimum of a 10-to-1 return on investment. In most cases, they've received 20-to-1 or more return on any money they've invested with me.

I've recently seen a fairly high profile long-time guru in the industry directly and indirectly bashing me and bashing NAPMA. He doesn't explain that he, in fact, learned how to run a school mostly from me and Jeff Smith. He doesn't explain that he never ran a particularly successful school, and, frankly, didn't enjoy it much when he did. He doesn't explain that his advice is mostly tailored to "be what small martial arts school operators want to hear" not what they need to hear to truly be successful. He doesn't explain that he always hated teaching kids, and longed for a return to an adult market that, frankly, never existed as he imagines it. And finally, he doesn't explain that he's so distanced from running schools and the day-to-day operations of running a school that he's totally in the dark as to what's working today in the current market and environment.

In fact, there are several "Gurus" coaching a "run to MMA" without truly understanding the market for traditional martial arts schools *or* the market for MMA. Is there a market for MMA schools (gyms)? You bet. Is it the right market for many or most traditional schools. No. Make sure you take advice from someone who understands the real forces at work in our industry.

And, to get back to point one: I freely acknowledge my "Debt of Gratitude" to teachers and mentors, such as: Jhoon Rhee, Nick Cokinos, Jeff Smith, and Ned Muffly. I acknowledge the incredible foundation laid for us by pioneers such as Pat Burleson, Chuck Norris, Ed Parker and others. I give thanks to stumbling across Guru's outside our industry such as Jay Abraham, Dan Kennedy, Tony Robbins, Zig Ziglar, Tom Hopkins, Lee Milteer and MANY others. I am eternally thankful to a wonderful group of peers who grew with me to run multi-million-dollar schools, including Masters Bill Clark, Tim and Dave Kovar, Keith Hafner, David Deaton, John Worley, Larry Carnahan, Pat Worley and others too numerous to mention. And, finally, to students of mine who recognize and give back to the industry, such as Toby Milroy, Lloyd Irvin, and MANY, MANY others. A few take all of the credit. However, for many years I had a quote from a fortune cookie taped in my DayPlanner (remember those?) "Expect no Gratitude and You Will Never Be Disappointed."

Consultation Certificate

This Certificate Entitles the Bearer to a Personal 1-on-1 Martial Arts School Business Analysis With a NAPMA-Certified Business Analyst. This Individual Consultation is Valued at $495.00.

Certificate expires 12 months from the date of purchase.
To schedule your personal business analysis, complete this form and fax to NAPMA at
1-800-795-0853; mail to 1767 Denver West Blvd., Suite A, Golden, CO 80401;
or visit www.PrivateCoachingSession.com

PLEASE FILL OUT COMPLETELY AND WRITE LEGIBLY

Name _____

School Name _____

Address _____

City _____ State/Province _____

Zip _____ Country _____

Phone _____ Fax _____

E-Mail _____

_____
Authorized by Toby Milroy
Chief Operating Officer, NAPMA

3 FREE GIFTS FOR SERIOUS SCHOOL OWNERS

FREE Personal School Evaluation

Two 30-minute Sessions A sure-fire way action plan to double your results or better.

FREE Two 90-Minute Seminars

with **"The Millionaire Maker Grandmaster Stephen Oliver** "The 5 Stupid Mistakes All Too Many School Owners Make that Kill Their Growth" and "The Key Step-by-Step Blueprint for Being a Big Winner"

FREE CD-DVD Package and Report

"How Hundreds of Smart School Owners Like You Doubled Their Revenue in the Last 12 Months Even in the Midst of the Greatest Recession since the Great Depresson, and How You Can, Too!"

Crisis Hits

When I say, "Crisis Hits," I am not talking about hurricanes, earthquakes or any other recent natural disasters. I am referring to a recent and dangerous trend in our industry, however, that is not only risky for individual schools, but also I'm afraid may just reawaken the staffs of state Attorneys' General offices around the U.S. (and their equivalent elsewhere).

What's that trend?

Recently, several of our industry "guru's" focused on CASH PROGRAMS as the ultimate panacea for anemic martial arts school operations.

This overwhelming emphasis on cash threatens to wreak havoc on the industry, especially when it is combined with arguably "hard-core" sales tactics and, often, disreputable or, at the very least, apathetic approaches to long-term customer service.

Please review with me the first example of the problem. I have spoken with many school owners recently, and some of them have aggressively adopted what I will characterize as the following:

Aggressive sales efforts focused on "cashing out" 100% of their existing students.

- Aggressive sales strategies to "cash-out" 100% of enrollments and renewals.
- Disdain for billing tuition and billing companies.
- Inadequate and/or heavily "labor-intensive" marketing efforts with limited "leverage."

Often, these strategies are combined with a "what-the-hell" attitude, regarding student service. These school owners have also adopted the viewpoint that their students will inevitably become dropouts anyway; they're not able to stop dropouts, so why try.

Adopting all or several of these methods and attitudes often results in the following scenario. A school owner learns these new tools, implements them suddenly and asks for cash payments from all of his students.

It's easy to predict what inevitably happens: the school owner doubles, sometimes, even triples his best month ever — nothing wrong with that as far as it goes. What happens next really wreaks havoc. First, without a very strong and effective marketing program, a school that has cashed out all its students, without big enrollment numbers, ultimately experiences serious trouble.

I've seen a school owner learn these new systems. Then, cash out every student in his school and hit the malls with a clipboard and a serious head of steam for two or three months.

Thrilled with his huge cash flow, the school owner buys a Corvette or a Porsche and a Rolex or two, spending all the money on rapidly depreciating assets, such as jewelry, cars, vacations, high-priced restaurants or, even in the best case, his own "McMansion," which locks him into a big payment, creating an asset that is not liquid. In straightforward terms, he has blown the money, quickly and completely.

What happens next? Inevitably, his record cash results cannot be maintained, and the monthly bottom line becomes just average months with 20%, 50% and even 75% less revenue than previously.

Now, "Mr. Cash-Out," the school owner, who has spent all the money, awakes one morning to realize a couple of horrible truths.

He has pissed off X number of students and his student body has decreased from 300 to 200 active or less.

He is cash-poor with a severely reduced cash

flow, and is on the brink of insolvency.

There are two schools of thought, concerning cash-outs, and each has its own rabid rank of supporters. Frankly, I don't endorse either; however, I am moving steadily toward the billing school of thought.

School of thought #1: Ask for cash. If your students pay you in full, then you have 100% of their tuitions.

School of thought #2: It's illegal, unethical and immoral to take the cash, so process your students' tuitions through a billing system.

Frankly, I like big cash deals. What I don't like is seeing school owners take hundreds of thousands of dollars in cash, and then, through financial mismanagement or miscalculation, are forced to close their schools, which is an invitation for regulatory scrutiny.

Nick Cokinos, founder of Educational Funding Company, has preached the correct strategy for years, and that is utilizing a contingent-liability fund. Quite simply, you deposit all paid tuitions for lessons that you haven't yet earned into savings accounts: liquid interest-bearing investments. You don't withdraw the money until you've taught the lessons and earned it.

Example: A school owner accepts a three-year, paid-in-full tuition. He deposits one-sixth of the cash-out in his checking account as current income; however, he should really deposit only 1/36th this month. Every month, he withdraws an amount equal to the lessons taught during that month (or would be taught if the student drops out) and deposits the amount in his checking account as earned income.

Too complicated? The alternative approach is just as valid:

Build your billing check to cover all of your monthly expenses.

When you take cash programs, invest the money personally to build wealth.

Create your lifestyle as your school and wealth grows — not from short-term bursts.

Are You Ready to Commit to Success?

I'm convinced that this year is going to be a *great* year for the Martial Arts Industry. More specifically for you, the fact that you are a NAPMA Member, and, frankly, opened your package and are reading this, means that you are really going to implement (more about that later) and grow.

It's certainly true that the last 24 months, between the recession in general and the credit crisis, has been really rough on any and all small businesses. In some areas, unemployment skyrocketed, and in general, their was a general "malaise" among consumers.

Now, the economy is creeping back. It's not roaring back yet, but that's on the way. Employment lags (not leads) the economic recovery, and while the housing market may not reach the previous "bubble highs," it's obvious everywhere that the economy is rebounding.

In retrospect, I'm sure it bottomed out and began rebounding long before President Obama tinkered with much or accelerated government overspending, however that's a topic for another time. The current reality is that consumer spending is back up; even the car companies are starting to show a profit again. My favorite, Apple, had their best first quarter ever, and their best quarter, excluding Christmas season, ever. And that was before iPad sold 500,000 units in a week. Even Martha Stewart on Fox Business was bragging about their sales and profits being way up in all channels, including at Macy's.

How's this year look?

Well, I'm hoping that *The Karate Kid* is a huge hit. Regardless, it's a great excuse for all member schools to pull out the checkbook and get out of bed a little earlier and do a *huge* amount of marketing internally, in the community and in the media to fill your school.

I'll share a little secret with you. The biggest part of my success with various movies going back to the original *The Karate* Kid (and, to *Enter the Dragon* and the *Kung Fu* television series (with the Jhoon Rhee Institute) is in having a great excuse to get my creative juices flowing, get my staff excited (and, out of bed), and to create excitement among my students. You may not need it — however, it's always good to have a reason to convince yourself and everyone around you that it's good timing for record enrollments, renewals, and grosses. It becomes a marvelous self-fulfilling prophecy.

Truthfully, I've always worked to have a good excuse for huge renewals at least a couple of times per year. I've looked for at least a quarterly reason to go "balls to the wall" (excuse the expression) on filling the school with new students. Maybe it's just me, but a key element of sales management always seems to be a good excuse for peak results and, something different to gain attention and focus on results.

What will guarantee your success?

Well, I hate to keep banging the same drum, but, go back and read "ten things you must do to be successful." They include: price your tuition at $200-plus each month, fix your sales ratios, offer continually better service to your students from their perspective, and market, market, market to add 20-plus new students per month.

The difference is *Implementation*.

I am continually amazed and flabbergasted by the number of people who pay lip service to a desire to be successful...who then do little or nothing.. I'm going to share with you today my two favorite quotes. Each of which occupied page one or two of my day-planner for years. Both have to do with truly accomplishing things rather than learning, hoping, planning, expecting, or otherwise preparing for rather than achieving successful outcomes.

The first favorite:

> *"Winners remember results, losers remember reasons."*

That's a very important one to anchor in for yourself. I repeatedly talk to school owners who share with me all the reasons what I'm suggesting won't work in their town, city, for their students, or with their style. They create a long list of reasons for everything that could go wrong, might go wrong, should go wrong. Geeezzzz! If they put 1/10th of that energy into just going and doing it, they might accomplish something.

The next thing these same people do when asked about their stats or their past results is give me the LONG list of reasons that they did everything right and things didn't work out. The excuse du jour is, "The Economy." Everyone's unemployed, has no money, isn't willing to pay for lessons, and it goes on *ad nauseum*. Interesting that at the same time 500,000-plus "early adopters" paid $500 and up for an iPad without knowing what they were going to use if for or even really what it would do.

Now, don't miss the point. If you are in downtown Detroit with 40% vacancy and 35% unemployment — then you may be right. Question is — why isn't your U-Haul packed and headed to areas with more opportunity?

The second quote is all about commitment. Are you truly committed to being a success as a martial arts school owner/operator? Well, I've got to remind you, wait and see always leads to failure. You have to be an active and committed participant in your own success. Unless you set a real goal and publically commit yourself to be in the top 20% of our industry you are doomed to mediocrity, and frankly to struggling financially.

The quote is this:

> *"Until one is committed, there is hesitancy, the chance to draw back, always ineffectiveness.*
>
> *Concerning all acts of initiative and creation, there is one elementary truth the ignorance of which kills countless ideas and splendid plans that the moment one definitely commits oneself, then providence moves too.*
>
> *All sorts of things occur to help one that would never otherwise have occurred. A whole stream of events issues from the decision, raising in ones favor all manner of unforeseen incidents, meetings and material assistance which no man could have dreamed would have come his way. I have learned a deep respect for one of Goethe's couplets:*
>
> *'Whatever you can do, or dream you can, begin it! Boldness has genius, magic, and power in it.'"*
>
> — W.H. Murray, of the Scottish Himalayan Expedition

Maybe, a final point worth making is about possibility and expectations. I met with school owners in San Diego, Los Angeles and San Francisco earlier this spring. Most of them had a very limited perspective about what's possible in their own industry.

I remember back — to probably 1986 or 1987, I'm not sure exactly — Nick Cokinos launched the EFC Top 10 list (now, I believe it's called the EFC All Stars.) On the early list I remember having three or four of the top 10 schools on the list. Now the "All Stars" list have often been controversial, with schools not wanting their numbers shared (either from embarrassment or hiding from the IRS, I guess). However, I'm convinced it was one of his best ideas ever. Suddenly, the real numbers of schools from all over the U.S. were right there in front of everyone. Whether it was me having several $15,000—$25,000 a month (in EFC collections) schools or Keith Hafner having a $75,000 single school (or Will Maier, Greg Silva, etc.), it created immediate "social proof" of what was possible. At conventions you could almost spot school owners pointing at individuals grossing double what they were grossing saying: "geez, that guy's not that bright, if he can do it I can do it." Now that's pretty powerful.

My group in California had mostly not had the benefits of Inner Circle, Peak Performers or Coaching. These $7,000—$12,000 schools were pretty happy with their results, not realizing that others "not as smart as them" in locations that were no better were netting more than they were grossing. And that others were running $35,000—$100,000 a month schools with their same style and similar clientele. That belief in what's possible is extremely valuable. It's why you've got to surround yourself with people who are doing better than yourself.

A similar example is I engaged in an industry discussion board recently about MMA and school operations. A school operator in my home state of Oklahoma chipped in and bragged about running a very successful MMA school that was doing $15,000 a month. Well, I guess very successful depends upon your perspective. While in Atlanta I spoke with two different MMA/BBJ school owners who were grossing over $100,000 a month (one from Miami, the other from Nashville or Memphis). One was open seven days a week, 24 hours a day. While in San Antonio, we visited a Krav Maga location with over 3,000 members.

Now, the $15,000 a month school thought they were setting the world on fire. Since they are not NAPMA members, they are not reading this newsletter, and really are only interacting with school owners who are, to quote Tom Hopkins, "More screwed up than they are," don't have an understanding of the six-figure income potential of their school. It's the same school owner who only wants free advice and won't invest to learn from those who have really been there, done that in our industry. Their loss, your gain.

Manage Your Time, Live Your Life

In a martial arts school operation, there are two major time-management problems that school owners encounter.

First: Deciding that their workday is from 5 p.m. to 9 p.m., then spending their day with a variety of time-wasting activities. There are many important activities that should be accomplished during non-prime time hours.

Remember that during class hours if you are not teaching or personally interacting with students and parents, then you are misusing your time. These are typically the only hours when you can communicate with your students.

What should you do during non-class hours?

- External promotional and marketing activities:
- Meeting with local elementary school administrators and teachers.
- Meeting with local merchants to develop co-promotional opportunities.
- Researching advertising and marketing opportunities.
- Writing marketing letters to your old prospects.
- Organizing your exam list and reviewing attendance records of your students.
- Reviewing your inactive student list— and making a plan to reactivate those ex-students.
- Updating your computer system and keeping your stats up to date.

The main issue is to distinguish between prime-time activities and non-prime time activities. All administrative duties should be accomplished only during non-prime time hours.

Second: Failing to manage time effectively on an hour-by-hour and minute-by-minute basis.

How do you manage your time effectively?

Use an effective planning system. I prefer Franklin Planners. They are more expensive than some of the other systems, but, given the value of this system to your life, it is well worth the expense. When using the Franklin system, I plan many activities quarterly and monthly — more so than focusing on every quarter hour. If you keep your objectives clear, then it can be relatively easy to manage your evening hours.

Use an adequate school management software system to keep your intro appointments and prospects' stats under control. Currently, there are several fine systems on the market. Naturally, I prefer the system that I completely designed, Master Vision; however, I would be the first to admit that other systems have similar capabilities to organize your day effectively.

Prioritize appropriately. I highly recommend that you read *First Things First* by Steven Covey, or, at least, study this chapter in 7 *Habits of Highly Effective People*.

To summarize Covey's concepts, all activities fall into one of four quadrants:

1. Urgent and Important.
2. Not Urgent and Important.
3. Urgent and Not Important.
4. Not Urgent and Not Important.

A martial arts school, during prime-time hours (4 p.m. to 8 p.m.) is full of quadrant-1 and -3 activities. On a minute-by-minute basis, the evening is full of ringing telephones, constant questions, classes that must begin and end on time, and the constant parade of important and unimportant urgencies.

For your evening to be effective, remember there are really only three important elements:

enrollments, retention and renewals. If an activity does not positively contribute to one of these elements, then it falls into the "Not Important" category.

Mediocre school operators fail to focus on those important areas, that are not urgent. Generally important, but not urgent areas include:

- Internal and external marketing efforts.
- Student retention.
- Renewal preparation.

A note about students and your time: With few exceptions, students, of one or two types, can consume your time. Your AAA Black Belt Club, 5-days-per-week loyalists and your D-negative and disgruntled students. You must be careful not to devote too much prime time to students in either of these categories.

Your AAA students will spend time talking, and in your presence, just because they can't experience enough of your school and you. Your D-negative students often have a negative outlook of their lives, and just want to complain to anyone who will listen. In any conversation of this type, work on keeping the conversation short and on subject.

A few ways to accomplish this is don't sit down, don't go in your office — address the issues at hand quickly and directly, suggest scheduling a specific appointment time when it's appropriate for your schedule.

Third: By spending excess time on "hobby" marital arts activities while rationalizing that you are working on your school business.

Fourth: Failing to structure your day effectively. To structure your day effectively, it's important to determine how you personally function best, and then plan your activities during your own peak times of efficiency.

A few years ago there seemed to be this myth that successful school owners rose at dawn and were in their office by 8:00 am. This works quite well for some of my closest friends, but, for me, this has always been massively counter-productive.

All martial arts school operators must be at their absolute peak between the hours of 4 p.m. and 8 p.m. You must determine which of your creative hours are for planning and development, and also structure your days to hit your peak during prime-time hours.

For myself, I am mostly creative late at night. When most of my friends are climbing into bed, I am just starting. This article was probably written between 11 p.m. and 3 a.m. I like to start my day mid-morning, take a break mid-day, and then hit school operations hard during prime time.

Depending upon what I need to accomplish, I will either take a break and go to a movie, or grab a quick bite to eat, and then work on my creative projects, either writing lesson plans, designing ad campaigns and writing.

For best time management, you can do much more work when no one is around to interrupt and the phones aren't ringing. If you are an early bird, then 5 or 6 a.m. might be best for you. Again, for me, my creative tasks are accomplished after 11 p.m. If I return your e-mail, then it may be at 2 or 3 a.m.

"Positioning" Your Martial Arts School

Years ago, I read a really interesting book, *Positioning: the Battle for Your Mind*. Now, some of the concepts presented conflict with the general direct-response position that I hold and propose throughout this column; however, a couple of concepts are worth revisiting.

What Are You Promoting?

The example used in the book (keep in mind that this book was published years ago) was about IBM's introduction of the personal computer (PC). You may be old enough to remember that when IBM introduced its first PC, there were quite a number of different makers pushing various systems. Apple had already made a splash with the Macintosh computer. The Osborn computer was big. Kaypro, Tandy, Commodore and others already had systems available, with competing operating systems and structures. The industry was fragmented, with no standards.

IBM could have introduced its new product by positioning it against its direct competitors — for example, why its product is better than Apple's or Tandy's; however, IBM did not choose that approach. Its management realized, quite appropriately, that battling over the very small number of hobbyists who already owned or were ready to buy a microcomputer was futile.

Instead, IBM took the tact of promoting why everyone should have a PC. IBM created a non-threatening mascot of sorts (the Tramp of Charlie Chaplain fame), and began a series of ads that explained the value of a PC in the home or office — always without reference to their direct competitors or other manufacturers.

IBM's logic was that, if it promoted the virtues of these machines, then IBM would gradually be recognized as the leader in the industry; and it would expand the number of people using computers rather than battle for market share.

Personally, I think this would be a very lousy approach for beer-makers or soft-drink manufacturers that are battling for market share in declining overall markets; however, for martial arts schools, this is, generally, a great approach.

Beginning in 1983 in Denver, I made an effort to emulate IBM's approach. My ads always touted the benefits of martial arts instruction, explained the benefits of our approach and never mentioned that any other business taught this content but us. During the years in Denver, if someone thought of martial arts lessons (especially for kids), then at least nine times in ten, they would think of us.

Do any of us think that we have impacted the market for kid's instruction as thoroughly as is possible? How about for adult lessons? I'd rather fight to convince a higher and higher percentage of the population to consider our activity, rather than fight other schools for a percentage of a small market.

If my competitors do a great job, then our market will expand. If they are hucksters or just lousy teachers, then our market will suffer — and that will hurt everyone. Again, the early days of the personal computer industry provide a great parallel.

What Is Memorable about Your Business/School?

If you plan to advertise and promote your business repetitiously for many years, then you should definitely be concerned about a number of details.

Your ads should have a consistent look and feel, so that they become recognizable and memorable. There should always be some constant pieces of content — perhaps, the format of your school name or logo and, perhaps, a common tag line.

Your ads should have a consistent appeal to a specific audience. If you try to be all things to all people, then you'll be nothing to no one! I'd rather be consistent to a target audience and become known for that niche than be spread across the board.

Your school should have an easy-to-remember name. Many schools use names that are not only difficult to remember, but also are downright unpronounceable by the general public. Be sure to choose a name that will be easy to remember and pronounce.

Years ago, combining these ideas, I chose the name Mile High Karate for my base in Denver, which is called "The Mile High City." This was somewhat common and, thus, easy to remember. At the time, I also felt that it helped to position my schools as the Denver martial arts schools.

Now is the Time to Hustle Like Never Before

I sincerely believe that we are at a marvelous "Inflection point" in our industry. I've seen this twice before. First in 1985, second in 1991. We combine two things right now that make the next 18 months considerably different than the last 18 months.

First, is the economic recovery. Since the run-up to the presidential election, generally we've been in one of the worst recessions in this century. That obviously makes it difficult for all businesses, especially those that rely on "discretionary spending" to get rolling. Although our market (kids' education) is somewhat recession resistant, still — it's made it difficult.

The economy isn't fully back, but consumer optimism is up, and overall consumer spending is coming back. Some areas such a real estate and employment are "lagging, not leading" indicators, and it will be a long while until real estate returns to "bubble highs" (if ever, in inflation-adjusted terms). However, the economy is recovering and consumers are starting to spend, again. Some of Mile High Karate's record years were in the early Clinton administration as the economy recovered from the last "banking crisis" (S&Ls), and the harsh recession that made Bush 1 a one-term president in favor of Clinton.

Second, is *The Karate Kid*. which changed the complexion of our entire industry. It moved the industry to 80% kids from 80% adults, and allowed for the type of pricing and structure that we use now. I'm thrilled to see that the new *The Karate Kid* doubled expectations on opening (thanks in part to NAPMA's efforts to enlist the martial arts industry). The new movie is on track to hit or exceed the revenue numbers of the original, even in inflation adjusted dollars (i.e., the original did $90,000,000, or $200,000,000 when adjusted for inflation).

With an opening weekend of $56—58 million and $113,000,000-plus gross box office in the first 10 days, and *extremely* positive word-of-mouth, I believe the movie and the huge marketing budget that Sony has invested is going to take us back to the original *The Karate Kid* boom. That was a time of 2,000- or 2,500-square-foot schools with 560—650 active students, and with *all* marketing efforts working well due to a receptive audience.

You can't sit on the sidelines. You *must* be spending on direct mail (mail multiple "Grabber Mailings" to your prospect database), you must be in summer camps, day cares, churches (target 2,000—3,000 leads from these this summer), and theaters. You must be on TV and in newspaper inserts.

These are all things that I did in 1985, 1986, 1987 with *huge* results. However, I believe many (not all) of our schools will be at 500 active and $100,000-plus-plus-plus revenue by early or mid fall.

Now's The Time To Hustle Like Never Before.

Now, let me take a deep breath and recognize a couple of things that may not be obvious.

First: A bunch of school owners are running around adding MMA Programs and other programs thinking that as a traditional stylists they must follow this trend to stay afloat. Oftentimes they rush to add curriculum or add programs without asking if there is an overwhelming demand for that program. Don't get me wrong —

I do believe that there is a market for quality BJJ programs and for adult-oriented programs, including fitness-oriented MMA. However, I think it's a huge mistake to layer contradictory programs onto your school or adapt a curriculum "because everyone else is doing it," rather than focusing on a market and pursuing it effectively.

Second: It's difficult, if not impossible, to be "all things to all people." Think of any brand that comes to mind. I'll throw a couple of examples. What's BMW? "The Ultimate Driving Machine," i.e.: sporty, responsive cars that are fun to drive. What's Apple? Quality, easy to use stuff. Certainly not the cheapest (I read that they have a 75%-plus market penetration of laptops priced at $1,000 and up).

Pick any other strong brand and see if they are trying to be all things to all people.

What should you do? Pick a market that you are competent and excited about servicing and focus all your efforts on that market. If you are excited about supporting and focusing on the "kids and family market," you now have "The Karate Kid Era Part II," with a $200,000,000, two-hours and 20 minute "Infomercial for Martial Arts Lessons." There are more than 10,000,000 people who will see *The Karate Kid* this summer. That's approximately 10 times the average viewing audience of a major UFC Pay-Per-View event, and probably up to five times the number that will see a UFC Pay-Per-View event this year.

Add that the movie is really a well-crafted infomercial for how fun martial arts lessons are (for the kids) and how valuable it is for personal discipline and respect (for the parents). It's pretty much impossible for a child five to 15 to leave the movie and not be interested in learning martial arts OR for the parents not to view martial arts as a valuable activity for their children.

Keep reading…

To put my rants and enthusiasm for *The Karate*

Kid in perspective take a look at the following results:

Box Office History for Karate Kid Movies

Released	Movie Name	1st Weekend	US Gross
6/22/1984	The Karate Kid	$5,031,753	$90,815,558
6/20/1986	The Karate Kid II	$12,652,336	$115,103,979
6/30/1989	The Karate Kid III	$10,364,544	$38,793,278
8/12/1994	The Next Karate Kid	-	$8,751,228
Totals			**$253,464,043**
Averages			**$63,366,011**

Total Lifetime Grosses

Domestic	$107,130,239	94.4%
-plus Foreign	$6,386,356	5.6%
= Worldwide	$113,516,595	

Domestic Summary

Opening Weekend: $55,665,805

#1 rank, 3,663 theaters, $15,197 average

% of Total Gross: 52.0%

Widest Release:	3,663 theaters
In Release:	10 days / 1.4 weeks

Through the weekend, we signed up 64 students for trial memberships (went into the weekend with 23 students).

I thought I would share our results here in Loveland. Through the weekend we signed up 64 students for trial memberships (went into the weekend with 23 students). We have already started converting them to regular memberships. Not bad for a smaller town. Last night, our dojang was nearly busting at the seams. For a brief moment or two I was a little worried because there was a line at the door waiting to get in. I started thinking I hadn't thought this through enough (making room for everyone).

The demographics amaze me. It's a farm(ish)-type town, but we have had an extremely diverse group of people signing up and coming through the door. Ages 4–56, mostly women and children, but some men, and varying economic groups. Had a few Black Belts come to the table as well that have been out of it for a while wanting to return.

I'm pretty happy with the results. I'm expecting to keep about 40% of these new students, but I'm going to give it my best effort to keep all of them.

We used the NAPMA information to get the results. It's a shame The Karate Kid, The A-Team *and the* The Last Air Bender *are so close together. To varying degrees, they can all be good opportunities to bring in students.*

SCOTT GRANGER,
MANAGING PARTNER
KOREAN ACADEMY OF TAEKWONDO NORTH

There's an interesting trend, happening again throughout our industry.

I've seen two types of martial artists with "blinders on" and "failure mechanism fully engaged" arguing against reality.

The first type are the "false gurus" trying to slam me and NAPMA. They deny reality. Accuse us of making up numbers. Or, claim that they have just as much claim to *The Karate Kid*, and that they have put together a comparable promotional package — at a cheaper cost.

Now, let me make this clear: NO ONE ELSE walked you through the complete promotional opportunity A–Z the way that we did. No one else had PROVEN through previous movie promotions starting with *The Karate Kid* I, II, III, and IV. I pity those who looked for cheap or who

thought one of the other self-proclaimed gurus had the secret.

Want to know the truth?

I'm expecting some Mile High Karate schools to set as many as 1,000 appointments for introductory lessons from *The Karate Kid* and related promotions. I've seen others who thought they were doing a great job by passing out 250-1,000 flyers in and around the movie theater. Our Mile High Karate record to date was 262 appointments set in three days during the opening of the movie. In the first 10 days we had several schools who broke 350 appointments scheduled for introductory appointments.

Quantum Leap attendees, along with Inner Circle and Peak Performers members, received a complete outline to accomplish hundreds of introductory lesson appointments. If you missed out on this, then you really just didn't implement. Don't miss out on the insider track through Peak Performers, Inner Circle and the upcoming Extreme Success Academy.

To finish for now I'll leave you with this note. I'm hoping that you were at "Quantum Leap," and if not, at least watched the video of me discussing *The Karate Kid I* as well as the music business, and the poverty mindset. If not see the member website and watch it now.

I also wanted to commend you for the Brass Balls Factor...

Just wanted to say "thank you" for all you do for the industry and what I gain from it personally.

I know I'm not the most vocal NAPMA member but I still listen to as much as I can and implement as many ideas as I can. The audio from your special Quantum Leap presentation was very inspiring and prompted this message. I LOVED it!

You described my former approach to

the "art" of JKD to a tee!

I also wanted to commend you for the Brass Balls Factor you displayed in your recent "anti-MMA" cover story. As usual you're correct and it was the best expression of my own thoughts I've seen.

Down here in Miami (65% Hispanic) you can imagine how MMA "dominates." So I'm strategically working on attracting the contrarian remainder in our community who think differently through our websites and direct mail reactivation efforts.

Keep Blastin'
Dwight Woods

How To "Turbo Charge" Your Results

The key components are simple.

Know what you want to accomplish.

Learn the necessary skills.

Then VIOLENTLY EXECUTE your plan.

It's amazing to me how many people sit on their butt—and then complain about how hard they are working.

TAKE ACTION! BE BUSY! MAKE IT HAPPEN!

What is that step? I hate to be a broken record on some subjects, but you must increase your prices; and, to do so, certain factors must be in place.

For example: After reviewing the revenues of one my coaching clients recently, I calculated that if he would just increase his down payment, then he'd add $98,000 in revenue with the SAME number of enrollments.

Guess what happened? I spent three months banging on my drum before he did anything. He added $0.00 revenue.

Then, he finally "took the plunge." Now guess what happened?

His enrollment ratios (which is the percentage of prospects who arrived for introductory classes and were enrolled) INCREASED. Yes, at a higher price point, MORE prospective students enrolled. His staff (he has multiple locations) told him that my strategy made the enrollment conference much EASIER.

As they say in direct-response TV commercials – "But wait, there's more!"

Before you think that he is an isolated example, please let me explain that more often than not I find this to be the case. The only limitation is in the minds of the owner, program director or whoever is running the school, not in the minds of prospective students.

What should YOU charge? Obviously, it depends on multiple factors.

What's the most important factor? That would be creating a perception of value. You must present your program as being valuable — VERY valuable. Once you've established that value, then it's only a matter of what I refer to as "fishing in the right pond," i.e., marketing to families that are able to afford your tuition instead of those unable.

If I were to provide a blanket recommendation, then your tuition should be at least $149 per month for new enrollments. For an upgrade, I'd like to see you bump the tuition a minimum of 50% from the enrollment price point, i.e., $225 or more.

I can almost hear the one or two "Doubting Thomases" now.

What are the typical responses of these "doubters?" Two responses head the list.

"I can't charge that much because my competition charges $X."

"My students cannot afford that much."

Frankly, my concern about your competition is exactly Zip, Zilch, NADA. Who cares what they are charging! If your prospects are making price comparisons, then it is due to one of two problems: Either you are not very impressive during your intros (review and revise your grooming, the appearance of your school, the content of your intro, etc.) or are you are failing to "Market in a Vacuum."

The "Market in a Vacuum" concept is one that I have addressed before. It is basically what occurs when you rely on the Yellow Pages or some similar marketing resources for most of your students. They will be prone to make price comparisons. If you are following my advice, however, then you won't experience this problem.

The other concern is typically a figment of YOUR imagination: "They can't afford it?" Take a minute and observe and understand the spending habits of your students. Maybe you are located in a poverty-stricken area — in which case you should MOVE. Otherwise, I'll bet your students (and prospective students) are spending much bigger sums on many other purchases than what I suggest you charge.

A family recently explained that they couldn't afford their renewal since they had spent $12,000 on a Disney World vacation! A couple of weeks with the Mouse and $12,000 were gone! Compare that to the lifetime value of martial arts training!

Just a bit of caution about your current students. Keep in mind that your current students have already been very solidly sold on what you are worth. You have "pre-framed" them to think of your lessons — no matter how much they love them — to be worth what you've asked them to pay.

It's difficult (not impossible, but difficult) to increase the price they pay to receive the same training that they are receiving now.

There is a strategy that will allow you to increase their tuitions as well, but I won't go into that now. We've made those increases at Mile High Karate many times with HUGE financial results.

Who Is Our Competition?

I've addressed how shortsighted it is to focus on other martial arts schools as your competition. To help further your understanding, let me share with you several real-world observations.

Price is irrelevant when compared to what other schools charge. Starting in 1983, I moved into Denver and grew from zero to 1,500 students during a little more than 18 months, while charging between 50% and 100% more than the average tuition of other martial arts schools.

How was I able to do that? Obviously, there are many factors, but some of them are:

1. Predominantly "Marketing in a Vacuum," i.e., creating the market for martial arts lessons and drawing them to me, rather than actively competing for individuals seeking martial arts lessons. Few of those students came from the Yellow Pages, the sign on the building or more traditional marketing methods. Almost all of them were generated by aggressively pursuing "suspects" that fit our profile and convincing them that martial arts instruction was valuable.

2. An early recognition that few prospects (or active students, for that matter) actively shop price. Clearly, many people who call the school or walk in the door ask about price; however, anyone even marginally skilled in telephone sales skills quickly makes that a non-issue.

3. A clear understanding that price is only important to most people in relationship to "value." With any service like ours, the prospect has difficulty equating a value to what he or she is receiving. With a tangible product, customers are more likely to try to compute an expectation of the cost of materials and difficulty of manufacture.

Their only ability to assess the value of your training is your presentation of your program, your facility, and, most importantly, your staff and you. They will judge value mostly on whether they like, respect and trust the people that they meet.

Next, they will judge value, according to the benefits of your program and the amount of "social proof" that you provide to increase their believability of that outcome for them.

"Price determines perception of quality." As counter-intuitive as this may be, prospects that do shop schools will often choose the more expensive — knowing nothing else. The reason is that whichever school is most expensive must be the "best"; and, frankly, most of us want the best products and services that we are able to afford, not the cheapest. Granted, there may be exceptions to that statement; however, just because you shop at Wal-Mart or Sam's Club doesn't mean you don't want the best. It just means you want the lowest price on a quality branded product.

Consumers have been taught the "knee-jerk" reaction, attributing price and known brands with quality — and "inexpensive" to being "cheap." Quick: which do you emotionally want, a Porsche or Subaru sports car? How about a Rolex or Timex? The Timex or Subaru may have all of the features you want, and may be better.

In my case, I have several very expensive watches, but my 25-year-old Seiko with a battery keeps much better time. In fact, I have a $19 wall clock that keeps much better time than the Rolexes or the Brietling. I drive a 911 Twin Turbo, but could have bought a Subaru with nearly comparable performance for much less than half the cost.

Examples: For our household, we often purchase branded food items from Sam's, but not the cheapest "generic" or "unknown" products.

A service, such as martial arts training, is selling the unknown. Consumers are unable to judge quality in a systematic way; they're only able to judge based upon the factors in Item 3 above.

Our competition is other uses of time and money. Adults evaluating a program for themselves or parents considering one for their child more likely compare us, at the low end, to a fitness center or other sports activity. At the high end, they compare us to a personal trainer, tutoring at Sylvan Learning Centers or even a child psychologist.

In reality, our mission should be to show the incredible benefits of martial arts instruction, charge "premium" prices to make teaching martial arts for a living attractive and lucrative, and make martial arts instruction an endeavor that parents see as a "mandatory" activity for their kids.

Big Winners, Winners, and the Mediocre Majority

In extensive conversations I had with Toby Milroy and Jeff Smith, we reviewed results that I had from several years working with coaching clients. It's interesting to review the results of these past experiences and extrapolate them into how to help members in the future develop their schools.

Results from coaching clients tended to be in one of two groups:

Starting point of $12,000 a month or less. Typically would argue implementation (that won't work in my town, city, with my style, with my staff, with my students) or they would change things to the point of being unrecognizable, then do nothing until their credit card maxed and they bailed out.

Starting point of $13,000 to $20,000 a month. Typically would get to $30,000 to $50,000 QUICK. Quickest, 90 days; more typically, 7—10 months.

These results were accomplished from one coaching group teleconference a month, The Millionaire Skills Call monthly, a coaching members private website and discussion board and a 30-minute one-on-one monthly call. Coaching members were also invited to a live event twice a year for a day or two, typically with Mile High Karate school owners and staff. They were typically receiving a fax a few times per month about current priorities as well.

First, let's talk about those who failed in that process. The failures in any business tend to share commonalities.

Let's start with a couple of universal realities. The world generally is divided into 5% big winners, 15% winners and 80% in the mediocre (or worse) majority. Using those numbers in a typical year, our industry will have 900 top-level schools, 2,700 good schools, and 14,400 mediocre or worse. In a typical year 3,600—4,500 will go out of business. Now, knowing our industry as I do, I think the 5% and 15% ratios are generous for the martial arts business. There's a relatively small number of school owners who are investing large sums of money and time in themselves and their school to make massive improvements. Most spend little or no time or money to improve their school or their financial results.

What are the commonalities of the losers?

First and most common is that for 80% or more, much of the 15% spend the bulk of the time and money that they do spend on personal and professional improvement on technical skills. They fly to Brazil or China to train in their chosen art. They spend 10, 15, 20 or more hours per week on their personal training and on perfecting their personal athletic skills. Don't get me wrong: your technical knowledge is important. However, low-performing schools can't see beyond that to the skills that are truly necessary for their own professional growth.

Second, common at least among the 80% who achieve little or nothing is the tendency to discount professional skills and systems with erroneous excuses. They say things like "… that's in a big city, it wouldn't work in my area. That's East Coast, that won't work in the Midwest. That's Tae Kwon Do, that wouldn't work for BJJ." You get the idea. They say that won't work with my students, in my area, with my style, with my staff and then do nothing.

Third, they want everything for free. Look at the free internet martial arts business discussion boards and Facebook groups. Many of the participants are looking for free advice and are unwilling to pay for quality training. It's trite but true, you get what you pay for. In the Internet world there's an often misquoted line that's "Information Wants to be Free." The concept has led to many failed business ventures and ultimately is a foundation for a media battle going on that's costing big media companies billions of dollars as things transform. You've seen Steve Jobs and many others chip in on this conversation that the problem online is that free information is most often worth exactly that…nothing. In a world of bloggers, how do you sort fact from fiction, value from rubbish?

The exact quote, by the way, was by Stewart Brand:

> *"In fall 1984, at the first Hackers' Conference, I said in one discussion session: 'On the one hand information wants to be expensive, because it's so valuable. The right information in the right place just changes your life. On the other hand, information wants to be free, because the cost of getting it out is getting lower and lower all the time. So you have these two fighting against each other'."*

Those who are unwilling to invest in their own education and in tools and systems to grow their business will be left to complain on the sidelines about all those who were willing to invest in their own growth and development.

Fourth, ultimately, most people fail to achieve much because they have a belief system about what they are capable of achieving. They limit themselves to that level. No matter how often they see others running $500,000 or $1,000,000 a year schools, they get stuck at $100,000 a year and can never rise above it because of the belief about themselves that they've internalized and never changed.

In our own industry, there's a new group pitching a "Please Don't Sell Me Anything" convention in the home of past NAPMA World Conferences, and selling their wares with the slogan, "there's nothing new in the business, and we've got all of the old stuff, cheap," or something like that. Their event I believe should be retitled: "Let's all go get drunk on the beach for 'old time's sake' and lament that we've learned nothing new in the past 10 years."

Frankly, some of the biggest leaps I've made in my career were when I was introduced to a new speaker or consultant through a live event during their 45-minute or 1-hour presentation then was offered an opportunity to study the topic more in depth. One that leaps to mind was Jonathan Mizel (an "internet marketing guru") who sold me a box of materials containing probably 30 hours of training, following a 45-minute presentation that I was impressed with, then a membership in his newsletter. I managed to meet him for lunch later, but took special care to read the entire archives of his newsletter website (two three-ring notebooks full of written material) so that I'd be prepared to ask intelligent questions.

Frankly, if someone listens to me or anyone else for an hour or two, they've been introduced to a topic, but are far from mastery. Imagine a new martial arts student attending a two-hour seminar on self-defense and thinking that they'd learned the topic.

As for the "there's nothing new" comment, that one's interesting. One the best direct response marketing books that you should read was written in 1923 by a gentleman by the name of Claude Hopkins. It's called *Scientific Advertising*. Another one, *Oglivy on Advertising*, was written in 1985.

So some of the major concepts that you should be using in your business were first articulated in 1923 or before. However, if you have not read those books and the many others on the topic, and applied them to a martial arts school through extensive testing and experimentation, then the concepts are new — to you. And frankly, to 99% of martial arts school owners as well.

At the other extreme, obviously there are new things happening in many areas. An easy example is with internet marketing that's clearly changing every month where there are LOTS of new things happening that you should know and that are useful to your business.

Honestly, one of the biggest impediments to martial artists is believing that teaching methods of 10, 20 or even 100 years ago were as good as it gets. In that area, learning and adding modern teaching methodology is essential to your growth, and is not available from anyone who's not currently working directly with hundreds or thousands of students. It's important to combine modern educational technology with constantly updated curriculum and structure to maximize both your student retention and the quality of their skills.

Another past guru in our industry ranted and raved recently about there being no "secrets" in our industry, noting that we'd promised to reveal the "secrets to success" at a coming event. Well, I heard that one described recently to me by a knowledgeable expert this way: "It may not be a secret to you…but if the student does not know it or understand it, then it's certainly a 'secret' to them."

Are there "secrets" to success? Well, there certainly are things that the top 1% of our industry know and apply that the other 99% haven't been taught or haven't applied properly. There are certainly "subtle distinctions" that are the difference between mediocrity and success. In a book I'm reading right now, David Oglivy described a 19

times improvement in an advertisement from one change — that's 1900% improvement.

That having been said, how do you value advice? That one's difficult. I like to look at it as return on investment. I've seen really BAD advice that was free cost school owners many thousands of dollars. Some "lesser gurus" cost some school owners $100,000 or more in lost opportunity just this last summer with bad advice about how to handle *The Karate Kid*, *The Last Airbender* and others.

With my coaching clients, I've always promised a "10 X return on investment," or, in other words, for every $1,000 they spend, they could expect $10,000 back — IF AND ONLY IF they applied what I taught them. Anyway, most typically the advice from free Internet sites and the guys who charge you $29 to $100 a month for a "bunch of stuff" are really costing you thousands of dollars. In our case, we have many years of real world experience at the table teaching you how to be a true professional in running your business, if you choose to, and how to earn a solid six-figure income along the way.

Oh, and back to the point number two. Those coaching clients who went from $15,000 to $30,000 in 90 days or in nine months, and those who went to $50,000 or more. What were their commonalities? Well, mostly they IMPLE-MENTED. They took direction on faith and just went and immediately got going. They didn't look for reasons why it wouldn't work. They didn't let their employees get in the way. They took the ideas and immediately ran with them.

The specific implementation process that I gave everyone who got to $50,000 a month or more was as follows:

- Keep good statistics (for a monthly review with me).
- Fix pricing (raise their prices).
- Add an upgrade process (50% to 100% bump from enrollment monthly payment

with pre-pay and accelerated options).

- Renewal blitz among existing students (this was often good for $100,000 to $250,000 in added revenue).
- Review and fix (if necessary) enrollment process.
- Add bigger down payment and bigger monthly payment to enrollment.
- "Open the Floodgates" to introductory process.

Along the way, these coaching clients learned more sophisticated marketing and advertising theory and strategies and applied them to their own business.

Suggested reading for you:

Tested Advertising Methods; Caples.

Oglivy on Advertising; Oglivy.

My Life in Advertising and *Scientific Advertising;* Hopkins.

Consultation Certificate

This Certificate Entitles the Bearer to a Personal 1-on-1 Martial Arts School Business Analysis With a NAPMA-Certified Business Analyst. This Individual Consultation is Valued at $495.00.

Certificate expires 12 months from the date of purchase.
To schedule your personal business analysis, complete this form and fax to NAPMA at
1-800-795-0853; mail to 1767 Denver West Blvd., Suite A, Golden, CO 80401;
or visit www.PrivateCoachingSession.com

PLEASE FILL OUT COMPLETELY AND WRITE LEGIBLY

Name _____

School Name _____

Address _____

City _____ State/Province _____

Zip _____ Country_____

Phone _____ Fax _____

E-Mail _____

_____
Authorized by Toby Milroy
Chief Operating Officer, NAPMA

3 FREE GIFTS FOR SERIOUS SCHOOL OWNERS

FREE Personal School Evaluation	**FREE Two 90-Minute Seminars**	**FREE CD-DVD Package and Report**
Two 30-minute Sessions A sure-fire way action plan to double your results or better.	with **"The Millionaire Maker Grandmaster Stephen Oliver** "The 5 Stupid Mistakes All Too Many School Owners Make that Kill Their Growth" and "The Key Step-by-Step Blueprint for Being a Big Winner"**	**"How Hundreds of Smart School Owners Like You Doubled Their Revenue in the Last 12 Months** Even in the Midst of the Greatest Recession since the Great Depresson, and How You Can, Too!"**

A Great Experience

An interesting and very important topic, "Abundance Mentality," was addressed at a recent business event. That was why I hired Lee Milteer, professional speaker and trainer, to work with my Mile High Karate staff, franchise school owners and personal coaching clients, and provide you, our NAPMA members, with exclusive information on the subject of the "Millionaire Mindset."

It's just amazing how many school owners think of money and other resources as being finite rather than infinite. In general, martial artists seem to suffer from several major hang-ups about money.

First, they think that there it is wrong to make money teaching the martial arts. To me, that's silly. Actually, it's no more inappropriate than a singer being paid for concerts and records or a racecar driver being paid for a driving career.

Second, school owners think there's a point at which their students are paying more than they should be paying. Clearly, they've made three erroneous assumptions: 1) That charging what students are willing to pay might, in fact, be charging too much; 2) that charging more than other school owners are willing to charge for a similar service is inappropriate; and 3) that excluding some students who are unable to pay is somehow inappropriate.

Third, school owners think that being "in it for the money" is somehow at odds with being the best instructor and martial artist possible—another strange and erroneous concept.

You must convince yourself that there is as much money and other resources available as you expect, need and request. Finances are not limited. We live in an affluent society; and there's no reason why you should not to receive a share of that affluence.

Do me a quick favor and count how much cash you have in your wallet, money clip or wrapped around your credit cards with a rubber band. Go ahead; I'll wait.

I'm willing to bet you have less than $500, most likely, less than $100. I have $2,132 in cash in my wallet (you know, that green paper money they still make.)

Now, let me ask you a few questions: If you have $32 in your wallet and I have $2,132 in mine, then who do you think will recognize opportunity faster? Who do you think will think in terms of "there's plenty" first? Who do you think will panic quicker when the next little crisis hits?

If you want your school to be financially viable, then consider carrying more cash, and stop feeling broke when you pull your wallet from your pocket.

Make friends with people who make more money than you do — preferably much more money than you do.

Take a millionaire to lunch and ask how he or she thinks about his or her business.

Travel to places where wealth is abundant. Instead of taking the dirt-cheap trip to an out-of-the-way place in Mexico, surrounded by the natives where you feel like a rich American, go where wealth accumulates.

Pop down to the dealership and take a Porsche 911 for a test drive, or the new Mercedes AMG SL.

Well, I could continue, but I won't. I want to share a short conversation I had with Mark Victor Hansen, author of *Chicken Soup for the Soul* book dynasty. He told me during lunch that he asked Tony Robbins one time why he was making hundreds of millions of dollars and Mark (at that time) was only making one- to two-million dollars a year.

Tony responded with questions: What's your "mastermind" group? Who are your professional and personal acquaintances?

When Mark said he spent time with others making approximately what he was currently earning, Tony replied, "That's why!" Tony spends time with billionaires.

That should cause you to think!

Don't Be a Loser. Rise to the Occasion.

I'm sick and tired of seeing good martial artists struggle financially, day to day.

It's been frustrating in the past year to watch so many otherwise great people, accomplished martial artists, and sincere teachers struggle financially. At least 25% of the industry went out of business during this prolonged recession. Others just struggle along making working a day job while running their school at night or just sacrificing along the way and less running a martial arts school than they should (and often than they could doing something else altogether).

Now, don't get me wrong. The conversation among the "consultants" is that "you can't fix losers," that some people just won't rise to the occasion. It's also that the population skews 5%, 15%, 80% with 5% big winners, 15% winners, and 80% who'll just do little or nothing. Frankly, nothing that I've seen contradicts these bleak assessments of human nature. However, I've also got to assume that you are a 5% type, or at least a top 20% in reality or in potential, or you wouldn't be reading this (and be a member of Peak Performer, Inner Circle or on that fast track). The 80% wouldn't bother.

Now, to point out what may already be obvious to you.

The transition to a winner as a martial arts school owner requires that you move from being an athlete (i.e., physically accomplished martial artist) to being that and an excellent teacher, to be that and an excellent teacher of teachers, to being that and an excellent leader and communicator of the values of martial arts training (some call that salesperson), to being that and an excellent promoter of the values of martial arts throughout your community (some call that marketer of martial arts). By the way, you also must master at some level keeping track of your results (accounting and keeping stats), hiring and managing employees, and other administrative and management functions of your business along the way.

The vast majority of the 80% types will never move beyond athlete and teacher to mastering any of the other skills. Frankly, many never move beyond their own athletic development. Those types rebel against learning to be a "salesperson" and believe if you are a good enough martial artist or teacher of martial artists that you will get enough students by "word of mouth." Both are failure mentalities that you must avoid at all costs.

Frankly, what you probably also know is this: The vast majority of your time and focus as a successful school operator must really be on two things.

First, have "RAVING FANS" among your own student body. Not just those who are developing quality techniques. Not just those who are learning and mastering your art. But, truly RAVING FANS who are developing the highest quality physical skills, in a fabulous environment, surrounded by people who they consider almost to be family, led by people who are truly a "product of the product," who show them and teach them leadership skills, life skills and success skills. As an aside, it's difficult to teach people success skills if you don't have them yourself. It's why I've always focused more on teaching my staff life skills than on having specific scripts for them to parrot in class.

Second, the majority of your time and effort, if (and only if) you are developing "Raving Fans," has to be spent on marketing. You must be constantly thinking about and working on how do I get more and more new students into our school.

If you are developing "Raving Fans" and sharing life-changing skills with your students, then you must be a "Raging Thunder Lizard Evangelist" for your program and insist that your staff and senior students are as well.

Now on this point, there's a couple of issues. What marketing effort will you master? And, how many different ways can you implement to get new students? It's important to have a few things that you truly master to generate new students and it's important to always have a "parthenon" of marketing activities. In other words, 10 or more different ways you are attracting new students each and every month. Never rely on just one mechanism.

The broad categories for attracting new students might include:

1. Internal Promotional Activities.

This is anything from Birthday Parties to Buddy Days designed to create either family add-ons (mom, dad, sister, brother, wife, husband) or referrals. I've seen schools who master one or several mechanisms for referrals who can fill their school with only referral activities.

One friend has been fabulous at VIP enrollments, mostly generated by hosting each belt graduation as a big show. Having students invite their friends as witnesses and then asking them when they attend for contact information and then inviting back to an "open house and introductory class" a few days after the graduation.

Another friend (Steve Doyon) has done a fabulous job hosting a huge number of birthday parties at the school and using that as a mechanism to convert attendees to immediate introductory students and to add the rest to a fabulous follow-up sequence (mail, calls, email.) That converts a huge number anywhere from week one to month 24, or beyond.

2. Community Outreach Activities.

This can range from School Talks (or my origi-nal version, "Gym Teacher for the Day") to programs with area scouts, churches, day cares, etc. The marketing crowd calls this "host-parasite" relationships.

However, for our purposes, it's all about finding a crowd of YOUR prospective students and finding the best way(s) to introduce your school to that group. Back when I was running Kickboxing fitness programs, I worked with nail salons, tanning salons, and other businesses that attracted 18-to-35-year-old women (who cared about their appearance). For the kids market I target elementary schools, day cares, churches, Boy Scouts, Girl Scouts and other youth activities both non-profit and for-profit (think Chuck E. Cheese's to the local Catholic Community Center).

3. Advertising. This is anywhere you pay for media. It ranges from direct mail to targeted lists to newspaper advertising. I've set out to master every facet of this and have driven huge volumes to my schools by newspaper advertising, newspaper inserts, direct mail, marriage mail (Val-Pak, Money Mailer, etc.), television — short form (30-second spots and long-form (infomercials) — and internet marketing (search engine optimization, site development, and pay-per-click).

4. Publicity.

This is finding ways to attract television stations, radio stations and your local newspapers to feature your school or your students in stories. My teacher/mentor Jhoon Rhee was perhaps our industry's master of this form of promotion. He was constantly on television and in the newspapers (the *Washington Post*, among others) gaining publicity for the Jhoon Rhee Institute. He also ended up using this form of promotion to be in front of HUGE audiences, such as on the Washington Mall during the fourth of July festivities. Another friend of mine, Chris Rappold, had over 500 articles on his school appear in area newspapers over the years. He paid for a PR rep but the features were free.

At different times and in different markets each advertising mechanism can be effective. Over the years I've had from moderate to HUGE success with all of these.

Many in our industry during the past 10 years became convinced that advertising doesn't work. In that they are wrong. However, it is my opinion that you should develop your marketing efforts by FIRST mastering community outreach and second, mastering internal promotional efforts (which become useful only at 100 to 150 active students anyway).

To conclude on this subject, let me add a brief note about the Internet. Keep in mind that you've got to think of the internet by it's sub components.

First, your website for your students. That's a resource that's different than selling video tapes of the curriculum, giving handouts to support your testing requirements and putting your calendar of events on a white board. That section of your website really is designed to help on the "Raving Fans" component.

Second, is the website for prospects? I've rarely seen this done well. The site for prospects really has a VERY limited purpose. That purpose is to take a HIGH PERCENTAGE of visitors and convince them to share contact information with you (name, email, phone, mailing address), then to take a high percentage of those visitors and convince them to schedule a free or paid in-troductory class with your school. Your purpose is the SAME as an info call. They need to know little or nothing about you, your school, your style, your schedule, your curriculum or your lineage, UNLESS that facilitates them giving you contact information and scheduling an introductory class.

Finally, the Internet is media: it has several components designed to drive clicks, that is, prospects clicking a link to arrive at your prospect website. You can drive clicks through search engine optimization and through pay-per-click advertising –– in other words coming up on search results if when someone searches the proper key words.

These two options are the modern equivalent of the Yellow Pages, being found quickly when someone is looking for martial arts lessons. You can buy banners, articles, videos and other more traditional advertising methods to be in front of people who may be good prospects but are not really looking for you. Many traditional medial outlets are trying (and mostly failing) to get this to work now.

The search engine and pay-per-click marketing approaches are well proven on the internet — if there are adequate numbers of people looking for what you offer. The other more traditional advertising forms are yet to be proven on the internet but soon may work well, either normally online or through smart-phones or other mechanisms.

Recommendations to My Coaching Clients That You Can Use

I want to share with you a few of the recommendations that I have made to my coaching clients. They likely apply equally well to your situation.

First: Use a Billing Company

Many of you use too MANY METHODS to chase pennies and ignore dollars.

If you are not using a billing company, then I recommend that you talk to Member Solutions and ASF. Both offer excellent software-billing integration and additional value-added services.

I especially like the birthday cards, membership cards, pass-a-friend program and other value-added services that ASF provide. I recommend both highly and always have.

The other choice is EasyPay. It is a great company. Call and ask for Rick Bell (tell him I sent you). EasyPay is simple and easy — less expensive than the others, but with fewer value-added services. The fourth and final option is EFC. I was their first client after they separated from the Jhoon Rhee Institute and a member of its board of directors from inception until a few years ago. Many clients like EFC.

My opinion is that EFC offers excellent networking and some valuable consulting of value; however, as a member of NAPMA, you would receive much higher quality and unfiltered information. EFC's billing services are not quite on par with ASF or Member Solutions. It's your choice, but you should use one of them, and not software alternatives that don't manage the process. I wholeheartedly endorse any of these four choices.

Second: Pricing, Programs and Contracts

Rule of Thumb: You should be grossing $200 to $300 per active student in your school.

There are three or more important points to learn from this "rule of thumb."

If you are not using membership agreements, with a minimum initial commitment of six months (preferably 12 months), then start doing so. If you have a problem of some sort with contracts, then look in the mirror, take a deep breath and realize you are running a business not a club.

Enrollment Pricing: My recommended MINIMUM for new enrollments, which you should start now is $200 down and $149 per month, or a total of $349 to enroll and $149 per month for 12 months.

Upgrade Pricing: I recommend that your first upgrade occur two weeks to two months from the initial enrollment—at a minimum. I recommend the following minimum upgrade pricing: $499 down and $229 per month.

What you title your upgrade program is your choice.

I used to call mine a Black Belt Club, which was a 36-month program (or shorter, if Black Belt was achieved in fewer than 36 months). My Master Club program led to a 2nd-Degree Black Belt.

My newer upgrade strategy is two levels or more that require the same amount of time, but with different (enhanced) services.

MASTER CLUB = 2ND DEGREE BLACK BELT: $249 PER MONTH.

LEADERSHIP = 2ND DEGREE BLACK BELT: $349 PER MONTH.

LEADERSHIP/COACHING = 2ND DEGREE BLACK BELT: $997 PER MONTH.

Third: Expectations

Many of my coaching clients aspired to $25,000 to $30,000 a month. The current standard is $50,000 -plus per month in revenue. If you are struggling for small increases — or fighting the basic system — then it's time to adopt my strategy.

Fourth: The Mythology of Martial Arts.

Forget about how great you think your style is and your awesome name (especially if it includes words, such as "dragon" or the name of your otherwise unknown style).

Your business won't pay your bills if you think:

- That the market cares about your martial arts rank or martial arts résumé.
- Your 10 or 20 years as a failing school has positioned you well for the future.
- Going it alone or doing things your way is a great idea.

During the last couple of months, there's been much time wasted on one-on-one calls with school owners with $7,000 to $15,000 schools who brag about how long they've been in business, their ads, their knowledge or their great curricula.

Several of them — who haven't done much two or three months later — complain they need more of my time one-on-one.

Some of my favorite quotes:

"Winners remember results—losers remember reasons." (Source unknown)

"Most people would rather have a good excuse than good results." (I heard this one from Dan Kennedy, quoting someone else.)

"But when I said that nothing had been done I erred in one important matter. We had definitely committed ourselves and were halfway out of our ruts. We had put down our passage money— booked a sailing to Bombay. This may sound too simple, but is great in consequence. Until one is committed, there is hesitancy, the chance to draw back, always ineffectiveness. Concerning all acts of initiative (and creation), there is one elementary truth, the ignorance of which kills countless ideas and splendid plans: that the moment one definitely commits oneself, their providence moves too. A whole stream of events issues from the decision, raising in one's favor all manner of unforeseen incidents, meetings and material assistance, which no man could have dreamt would have come his way. I learned a deep respect for one of Goethe's couplets:

'Whatever you can do or dream you can, begin it.

Boldness has genius, power and magic in it.'"

W. H. Murray in The Scottish Himalaya Expedition, 1951.

The accurate Goethe quote is:

Then indecision brings its own delays,

And days are lost lamenting over lost days.

Are you in earnest? Seize this very minute.

What you can do, or dream you can do, begin it.

Boldness has genius, power and magic in it.

Fifth: Know Your Business Statistics!

You must gather and maintain your operational and business statistics, and know your current situation every week. Are you on-target to achieve your daily, weekly, monthly, quarterly and yearly goals? How many enrollments do you need per day, week and month to match your projections?

How many renewals/upgrades do you need? What is your target student retention rate? What are your daily break-even cost and daily profit goal?

Many schools owners don't know their basic statistics, such as intros, conversion rates, upgrades, new monthly payments or contract amounts.

If I asked you, "What are your totals for the month to date?" Would you have to refer to a ledger or computer, or ask someone? If you do, then you have a problem.

Sixth: You Can't Do Anything Without New Students.

Your target must always be 20 or more new students per month — every month — or 240 or more new students every year, forever.

If you have plenty of cash flow, then educate yourself about copywriting, TV, radio and direct mail. Improve your marketing skills and spend more time on grassroots promotional efforts and internal marketing.

My personal record is 35 enrollments (12-month contracts, signed and down payments, collected by EFT) during one day, back-to-back.

I remember an otherwise intelligent school owner who joined my coaching program — with the intent of earning $60,000 to $90,000 a year in income, which is a reasonable goal, considering many school owners in my coaching program are able to earn similar amounts. During the first month in my coaching program, the new member sent me a barrage of emails, stating among other things:

"I'm not willing to do contracts" and, "I don't believe in 'upgrade or renewal' systems."

Geeezzz!!!!

Why not just email me the following message?

"I have decided to take a permanent 'vow of poverty.' I will only teach martial arts for the fun and fulfillment of working with students. I have absolutely NO expectation of making more than a meager income teaching martial arts, even though I've devoted the majority of my life to learn and master this art."

It amazes me that otherwise intelligent human beings will decide to ignore intelligent business practices due to ignorance or the "unscrupulous" application of otherwise valid business systems by some operators.

If you remember nothing else, then please remember the two things that every intelligent and rich business owner in the martial arts industry knows:

- Student service and retention are essential for long-term success.
- Aggressive renewal and upgrade systems account for 60-75% of all revenue of a successful school.

You will greatly improve your understanding of some of the fundamentals of "how martial arts millionaires create 75% of their incomes," but I encourage you to keep an open mind and approach your school's business practices with both "enlightened self-interest" and the highest levels of integrity.

Most school owners who join my coaching program generated an average of $15,000 to $17,000 in gross income per month; however, after eight to 12 months of working together, that average dramatically increased to $45,000 to $50,000 per month. Be aware that this three-fold increase is not magical; it requires your willingness to "empty the cup" and immediately apply intelligent, proven business systems to an otherwise quality program.

Wow, Extreme Success Academy!

Just got back from San Diego. Wow, what a great event. Our surprise guest was "Blast from the Past" Andrew Wood. He was, as usual, fabulous on Saturday Night. The obvious difference between the "winners" and "losers" starts with showing up. Everyone at the event learned enough to add $10,000.00 or more to their monthly revenue (in some cases MUCH MORE) in the next 90 days, if they actually implement what they learn. Several members that I talked with have DOUBLED their revenue using what they learned at Extreme Success Academy last year in San Antonio! That in a serious recession — imagine what would have happened in "boom times!"

As you would have expected, Brian Tracy was fabulous as always, and shared some great insights both into his martial arts background as well as into what you, as a martial artist, must do to maximize your results and grow your school. Frankly, the entire roster was brimming with such fabulous information that it's hard to know where to start. I'm told that I really changed many people's thinking on Friday and Sunday about how a school operator should think and about what it takes to move to the highest levels of our profession. Toby Milroy really gave a ton of "meat and potatoes" information all day Friday to start everyone off strong. Many folks commented on the huge value they received (as always) on the nuts and bolts of effective grass-rooms marketing efforts.

Please, Please, Give me Permission to FAIL!

It's just amazing to me how aggressively some people will argue with you when you are trying to help them be successful — they are literally arguing for failure. If you've studied much of Tony Robbins' materials, he talks about "my delusion" — meaning that he believes that his goals are achievable and that external events will help not hurt his progress. You can have the opposite delusion — that everything external is conspiring against you. Your belief system either way will conspire make sure you get what you expect.

It goes back to the great quote:

> *"Most People Would Rather Have a Good Excuse than Good Results."*

Here's a recent e-mail I received (I won't share with you the name, for obvious reason).

> *"… your numbers have a snowball's chance in hell down here. In case you haven't heard, Arizona has not only the second worst foreclosure rate in the country, but is now the second POOREST state in the union! Only Louisiana beat us for the top spot! Sometimes you remind me of Nero watching Rome burn. I know you are trying to help, but castigating me for not showing "your" numbers is not only frustrating, but counterproductive.*
>
> *"There are NO down payments because people can't/won't pay them.*
>
> *"Zero PIFs because nobody has that kind of money. Despite what we show them we have and can do, most simply walk down the street to the next little TKD hole-in-the-wall and sign up for $50/month.*
>
> *"$99/month is considered "expensive" here in Tucson for martial arts…especially with a contract which scares the crap out of people."*

Anytime you say nobody can do something, you're wrong. Some can or will. If you say people won't pay something, you are probably just reviewing your belief system not the reality of the market.

I'll share with you part of my response to the letter above, where I looked into Tucson's numbers in comparison to two Mile High Karate schools whose current numbers I had handy: It's easy to conclude that the "economy sucks," and frankly, if you watch the news or listen to popular opinion, it's a reasonable conclusion. However, such "externalization of blame" for results does nothing to improve your income or your overall results.

A consideration is the demographics of income issues. Approximately nationally: A person who is 30-plus years of age, with an education level of college or better, has an unemployment rate of less than 4.5%. That same person with a high school or less level of education, less than 30 years old, is close to 20%.

Therefore, targeting white collar, educated parents is vital for marketing success, both for income and employment purposes. Single, young adult males are the ABSOLUTE worst in the current environment as a market target.

As an economist by educational background (BA Economics, MBA), I always feel compelled to investigate and evaluate comments such as this to see if there is in fact a kernel of truth buried in it.

I dug around a little and went through the Bureau of Labor Statistic numbers and did a comparison against Mile High Karate Fresno, CA, and Mile High Karate Mission, Texas. BOTH are FLOODED with traffic. If fact, the problem is too much Introductory traffic and slipping ratios due to volume.

Mission is coming on strong from a "SMALL SCHOOL" with less than 100 active students, to a strong school with the volume they are generating. That school enrolled nine new students just on Friday night. That puts them at 24 enrollments for the month to date.

Sascha Williams in Fresno is way up this year over last year, and is looking at a $500,000 year with a little continued momentum.

Both schools, by the way, are charging $400 as a down payment plus $197 per month for a 12-month enrollment. Masterclub Renewal is $750 down and $259 per month. Leadership Renewal is $1,000 down and $359 per month. Paid in full, that is approximately $13,500.

In comparing the Tucson area with those two schools, the most recent Bureau of Labor Statistics numbers are the following:

Income:

Tucson, Arizona:	$40,870
Fresno, California:	$40,460
Mission, Texas:	$31,060

Unemployment:

Tucson, Arizona:	9.2%
Fresno, California:	16.1%
Mission, Texas:	12.3%

It's easy to look externally for an excuse, but I'd really suggest we fix your systems and processes from the inside out. What must you do?

- Target the RIGHT audience, those who are likely to both value your program and be willing and able to pay for it.
- Market extensively throughout targeted areas in your community and draw from communities with the income and stability that you need for your school.
- Then, continually upgrade the quality of your program to increase it's value to your students and prospective students.

The Quickest Way to Kill a School

It's a rather simple: The quickest way to kill a school is to become good at sales and marketing without mastering service and education.

Let me say that again, differently. If you are not an excellent teacher and motivator, then the absolute worst thing you can do is expose your school to a huge number of prospective students, so your community learns about how poor your school delivers this critical service.

Let me give you this example from a couple of other industry perspectives. Dan Kennedy is one of the many "marketing gurus" that I've studied. He shares a story about opening a new restaurant. After exploring all of the many advertising options — Val-Pak, money mailer, flyer, direct mail, etc. — the restaurant owners decided to print certificates, instead, good for a free meal (absolutely free — not two for one, no cost for drinks, etc.). These certificates were delivered to every home and office in the restaurant's immediate vicinity by hand, with a personal invitation to try the restaurant.

The restaurant was swamped with traffic during its first month, with very little revenue, because it gave away the lion's share of the meals. What do you think happened next? If this were as much of the story I knew, my first answer would probably be there is no business the second month, or thereafter, and the restaurant quickly closes. My second answer is that during the second month, it would be just as busy, with happily paying customers; and the restaurant's business quickly grows from there. What's the difference? By now it should be obvious: Good food and fast, friendly service.

If the restaurant had good food and fast-friendly service, then its expensive marketing effort was well worth it. If not, then the management just proved to everyone in its neighborhood that the restaurant was not worth revisiting for a free meal or any other reasons.

How about another example: One of my executive staff members worked for a branded oil-change business for many years. Its absolute best strategy to grow a new location was the same as explained above. The company would distribute certificates widely that were good for a free oil change, with no strings attached.

Once many of its neighbors visited the location and were treated professionally and courteously with quality service, they were very likely to return again and again for service, but paying the standard rate. Again, this strategy would backfire quickly for a poorly run location.

What if the location was poorly maintained, with a grumpy staff that performed the service poorly and looked up a female customer's skirt while changing the oil? Well, the word would spread quickly, but not positively. The company would be ensured a tough launch, and have difficulty overcoming its bad reputation.

Our industry has experienced this situation often enough that many excellent martial artists, who are also excellent teachers and mentors to their students, are afraid of developing their marketing talent or sales skills for fear of becoming like those other "shady operators."

In contrast, I would say that the two biggest sins in our industry are first, quality teachers who are afraid of or unwilling to learn to promote their school and grow their student base; and second, lousy martial artists and teachers who master the art of marketing and sales and, therefore, poison the experience of martial arts for their students.

No business ever thrived without mastering three key functions: marketing, sales and service delivery. Miss any one of these key areas and you are doomed to financial failure.

I highly recommend that you start with a top-to-bottom overview of your school. Forget, for the moment, your own mastery of your chosen art. It's not very relevant to your student's experience. Focus, instead, on every aspect of your service delivery, starting with the most important, and then reviewing all of the supporting areas. Start with your rapport with students and their parents, and then look at your communications skills. Next, evaluate your ability to segment your curriculum properly for student mastery. Next, how are your classroom pacing and structure and your facilities, training, support equipment and curriculum support materials? How's the appearance of your key staff members and you?

After you've reviewed all of these areas, it's time to master the marketing and sales functions, and then grow your student base dramatically.

Important Issues for Large Operators

As your school expands, and you can no longer personally control every aspect of your school operation, there are several important issues that begin to arise that you may never have previously considered. The first of these that I'd like to address is how to ensure control, as you develop strong Black Belts and strong staff members.

Once you expand to multiple locations or your single school increases to a large student body of 300 or more students, you will find it necessary to delegate much, or perhaps all, of the teaching to an employee. In a martial arts school, personal loyalty and respect for the instructor is an important component of your developmental process. Martial arts schools, especially more traditional schools, depend on a strong hierarchy and obedience to the instructor.

The same structure that helped you maintain order in the early stages of your growth can become a problem as you grow if not managed properly. Industry horror stories abound.

A common story is the development of a student, from White Belt through the coveted Black Belt. Next, you begin to teach him leadership skills, and allow him to teach more students. Often, this is in parallel with developing the student's athletic prowess, and he becomes a cornerstone of your school and a respected champion of the tournament circuit.

Once your confidence in this student's skills and leadership abilities has grown, you offer him a "career" position with you, and he begins to teach for you full-time. Gradually, he becomes the head instructor and teaches most of the classes, while you become increasingly focused on the sales, marketing and administrative aspects of your school.

Gradually, your students begin recognizing your Black Belt student as their primary teacher and mentor, and the teacher starts to take great pride in "his" students' achievement.

What comes next is that this instructor often begins to hear from students that he should have his own school. Perhaps he marries and his wife continually complains that he should have his own school, and that he's not being paid enough; and, of course, that he is responsible for the success of the school, since all the owner does is sit in the office and talk to people all day.

Then one day, like a lighting bolt from the blue…

Well, you can probably finish the story. I've seen cases where your previously loyal Black Belt employee has moved across the street, and, in one case, actually announced at the monthly belt test that the students should join him across the street on Monday — perhaps, followed by letters and phone calls to solidify the solicitation of your clientele.

The question becomes, how do you protect yourself from such a disaster?

Well, there are many ways that school operators attempt to protect themselves. What doesn't work is always to be your students' primary contact and work aggressively to make sure you are always seen as the top athlete, teacher and main student contact. That approach is fine when you have as many as 100 or 150 students, but then you must delegate authority and let others take some responsibility.

What must happen, then, are several things.

First, your school must be built on a formal hierarchy, with you visible at the top. It must always be clear that you are the senior person in your school and that all others report to you. This is where larger organizations and affiliations often help to solidify everyone's relative position.

Second, before hiring anyone, it is important to have a clear understanding. That written understanding must include several points:

- Your enthusiasm about helping this budding martial arts instructor develop a substantial career in the martial arts.
- Your willingness to help him grow in any way possible.
- Your willingness to compensate continually his relative contribution to the financial outcome of your school.
- His commitment to support now and always your school and you.
- His understanding that it is unacceptable ever to teach any of YOUR students outside of your school environment and, regardless of how the future unfolds, he will never solicit any of your students.
- His understanding that it is acceptable for him to open a school in the future under your banner or independently, but he will not open it within a reasonable distance, so as not to compete with you, or you to compete with him.

In conclusion, there are many landmines to avoid as your school grows. Developing your competition is certainly one that is important to control and monitor.

We're in a REALLY Simple Business.

I remember while working on the MBA (Master's in Business Administration) thinking about what a really simple business a martial arts school is in reality. During the program one class we were working on multivariate scheduling programs (how to program traffic lights in London or schedule flights for United Airlines) and then Pert Charts, Gantt Charts and stuff like that. The next class was all about "Managerial Accounting," determining costs of a product by allocating overhead by Machine Hours and stuff like that.

A couple of things dawned on me then. First, we're in a really simple business. Second, many martial artists who struggle do so by over-complicating their business and confusing simplicity with a lack of sophistication — or, confusing complexity with substance.

It's important to keep in mind with our business that there's really three primary drivers of your business: enrollments, renewal and student retention. If what you are working on during any given moment does not directly impact attracting new students, renewing existing students or keeping existing students for a longer period of time, then you are wasting time.

Take those three "drivers" and overlay your tuition rate and structure and you have all of the key elements to increase (or decrease) your gross revenue.

In my efforts with consulting, I'm often confronted with school owners who are busy confusing "activity with accomplishment," or who have over-complicated their life and their school by ignoring the basic premise above.

How in practice does this work?

One way is to determine what curriculum you are going to teach in your school and whether to add a piece of material. The first question is always, "will this encourage students to stay longer with our program or will it accelerate attrition?" If you reasonably expect any piece of curriculum to improve your overall student retention, then consider it. Next, ask yourself if it can be used to enhance renewals. Often something new or different is a marvelous "hook" for the renewal, for instance, "once in leadership you also get to learn '_____.'"

I've made this mistake occasionally. Once was in adding too much BJJ for our Black Belts. The concept was enticing for them, but once they ended up with too much ground work, 85% dropped out. Another time was in explaining the actual "knife-fighting" meaning behind the stick work we were teaching. They enjoyed the stick movements — they were massively turned off thinking about it as a knife scenario.

For most people, the more realistic you make "self-defense" scenarios, they less enthusiasm they have for what they are learning. It's a reasonable human reaction to be turned off by knives, guns, injury and potentially being attacked.

Most important is that you are not your market. What you are excited to learn has little or nothing to do with what will be a nice addition to improve retention or to be an attractive addition to enhance renewals. Personally, I've always enjoyed fighting. Tournament point fighting. Kickboxing. Full-Contact Karate. I've always been aware enough to know that hitting at full-power or, for that matter, getting hit, is not what most (99.9%) of my student base wants.

Throughout the last 30 years I've seen many, many cycles of adding curriculum (or pretending to do so) hoping to attract more students. The MMA trend recently is nothing new. I remember schools adding "Kung-Fu" to their signs during the run of the *Kung Fu* TV show (and more recently during *Kung Fu Panda*.) When Tae Kwon Do showed up in the Olympics, schools promoted Tae Kwon Do (including many who actually taught Tae Kwon Do).

There are times when "media trends" lead to a BIG upsurge in all martial arts training. Certainly *The Karate Kid* in the 1980s was one of these. *Kung-Fu* and *Enter the Dragon* led to an upsurge in the 1970s. Then there are times when a specific type of training gets driven by the media. "Tae Bo with Billy"'s frequent infomercials drove huge interest for Cardio Kickboxing. Most of these efforts miss several important points.

One point is that you should first pick a "target market" and then decide what to offer that target market that it will be receptive to learning and paying a reasonable tuition rate to learn.

The next point is that in most cases, students who approach you do so from a point of near or total ignorance about martial arts. Never assume your level of knowledge about martial arts, styles, approaches when approaching a market. They may use a current "buzz word," but frankly, they almost never know really what they want. It's up to you to help them hone in on what they want to learn and why.

Third, evaluate each "media trend" and ask: "Is this driving a surge of people looking to pay to train in this particular art or style?" I can tell you from experience that there was a HUGE surge in people looking for cardio kickboxing. There is not a surge of people looking to be the next UFC fighter.

You make HUGE headway in your school by focusing in on the three drivers and avoiding anything that distracts. The most successful schools that I see (at the "bottom line") focus on one curriculum. They add to or enhance that curriculum based upon having more stuff to teach to entice renewals or to keep the program interesting for their students. They focus on their "bread and butter" and target creating $30,000, $50,000, $75,000 or more monthly TUITION from that one curriculum. They focus on constantly improving their student experience while expanding their reach into their immediate community.

If the focus is the adult audience they get better and better at attracting that target audience. If their focus in the kids market then they get better and better at attracting and keeping kids. Mostly successful schools do not try to attract ALL markets. You'll see very few huge schools with Tai Chi for the 50 and up crowd, MMA for the 20-30 year old crowd and family-oriented life-skills for the under-12 crowd. One offsets the other. It would be like seeing a combination McDonald's, Morton's and Chili's. Different target audiences. Different branding. Different facilities. Different approaches.

Critical Success Skill: Build Immunity to Criticism

Here's a business tip that you must learn, and learn well.

Recently, I "Googled" my school name, Mile High Karate, on the Internet just to learn if anyone was misusing the name or stealing my content, which is considered "intellectual property."

Can you believe that this happens? It sure does. Here's what I found.

There are schools that have copied the contents directly from my FreeKarate.com and MileHighKarate.com Websites, word for word! Often, the perpetrators are so blatant that they even use my name and our testimonials.

This is a very clear case of plagiarism. Keep in mind that you're allowed to copy concepts, but you are not allowed to duplicate/steal the text or the pictures/images.

I also found the comments of a person from Oregon who had posted his opinion at Defend.net in response to someone looking for a school in Colorado:

> *"Whatever you do, and I'm sure you won't, don't go to Mile High Karate,"* this person wrote. *"There is a terrible chain down there that doesn't even proclaim to teach martial arts, but character building, and every single instructor is called a 'master.' I hate McDojos like these…"*

Jeez, what an idiot! You must always avoid the attempt to rebut people who make these kinds of pronouncements. What a whacked-out comment! Yes, my school's focus is character development for kids — through quality martial arts training and the mental disciplines that are taught as part of that training.

My response to his comment about all the instructors at my schools calling themselves "master" is that, during the last 22 years, we've developed a bunch of Black Belts, and we have a number of instructors 24 to 26 years of age who have been training with us since they were seven. To be referred to as "master," they must first have achieved their 4th-Degree Black Belt, which requires an average training time of 12-plus years to attain.

I guess the word "McDojo" is his attempt to slam both McDonald's® and Mile High Karate® in the same comment. There's a weird idea that anyone who runs multiple martial arts locations must have low-quality instruction. That is just not the case any more.

The important point is that to build your school to a professional level requires that you do two things:

1. Systematize and professionalize, which will create a more consistent student experience and a higher quality operation.
2. Ignore the idiots who don't understand why you are successful. Learn to build immunity to criticism. It's a critical success skill.

When I was reading that idiotic Web posting, the following letter appeared in my e-mail:

Dear Mr. Oliver,

I recently purchased your Extraordinary Marketing Program with the audio CDs of your boot camp. Wow! I have been searching for the path to take my school to the next level, and this is it! Everything I implemented that you recommend has produced successful results and it saves me the time of learning the hard way.

What I like best is how you speak about quality of life. You have given me the tools to have fewer students and make my school more manageable for my wife and me, and to be virtually the only staff members. At the same time, you have also given me the tools to generate optimum profits, so my wife and I may live a decent financial life of security, and, of course, have quality time outside of the martial arts school.

There are school owners and people who make negative remarks about what you do, and I wonder why these individuals mock what they do not understand. In following your work at numerous NAPMA conventions, you repeatedly mention the words, "There is an ethical component to all of this..." You certainly do promote that we, as martial art teachers, individuals and business owners, must render useful service worthy of exchange for our financial success.

I applaud your dignity and I thank you for helping me follow my dreams!
DANIEL ROMINSKI
OLYMPIC KARATE INSTITUTE
RUTHERFORD, NJ

Consultation Certificate

This Certificate Entitles the Bearer to a Personal 1-on-1 Martial Arts School Business Analysis With a NAPMA-Certified Business Analyst. This Individual Consultation is Valued at $495.00.

Certificate expires 12 months from the date of purchase.

To schedule your personal business analysis, complete this form and fax to NAPMA at 1-800-795-0853; mail to 1767 Denver West Blvd., Suite A, Golden, CO 80401; or visit www.PrivateCoachingSession.com

PLEASE FILL OUT COMPLETELY AND WRITE LEGIBLY

Name _____

School Name _____

Address _____

City _____ State/Province _____

Zip _____ Country _____

Phone _____ Fax _____

E-Mail _____

_____

Authorized by Toby Milroy
Chief Operating Officer, NAPMA

3 FREE GIFTS FOR SERIOUS SCHOOL OWNERS

FREE Personal School Evaluation

Two 30-minute Sessions
A sure-fire way action plan to double your results or better.

FREE Two 90-Minute Seminars

with "The Millionaire Maker Grandmaster Stephen Oliver" "The 5 Stupid Mistakes All Too Many School Owners Make that Kill Their Growth" and "The Key Step-by-Step Blueprint for Being a Big Winner"

FREE CD-DVD Package and Report

"How Hundreds of Smart School Owners Like You Doubled Their Revenue in the Last 12 Months Even in the Midst of the Greatest Recession since the Great Depresson, and How You Can, Too!"

Marketing your Martial Arts School: A Key Is Repetition

Keep in mind an advertising rule of thumb: Until you have exposed a prospect to your message at least seven times, he or she doesn't understand what you are trying to communicate.

It often works in this manner: A mother in your target audience glances at your ad in a local newspaper. The headline is somewhat interesting; however, the phone rings, her kid spills his milk or one of 10,000 other potential distractions catch the mom's attention and she forgets your ad.

A postcard from your school is delivered to her family's mailbox. She glances at your postcard while she sorts the mail into two stacks. Pile A is personal correspondence, bills, etc., which she must keep. Pile B is junk mail and other non-requested materials that she typically throws in the trash. Your postcard is discarded too, but it has had a minor impact on her mind and some vague familiarity of having seen your ad before.

The neighbor pulls into the driveway and his five-year-old hops from the car, wearing his martial arts uniform and his equipment bag in tow. The mom sees the neighbor child and vaguely remembers a conversation with his mother about his great improvements in behavior since enrolling at a great local martial arts school.

Glancing through the local paper, she sees your ad again. This time it looks a little familiar. The headline seems targeted at her personally. She reads most of the body copy and decides to discuss the idea of martial arts lessons as a family. This is quickly forgotten when she must manage 10 other daily crises before her spouse arrives home after work.

A friend at the gym mentions that her child is taking martial arts lessons, and loves it. She mentions a local school — it's a familiar name now.

Another letter from your school appears in her mailbox. This time, during her mail sorting, she saves your letter in the "A" pile. The letter is opened. She glances at the contents, and thinks it looks interesting. She decides to investigate this idea and the letter is attached to the refrigerator to be discussed later. Nothing happens.

The next-door neighbor's kid comes home again in his martial arts uniform. The child of the first mother expresses an interest in his friend's fun at martial arts classes. The neighbor kid gives them a pass, some information or invites them to visit the school.

The mother then finds your third promo letter in her mailbox. This time, the letter is placed by the phone. She calls your school that same day. If you've trained a staff member to answer the phone professionally, then he or she schedules an appointment for the mother and her kid. They arrive for the introductory class and they enroll, assuming that you greet them well, teach a great intro, build rapport with the parent, present your program effectively and keep their attention.

Remember, when tracking your results try to determine not only why the prospect called today, but also how she learned about your school originally — and all of the materials that she has seen.

Whatever advertising or promotional medium that you choose to use, determine how to expose prospects to your message a minimum of three times and, preferably, seven to 10 times.

A Dumb Statement!

A coaching client of mine had increased his revenues from $17,000 to more than $30,000 a month. The methods his used to grow his school are those he learned from a one-on-one consultation and attending a Boot Camp. He never attended any of our other mastermind sessions or took advantage of many other opportunities I provided. He then decided that once his gross doubled that there was nothing more to learn. He had learned "one or two" secrets and was done.

Dumb, real dumb.

What could he have accomplished?

For starters, he could have increased his revenues from $50,000 to $75,000 to $100,000 a month. Maybe he thought that he now knew everything I knew — frankly, he hadn't even scratched the surface. Maybe he thought he knew enough. It seems stupid to me to "leave money on the table."

Frankly, many school owners hit revenue numbers that they otherwise thought were impossible, and then they lose perspective.

They suffer from one of two syndromes:

The legend-in-their-own-mind syndrome: Suddenly, they've decided that they know so much that they should be the "guru" and learn no more. That's a dangerous egotism that must be avoided at all costs.

The second syndrome is just as dangerous: They decide they've "arrived," and know everything that they need to run and maintain their businesses. A successful business can never be static, and a successful business owner can never be satisfied with the status quo. I've COMPLETELY reinvented my business at least every seven years, and I did so once again this spring. Once you stop evolving, you die. Our industry is constantly changing—and so should your preparations and expectations.

My own expectations have changed dramatically during the past 25 years. What would have seemed unbelievable gross revenue 13 years ago now seems a rather mundane NET profit this year, and the pace is accelerating.

Don't become comfortable or think that you have nothing more to learn.

"Entrepreneurial Seizures" and Other E-Myths

Gerber in *The E-Myth* described that all businesses are started by a technician who one day had an "entrepreneurial seizure" and went from being technician to business owner. He describes the phenomenon of new business owners who think that the technical aspect of their business is going to encompass the vast majority of their business who are discouraged and dismayed to discover that they now have to wear multiple "hats." They suddenly discover that they must be the head of HR (Human Resources,) Marketing Director, Sales Manager, CFO (Chief Financial Officer,) and on and on all of which has little or nothing to do with baking cakes, repairing cars, or even training in martial arts.

In our case I like to make it a little simpler.

90-95% of our time as a school owner is focused on three outcomes: 1.) New Student Enrollments; 2.) Student Retention; 3.) Renewals or Upgrades.

If you are considering doing anything in your ask first if it will help you get more students, keep them longer, or move them into higher (and, more expensive programs).

That having been said, it's important to recognize that you as the owner (and, any and all full-time staff) will likely spend as much time focused on marketing efforts as on teaching. The way I teach staff in my schools is this: From early in the morning until 3 or 4 p.m. is almost 100% focused on external marketing activities. From 4 p.m. until 9 p.m. (Monday through Friday) is time for classes, which means opportunity to interact personally with existing students and prospective students. You now focus on personal rapport with students looking for opportunities to student service (retention), for goals focus and student interaction for long-term achievement (renewals), and for introductory classes, enrollment conferences, family add-ons and generating referrals.

So to summarize a couple of things before moving on:

1. **Mistakes that BROKE school owners make:**
   A. Spending more time on personal martial arts training and on technical training than on learning and training on sales, marketing and advertising.
   B. Delegating sales and marketing (hiring a "Program Director" more below)
   C. Deciding that they are "Not a Sales Person" and therefore not learning communication and sales skills.
   D. Showing up at the school at 4:00 or 5:00 p.m. and thinking that the appropriate workday is 4:00 until 8:00 or 9:00 p.m.). Working only 16 to 20 hours per week.
   E. Implementing only one or two things a month to attract new students.

Ironically, it's true that most school owners would rather sit in their business broke and slowly (or, quickly) going out of business rather than leave the school and go find new students. You've got to be willing to get out into your community and connect with people and organizations that can help you fill your school.

2. **Traits of successful school owner:**
   A. They treat their school as a full-time, lucrative career. They set their alarm, get out of bed and go to work promoting their business.

B. They understand that a martial arts school is as much about marketing, sales, and customer service as it is about athleticism or martial arts proficiency.

C. They extensively invest in their own education in each of the key areas of their business including: Sales, marketing, teaching methodology, hiring/training/supervising employees, and personal goal setting and motivation among others.

D. They network with other successful martial arts school owners and avoid hanging out with unsuccessful school owners.

E. They keep track of all of the key "statistics" to monitor their business.

Admittedly, neither list is extremely comprehensive, but you get the basic idea.

Now, back to the "Program Director" comment. I've seen very few single or multi-school owners who are the full-time head instructor for 20 to 40 classes per week in their school. One of the first staff positions that they tend to fill is first a part-time, then a full-time head instructor. It's really a bad idea in most cases to first hire someone to "take care of sales." First, you should master each and every function of your business before hiring someone else to do it for you. You must be on top of the key skills in order to teach them or to delegate them.

With school owners that I work with most that are grossing $10,000 or under are teaching most of the time. Most that are grossing $20,000 to $50,000 a month are focusing on marketing, selling and customer service primarily. Most over $50,000 a month or with multiple locations spend their time training and supervising staff rather than doing the teaching or selling themselves. That having been said, I've seen schools up to $100,000 a month where the owner handles most, even all of the sales processes (enrollments and renewals).

Anyway, to conclude it's vital that you be constantly investing in your own training and development in all aspects of your business operation. Likely you need to focus first on marketing and sales as a primary study.

Next, you need to realize that you are ultimately in a selling and marketing business. You'll need to invest more training and time in implementation on those functions than you've invested already in your martial arts training and development. Most instructors think nothing of training seven to 10 hours a week on their own physical skills but, fail to invest an equal amount of time on improving their career and income.

Move into the top 20%, then the top 5%, and ultimately into the top 1% by developing your business, teaching, sales and marketing skills every day.

Focus Your Marketing Dollars on a Specific Target Audience

I remember a long talk I had with Bill Clark, followed by similar conversations with Lloyd Irvin and Jeff Smith. We all basically agreed on the following.

My conversation with Master Clark was focused on the misadventures of many schools that should be marketing benefits to specific markets. Your school must be clearly in a category and your marketing dollars focused on a specific target market.

Master Clark's Black Belt Academies and my Mile High Karate schools might be described as "Sylvan Learning Centers with martial arts." He's incorporated a kids development program and I've created our "Building Successful Kids" program and an extensive character development and leadership program for kids and families.

Both of us have claimed a territory and developed a clear image of what we do. Our focus is on kids, families and character development, not on MMA events (though, truth be told, we've both practiced and taught mixed martial arts since the 1970s).

At the other end of the spectrum are BJJ schools and MMA schools that are clearly and unabashedly targeting the young adult male market. They satisfy that specific market's expectations for vigorous workouts and a broad-based curriculum. They teach high-quality MMA and charge $200 a month and more.

The commonality of schools doing very well is based on several factors. Clearly, one of those factors is deciding whom you are targeting and, in essence, "the side of the industry you've chosen," and then being very clear about your position and very focused on your market.

Many other school owners should clearly think about one of my favorite lines from an otherwise forgettable movie (*The Stepfather*). "Wait a minute, who am I here?" Those who fail, try to be all things to all people. Those who succeed focus on being very good at what a segment of the market wants to learn.

Marketing Your Martial Arts School: Media and Promotional Activities

Here are a few questions that will help you decide where to spend your dollars, time and energy on marketing, advertising or promotional efforts.

Is the marketing campaign or promotion targeted specifically for your school? (This question addresses geography.)

Does a demo or ad attract too many people who are not qualified prospects for my school, or is it targeted directly to your neighborhood? (Addressing people.)

Are the people who will see the demo or read the ad your exact target prospects? (Addressing income.) You can spend your time doing demos at high schools, but I'd rather present demos to K–4 children any day. Make sure you aren't sending flyers to retirement homes and expecting enrollments!

I've wasted plenty of time doing demos and after-school programs in academic schools with low-income children or advertising to or mailing to low-income households. I'm all for making a contribution to the community; however, a better alternative is to grow your school to 500 students and gross $50,000-plus per month, and then donate 5% or 10% to scholarships.

Focus and Responsiveness

Will the audience pay attention to your ad? Is the publication where your ad runs a free newspaper that lands in mailboxes or driveways unsolicited, and remains unread or a subscription periodical that your audience is more likely to read and see your ad?

Are you on the sidelines during a demo or promotional activity, hoping someone will talk with you or are you the main event?

Is your presentation "laser-focused?" Too many school owners think, "There will be people of all ages and types in the audience, so I will create a generic presentation [letter, ad, demo], so it applies to everyone." Big mistake! Trying to be everything to everyone is being nothing to no one.

It's much better to "rifle shot" your advertising that is very appealing to 5% or 15% of your general audience, and ignore the majority. During your demo, highlight one aspect of your program targeted to the most likely prospects in the audience. Don't present so many points that no one will remember any of them; instead, always focus on one target market at a time.

Entertainment, Education and Persuasion

Trying to entertain your audience is a huge temptation in demos, presentations and advertising. Entertainment is always interesting; however, it doesn't persuade the audience to participate.

Example: When I saw the acclaimed stage show *Riverdance*, I had great seats, enjoyed the show and was amazed at the choreography, lighting and talent. It was a wonderful night of entertainment; however, personally, it did nothing to inspire me to learn Irish dancing. Now, the theater was charging $35 to $75 per seat, and 2,500-plus seats (the theater's capacity) were sold — six times a week.

I know why they were doing the show and it had nothing to do with motivating audience members to become dance students. Don't imitate the theater and show's methods unless you can do $125,000 at the gate per night.

It's great to educate your audience about the value of participating in your activity, why they should participate and what they will experience as students. Again, think in terms of targeting your audience, and teaching them the benefits of participating in your program.

The education that you provide must be about "what's in it for them" — and not about you, your style, its history, why it's better than other styles, etc. They just don't care about any of that stuff.

Students generally don't enroll in your school because of a history lesson, your style or the prestige of your grandmaster. They enroll because they expect some benefit and believe that you'll be concerned and capable enough to provide that benefit.

Capturing the "Slight Edge"

'd like to share an important "success secret" understood by Bill Gates, Donald Trump and most all self-made millionaires and billionaires. First, though, a little personal background is necessary.

During recent months, I've been to four major marketing, management or Internet-marketing boot camps or multi-day seminars. Total cost? Much more than $10,000, not including travel, hotels, meals and rental cars.

Additionally, I just ordered approximately $1,100 in audio CD programs, books or reference materials related to my business and personal growth.

Now, during the past 27 years, I've done plenty of reading and studying, and spent much time in formal and informal management, teaching, sales, marketing and human relations education. In addition to my MBA degree, I've spent thousands of hours learning about how to run a business and teach people effectively.

The truth is I have so much information that I leave some of the seminars I've attended empty-handed. That's because there was nothing left for me to buy. Like other multi-million-dollar entrepreneurs in my same situation, we already owned all of the content — and want more.

Why, then, would I still invest in education and development at this elite level? That's the success secret. It's called the "Slight Edge."

Another example: Years ago, I remember sitting in rapt attention as Joe Lewis explained the minute details of his renowned side kick. At that time, I had the best kicks of those with whom I trained and, frankly, I knew quite a bit about how to execute a side kick. That wasn't just my opinion. World champions Jeff Smith and John Chung and many others whose opinions I respected also shared that opinion.

Why did I pay such close attention to Joe Lewis? Because he had one of the most powerful side kicks ever. He had developed subtle distinctions about his side kick and how he executed it that was way beyond my understanding of that technique. It was fascinating to try to enter his mind and determine how he thought and felt about kicking.

The school owners (and other small business owners) who fail or achieve just slightly beyond mediocrity will consider a book, CD, seminar or other learning opportunity as content they've heard or read previously. Those who are very successful will look for the subtle distinctions in those materials or renew their commitment to gain new knowledge by studying the material.

Every month, I talk with school owners who gross $8,000 a month or less and also school owners who gross $2 million or more a year. Frankly, it's not that the guys doing millions know 10 or 20 times more than the small school owners. It's that they've learned some subtle distinctions that helped them move to dramatically higher levels, and they've continued to remain open to and seek new material.

Don't ever look at an issue of *Mastering the Martial Arts Business* magazine, your monthly NAPMA member packages or my Extraordinary Marketing materials and say, "I've heard that before." Instead say, "What's the subtle distinctions that I can discover that will give me a huge leap towards success? What's in these materials that I may already know, but I'm not implementing effectively?"

Learn new material every month; internalize content that you've heard, but perhaps not mastered; and gain subtle distinctions to propel you to new heights and motivate you to even stronger implementation. You'll certainly benefit from the financial results!

Want Massive Profits? Implement a "Drip" System!

was listening today to one of Tony Robbins' *Power Talk* CDs today. Something he said struck a chord for me in relation to what I see every day in our industry. To paraphrase, he said someone asked him what the difference was between when he was broke and now. He said that the primary difference between when he was broke and now was a sense of urgency and positive expectations. Basically, what he was describing is a level of Entrepreneurial Urgency that's driven by a belief in the potential results. If you expect to fail it's easy to adopt a "why bother" attitude.

Let's take just one example of this statement applied to martial arts schools. An example that I've repeated several times is the story of a chiropractor who added on average 35 new patients every month. When asked what to do to add 35 new patients per month his response was that he didn't know anything to do to add 35 new patients, but he did know 35 things that would add one new patient or more.

I can't tell you how many school owners I've talked to who really just don't do much to build their school. I'll ask them month after month what they did in the past month to promote their school and they'll name one or two things. Ask them for progress since last month and they have a list of excuses for why they haven't started implementing the new marketing strategies they discussed the previous month. Month after month goes by and they get little or nothing accomplished.

It's important to make sure you ALWAYS have that Entrepreneurial Urgency that Robbins talks about. Always, always, always implement aggressively and immediately.

A good plan violently executed now is better than a perfect plan executed next week.
— GEORGE S. PATTON

Frankly, most people are losers. They look for reasons to justify their failure rather than find success.

All populations sort themselves into the top 5% (big winners), the top 20% (winners), and the bottom 80% (don't do much, look for excuses).

The BIGGEST difference between the top 5% and the bottom 80%? Implementation with a sense of URGENCY. It's got to be done now, not next week.

To use Zig Ziglar's line — losers wait for all the lights to be green before heading across town.

If you just set your alarm, got up, and got out and talked to people one-on-one OUTSIDE of your school every day for five hours, you'd practically be guaranteed to make $250,000 or more NET in the coming year. Better still would be a school with 500 kids — 100 in programs, 20 enrolled ALSO — 10 or 15 times in the coming year.

Will you take action? I don't know. Frankly, it's up to you.

We've given you EVERY tool you need (and a bunch more than you need). However, if you think, ponder, worry, try to understand everything 100%, you'll get to next year at the same place or worse.

Go IMPLEMENT. Add 100 students to your school. Renew them to leadership programs. That's good for $300,000 to $500,000 with nothing else.

For example.

- 100 new students x $397 down payment = $39,700
- 100 new students x $150 per month = $15,000 (monthly)
- 50 x $500-plus down payments on renewals = $25,000
- 50 x $100-plus increase in monthly payment on upgrades = $5,000 per month.
- 10 paid-in-full renewals = $13,500 x 100 = $135,000

Total: $39,700 plus $180,000 plus $25,000 -plus $60,000 plus $135,000 = $519,400.

The bottom line? It's worth your time to set your alarm clock, get your staff out of bed and HIT THE GROUND running EVERY day on marketing.

How do you get started?

Frankly, every month we are giving you lots of tools. Each Maximum Impact Teleconference will give you a bunch of great ideas — never miss a call.

Internal Promotions to Create Family Add-ons and Referrals.

The best way to get family add-ons? Assumptive. Stock up on uniforms. Give siblings a uniform and tell them it's their day to join a sister or brother. Nothing beats talking to them one-on-on, just giving them a uniform, and having them jump in class.

Referrals. Consistently the BEST way to get referrals is really from two main sources:

1. Hosting events in the school that's easy to invite friends to attend. These include (but are certainly not limited to):
   A. Birthday parties.
   B. Pizza parties
   C. Big belt graduation with friends invited to witness

D. Board breaking day
E. Buddy days of all sorts
F. Movie nights

The KEY in all of these is getting permission slips and/or name, address, phone and email and following up 24 or more times in the coming 10 months. They may not enroll this week but may in three, five or seven months.

2. Connecting through organizations that they participate in to do a class or demo. These include but certainly are not limited to:
   A. Boy Scout troop
   B. Girl Scout troop
   C. Day care
   D. Elementary or Middle School
   E. Sports team: soccer, baseball, football, hockey, cheerleading
   F. Dance or gymnastics school
   G. Service organization such as Jaycees, Kiwanis, etc.
   H. Company functions or, items like "Payroll Stuffers" for employees (Free Month Certificate sent in payroll or company newsletter)

See the new NAPMA Referral Program for a complete A-Z Outline for one such fabulous internal promotional program.

Remember, once you collect a lead, follow up, forever. Direct mail is a key. See below.

Suspects into Prospects ("Farming")

Find extremely targeted lists of "suspects" and work that list consistently and repetitiously.

Examples:

- School directory — local school with excellent demographics;
- Purchased list — income, $75,000-plus; kids, 4-12; owns home; geographically targeted.

Step 1. Letter or Postcard #1, #2, #3, #4 (within six weeks)

Step 2. "Drip System"* Monthly Mailer — Send forever.

Prospects into Intros

Example: Attended a birthday party, after-school, demo, etc.

Step 1. Letter or postcard with telephone follow-up.

Step 2. Mailer #2, #3, #4 within six weeks.

Step 3. "Drip System" Monthly Mailer — Send forever.

Step 4. January, May, September: Mailer #1, #2, #3 weekly plus telephone follow-up.

Lost Intros into Enrollments

Example: Came to First Intro, never came back. Cancelled when called.

Step 1. Follow-up letter with lots of testimonials.

Step 2. "Price Drop Offer," i.e., one month free or three months, $99; or 2-for-1 offer.

Step 3. Telephone call follow-up to "price drop offer."

Step 4. "Drip System" (Monthly Mailer) — Send forever.

Step 5. (January, May, September) — Mailer #1, #2, #3 weekly plus telephone follow-up.

Drop Outs into Reactivations

Step 1. (Week 1) — "Missed you in class" call from Asst. Instructor.

Step 2. (Week 2) — "Missed you in class" call from Asst. Instructor.

Step 3. (Week 3) — "Missed you in class" call from Head Instructor.

Step 4. (Week 3) — Personal letter from Instructor: "Miss You in Class."

Step 5. (Week 4) — Personal letter from Program Director.

Step 6. (Week 4) — Personal call from Program Director.

Step 7. (Monthly) — "Drip System" mailer.

Step 8. (January, May, August) — Mailer #1, #2, #3 weekly.

Reactivation Class — call everyone past 24 months

* "Drip System" continuing to follow-up on a "suspect," "prospect," "lost intro" or "drop-out" on a very regular basis monthly or more in peak seasons.

The Good Old Days That Never Were!

Maybe you, like me, remember the "good old days," when "true" martial arts training was the rule, not the exception, and you had to be "dedicated" and have incredible "perseverance" to learn the martial arts.

I remember my first or second lesson — and the joys of free-sparring as a White Belt. Now, I know that I'm dating myself a bit, but this occurred before safety pads. Our only padding was a baseball groin cup that we wore. Groin kicks were rampant as well as supporting-leg sweeps on tile floors. Oh, and you could — by accident, of course — be hit or hit your sparring partner in the face at full power!

It's an interesting commentary for those of us who have been training since the 1960s or 1970s. If you haven't been around that long, then just take my word for it: You had to be either nuts or stupid to continue training in the martial arts during those "good old days." When I think about what I accepted as "normal," I am just absolutely amazed that any of us lived through it all.

An example: I remember speaking with Allen Steen at a Jhoon Rhee reunion event in Washington, D.C. Allen is the "Father of Texas Karate" and the man primarily responsible for spreading the martial arts throughout the southwestern U.S. I talked with him about his former tournament in Dallas, which was one of my early competition experiences.

With Allen, I laughingly recalled the rules. This particular event was one of the early tournaments to use the then-new Jhoon Rhee Saf-T-Pads. In those rules, supporting leg sweeps were legal and you had three seconds to score on an opponent once he hit the ground. Head gear wasn't required — in fact, I'm not sure anyone had heard of the concept — and the tournament was conducted on a concrete floor!

Oh, did I mention it was "full-contact?" If you knocked your opponent out, then you won — including, I might add, if the floor knocked him out during a sweep.

Allen laughed and said. "Yeah, we had forty-two ambulance calls that day!" You know, if I hadn't been so young and enthusiastic, I would have rethought participating in that event — or in the many other wacky activities.

I remember one of my instructors, Gran Moulder, a 2nd-Degree Black Belt at the time with the Jhoon Rhee Institute. Now, I'm not saying that Gran was wound "too tight," but he was one of those Marines who enjoyed Vietnam a little too much.

After two or three tours of crawling through the Vietcong caves with a bowie knife and staking bodies at night to set ambushes, the Marines decided he probably shouldn't go back. Instead, they sent him to Tulsa to abuse my classmates and me.

I remember fondly the knife-defense demonstrations we did when I was 13 or 14. With that very same bowie knife that Gran had used to hunt the Vietcong in Vietnam, I would be the attacker and he the defender. Soon, the knife would come streaking past my testicles, and then come slashing across my throat. Looking back, I'm not sure which one I cringe about more!

These memories were brought back vividly several years ago while sitting with Jhoon Rhee and Bruce Lee's widow, Linda Lee. Another old-time martial artist was doing a knife-defense demo just like the ones I did many years ago. He ended up slashing the throat of his assistant!

Oh, the "good old days." Comparing now versus then, I am absolutely sure about a few things.

First, if you were to watch the old films of or had been there to see the champions of the 1960s or 1970s, then it's apparent that today's fighters could run rings around them, in any arena.

Second, if you were to look at the average quality of a Black Belt then versus today, then you'd see that my Black Belts are now much better.

Don't even try to compare student retention. Of the hundreds of students that came through our schools in Tulsa, I was the only one from the time I started to ever earn a Black Belt. Everyone else dropped out, usually at Gold or Green Belt.

Finally, I'm not sure how I survived, but I do know that the craziness never helped anyone achieve mastery at any higher level.

Focus Your Attention on These Issues

Sales

Many instructors and school owners think that sales is a dirty word, and openly rebel against learning effective sales or closing methods. Unfortunately, there's also been a group, during the last couple of years, which basically teaches only "high pressure" sales techniques and thinks that they are the end-all and be-all of running a profitable school.

The reality is a little different.

You cannot be a successful business owner without mastering marketing and selling methods that are appropriate to your business. You must also know "generic," or general, sales and marketing knowledge. You must be aware of how other businesses, especially similar businesses, sell and market.

Dan Kennedy says you are committing "marketing incest" when you only learn sales and marketing from your industry. Just because a method is an industry norm doesn't mean that it's the right or only way of doing business. At a minimum, you should watch how chiropractors, dentists, dance schools and many similar businesses market and sell themselves. I can almost guarantee you will learn something.

That having been said, long-term success in our business is about customer service, long-term student retention and quality referrals.

You must be a well-respected educational institution and be highly regarded by other businesses in your area, by educators, doctors and other opinion leaders.

Mastering sales methodology without focus on customer service and satisfaction will allow you to suck plenty of money from your community during the short run, but ensure mediocrity or self-destruction in the long run.

Quality Student Service

Many of the quality and service problems that martial arts schools experience are due to the industry being greatly personality-based, which is combined with teaching curriculum in a way that has not been reviewed and structured by educators rather than athletes. Many schools with which I've worked have curriculum structures and content that are guaranteed to cause most students to fail, rather than succeed.

One of my top priorities in my personal learning during the 1980s was pedagogy and curriculum design. I hired a Ph.D. educator, buried myself in the research and went to work on curriculum structure and "chunking" that made sense and was repeatable.

While it's always important to have an instructor who is personable and charismatic, much in student development can be addressed by teaching the right thing at the right time, and in scientifically designing your system and structure to match the current educational methodologies.

The next area is creating systems that improve student perception of interest and concern.

Studies have been conducted on why people stop patronizing businesses. The leading factor again and again is NOT dissatisfaction with the quality of service received. The leading factor cited is "perceived apathy." What are YOU doing to make sure your students know that you believe they are valuable and you are paying attention? Do you do that systematically or irregularly? Do students "fall through the cracks"?

The TREMENDOUS improvement to the bottom line that can be achieved with only small improvements in long-term customer loyalty has also been scientifically studied and validated. Remember, you spend the most to acquire new students. If it costs $500 or more to enroll a new student, then would it be worth similar investments in additional recognition to improve long-term retention?

I've seen a very small number of schools do this very well. Most do not do it very well. The "sales-is-the-only-thing" trend in our industry leads school owners to believe that student service doesn't matter. That is a tremendous disservice to everyone involved.

Back to Basics

Recently, I've seen much industry press coverage about "Big Schools" that I would not consider successful. Keep in mind that there are ALWAYS two factors that must be in place at any performance level to be considered successful.

First: Profit.

It doesn't matter what your gross revenues are unless you keep a reasonable percentage for the bottom line. Don't be seduced by a bigger-is-better mentality. (Study the numbers below carefully. They are based on a 2,000- to 3,000-square-foot location with two full-time staff, one or both of which could be the school owner/operator.)

Second: Sustainability.

One-month numbers may be impressive, but I'd rather see a big billing check that MINIMALLY covers 100% of your fixed monthly expenses and DOUBLE that number regularly in total gross.

Definitions of Success:

(Based on monthly average gross revenues for a 2,000- to 3,000-square-foot martial arts school)

- Outstanding: $75,000 and more
- Successful: $50,000 to $74,000
- Foundational: $30,000 to $49,000
- Breakeven to Marginal: $18,000 to $29,000
- Imperiled (on the brink of financial disaster): $17,900 or less

Mile High Karate standing records for performance:

- One-month enrollments: 77 (Littleton, CO)
- One-month renewals: 53 (Lakewood, CO)
- One-month cash: $123,000 (Arvada, CO)
- One-day cash: $33,233 (Aurora, Arvada, Lakewood and Littleton, Colorado have achieved similar numbers.)

In Marketing, What's Old is New Again

What's new? In the coming things really are a lot different when it comes to marketing your martial arts school — but, really no different than they ever were. OK, I know that's contradictory, but let me explain.

In marketing, all of the rage right now is "Social Media." Consultants and pundits are running around claiming the way of the new world is to "have a conversation" with your customers. The interesting thing about that is that everything old is new again. Really, in the 1960s, 1970s and 1980s the important elements to running a school (and really just about any retail or service business) was to "have a conversation with your customers." Honestly, for most service or retail businesses, no one had to create the internet or Facebook®, LinkedIn®, Ping® or whatever, to have a conversation with their customer.

Maybe if you are selling Doritos®, Pepsi®, Tide® or are some other product company, creating a direct channel of communications with your customers without relying on the big retailers or whoever is selling your stuff is probably useful. However, in our case, you should be having a personal conversation with your student and their family a couple of times per week.

There is, after all, a lesson there. The product that we have is more about the rapport you create with your students. It's about you knowing as much as possible about them. It's about creating a story and personality for your school that they enjoy and appreciate. It's even about expanding your reach with your students so that they want to share your story with their friends and family members.

Now, don't get me wrong.

There's a bunch of NEW stuff you have to know when it comes to media, marketing, contacting prospective customers, etc. There may even be a few new opportunities and tools to stay in better touch with your current customers. However, I will caution you rounding up all of your students in a public forum and networking them together with your staff and senior students can be downright dangerous. Keep in mind that anything online is ultimately public. That means that your disgruntled former employees as well as competitors down the street can find your students and friends online if you are sloppy enough to round them up in a public forum.

I'm going to be sharing with you each month everything that's new now that you need to be doing online and in various media. There's a bunch of stuff you have to be leery of when it comes to social media and discussion forums. You also have to be eternally vigilant about defending your reputation and managing your "ratings" at Google®, Yelp®, Yahoo®, Bing®, the BBB® and the many other online ratings services where anyone can anonymously slam your school or your character.

I'd suggest that you start with a couple of "vanity" searches for your name and your school's name in Google, Google Maps, Yahoo, Bing and Yelp. See if anyone has rated your school. Take the time to rate yourself a five-star. Get your staff and enthusiastic students to give you a five-star rating. Keep an eye on each of these regularly. Obviously you want to have great student service. However, there's little you can do about a competitor or a single disgruntled student, parent or staff member posting one or many negative ratings. In most cases if you get a bunch of positive ratings it will wash out the negative. Most of the various ratings are posted in chronological order. Therefore, the more recent drowns out the past.

Keep an eye out next month as we discuss Facebook, the BBB, and the many online ratings and how to position your school properly in each.

Finally, one of my favorite quotes. This one by Bruce Lee — that frankly applies not only to your curriculum but to your martial arts school business development:

In JKD, one does not accumulate, but eliminate. It is not daily increase, but daily decrease. The height of cultivation always runs to simplicity.

Before I studied the art, a punch to me was just like a punch, a kick just like a kick. After I learned the art, a punch was no longer a punch, a kick no longer a kick. Now that I've understood the art, a punch is just like a punch, a kick just like a kick. The height of cultivation is really nothing special. It is merely simplicity; the ability to express the utmost with the minimum. It is the halfway cultivation that leads to ornamentation. Jeet Kune-Do is basically a sophisticated fighting style stripped to its essentials.

Consultation Certificate

This Certificate Entitles the Bearer to a Personal 1-on-1 Martial Arts School Business Analysis With a NAPMA-Certified Business Analyst. This Individual Consultation is Valued at $495.00.

Certificate expires 12 months from the date of purchase.

To schedule your personal business analysis, complete this form and fax to NAPMA at 1-800-795-0853; mail to 1767 Denver West Blvd., Suite A, Golden, CO 80401; or visit www.PrivateCoachingSession.com

PLEASE FILL OUT COMPLETELY AND WRITE LEGIBLY

Name _____

School Name _____

Address _____

City _____ State/Province _____

Zip _____ Country _____

Phone _____ Fax _____

E-Mail _____

_____
Authorized by Toby Milroy
Chief Operating Officer, NAPMA

3 FREE GIFTS FOR SERIOUS SCHOOL OWNERS

FREE Personal School Evaluation	**FREE** Two 90-Minute Seminars	**FREE** CD-DVD Package and Report
Two 30-minute Sessions A sure-fire way action plan to double your results or better.	with **"The Millionaire Maker Grandmaster Stephen Oliver** "The 5 Stupid Mistakes All Too Many School Owners Make that Kill Their Growth" and "The Key Step-by-Step Blueprint for Being a Big Winner"	**"How Hundreds of Smart School Owners Like You Doubled Their Revenue in the Last 12 Months** Even in the Midst of the Greatest Recession since the Great Depresson, and How You Can, Too!"

Making Direct Mail Work for You, Part 1

There are two types of mailing lists that you can buy, "compiled lists" and "response lists."

A compiled list is what most martial arts schools that have had success with direct mail tend to use, including myself. A compiled list is typically organized from publicly available data. For instance, a compiled list would be one with an organized "sort" of recipients, such as:

- Individuals within a 3-mile radius.
- Individuals who own their homes.
- Children three to 12 years of age in households.
- Individuals with incomes of $50,000-plus yearly.

There are many list brokers, but I typically buy lists from InfoUSA, such as those with the sample sort above. They are the largest supplier in the industry for these types of mailing lists. For information, visit InfoUSA.com. Other sources exist that may be as good or better, such as Donnelly.

A response list is a list of individuals who have responded to an offer — either as a prospect or customer. For instance, you can buy the list of subscribers to Black Belt magazine or the names of purchasers of any TV infomercial products.

Another example is the list of purchasers of Billy Blanks' Tae Bo™ DVDs to promote your fitness-kickboxing program. Additionally, you could have bought the "hot list" of purchasers of the last 30 or 60 days (i.e., those that are "hot to trot" to start the new program).

The advantage of a response list is that you know the individuals on the list will likely be "responsive" to a similarly targeted offer. The dis-advantage for martial arts school owners is that most of these lists are generated from a national or international audience, and, therefore, may only include a limited number or responses within a reasonable radius of your school.

Additionally, the list brokers typically require you to buy a minimum of 5,000 names at a considerably higher cost per name than a compiled list.

You can overcome these challenges by working cooperatively with similar local businesses. For example, if a parent is willing to spend money for her child to be tutored at Sylvan Learning Centers®, then she is likely responsive to other personal-development offers for her child.

There are many thousands of lists available for purchase. You can search for them through Standard Rate and Data Service (SRDS). You can subscribe to its lists, or search online at its Website; however, SRDS's lists are rather expensive, so your best option is probably to visit any major library. Ask any librarian in the reference area for Standard Rate and Data, and then plan to spend several hours there.

After what I've explained above, it's very important not to forget a simple and powerful fact: The best list of all is your school's lead list of people who have expressed an interest in your school by providing contact information on your Web site, calling you on the phone, registering for a special seminar, attending a demo, accompanying a friend to a graduation or taking an intro lesson without enrolling.

Your highest priority of the various grassroots marketing efforts that you undertake should be to build your mailing list of interested prospects and to make sure you're in front of them when they are ready to "take the plunge" and enroll.

That's the group that you definitely want to "drip on," with a never-ending series of monthly mailings, and, perhaps, even more frequently during peak seasons.

Making Direct Mail Work for You, Part 2

During part one, I recommended that the best lists come from your leads or prospects.

What Determines Response?

Your response from any mailing is will be directly affected by the following:

1. *The list.* If you mail to the wrong target audience, then you can't expect many responses.

2. *Your direct mail piece being opened.* The biggest direct mail hurdle is your piece being placed in the A pile, or the mail that is considered important enough to be opened. You can help to make sure your piece is opened with copy on the envelope (i.e., teaser copy, headlines, testimonials, etc.).

3. *The headline.* If the headline and first sentence of your letter or piece fails to motivate recipients to continue to read, then the letter is a waste of time.

4. *The offer.* The offer must be both compelling and time-sensitive, using an expiration date, limited time only and any other perceived urgency to respond.

Thinking about Response

A successful direct-mail campaign is all about "ROI" (Return On Investment), not Percentage Response Rate. Instead of being concerned about the percentage of responses you are likely to receive or a low-percentage return, focus on your return on investment.

For example, your average student value is $2,000 (i.e., how much the average student will spend at your school during his or her lifetime as a student). If you decide to place a Val-Pak ad that cost $320, then your ROI is 600% if just one student enrolls.

That's a much different way of looking at the value of advertising: 10,000 direct mail pieces may only generate two calls and one enrollment (i.e., a 0.12% response), but your ROI is 600%.

Almost all martial arts school owners don't understand two distinctions about the use of direct mail.

1. The best way to increase your gross revenue and net income is to learn and implement the methods that result in a higher average student value. You must determine how to ask for larger down payments, higher monthly payments, more expensive upgrades — and, of course, student retention.

2. How much you can feel good about spending advertising dollars is in direct proportion to your average student value. Increasing that student value increases your options to fill your school.

I recommend two programs that will help you learn how to use direct mail more effectively.

1. Dan Kennedy's "Copywriting Seminar in a Box." This is a huge program that covers the topic of writing letters and ads more effectively than any others I've seen. You can find it at KennedyCopy.com.

2. Dan Kennedy also offers an excellent introductory program for direct mail follow-up. You can access his "Magnetic Marketing" program.

There are many excellent books on this subject. I recommend Ted Nicholas, Joe Sugarman, Gary Halbert and John Carlton. Joe Sugarman also wrote an excellent book on infomercials.

Other Suppliers

I regularly use a variety of suppliers for various activities. For postcards, I use Get Members. Visit GetMembers.com. It provides comprehensive services: design, purchase of the compiled list, printing, assembly/preparation, postage and fulfillment. The other is 1800postcards.com, which offers quality full-color printing, but not mailing services.

As One Martial Artist to Another, Let's Talk Frankly About Money: Part 1

I know what you may be thinking, "Is it really possible to make a big income or even be rich in the martial arts industry?"

I'm no different than you. When I graduated from Georgetown University, I put together a business plan and showed it to my first instructors (Gran Moulder and Bob Olinghouse — both Jhoon Rhee Black Belts from the Alan Steen-Pat Burleson lineage). I was 22 and excited about moving from Washington, D.C., to Denver, Colorado, to open my first school.

I asked Gran for his feedback on my business plan. (At the time, he was president and owner of a family business, Moulder-Oldham Janitorial Supply. Bob, my other instructor, even worked for him for a while.) I mistakenly thought that as a "real" business person/business owner he might give me some useful ideas.

When I asked his opinion he was very helpful! You know what he said? "You can go to Denver and 'play at Karate' for a while, and then find a real job." Obviously, very helpful feedback about my career objectives! This wasn't the first time I had heard the "How-do-you-expect-to-make-a-living-doing-martial-arts" line, but this time I was informed, and prepared enough to ignore it and just execute my plan.

By the way, a few years later Gran came to visit me in Denver. I had a new Corvette and a huge house on the side of a mountain overlooking Denver. I had 1,500-plus active students in five locations. I made him "eat crow," although I felt bad about it later when I learned that his family business in a "real industry" had folded.

It's unfortunately ingrained in many of us that we've chosen an industry where the love of what we do trumps the fact that we'll probably never make much money doing it.

Many martial artists have never been able to move past this early, negative "programming." It may have been drilled into you by teachers, parents, siblings, friends, and even your wife or girlfriend that it's just not possible to make a comparable or better living than the "professionals" (doctor, dentist, lawyer, etc.) in your family or circle of friends.

Now, I'm sure I don't have to tell you there are many people who have become rich as martial artists, and within martial arts. I'm sure you don't think that Chuck Norris, Jackie Chan, Jean Claude Van Damme or Steven Seagal have "suffered for their art" — financially. (I asked Chuck once while at his ranch in Texas whether all the fortune was worth all the fame — predictably he said, "I've been rich and I've been poor. Rich is better.")

Certainly, those examples don't help us much, unless we're planning to start acting lessons, so let's look at some other examples within martial arts. You may not know them — I do — but I can certainly tell you that Nick Cokinos, founder of Educational Funding Company, and Master Alex Reed, founder of ASF International, are both incredibly wealthy. Nick drives a new convertible Rolls Royce and has a huge amount of real estate and stock investments. Master Reed lives full-time on a cruise ship — and bought another home on the Palm, a man-made island in Dubai!

Another example certainly is my friend Mike Dillard who owns Century Martial Arts Supply — and a considerably amount of commercial real estate in Oklahoma City.

I could continue, but your response is predictable, "OK, I can become rich as a martial artist, but can I, running martial arts schools?" Well frankly, I believe, in many ways, that is an easier, more predictable and practical route.

How do you really become rich running martial arts schools?

There are names in the industry you would know — and, probably more that you wouldn't know — that have run single locations or small multi-location chains effectively. There are others who have run bigger organizations: Danny "Tiger" Schulmann, Master Bill Clark and myself. These are individuals who have mastered multiple-school operations and became rich running martial arts schools and teaching instructors how to teach and how to manage their martial arts schools. You probably know one or more of these names and there are others. I'm sure you would agree that they've achieved high income and wealth from running martial arts schools.

I can teach you how to do the same thing.

Our Regional Developer program gives you the opportunity to become the equivalent of "Tiger Schulmann" in New York, Bill Clark in Jacksonville or Stephen Oliver in Denver. It provides proven systems for large school operations without the headaches of a large staff and without spending $100,000 to $200,000 to open each school from your personal resources.

OK, maybe you acknowledge that you can definitely make plenty of money from a multiple-school operation, but maybe you only want to teach and work with students on a daily basis. Is it really possible to run a single school and make a LARGE income?

Certainly it's very possible. I could list some of our school owners who, by following systems, focusing on priorities and managing their expenses, make very good incomes from single schools. You probably haven't heard of them, however, since they're not in the public eye seeking exposure. By the way, there are many anonymous rich people in the martial arts industry; you just don't know them.

Some that you may know include Keith Hafner, my friend in Ann Arbor, Michigan. I could give you Keith's full background, but let me give you just a little "snippet." A few years ago, he built his "dream house," which is in the range of 8,500 square feet on a beautiful treed lot, with a built-in swimming pool, Jacuzzis, workout room and built-in, massive stereo system throughout the entire house.

He runs a school that does approximately $100,000 a month in gross revenues with a 50% net for many years now and still does every enrollment and renewal himself (with his son teaching the majority of the classes). There are many examples like that.

As One Martial Artist to Another, Let's Talk Frankly About Money, Part 2

Steve Doyon, my friend in Connecticut, is another anonymous, wealthy martial arts school owner that you probably don't know. He runs a $1,000,000 per year single-school operation. I could continue about single schools that are generating huge grosses, but also many that may not gross as much, but are running high net profits with proper controls and systems in place.

There are many schools with which I've personally worked that are about to grow to $10,000 or more per month net profit. Even in my case, my one remaining "corporate school" had a net profit last year of more than $90,000, AFTER paying two full-time Black Belts, running it for more than $100,000 and with almost no involvement from me. (I actually visited the school about seven times last year, did none of the teaching and none of the sales, and, frankly, none of the "grassroots" or on-site marketing either.)

In addition to the fact that many of us have been taught that you "can't make money teaching martial arts," many of us have also been taught that even if you can, you shouldn't.

I'd like to share another story with you.

Many years ago, Tom Callos, a close friend of mine (who was working with Jhoon Rhee to put together the book Bruce Lee and I) called me about going to the "Bruce Lee Auction." Linda Lee (now Linda Lee Caldwell) had decided to auction much of Bruce Lee's stuff, and Tom, Ernie Reyes and several of my friends planned to attend.

Tom urged me to attend with him. I was interested at the time and asked him to forward me the auction catalogue. After looking through the catalogue, something caught my attention. It was a beautifully hand-written goals statement by Bruce Lee.

It said:

> "*My Definite Chief Aim:*
>
> *I, Bruce Lee, will be the highest paid Oriental superstar in the United States. In return I will give the most exciting performances and render the best of quality in the capacity of an actor.*
>
> *Starting in 1970, I will achieve world fame and from then onward till the end of 1980, I will have in my possession $10,000,000.*
>
> *Then I will live the way I please and achieve inner harmony and peace.*"
>
> (SIGNED) BRUCE LEE, JANUARY 1969.

That piqued my interest.

Why did it interest me? I'm a big fan of *Think and Grow Rich* as well as much of the success literature. I know how important and powerful goal setting and clarity of purpose can be to achieve success. I was thrilled to see this representation of clarity of focus that Bruce Lee had created for himself (coincidentally, during the year I started in martial arts).

I was thinking seriously about attending the auction to buy that one piece. About that time, I talked to Jhoon Rhee and told him about the auction and the letter. He said, "Yes, I know that one. I was with him when he wrote it in Los Angeles. He was very excited about it, and we talked at length about how he would grow his career and achieve financial wealth."

I don't remember why now, but I didn't board the plane. Planet Hollywood bought it for $35,000. I'm not sure I would have been willing to pay that much at that time for a piece of paper written by Bruce Lee, but I certainly regret it now. You can see a color copy with a photo of Bruce in sunglasses, which is usually framed and displayed near the front door of just about every Planet Hollywood.

Why do I share this with you?

So many martial artists are hung up on the "history of what they do" and ignore what it takes to be rich.

Ask yourself now. When you are in your 60s or 70s, what will be more important to you? The physical specifics of what you taught or the fact that you helped thousands of students achieve tremendous results in their lives, while you earned a great living, providing for yourself and your family and creating wealth to retire comfortably with whatever toys you desire and knowing that your children are well provided?

Think about it for a second. Bruce Lee was perhaps the most accomplished and the most forward-thinking martial artist of his generation. He had no trouble with charging $250 an hour for private lessons (during the 1960s!); driving his new Porsche around LA at high speed (scaring Jhoon Rhee among others — something that I've also done in my Porsche Turbo, by the way, while Jhoon Rhee screamed, "you drive like Bruce Lee"); or setting a goal of $10,000,000 CASH in the bank.

Prior to receiving his acting break, Bruce was conspiring with Jhoon Rhee to open a chain of schools in the San Francisco-Oakland area. They shared ideas about advertising, marketing, pricing and business strategy. He regularly sent Chuck Norris and other martial arts schools' advertising to Jhoon Rhee, and then set their strategies for the best marketing practices!

Here's a serious question for you: Do you REALLY want to be financially successful?

To accomplish financial success, you must realize that you must focus on what the market will pay and a system and process that will deliver it most effectively to the most people.

With Mile High Karate, we know that there is a huge market for happy, successful well-behaved kids. We know that parents will pay just about any amount of money to protect their child from negative peer pressure and give them the tools that they need to be successful.

We also understand that the market is not clamoring for any particular style or methodology, but is enthusiastic about the "outcome" that we've created for our students. Your long-term career move may be to affiliate with us and leverage a true "national brand," with systems in place to teach what students and parents want to learn (and are willing to pay handsomely to learn).

As One Martial Artist to Another, Let's Talk Frankly About Money, Part 3

Mile High Karate has created a system that is easy to implement and creates a VERY high quality student physically, mentally and emotionally; and, frankly, more importantly, we've created a marketing process that will flood your school with students who want what you teach. We've created systems to help you provide the highest possible service with the minimum of headaches and the maximum profitability.

Look in any career area.

Is the number one box office draw at the movies star the most accomplished and technically skilled actor or is he or she skilled, charismatic and marketed well?

How about music. Were Madonna or Britney (and whoever is now taking their place) the most accomplished and technically skilled vocalists or have they just tapped into the "pulse" of what the public wants and been properly packaged and marketed? Surely, there are opera stars or other classical singers with better technical skills in an area that the market doesn't want.

Do you think Dr. Phil is the most capable psychologist or was he just a genius at packaging and marketing what the public wanted?

Does he do much more good than the psychologists who aren't willing to market themselves?

I'll bet there's a bunch of Harvard-trained "traditionalist" psychologists upset about him "commercializing" psychology.

That's right, they don't understand either. It's not about being right; it's about capturing the public's imagination and creating a powerful brand that satisfies their needs. Dr. Phil will have a much more powerful influence on the MILLIONS of people who learn from him than the trickle of patients the pissed-off guys will help during their careers.

Now, before you become self-righteous and think that I'm talking about diluting the arts and "selling out" on quality, let me share with you a quote from Paul McCartney: "Somebody said to me, 'The Beatles were anti-materialistic.' That's a huge myth. John Lennon and I literally used to sit down and say, 'Now, let's write a swimming pool.'"

Now, that's a quote from the most covered band of all time, which is still one of the most popular and profitable bands ever — more than 30 years after they disbanded. There's even a Cirque Du Soleil show of all Beatles songs. Regarding Paul McCartney, if you don't know, he's considered the most successful pop composer of all time. In the *Guinness Book of World Records*, he is cited for the most records sold, most number one records (shared) and the largest paid audience for a concert (350,000-plus people, 1989 in Brazil).

If Lennon/McCartney can become the most respected songwriting team in history by focusing not just on the "purity of their craft" but also on "let's write a swimming pool," then don't you think you should give yourself the right to be rich doing what you love and creating great results for your students.

In closing?

It's amazing to me that so many people (including and maybe especially many in the martial arts industry) ignore that great quote of Zig Ziglar's:

"You have to BE and DO before you can HAVE."

Don't misunderstand me; I'm all about skipping as many rungs as possible to leap to the top of the ladder of success, but there are many basics that must be addressed to reach the top rung and stay there. Ultimately, your long-term success is all about character. You must combine a thirst for knowledge and a willingness to implement aggressively and try new things.

I seem to have recently been "surrounded" by two types of losers, who will always remain losers until they reorient their worldview.

Type #1: "Win a Little Bit and Quit." I've seen multiple school owners recently implement a couple of ideas. Their GROSSES jump $10,000 to $12,000 per month; their nets jump $5,000 to $7,000 a month, and then just quit. They've decided that this new (rather mediocre) status quo is everything they ever wanted and more.

Certainly, it's great to move from near insolvency to a $75,000- to $120,000-a-year income, but achieving that goal first is much easier than maintaining it month after month, year after year. Second, the habits and actions that a school owner learns when almost insolvent don't support him well to the next level of success and, often, after an immediate flush of success, come back to haunt him. Finally, the next step is achieving these results through others — consistently. That's MUCH harder than it looks and has some ups and downs.

Type #2: The "Magic Pixie Dust" crowd. They lament, "Gee, this is too hard; I must work too many hours. Why can't you just do it for me and send me the deposits while I sit on my couch and watch American Idol?"

Some people watch my business from afar and conclude that they can take a few ideas and essentially — overnight — run their businesses by remote control. Interestingly, the ones who seem to "whine the most" are the 25- to 35-year-old crowd; its members have barely started their careers!

Frankly, the reality is that most "overnight" successes that I have ever known worked, learned, experimented and thought about their business 24/7 for many years before being recognized as an overnight success.

I can teach you to progress from a $50,000-a-year income to a $125,000-a-year income — then to double that to $300,000-plus, then to double that again to $600,000, but only if you are willing to KEEP growing — and to work hard. Remember, the skills and thinking that took you to your current level of success are different from the skills and mindset that will move you to the next level.

A Reveal of Ten Mistakes You Might Be Making

Toby and I just returned from the Financial Power Summit in Dallas, Texas. I'm honored to be joined on this tour by Grandmaster Y.K. Kim, Master Kirk Pelt and Master Keith Winkle. Other than the fact the my entire family ended up sick on the days before the event, myself included, and I ended up putting on my game face with a serious virus, the event was fabulous.

I have some take-aways from the event and some observations that I'd like to share. It was interesting. Bob Dunne, Toby Milroy and I went about really investigating everyone who was pre-registered for the event. I reviewed everyone's Website. Toby and Bob called all of the schools to do info-calls on them.

My intent was to play the audio of the calls and review the websites during the event. Toby hyperventilated on that one — sure I was going to offend everyone before the session even got going. I'm not sure I have the numbers exactly right, but on the calls, it was something like 20 calls placed, 17 "no" answers and 3 answered. Two of those three ended up chasing down a "rat hole," discussing the merits of their various styles and programs and not asking for a name, number, and appointment. Embarrassing. I explained that these are among other things that I've tracked for years when information calls come into our schools.

I can tell you definitively that moms call about lessons for their kids mostly between 9 a.m. and 11 a.m., Monday through Thursday. I can also tell you based upon outbound calls from NAPMA headquarters to schools that most schools do not answer their phones before 4:00 p.m. Therefore most information calls go to voicemail. Either the Mom does not leave a message, or a game of phone tag ensues. Many times they've lost interest or gotten distracted by the time they are contacted — if they ever are, in fact, contacted.

I will tell you also that the Websites were absolutely scary. A couple were mediocre. The rest were just horrible. They missed key points that I've been teaching members for years. They mostly spent a ton of time talking about their style and their biography. I irritated a few in the seminar by pointing out that no one cares. A mother doesn't want to read about Kenpo, Tae Kwon Do, MMA or any other iteration. She wants to hear about benefits, feedback from other parents and have an easy way to learn more.

In most every case they made no effort to capture information. Just about everyone confuses stuff that may be useful for their current students with information for prospective students. At the very least you want a clear path for prospects to learn about benefits of your school and to raise their hand to learn more.

I walked through with one NAPMA member looking at her Website. My comment was first: Who are your students? Answer. Mostly kids (60 percent kids, 40 percent adults). About half of the adults came in with their kids. If that's true then my point was to look at your Website from the perspective of a "soccer mom" of a seven-year-old girl. What does that mom think about the patch with a knife and sword? How about the photo of two kids sparring with one kicking the other in the knee. How about a listing of various styles and types of martial arts.

Well, you get the picture. You've got to look at it from the perspective of your prospective student who knows little about martial arts, but is looking to start lessons. Look at it from the perspective of a parent. Look at it from the perspective of an adult prospective student. Forget your preconceptions and look at it from the standpoint of a new prospect.

Another observation from the event. About half of the people in the room were from schools in the $5,000 per month range or less. The other half was in the $20,000 to $40,000 per month range. Several of the participants were ATA Schools, Premier Schools or Mile High Karate schools. They were all in the top level of schools from a standpoint of revenue, understanding of systems, quality Website, etc. In fact, I told one of them (not a Mile High guy) that the areas where he was screwing up were the areas where he was resisting what his organization was telling him to do, clinging to a variety of irrelevant curriculum and maintaining a "shadow" Website that didn't follow the parent organization's recommendations. One of the other "sharp" participants was Howard Nixon — a long-time Maximum Impact member — who frankly should be and, probably soon will be, a Peak Performers Member.

As usual, those who made the effort to hog time, tell everyone about their great ideas and argue simple points, were the school owners doing $5,000 or less per month. I was unusually diplomatic (for me) but, frankly, it gets annoying listening to failing school owners share their secrets of failure. These failing school owners are clear that the success skills shared won't work in their community, with their students, with their style (as if any of that matters).

The school owners in the room doing the best — the top 10% guys — were sitting on the edge of their seat, taking notes — in some cases brought an audio or video recorder — and asked specific, directed questions to have an action plan. I'd certainly like to express appreciation to the members who attended and contributed…thank you.

After the seminar, I took the time to do more thorough evaluations with several Maximum Impact members — as you know, that's unusual as I mostly personally coach our Inner Circle members, who range from $30,000 to $100,000 or more per month.

In one case for a school doing $4,500 to $5,000 per month, it didn't take long to find the problem areas.

The quick list:

1. No organized Info Call, Introductory Class, or Enrollment Process.
2. No contracts, strictly month-to-month.
3. Not outsourcing or automating billing. Having students bring checks in month for payment.
4. A poorly-designed tuition structure, with no down payment to get started.
5. An average monthly student value of $100 or less, rather than where it should be of $250—$300 per month.
6. No Renewal Program (aka Upgrade).
7. Complicated curriculum structure (multiple programs, multiple styles, confusing structure).
8. A predisposition about what their students and prospective students will and won't do.
9. A focus on teaching physical skills rather than "life-skills."
10. A near total reliance on "word of mouth" for new students, without a real referral system.

I don't have the space to go into all of these items here. I will tell you that members who have poor results focus primarily on learning new curriculum "stuff" from the materials that we share and don't really pay attention on the monthly tele-coaching calls and fail to study the material in your monthly "Maximum Impact" package. Developing teaching skills is vital, and you must have a focused approach to generating new students and creating maximum student value. To really thrive, focus on fabulous student service. Make sure you have clear and effective sales processes in place for prospective students and for renewals, and keep your pipeline filled with new students.

On the billing side, I'll tell you that I don't have a "dog in this hunt." What you must do is require that all payments be automatic through EFT or credit card. You can automate that with software applications or you can hire a billing company. Don't be "penny wise and pound foolish" on stuff like this. Hire an accounting firm, payroll service firm and automate or outsource your billing.

I will leave you with one thought. There's no excuse for having fewer than 100 students grossing less than $20,000 a month. Every school I've ever opened was at 100 or more students in the first six weeks. If you are running a small school full-time, make a decision and add 100 students in the next 60 to 90 days. It's completely doable.

You may spend 20, 30 or even 40 hours a week "beating the bushes" for new students. I will tell you that working HARD is a hell of a lot better than being lazy and broke. Frankly, you may have to really work hard on your marketing to build momentum, but it's a lot easier to keep a school rolling than to get it there in the first place.

Another point that many miss is that no matter how many "referral systems" you have in place, it's really tough to grow from within when you have a small student body. You've got to jump-start things with community outreach and advertising. In the early days, most of what I accomplished was through pure manual labor. It's easier to spend a big stack of money to fill your school, but, really, it's just about making a decision and getting to work.

7 Steps to a Flood of Introductory Traffic

I just returned from a couple of days in our school in Fresno, California. It was a great experience. Lots of fabulous students. A motivated and energized staff. Monthly new records being hit. And overall great momentum in the coming year. They are FLOODED with introductory traffic. Most of what I was working on was improving ratios that have slipped due to volume and renewal ratios.

In working with them — with a target of really being a million-dollar-a-year school by the end of the year — I reviewed our standard approach to going from mediocre to fantastic.

First step. Fix your teaching and curriculum. Take a look at your monthly retention rate. Get your monthly dropout rate to less than 3% of your active students. If it's 5% or above you've got to figure out where the problem lies. If you have a problem it really boils down to the quality of your teaching (and teachers) or the structure of your curriculum. Lots of schools have a really lousy curriculum. It's important to chunk it down appropriately. It's important not to teach too much stuff too early.

To improve your retention take a look at a couple of important considerations.

1. The first few months really are only about getting the student committed to Black Belt and beyond. Keep it fun and help them have success. If they feel successful, feel like they can master your art, then it's much easier for them to picture training to Black Belt and beyond.

2. Make sure there is REGULAR PROGRESS. Students should advance to a new belt every two or three months. They should be able to earn stripes on their belt and other rewards every four to eight lessons. Keep in mind that I'm not talking about only your Little Ninjas® or children's program. Adults need regular progress as well. Look at the typical four-year college. You have at minimum a mid-term and a final each semester — therefore you move forward to new curricula at least two or three times per year and have progress updates at least every two months — usually more often.

3. Make sure you hire staff who are more concerned about their students than themselves. Great athletes rarely make great coaches. Many of us make the mistake of hiring staff based upon physical talent. That's nice, but really empathy and sincere concern for your students is more important.

4. Keep track. What gets measured gets done. Pay close attention to who's gradually attending less regularly. Always know who's been gone for a week and go on a massive effort to get them back (phone calls, letters, etc.). Track your one week, two week, three week inactives. Know your average monthly dropout rate (percentage of students who drop out each month based on your total active count).

Ultimately student retention is more about rapport and sincere concern for your students and less about the content of your classes. If you like your students, know who they are, their names, details about them, their goals and needs, then they will like you and know you are sincere.

Second step. Fix your tuition rate. You should be charging $150—$250 per month for new students. Then you must have a Black Belt Program and Master Club and Leadership Levels. Typically you can have these upgrade programs where their tuition can increase by 50% to 100% or more. I typically have an option that's double and an option that's a 50% increase.

Again, we've seen schools who don't use contracts. I believe your initial enrollment should be six to 12 months, and your upgrade should take them to Black Belt or beyond.

Broken record on this: IT DOESN'T MATTER what your competition is charging. You can be double anyone else in town — if you are marketing properly — and it won't make any difference. My studies show that less than 5% of prospective students ever shop other schools. Frankly, most schools are so bad that if you have a quality teacher, structure and proper focus for your students, then it won't make any difference anyway. Much of what we teach is "Marketing in a Vacuum." They should be deciding if they like what you offer or not. Then they'll decide if they can afford it or not. Your real competition is other discretionary spending, other sports activities and other developmental activities.

Third step. Fix your RATIOS. Get your contact (info call or lead call)-to-appointment ratio right: 70% or 80% introductory to enrollment ratio in place.

Fourth Step. Fill your pipeline. Flood your school with new prospective students. There are MANY ways to do this, but I'll tell you it's SIMPLE. Perhaps not EASY, but it's SIMPLE. You've got to work hard. Beat the bushes. Get out in the community. Network with students. But it's SIMPLE.

Back to Fresno; they've generated 248 LEADS (contact with name, address, phone, email that's expressed interest) in the last two weeks. They've scheduled 148 appointments and have enrolled 14 of them so far, and are on track for 40 enrollments this month at $400 down and $197 a month on a 12-month contract.

There are many ways to fill your pipeline. Most take time, money or both. In their case, they've been making a bunch of appointments at carnivals, fairs and other community events. EVERY member school should be working on public relations, community outreach, internal events and advertising every month. You really must plan on spending the vast majority of your time out in your community finding prospective students until you get to 250 or so active students. You've got to continually beat the bushes and fill your pipeline.

Want to REALLY fill your school? Pull the trigger and get the Japan Relief flyers out to 50,000-plus people in your community next week. Then make sure you are hitting the *Kung Fu Panda 2* promotions in the theaters and in your school — a 100% effort. Each could be worth 50 or more new students. But you must IMPLEMENT VIOLENTLY.

Fifth Step. Once you've flooded your sales pipeline with prospects, go back to step three and fix your ratios — again. With volume, things start getting sloppy. You've got to step back and fix those ratios. Keep them tight, even with 100-plus introductory classes per month.

Sixth Step. Really review your new student (White and Gold Belt) classes and make sure they are fabulous. Make sure no one is getting lost in the shuffle. Make sure they all feel a lot of rapport with you and your school and staff.

Seventh Step. Take a look at your upgrade ratios. I want to target 75% of your new enrollments ending up in your next level in the first four months. Our target is 50% of new enrollments renewed in the first two months, 50% of those left renewed within the next two months.

You may need to reframe your perspective on this. The best way to improve your retention is to improve your renewal ratios. If they don't renew they are going to drop out. If you renew them early when they are ready, your ratios will improve.

An important note: It's essential to renew them when they are ready. If they don't renew when they are ready they may never renew. Jeff Smith's analogy is that it's like buying a watermelon. You thump them to see if they are ripe. Once ripe, it's time to renew. From there on they die on the vine and rot. You NEVER enroll someone for a year and wait until the end of the year. Frankly, in the early months of their lessons is when you must prep them for long-term follow-through. If you don't do it then, it will likely never happen

Keep It Simple and Focus on What's Important

At the most basic level, all businesses are simple. Management guru Peter Drucker said, "The purpose of all businesses is to create and keep a customer." I've expanded that for our staff just slightly to three points of daily focus: enrollments, renewals (or upgrades) and retention.

It's useful to keep it simple and focus on what's important. Obviously, each of these points can be expanded infinitely; however, what you must do every day is to focus on each of these areas: What can we do today to enroll more new students? What can we do today to retain students longer? What can we do today to renew more students into our upgrade programs?

From a time management standpoint, start the day with a blank legal pad and a brainstorming session (often with just yourself) on attracting new students. What internal and external promotional activities can you implement to add more students? What can you do immediately (today) to create leads, expand intros and improve enrollment ratios? With what groups or organizations should you be working to promote your school? Who must you know to grow your school? What labor-intensive activities can you do today to fill your school? What additional advertising or marketing efforts should you be undertaking to grow your school? Are you spending enough? Are you being smart about your advertising and promotions?

I've witnessed many school owners who'd rather sit and bemoan their lack of new students than to take action to find more students. Even on the most limited budget, you can still hit the streets, pick up the phone and meet individuals and groups who may be interested in your school. Make sure that every day you are doing something to find new students.

Next, during "prime-time" be careful on what you focus. Minute-by-minute, you must be taking the most productive actions possible. For each class, ask yourself (and your staff) these questions:

- Who's in class who won't be back if I don't take action to fix them?
- Who's in class that can be renewed?
- Who's in class that could help us with enrollments?

Everyone has had the experience of reaching the end of the evening without adding a new student or renewing anyone. Guard against that every day. Focus on making sure that you are maximizing results in every class with every method possible.

Consultation Certificate

This Certificate Entitles the Bearer to a Personal 1-on-1 Martial Arts School Business Analysis With a NAPMA-Certified Business Analyst. This Individual Consultation is Valued at $495.00.

Certificate expires 12 months from the date of purchase.
To schedule your personal business analysis, complete this form and fax to NAPMA at
1-800-795-0853; mail to 1767 Denver West Blvd., Suite A, Golden, CO 80401;
or visit www.PrivateCoachingSession.com

PLEASE FILL OUT COMPLETELY AND WRITE LEGIBLY

Name _____

School Name _____

Address _____

City _____ State/Province _____

Zip _____ Country _____

Phone _____ Fax _____

E-Mail _____

_____
Authorized by Toby Milroy
Chief Operating Officer, NAPMA

---

3 FREE GIFTS FOR SERIOUS SCHOOL OWNERS

FREE Personal School Evaluation

Two 30-minute Sessions
A sure-fire way action plan to double your results or better.

FREE Two 90-Minute Seminars

with **"The Millionaire Maker Grandmaster Stephen Oliver** "The 5 Stupid Mistakes All Too Many School Owners Make that Kill Their Growth" and "The Key Step-by-Step Blueprint for Being a Big Winner"

FREE CD-DVD Package and Report

"How Hundreds of Smart School Owners Like You Doubled Their Revenue in the Last 12 Months Even in the Midst of the Greatest Recession since the Great Depresson, and How You Can, Too!"

Have You Reached "Black Belt" Rank in Business?

I just returned from our second "Financial Power" seminar where NAPMA has teamed with AMS to give an industry appreciation and support seminar tour. Y.K. Kim and I have teamed up for the first time for an event series such as this. (He and I have been friends since meeting through Grandmaster Jhoon Rhee in the 1980s.)

After the event, Grandmaster Kim, Kirk Pelt, Keith Winkle and I were discussing the New York/New Jersey event and the participants of the event. The topic came up about the level of results that many of the school owners were having (many schools under $10,000) per month and the backwards way that many had structured their curriculum, their tuition and their marketing approach. Someone, I forget who, said that it's amazing given how much information is available to school owners and the huge advances that have been made by the top school owners in the past 20 years. After some discussion I pointed out that our industry "turns over" every 4 to 5 years — in other words, 20—25% of all schools go out of business each year. Therefore, the general knowledge of the industry doesn't date back to the 1960s, but really is on average only a year or two.

In terms of your martial arts school, most owners are only green or blue belts. They don't know what they don't know. Actually, that's giving most too much credit. Most school owners (probably the bottom 80%, certainly at least the bottom 50%) DO NOT seek out teachers and training on how to run their business more effectively. In a similar vein I heard a stat recently that said 80% of sales people have never read even one sales book. The head of a HUGE insurance company said the difference between his mediocre sales people and his top 10% was just reading two books per month. The unfortunate reality is that most people are ignorant by choice. They then blame circumstances for their failure rather than looking in a mirror.

In fact, the number one complaint that we get from members is that they don't have time to read all of the stuff we send them. In reality if you allotted 30 minutes a day to your own training, you'd go through all of our material plus an additional book or two each month. It's simple. Surely you should allot 30 minutes or an hour a day to improving your CAREER? Make sure you commit right now to being in the top 20%, then top 5%, then top 3% of our industry. More on that later.

Anyway, back to the seminar. There continue to be common themes among failing school owners. I point them out again here. (By the way, I'll also share some common traits of successful owners.) The failures do a couple of things.

First, they tell us their best source of enrollments is "word of mouth," aka, code for waiting and hoping. They say that in seriousness, but when asked what referral strategies and systems they have in place, you get a blank expression. To be successful you must "do more stuff." Frankly, you should be actively working on internal referral strategies (pizza parties, birthday parties, events tied to belt graduations, self-defense days, movie nights, etc.) and working on community outreach activities with churches, day cares, sports leagues, businesses, schools, etc. — and advertising regularly. If you're not doing 10 or 15 things each and every month to attract new students, then you are missing the boat.

Second, and keep in mind this was the NYC metropolitan area, they charge way too little. You really should be at least in the $125—$150 range for your lessons. I'd prefer closer to $200 or more for new enrollments. In almost any town or city, charging less than $100 is crazy.

Third, program structure. Most schools are making their initial enrollment too complicated. Many still shy away from contracts or offer "month-to-month" options. For many years (starting in 1983) I offered a 12-month and an 18-month enrollment option. I've seen successful schools that offer 6-month enrollments and others that offer 12-month initial enrollments. But don't make it too complicated. One school I talked to offered month-to-month, 3 months, 6 months and 9 months as options. Too complicated.

Fourth, no upgrade system. Many schools STILL just enroll students on a monthly tuition forever (i.e., until they drop out). Others enroll them for 6 months or 12 months and then just do a new contract. You must have a RENEWAL system in place to help your students set their goal to Black Belt and beyond. It's imperative for them to see that vision and buy into the idea of "graduating" to Black Belt and then to 2nd- and 3rd-Degree Black Belt.

You also need to have some upgrade system. What I mean by that is a mechanism to move them to pay more than you charged at the initial enrollment. There are several ways to do that, but I'll leave it at you can move them to Black Belt Club, Master Club, or Leadership at higher monthly or per lesson tuitions, or you can have "add-on" options such as demo team, weapons classes, etc. The objective is to add 25%, 50% or more to the tuition being paid.

Fifth, EVERYONE thinks they teach great classes, have great curriculum and have great student retention. MOST are fooling themselves. The best indicator is your monthly dropout or quit rate. If you are losing more than 3% you have room for improvement. So if you have 100 students and are losing more than three per month, you can get to work figuring out how to fix your student retention levels.

The most likely suspect in all cases for fixing the curriculum is to simplify your first-year curriculum (especially the first four or five months). Chunk it down into more "bite-size" pieces. Push things like free sparring into the second year of your curriculum.

Make your first few months about setting a goal to be a Black Belt and beyond. Make the first year about making sure they get so anchored to your school that they are still there in year two.

You only create fabulous students by having them stick with you for two, three, four or more years. The second thing to look at and really the biggest problem is RAPPORT. Most students ultimately drop out because of only one of two things. They are confused early on and get frustrated. Or they don't feel like part of the family. In your school the biggest problem is "perceived apathy." In other words, if they like you, like your staff, have friends in their class and feel like they'll be missed, then they are much less likely to ever drop out.

To wrap up on this discussion, let's talk about a reality of human nature and of our society in general. In the United States the top 20% of income earners (household income) are at $90,000 or more annual income. The top 5% are at $150,000 or more. The top 3% are at $200,000 or more.

Where do you want to be in your career?

Our target for my Inner Circle members is to make sure they are all in the top 3% or even top 1%. We want each and every one to have a PERSONAL income of $200,000 or better (often much better).

Our target for my Peak Performers is to make sure that each are in the top 5%, to make sure they are in the $150,000 or more income range in short order.

Finally, our target for ALL NAPMA Maximum Impact members is at MINIMUM to be in the top 20% — to be at $90,000 or more personal income. We're not talking about school gross but are talking about how much you keep after expenses.

Make a determination about where you want to be. Is it in the top 20%, the top 5% or the top 3% or better? I've personally taken many school owners on the journey from struggling to the top 3% or 1% of the industry. Others I've moved from being a top 20% school to a top 3% school in six or seven months. If you are ready to take the next step forward for your business then we should talk and get a game plan to radically grow your school — now.

Every 7 Years ... or We've Been Spoiled

In the heat of the media feeding frenzy about the economy, there is an underlying lesson. It's typical for the economy to cycle up and down during a seven-year more or less cycle. Many forget the shocks to the system right after 9/11. Most of you don't remember the "Carter years" of disaster, or the downturn during the late 1980s that was very similar (over-built office space, retail and housing and the savings and loan bailout).

While many school owners may have managed to survive or even thrive during the economic growth of the Clinton and Bush administrations, the real question about the strength of your underlying business is how you do when the mediocre majority are suffering or closing businesses.

In my book, *Everything I Wish I Knew When I Was 22*, I write about two items of interest to many of you.

One item of interest was "Things Are Never as Bad as They Seem." Human nature and the financial markets that reflect human nature tend toward euphoria or depression...not much in between. It's really like being "bi-polar," without the drugs.

Anyway, the stock market tends to overreact to bad news. You and your staff may also tend to overreact to a slowdown and having to struggle or at least work harder than you think you should. Make sure you step back and make an objective and optimistic assessment of where you are in your business and what needs to happen to move forward.

You must work to shield yourself from all of the real and exaggerated bad news, and stay focused on success. Make sure you also put more time and effort into your staff. Some will bail, looking for safer havens with bigger companies (although, obviously, that's a fool's mission).

The second item of interest is keeping failure in mind. Most of the famous and successful entrepreneurs that you read about suffered many financial ups and downs. Ray Kroc of McDonalds and Tom Monihan of Dominos Pizza were both broke and nearly threw in the towel during their early years (and, at least, in Domino's case later as well, when Monihan had to return and take back the reins). Jhoon Rhee, Jeff Smith, other friends of mine and I have all experienced ups and downs, although we may appear to be eternally successful from your point of view. Stories of bankruptcies, divorce, staffing problems and scandal brought on by careless staff are endless among the successful "icons." Often, you just don't hear that side of their stories.

In Jhoon Rhee's case, Jeff Smith moved from Texas with a group of his friends (Pat Worley, Gary Hestilow, Larry Carnahan and others), when many of Jhoon Rhee's staff members left with little or no notice. I had the same experience during the 1980s, and the S&L crisis. What seems like a crisis at the time often is for the best; however the financial and emotional struggle isn't much fun.

If you're feeling anxious or are struggling, then you're not alone. There are many of us, however, who have "been there, done that" supporting you through NAPMA. We can help you not only survive, but also thrive in the current economy.

As a final note, there's an additional situation that could sabotage your success that you should fix before it becomes an issue. It's the "Am-I-good-enough?" syndrome. In fact, the theme in John Graden's excellent book, *The Imposter Syndrome*, is that many people, even as they are experiencing success, sabotage themselves, thinking that success is not real or earned. They are afraid that, at any moment, they may be "discovered." Don't fall victim yourself. Add your visualization exercises. Set goals. Have positive expectancy and move forward undeterred.

Some Thoughts about Style, Part 1

Let me share a story about style and my thinking in having a consistent style throughout all Mile High Karate schools. You may know that both Jeff Smith and I studied with Grandmaster Jhoon Rhee, who's known as the father of American Tae Kwon Do. He invented musical forms and safety equipment, opening the way for every aspect of current sport karate — from the NASKA circuit to professional kickboxing.

Bruce Lee and my instructor Jhoon Rhee were close friends. They trained together and stayed at each other's homes; and Bruce even arranged a Hong Kong movie deal for Jhoon Rhee. Jhoon Rhee taught Bruce to do a powerful side kick, and Bruce taught him to think with more flexibility about styles and the nature of martial arts.

Jhoon Rhee insists that I met Bruce Lee while testing in the early 1970s — however, I'm not sure he's right. Regardless, I probably wouldn't remember. Unfortunately, Bruce Lee died in Hong Kong when I was 13. Prior to that he was recognized in martial arts circles, but certainly hadn't achieved "superstar" status in the United States. Frankly, among the martial arts community of the 1960s and early 1970s, he was not a popular figure. Only innovators, such as Jhoon Rhee, Jeff Smith, Chuck Norris and Joe Lewis, befriended him and supported his ideas.

I've spoken at length about Bruce Lee with Jhoon Rhee and others who were friends and associates of his, including Jeff Smith, Chuck Norris and Fred Degerberg, and with Linda and Brandon Lee.

While reading Jhoon Rhee's fascinating book, *Bruce Lee and I*, I was reminded of many things that martial artists then and now do to screw up their thinking about their arts, careers and long-term objectives.

Interestingly, with Bruce Lee and many others that have achieved such exulted status, the general belief about who they were, what they believed and what was true is often different. Chuck Norris and Jhoon Rhee shared with me many stories that debunk popular beliefs.

Anyway, much of the way martial arts is taught today can be traced to the influences of Bruce Lee and Jhoon Rhee as well as famous fighters, such as Chuck Norris, Jeff Smith, etc.

A Bruce Lee quote that encapsulates part of the shift in thinking of people like Jhoon Rhee (and me) is:

> *"Before I studied the arts, a punch to me was just like a punch, a kick just like a kick. After I learned the arts, a punch was no longer a punch, a kick no longer a kick.*
>
> *"Now that I've understood the arts, a punch is just a punch, a kick just a kick."*

The height of cultivation is really nothing special. It is merely simplicity, the ability to express the utmost with the minimum. It is the halfway cultivation that leads to ornamentation."

Maybe it's due to the fact that I've been at this since 1969 —39-plus years and trained directly with Jeff Smith and Jhoon Rhee — that I came to understand this quote fully 20 or so years ago.

However, I still don't understand many of the martial artists and school owners I meet and coach.

Personally, I have trouble identifying with school owners and Black Belts who want to introduce themselves by identifying with their narrow "stylistic" designation.

They say, for example, "I'm a Japanese stylist (BJJ, Kenpo, etc.). How will Mile High Karate work for me? My curriculum is Kenpo. How can I teach your curriculum?"

I've had to shake my head in bewilderment at several school owners for whom Mile High Karate was their most exciting possible career option because they were hung up on being a Goju or Kung Fu stylist…or whatever.

As you begin training, any good teacher will drill into you lineage, loyalty to style and association and appreciation for the "intricacy" of what you are learning. Clearly, we do the same for our beginner students at Mile High Karate.

As you progress in your learning and achieve levels of mastery, however, you must learn that what served you as a beginning or intermediate student handicaps you during your later growth.

Back to Bruce's quote: "Now that I've understood the art…. a punch is just a punch and a kick is just a kick." What does that mean?

First, to grow in your career, you must move beyond the detail and see both the simplicity and the "big picture." You must arrive at the "Why" of what we do, not the minutiae of the "What."

Why do we teach martial arts? Well, anyone who has thought even a little bit about it realizes that there are several reasons or target outcomes for our students.

Do you really care that they master the minutiae of one specific style or art? Isn't it more important that they accomplish the following:

Complete "Self-Mastery" — The ability to set and achieve goals, and to achieve positive outcomes. Isn't true personal accomplishment in all areas the highest value of martial arts training? If so, then isn't that neutral of some arbitrarily designated "style?"

Highly effective and appropriate self-defense skills — The ability to avoid an attacker, physically or verbally, and to protect yourself and your family in any situation.

Health and fitness — To achieve a high level of athletic prowess and maintain the highest level of health and fitness, you must encourage not only a fitness lifestyle, but also a peak fitness level.

It's important to think about this to move beyond self-limiting beliefs about what you are teaching and why.

Some Thoughts about Style, Part 2

Again, back to the Bruce Lee book and a quote from Grandmaster Jhoon Rhee:

"Martial Arts is 99 percent philosophy and 1 percent action.

Martial Arts without philosophy is merely street fighting."

What does this really mean?

Well, what we are teaching is much more about developing a way of thinking about life and human interactions. It's about really teaching success skills and a philosophy of personal responsibility and accountability and much less about more effective ways of kicking and punching.

Isn't developing Black Belts with unshakable character and a positive can-do spirit really the most important thing? Isn't it really more important that the highest percentage of your students follow through to that point?

The specifics of a form or a set of movements is really irrelevant to our objective, other than as a process to achieve self-mastery.

You must realize the level of thinking and understanding that brought you to where you are will not serve you well as you grow into the future. It's necessary to move past these narrow definitions and limiting associations to grow your career and your art to the next level.

Now back to the question.

Our purpose in the Mile High Karate curriculum is first and foremost highly effective personal development for our students. We complement that with teaching both a very high quality blend of "Americanized" martial arts that not only includes Tae Kwon Do forms and kickboxing-derived sparring combinations AND Kali, Escrima, BJJ, traditional martial arts weapons and a variety of forms and movements from many styles.

Our system is extremely strong, since it have been developed during many years to be excellent for student retention and to facilitate renewals as well as to create truly excellent Black Belt students.

As our system evolves, it benefits from the huge base of experience that instructors like you bring to the Mile High Karate organization.

Jeff Smith and I have incorporated a wide range of "styles" and types of martial arts into the system and we will continue to evolve our curriculum with your input and contribution.

Do you have to abandon what you've learned or stop learning and advancing in your arts?

Absolutely not, in fact, your mastery in complementary skills brings enormous strength to Mile High Karate.

We expect our advanced Black Belts to be truly masters of the martial arts (not of any one limited style or method).

Do I have to teach the Mile High Karate system to my students?

The answer is yes — most of the time. We clearly want all of the Mile High Karate schools to teach the same core curriculum.

Keep in mind:

We have a very clear and methodical system in place to convert your current students gradually and to thrill them with the new material and skills.

We have spent hundreds of hours designing the transition process, so that you keep your current students, renew a bunch of them and excite about all the new stuff they'll have an opportunity to learn.

Having all schools on the same core curriculum accomplishes several things.

First, as we stake out our target niche of the number one school for "Character Development for Kids and Families." We require a consistent curriculum that, in fact, accomplishes that result in the absolutely best way possible. Many schools SELL "self-esteem" and "character development"; our system not only sells it, but also truly and consistently DELIVERS it!

Second, to really create a STRONG NATIONAL BRAND, the schools all must have the same look and feel and the same teaching systems and methods. This is very much to your benefit. Our strong national brand will enhance the value of your business and will make you the #1 choice for prospective students in your territory.

Third, to continue to be highly effective at instructor and staff training AND, even to allow you to become an absentee owner someday if you wish (or to sell your school for real monetary value), then your operations must be truly "systematized." This includes teaching systems, curriculum and student retention processes.

Fourth, to create a powerful system, where locally, regionally and internationally, all of our schools can get together for big events (intramural tournaments and seminars) and Black Belt tests. In each region, we certainly want to "clump" schools — each with protected territories to ben-efit from the massive synergies that I experienced in Denver for 30-plus years and that we experienced with the Jhoon Rhee Institute, as well.

Fifth, a really important component of making you rich from your chosen profession is to have the curriculum work with retention and upgrade systems. We have this down to a science and, frankly, this is one place that will really grow your income.

All of our curriculum systems are designed to keep students training and excite them massively for the new renewal of upgrade.

Sixth, and this is really important, we've already created a wide array of support systems that create consistency and help students learn quickly. These systems help them reach their maximum potential, while minimizing your one-on-one time needed with any student.

Powerful technical advances, such as a student's ability to enter their password at MileHighKarate.com and then download their next bit of curriculum onto their video iPod to watch anywhere, to download the paperwork needed for their next testing, or listen to a teleconference about how to really dedicate themselves to maximum results.

The support systems are in place and work great!

Some Thoughts about Style, Part 3

Finally, we've designed a system that minimizes your staffing needs, while maximizing your income, and that makes students better faster. We've honed down the class structure, so that you don't need a huge number of instructors (or a high payroll!) to support a big and very profitable school.

OK, back to the "most of the time." What's that about?

In your school, you'll always have need for "exciting, extra material." In Denver, we've taught stuff from Ninjutsu to Samauri Sword to Aikido and an incredible amount of other material that's not formally in the curriculum, but is exciting and new.

Your leadership students, Black Belts and demo teams all need to learn new and exciting things.

There's room throughout the system for lots of additional material to be taught at special leadership classes, Black Belt seminars and as special modules that students can enjoy to keep classes fresh.

Your students will benefit from a huge team of quality Master Instructors and have a very powerful curriculum to make sure that we are all proud of every first-, second-, third-degree and higher Black Belt who is allowed to hang diplomas and claim association with you.

To reiterate, you'll be working with former World Champion Jeff Smith and all of our senior Master Instructors. Your skills and mastery will strengthen our system and expand everyone's capabilities!

There's something else that you must consider that is a very important personal success principle.

> *"We can't solve problems by using the same kind of thinking we used when we created them."*
> —Albert Einstein.

Ask yourself now: Are you completely happy with where you are in your life and your career?

It's rather clear, isn't it that if you were, then you wouldn't be exploring a positive career change with Mile High Karate?

It's important to realize that if you keep doing what you've done, then you'll keep getting the same results.

This concept is important for your next step in career growth.

As a child and a young adult, we learn many valuable lessons.

They serve us well at that point in our development…however, unless abandoned at some point, they handicap us.

Imagine the lesson as a child, "Don't Talk to Strangers." Now, move that lesson forward as an adult in any sales, teaching or leadership position (such as running a martial arts school). The "Don't Talk to Strangers" lesson, while protecting the child, handicaps the adult.

There are many examples of this. Unfortunately, most martial arts school owners and teachers are stuck in lessons that served them well as students, but handicap them as a career school owner/operator.

Narrow definitions of your "style" and a close affiliation with the lineage of your teachers and association were valuable to you in the past. Just as a child is taught lessons that later handicap them, your past affiliations and ways of thinking about your style and system may handicap your future career growth and development. They clearly will prevent you from becoming rich in the martial arts.

What about your association or affiliation?

I know well the many fine martial arts associations and narrowly defined styles.

The question is: Does your past affiliation support your future career goals?

Do you think that the organization that you are involved in can help you create industry-leading business results and help support the long-term wealth development that can be your potential?

Does it create a truly national brand identification that will help you attract and keep students?

Do you look around at your industry events and see a bunch of "Martial Arts Millionaires?" If you are hanging around with the Holiday Inn or Motel 6 crowd rather than the Four Seasons crowd, then you are in the wrong place to truly achieve wealth.

If you think about your situation clearly, then you will clearly understand that continuing what you've always done won't help you get where you want to go.

Unfortunately, most associations support that middle ground that Bruce Lee described — complicating the art and supporting outdated beliefs about style and lineage.

Back to his quote: *"It is the halfway cultivation that leads to ornamentation."*

Your current associations are, unfortunately, not run by professional educators and business people who understand effective marketing, sales and business methods that support state-of-the-art curriculum structure and teaching methods.

Do they really encourage and support truly high performance? Unfortunately, more often than not they actually encourage or even insist upon mediocrity. Clearly, making an amazing living teaching martial arts is not on their radar screens or encouraged.

Unfortunately, the martial arts associations tend to insist upon curriculum and systems that don't work in professional school environments.

It's really not their fault. The leaders at the top have never run a chain of highly profitable schools.

They've never really had to evaluate their organization relative to supporting a very profitable professional school.

In all cases — no one is there to take care of all of the business and legal processes and to take them completely off your hands.

In all cases — industry leading marketing systems don't exist to support your growth.

In all cases — the vast majority of schools are either abject failures financially or are part-time sidelines for their owners.

We're different.

We've created a completely integrated marketing, sales, business and teaching system. The Mile High Karate system not only produces students that are better than those under these old systems — but also creates financially successful martial artists.

Don't Make These Stupid Mistakes in Your School!

Stepping over dollars to pick up pennies — and other stupid mistakes that school owners make.

To follow-up from last month, I've been talking to a bunch of school owners one-on-one. I notice those least likely to succeed are really TIMID in being willing to take chances and invest in their own education and development. Those who end up being BIG winners invest first in their own business knowledge and into ideas and systems that will allow their school to grow in the short- and long-term.

After talking with many members in the last 90 days, I've noticed that many really don't "GET" what the new NAPMA is all about.

First of all our "point of entry" for new members is Maximum Impact. We do have MANY old "legacy members" who are essentially still on the OLD memberships, but we've decided to bring new members in at Maximum Impact (previously called NAPMA Squared) only. Why is that? Well, we've found without the monthly telecoaching and without the MUCH higher level content about tuition structure, understanding Internet and direct response marketing, and without the high-level sales training provided only through Maximum Impact (or above), school owners really get stuck at a LOW level with little understanding about what they are missing.

If you are one of those members who's been around forever but aren't getting the second Maximum Impact mailing each month and aren't participating in our monthly telecoaching calls (and have access to the Maximum Impact Member NAPMA member site), then you should call Bob Dunne right away and make sure that you are upgraded. Call Bob Dunne at NAPMA Headquarters at 727-540-0500, ext. 202. If you have questions about your membership, be sure and ask him.

The next level above Maximum Impact is Peak Performers. The Peak Performers team adds two things to your membership with NAPMA that have been proven to be extremely valuable. The first is the mastermind effect. The Peak Performers meet together live and in person three or four times per year. They learn directly about how to grow their school at an accelerated level from myself, Toby Milroy and other special guests. Just as importantly they learn from the successes and failures of each other and go to work on each other's problems and opportunities like an expert "board of directors."

In addition to that mastermind effect, they benefit from PERSONAL coaching every month. Each month they talk with an EXPERT (myself or Toby) to focus in on their problems and opportunities in growing their school. These coaching sessions added to the mastermind effect have proven VERY effective in helping school owners GROW quickly. The value often lies in expert help in nailing down the list of priorities to the top two or three action items to be immediately accomplished. At other times it lies in having someone "Looking over your shoulder" to hold you accountable for IMMEDIATE ACTION. Other times it's just valuable from the standpoint of having a few questions answered immediately to get traction on immediate implementation.

The next level is my Inner Circle team. The

MINIMUM threshold for consideration for membership for Inner Circle is $30,000 per month in revenue. We have schools in the Inner Circle that gross $400,000 a year — and others that likely will do $2 million this year. It's the crème of the cream.

My personal objective is for EVERY NAPMA Maximum Impact member to be in at least the top 20% of the martial arts industry. That means no less than $90,0000 a year in NET INCOME from their school. My personal target for Peak Performers is that each school be in the top 5% — which is a NET INCOME of $150,000 or more. My personal target for the Inner Circle is for each and every one to be in the top 3% or our industry with personal incomes from their school of at least $20,000. I've been lucky for the past 28 years to mostly only associate with the top 1% of our industry.

I was lucky enough (then focused enough) to associate myself with ONLY the big winners in our industry. Trust me. They aren't smarter than you are or more capable. They do think differently than most about their business. That I can teach you. They also have a ROBUST understanding of each element of their business. Not just martial arts curriculum, but truly each element from marketing and sales to student retention and educational psychology. Some have been self-taught; most were lucky enough to find the right mentor early on. In my case that was Jhoon Rhee, Nick Cokinos and Jeff Smith.

The benefit you have as a member, which is expanded DRAMATICALLY in Inner Circle or Peak Performers, is that you have me teaching you both the necessary skills and acting as a personal mentor to move you to levels greater than you ever thought possible.

Since the first leg of our national seminar tour I've been doing several one-on-one calls with school owners. I've heard a lot of excuses for fail-ure and have also seen some winners. Many of the winners have come on board our Inner Circle or Peak Performers team. After speaking with Jeff Smith, Toby Milroy and Bob Dunne, they convinced me to do some more of these personal school evaluations with members who haven't been able to attend one of the Financial Power Seminars. Typically I charge $1,297 hourly for consulting, but will do a small number of thorough evaluations with members at no charge. There are, however, "strings attached."

I hate wasting my time! In order to qualify to do one of these calls, it's important that we BOTH be prepared to make it of maximum value. From YOUR side I require that you do three things. First is to watch the confidential video from my seminar recently held in Chicago. This is a 90-minute excerpt from a full-day event — however, I think you'll find it extremely valuable — especially my part on things that school owners do to screw up. To watch that valuable video go to www.PrivateCoachingSession.com. The second condition is that before our call, you go re-read (or read for the first time) my book, *Everything I Wish I Knew When I Was 22*. It's available as a digital download, I'll send you a free copy. The third condition is to make sure I UNDERSTAND YOUR SCHOOL. You must give me as much information as possible before our call. I have a special questionnaire that you can complete and fax back to help with that process. To learn more and see if you've called in time to reserve a spot (again, I'm only going to be able to talk to fewer than 10% of our members before running out of time), then call Bob — he'll schedule an appointment time once you've completed the three steps above. Call Bob Dunne at NAPMA headquarters at 727-540-0500, ext. 202, to learn more about this, to get a copy of the questionnaire and to request a free copy of the printed book, and to schedule an appointment. PLEASE DO CALL QUICKLY.

As a final note, I'd suggest you review the special report I did a few months ago entitled the "10 Things You Must Do to Thrive." If you don't have it, ask Bob when you call and we'll resend it to you. You really must take a look at your results and make sure that you are running your school in a profitable manner.

Rules of Thumb?

1. Total monthly gross divided by total active students = $200 (or more). This is the average value per active student in your school. The failing schools I've talked to tend to be under $100. Our Inner Circle and Peak Performers tend to be $200 or more.

In other words, if you have 200 active students you should be grossing $40,000 or more per month.

2. Active students. "Critical mass" really doesn't kick in until you are at 100 active. Every school I ever opened from scratch was at 100 in the first 4 to 6 weeks. If you are below 100, you really must "kick-start" things and break the low-end barrier as quickly as possible.

3. There's magic in 300. I'd rather, in most cases, see a school with 300 active grossing $75,000 to $100,000 a month than see a higher active count with a lower revenue per student. Once you break 300 it's harder to keep track of everyone and to maintain strong student retention numbers. It certainly can be done. However, there's a line where you REALLY need to be organized. I've seen schools with 750 students grossing $75,000 and schools with 250 students grossing the same amount but with MUCH higher net profits. Your goal is to have a HIGH net, not just to be bigger for the sake of being bigger.

Opinions About Running Your Martial Arts School…Everyone's Got One!

Asking someone's opinion killed many great ideas.

Ideas are proven or unproven by aggressive implementation. Whenever you have a "brilliant" idea that doesn't cost much and won't require hundred's of hours — JUST DO IT! If it works great — tell your mentors, consultants, peers and friends. If it fails — well, either tune it or at the very least — don't tell anyone!

More great success was killed by second guessing every idea — running through the gauntlet of other people's opinions — and by attempting to be perfect.

I have two regular roles: one as a coach and mentor to my Mile High Karate Regional Developers and franchisees and NAPMA members; the other, as a coach and mentor to my personal coaching and Millionaire Wealth group members. In that role, I must constantly remind myself to give guidance, and be a catalyst for action. I'm constantly concerned not to shoot any potentially good idea just because "I've tried that before and it didn't work." Frankly, it may not have worked for me, due to poor implementation or even different market circumstances.

As General George Patton said (or, at least is purported to have said): "Once you've decided, don't delay. The best is the enemy of the good ... a good plan violently executed now is better than a perfect plan next week."

As a manager — improve your skills to enhance and bring clarity to the ideas of your employees — without squashing their initiative and enthusiasm.

Recently, I've become quite good at this response: "Gee, I don't know if that will work or not — but, if you really think it will, then why don't you try it, and let us know what happens!"

Often accompanied by: "A couple of things that might help are _____, _____, _____, and _____."

And: "My friend, _____, has had some real success with something like that — let's call him/her on the phone and brainstorm the idea a little."

Remember: No matter how skillful you are at advertising — you will only know if it is a good ad, once the phones start to ring (after spending money to place it!).

No matter how great an educator you are — your students' results are the only indicators of the quality of your methods.

RESULTS prove whether any idea was a good or bad one. No amount of armchair quarterbacking will make any difference.

Another General Patton quote: "Never tell people how to do things. Tell them what to do, and they will surprise you with their ingenuity."

ALSO, REFRAME your worldview!

Often, we listen to good ideas and are unable to HEAR them because they conflict with our predisposition.

If you hear an idea that doesn't seem to make sense — try stepping into that person's "frame of reference" for a few minutes and determine why it makes sense to them. You may find a real gem — and create some flexibility in your thinking, as well.

Some "Action Quotes" for you:

George S. Patton: *"A good plan implemented today is better than a perfect plan implemented tomorrow."*

Rosalynn Carter: *"A leader takes people where they want to go. A great leader takes people where they don't necessarily want to go, but ought to be."*

Kahlil Gibran: *"A little knowledge that acts is worth infinitely more than much knowledge that is idle."*

Mahatma Gandhi: *"A man is the sum of his actions, of what he has done, of what he can do. Nothing else."*

Baltasar Gracian: *"A wise person does at once, what a fool does at last. Both do the same thing, only at different times."*

Turkish proverb: *"Abundance is from activity."*

Immanuel Kant: *"Act as if the maxim of your action were to become, through your will, a general natural law."*

William James: *"Act as if what you do makes a difference."*

A few more reading suggestions: *Reframing Organizations* by Bolman and Deal, *Executive EQ* by Robert Cooper and Ayman Sawaf and *The Loyalty Effect* by Federick Reichheld.

"There are men in the ranks who'll stay in the ranks. Why? I'll tell you why — Simply because they don't have the ability to get things done."

I remember many years ago, it was an EFC Board Meeting and small seminar, frankly I don't remember where. I do remember it was an early event attended by Tom Callos, Buzz Durkin and Tim and Dave Kovar, perhaps their first Board meeting.

I remember those of us more senior laughing while Nick had them each stand in line and come up front and repeat the line above: "There are men in the ranks who'll stay in the ranks…Why? I'll tell you why: simply because they don't have the ability to get things done." One at a time, over and over. Now, I wasn't one of the newbies being "indoctrinated," but the phrase and the event have stuck in my mind for what's probably now 15 years.

The same quote in different guises has popped up in each environment that I've been in. While at a Dan Kennedy event as one of his "Platinum Members," I heard him describe our group of his top members (the top 10 of about 25,000 clients) as not being doers but "doners." In reality the Platinum group often implemented within minutes, not days, of hitting upon a new idea. Members of the group (myself included) often were on their BlackBerry during the meeting, giving directions for new strategies or on the phone during each break, to the point that Dan loudly boycotted phones, BlackBerrys, iPhones and laptops from all meetings.

As I've continued to talk one-on-one with various members and seminar attendees, I've recognized a huge gap between knowledge and implementation — in other words, between "knowing" and "doing."

I've been pondering where the gap lies, reviewing NAPMA's content, our website, the various packages we deliver, the CDs, the DVDs, etc. Racking my mind to figure out why so many school owners don't do what they've been taught. Why they don't implement the incredibly valuable content that we provide each month. Frankly, many of those I've talked to don't even seem to know the basic concepts that seem to me to have been repeated over and over to the point of massive redundancy.

After many sleepless nights, conversations with 117 school owners, conversations with my personal top 10 school owners in our industry (Jeff Smith, Bill Clark, Keith Hafner, Greg Moody, Buzz Durkin and several others) and an extensive discussion with my NAPMA Inner Circle members about how to fix this obvious problem, finally something became extremely clear to me.

In our day-to-day lives and as instructors we know what it takes to develop a student to their highest level. Clearly we know that it's not enough to give them a book and a DVD and tell them to show up for testing without any personal lessons in the interim.

As a teacher we know that there are a series of necessary elements for a student to achieve at their highest level. You know as well as I do the key elements, but let me outline them here anyway.

The key elements are:

A concerned teacher who not only explains and demonstrates the various techniques but who also monitors and gives real-time feedback. The most valuable aspect of a quality teacher lies not in sharing knowledge. That can be done in a book, CD, DVD or online. The value is in providing encouragement, support, clarification and feedback.

The next key element is in "social proof." As a student it's incredibly valuable to be surrounded with others — some ahead of you, others behind — that are mastering the same skills and are available for practice and implementation. To have partners for drills and grappling or sparring partners for free-style practice.

Another element is that of "positive peer pressure" — the benefit of training with a team of people who help to hold you accountable to your own commitment. Someone to look forward to training with and someone who will push you to new heights.

As I started to think in these terms it became clear to me why so many schools that are surrounded by information really haven't had much "efficacy" in implementing what they've been taught.

Thinking back to my own development it's clear that I've always had the three elements in each area of my own development. I've always had a quality Master Teacher who encouraged me, gave me continuous feedback and was available to look over my shoulder and answer questions. Those included Jhoon Rhee, Nick Cokinos, Jeff Smith, Dan Kennedy and others. But in each case I had direct access to and direct feedback from a "Master Teacher."

I also have always been surrounded with HIGH-QUALITY fellow students, whether that was through the EFC Board of Directors, the NASKA Board of Directors, Jhoon Rhee's Inner Circle, Dan Kennedy's Platinum Group or my top 1% circle of Jeff Smith and my friends in the industry. I've always been surrounded with peers who were moving along the same path and who were mutually supportive.

Finally, these circles of friends became both a mastermind team and a source of accountability.

After putting together the pieces it has become clear to me why most school owners are not having the kind of results that I've seen over and over with coaching clients, my Peak Performers and Inner Circle Members, and with my Mile High Karate Franchise owners.

School owners such as yourself are overwhelmed with information but often lack "efficacy" — lack implementation. The difference between access to knowledge and effective implementation that creates massive wealth and improves lifestyle turns out to be personal teaching/coaching along with a mastermind/peer group. That's what we're providing to Peak Performers, which makes a HUGE difference in results and implementation. I'd love to set aside some time to talk with you one-on-one about your growth and development. If you'd like to take some time and have an implementation outline then go to: www.PrivateCoaciungSession.com. Watch this excerpt from a recent "Financial Power Summit" seminar. Next take some time to read my book *Everything I Wish I Knew When I Was 22* (free digital copy at the site above and in your member website or physically available from Amazon.com or BN.com). Finally, complete the evaluation form on the website and fax to 1-800-795-0583. Bob Dunne will give you a call and we'll schedule a one-on-one evaluation where I'll give you an action-implementation plan.

Let me leave you with just one other thought. Too many school owners teach self-esteem, confidence and motivation but frankly lack it themselves. What we really want to be teaching — and personally developing — is Positive Self-Efficacy.

Here's a quick definition of "Positive Self-Efficacy"

Perceived self-efficacy is defined as people's beliefs about their capabilities to produce designated levels of performance that exercise influence over events that affect their lives. Self-efficacy beliefs determine how people feel, think, motivate themselves and behave. Such beliefs produce these diverse effects through four major processes. They include cognitive, motivational, affective and selection processes.

A strong sense of efficacy enhances human accomplishment and personal well-being in many ways. People with high assurance in their capabilities approach difficult tasks as challenges to be mastered rather than as threats to be avoided. Such an efficacious outlook fosters intrinsic interest and deep engrossment in activities. They set themselves challenging goals and maintain strong commitment to them. They heighten and sustain their efforts in the face of failure. They quickly recover their sense of efficacy after failures or setbacks. They attribute failure to insufficient effort or deficient knowledge and skills which are acquirable. They approach threatening situations with assurance that they can exercise control over them. Such an efficacious outlook produces personal accomplishments, reduces stress and lowers vulnerability to depression.

In contrast, people who doubt their capabilities shy away from difficult tasks, which they view as personal threats. They have low aspirations and weak commitment to the goals they choose to pursue. When faced with difficult tasks, they dwell on their personal deficiencies, on the obstacles they will encounter, and all kinds of adverse outcomes rather than concentrate on how to perform successfully. They slacken their efforts and give up quickly in the face of difficulties. They are slow to recover their sense of efficacy following failure or setbacks. Because they view insufficient performance as deficient aptitude, it does not require much failure for them to lose faith in their capabilities. They fall easy victim to stress and depression.

Consultation Certificate

This Certificate Entitles the Bearer to a Personal 1-on-1 Martial Arts School Business Analysis With a NAPMA-Certified Business Analyst. This Individual Consultation is Valued at $495.00.

Certificate expires 12 months from the date of purchase.
To schedule your personal business analysis, complete this form and fax to NAPMA at 1-800-795-0853; mail to 1767 Denver West Blvd., Suite A, Golden, CO 80401; or visit www.PrivateCoachingSession.com

PLEASE FILL OUT COMPLETELY AND WRITE LEGIBLY

Name _____

School Name _____

Address _____

City _____ State/Province _____

Zip _____ Country _____

Phone _____ Fax _____

E-Mail _____

_____
Authorized by Toby Milroy
Chief Operating Officer, NAPMA

3 FREE GIFTS FOR SERIOUS SCHOOL OWNERS

FREE Personal School Evaluation

Two 30-minute Sessions A sure-fire way action plan to double your results or better.

FREE Two 90-Minute Seminars

with **"The Millionaire Maker Grandmaster Stephen Oliver** "The 5 Stupid Mistakes All Too Many School Owners Make that Kill Their Growth" and "The Key Step-by-Step Blueprint for Being a Big Winner"

FREE CD-DVD Package and Report

"How Hundreds of Smart School Owners Like You Doubled Their Revenue in the Last 12 Months Even in the Midst of the Greatest Recession since the Great Depresson, and How You Can, Too!"

Powerful Commonalities in Our Differences

In the last 30 days, I've completed extensive interviews with the Inner Circle Members who are setting the world on fire with huge single schools, powerful multi-school operations and everything in between. From traditional Tang Soo Do to massive adult MMA programs they're the top 5% of the industry and the top 5% of income levels among all professions in the United States and around the world.

I also completed interviews with our $1,000,000 mission of Mile High Karate schools. The number one school in Australia, the number one school in New Zealand, and schools ranging from Fresno to Sterling, VA, all of whom are on a mission (and, on track for $1,000,000 results in the coming year).

Next, I interviewed a bunch of "old farts." Well, OK, that's not fair, but if they are even a day older than I am, then it makes me feel good at this stage! Anyway, all old friends but none who have been thriving in the martial arts business for less than 25 years — some much longer. Sharing freely their lessons learned along the way. This group includes one school that enrolls only four students per month while maintaining 380 active students at $200 a month average tuition per student, and another with 11 personally-owned locations and a chain of close to 30 licensed locations.

OK, yes, I've been busy, busy, busy prepping fabulous content to share with you in the coming months. Great content for our Maximum Impact, Peak Performers and Inner Circle Members.

Across all of these conversations there are vast differences — but, still, powerful commonalities.

As for differences, they range from schools running huge numbers in the adult female fitness/martial arts market to schools that focus primarily on Little Ninjas through early elementary. There are million-dollar operations that teach adult men MMA and host live events on the side, and school that only accept families.

The differences are ONLY important to you for recognition of the proper model, marketing, teaching, tuition structure can achieve STELLAR results no matter what your target market or base curriculum.

The similarities are much more profound for you to study and implement in your school.

What's common among the top 5% in each arena?

Well, the first thing is, and I hate to say it out loud again, but really, the most important thing is "Your Personal Belief System." This is true in general about your own success, and more specifically about a range of more narrow pieces of your business. The successful school owners first really BELIEVED it was possible then behaved as if they were already there.

In EVERY case their success and their ability to believe in their own abilities came through having a PERSONAL MENTOR who helped them develop their school — sometimes that was their martial arts instructor — but, usually it wasn't.

In all cases the success stories came through personal guidance from a financially successful coach on how to operate their school. For some it was me. For others it was Jhoon Rhee, Jeff Smith, Nick Cokinos or Richard Reid. Others grew up in highly successful schools and learned from success — as I'm sure you would guess — most did not grow up in a financially successful school. Most struggled for months or years until connecting with me as a coach or some other capable mentor.

The next aspect was in having a "Success Peer

Group." A personal "Master-Mind" and support team of like-minded, positive individuals who contributed to each other's success. It's important to note that in all cases these were other martial artists on a common quest for a quality and profitable martial arts school; a group of other business people unrelated to our profession is sometimes helpful and sometimes confusing. Sharing ideas with other high-performing, high-income people is always valuable.

However, for QUICK results, have a peer group of profitable martial arts school owners to share with on a regular basis.

The next commonality among all of these individual was a SINCERE desire to help their students. A focus on retention, quality teaching, and long-term service to their community. They ALL teach very high quality martial arts from anyone's perspective. The quality of Black Belts among this group are ALSO in the top 5% of the martial arts industry. However, they focus on the student first and recognize that acceptance and enthusiasm must come before quality athletic skills.

Now, I don't want to gloss over this point. With the veterans of the industry the vast majority of our conversation is almost always about quality service and sincere interest in students. To grow a young school quickly it's necessary that you become fabulous at internal marketing, community outreach and advertising. However, some veterans have such high quality and long-term retention that they have no need to think about marketing at all to maintain a $250,000 to $500,000 per year

income. Incredible? Try running with the above mentioned 380 students in a community of less than 8,000 with fewer than five new students a month. That's life-long student devotion.

You'll hear in the interviews the sincere and deeply held belief that devotion to students trumps direct financial considerations. Trumps "stylistic purity." Trumps everything else. You don't get there overnight. Frankly, you certainly don't get there by hiring the best "athletes" as teachers. By having the students spar early. By having the highest quality Gold or Green Belts.

You do get there by long-term devotion to the culture of your staff, your Black Belts and your senior students. It's constant vigilance of the language you use and of the decisions you make on a minute by minute basis in interacting with your students, their families, and your community.

To be fair, this is harder to achieve in multi-school chains than in a single school owner-operator operation. It's harder to achieve with 1,000 students than with 200 or 300, but doable and ESSENTIAL in all cases.

Clearly there are more commonalities among the top 5% that I've covered here, but I'll leave you with one other thought to consider. All of the successful school owners moved from being an athlete to a "Master Teacher." They then understood that a thorough understanding of key business concepts are essential. Most looked to someone like myself to help them master marketing. They then focused on managing sales, managing service then on developing and training staff.

Stepping Over Dollars to Pick Up Pennies

Sometimes, it's amazing to me what concerns school owners of small and barely profitable schools. There's a big difference between the way that successful school owners think about issues big and small versus how failing school owners think about the issues in their businesses.

When speaking at an industry event, I was inundated with comments and questions from small school owners that belied two common problems:

- A lack of an abundance mentality.
- A focus on saving pennies, rather than earning dollars.

First: **Most school owners have expectations that are much too low for their businesses, and lack faith in their abilities to achieve at a high level.**

They ask how to run their schools more effectively, while working full-time jobs in other careers. Rather than looking at the real potential of their businesses, they try to coordinate their day jobs to support their lifestyle needs, with working at their schools 40 hours a week.

While they are struggling with two jobs, other schools are thriving.

Just this month, three of my close friends' schools grossed more than $100,000 in a single month. They are spread across the country and have different programs, curriculum and strategies for attracting new students, and much different personalities. These school owners, however, are not just surviving — they are thriving.

It is important that school owners make the decision that they will not just survive, but thrive in their schools. School owners who are running their schools on a part-time basis must decide to thrive, and then "jump off the cliff" and run their schools on a professional, full-time basis.

Second: **Saving pennies, rather than earning dollars, works in two specific ways.**

A. School owners try to do everything themselves, rather than delegating critical support tasks. School owners go through their daily routine looking for small, incremental gains in their businesses and hoping to save a few dollars here and there.

School owners who are grossing $5,000, $7,500, $11,000 or $13,000 a month patiently explain how they are saving a dollar to two per payment, by doing their billing in-house, rather than contracting with a service provider. They explain that they do all of their payroll and bookkeeping, instead of paying $60 or $70 per month that a service firm, such as Paychex or ADP, would charge.

Focusing on tasks such as billing, payroll or accounting and taxes expends valuable time that could better be spent on the important elements of growing a school.

Every school owner must master three key elements and effectively attend to them every day.

1. Marketing to generate new students.
2. Sales — enrollment and renewal or upgrade processes.
3. Motivational teaching.

The owner's main role is marketing his school, and then monitoring for quality student service, everything else is secondary.

B. School owners fail to invest in crucial points for growth.

Every school owner must spare no expense on two items:

1. His or her education, as a martial arts businessperson.
2. Marketing and advertising his or her school.

Owners of small schools often patiently explain to me how attending a worthwhile seminar is just not in their budgets. They are not willing to spend $1,500 to $5,000 on their education—even if they might learn enough to add 10 or 20 times in revenues, compared to their educational investments. Often, I see even a more perverse spin on this phenomenon: martial artists will spend huge amounts of money on curriculum-oriented training to develop their athletic talents, but fail to see the value of business education to support their schools' growth.

The most frustrating aspect of attempting to teach school owners about marketing is their lack of willingness to invest effectively in the growth of their schools. Proven concepts, with a 3-to-1, 5-to-1 or even 10-to-1 return-on-investment, are ignored or derided as too expensive or ineffective. Smaller school owners often combine unrealistic expectations with a lack of willingness to invest effectively.

In conclusion, we are in a wonderful business. The more students we have and the more effectively we develop our students, the more income we will earn. Financially successful school owners are impacting high numbers of students in a very positive way.

To grow your school, you must believe in the opportunity provided by your school, and be willing to invest in both your education as well as marketing your school.

It's essential that you make a clear decision to believe that you can make a great living running your school. Once you make that decision, seek the best mentors, coaches and mastermind teams available. Money spent on productive success coaching will multiply itself tenfold or more.

Prepare to Review Your Year

As the year is coming to an end, it's important to review this year objectively, look at your ratios and study important operating numbers.

Review these specific numbers:

- Your student retention rate (i.e., quit rate).
- Total average monthly dropouts (number) divided by total average monthly active
(a percentage).
- Each month, quarter and yearly average.

How do you evaluate?

First, did your number improve this year?

Second, what's a reasonable target? Some schools have dropout rates as low as 1–2% per month. Most schools (and most are very bad) probably average 7–9% per month. If you're at 7% you are average, then 4% or less is quite good; 2% or less is VERY good.

Sales Ratios: Percentage from Inquiry to Enrollment.

Review your basic numbers, such as info calls/walk-ins, intros and enrollments. What's your ratio from first contact to intro? What's your ratio from intro to enrollment? Again, look at each quarter and yearly averages and determine what are you doing well and what needs to be fixed.

If you don't enroll at least one-half of prospects that have contacted you, then it's a real problem. What's good? 75%–80%. There are many ways to improve this ratio, but focus on building rapport with everyone and benefits, not features.

Enrollment Volume

If you aren't enrolling enough people per month, then it could be because of your ratios above, or it could be just inadequate volume. The solution depends on your objectives. Mile High Karate schools' targets are an average of 20 new students per month. That could be the right number for you; but if you have a 20,000-square-foot super school, then that's not enough. If you have a small school, then it might be more than you need.

Average Student Value

When you compute this average, make sure you compare "apples to apples." For example, the average monthly gross revenue divided by the average total monthly active. The Mile High Karate schools' target is $300 per month on average. Most of my coaching clients hit $200 or more per month within 12 to 18 months. That doesn't mean that your monthly tuition is that amount, but the average per students is the total of down payments, paid-in-fulls, accelerated tuition, retail sales and monthly tuition.

Once you've reviewed all of these numbers you should be able to decide what to do next to grow your school.

Profit and Loss Review

Hopefully, you have complete up-to-date financial statements. For the end of the year, you should review all of your expenses relative to your revenue.

- The ratio for your major expenses:
- Rent: 12-15% of gross revenue.
- Payroll: 25-33% of gross revenue.
- Advertising: 12-15% of gross revenue.

The following factors contribute to a martial arts school being operated incorrectly.

Overpaying for facilities: Don't pay for too many square feet; instead, I recommend a better and more highly visible location with less space, if necessary.

Hiring too many people, but not paying the good ones enough. You should be looking for high performers and pay them well as a percentage of gross revenue (10-12%).

Not advertising effectively: An industry myth has been that advertising doesn't work. In fact, with realistic expectations, many media can work very well. If you err, then err towards being more promotional and aggressive in your marketing efforts than you would otherwise if your student retention, quality and pricing are properly in line.

Finally, Review Pricing

Make sure that you "know your stuff," are a walking "product of the product," your student service is the highest possible and your facilities and staff are first rate. Then, review your pricing.

Just about everyone under-prices and is too timid about tuition rates.

Remember that you are likely not in the business of operating a martial arts school as a charity. If you are, then this doesn't apply to you. If you are in the business of operating a martial arts

school to make a living for yourself, provide for your family and offer your community a quality service for many years, then you have absolutely no responsibility to make sure everyone that walks through your front door can afford your service.

If you don't price your lessons so some people can't afford them, then you are leaving too much money "on the table." Review what you are charging for new enrollments, upgrade or renewal programs and your Black Belts. The beginning of the year is an excellent time to raise your prices.

I hate to dictate, and certainly it may vary, based on where you are located; however, for a new student, you should be in the $150–$250 per month range. You should also have some level of "upgrade" programs available at no less than $250 per month. I've seen schools with programs that run anywhere from $250 to $1,000 a month (for some type of special private, individualized executive program).

Now, if you don't think that anyone will pay those types of rates, then I highly recommend that you go participate in a presentation at Sylvan Learning Centers® to see what they are charging.

Lessons Learned from Apple's Steve Jobs

As I write this, five days past deadline, the breaking news is of the death of Steve Jobs on the day following Tim Cook's first turn at handling new product release with the iPhone 4S, among other things.

In retrospect, there's much to learn from Steve Job's career and the incredible results he accomplished at Apple computer. As you may know, I've spent hundreds, if not thousands, of hours studying the biographies and autobiographies of successful entrepreneurs over the years, and impatiently await delivery to my Kindle app on my iPad of the first authorized biography of Steve Jobs, written with his cooperation and blessing. I've absorbed at least 20 books separately about Jobs and Bill Gates. Both have a fascinating story and incredible genius.

In Jobs' case, there are many lessons applicable to you as a martial arts school operator.

Let me start with a story that was reported in a recent feature in *Fortune Magazine*. The story goes like this:

At Apple, Jobs personally assisted in selecting each vice president (there are approximately 70 at Apple). With each new vice president he'd sit down and share a brief story.

"Somewhere between janitor and CEO there becomes a point where excuses don't matter and all that counts is results. You see, if the janitor who cleans my office fails to empty the trash for a couple of days, it's acceptable if he says, 'the locks were changed and no one gave me the keys, so I couldn't empty it.' However, at some point no one cares about excuses, only that you got it done. That point is at vice president."

It's about a culture of total accountability and personal responsibility. At Apple, under Jobs, there was always ultimately the "person in charge" of each product or project. Someone to ultimately take the credit or the blame for success or failure.

Another story was about the release of "Mobile Me." After the rather shaky release and frustrating performance of that product, Jobs had a tense meeting with the team and immediately fired the "person in charge," and transferred or fired just about everyone on the team. The joke was that no one at Apple took the elevator because Steve used the elevator and they were afraid they'd end up fired somewhere between the fifth to the first floor.

On a different note, there's a quote that I like:

> *Genius is the ability to reduce the complicated to the simple. — C. W. Ceran*

Ultimately the product design genius was not in creating products with better technical specs or a level of complication. It is the genius of taking complicated machines and making them extremely simple to use. The ultimate genius of the Mac, iPhone, iPad, and iPod are in simplification of the interface. Of the bravery to leave out features if necessary to insure ease of operations.

So, what are the lessons of Jobs to martial arts Schools?

Well, first is recognizing what the market wants — not what the technical people think are important. Our industry is mostly populated with individuals who take the technical specifications of what they teach extremely seriously. They believe that by teaching a more effective form of self-defense or by having a more impressive lineage, that students will flock to their door. Unfortunately for the purists among us, the market — the prospective students — don't know and don't care about those technical details.

Jobs was a genius in ultimately figuring out what his customers would want to do with his "gadgets" and then designing them so that it was intuitively obvious. The proof of that concept is the fact that my three-year-old can use both my iPhone and iPad like an expert. He hasn't figured out how to use the DVD player in his room, but can expertly stream Netflix from my iPad and find and play "Angry Birds," among other things, on my iPhone.

It's difficult to remember now, but Jobs was ridiculed and second-guessed on many of what turned out to be his greatest accomplishments. His perfectionism and a flamboyant management style led him to be fired from the company he founded. Ultimately, Apple floundered and was near bankruptcy when Apple bought his company, NeXT, in order to turn its operating system into the next generation Mac operating system. Even upon returning the to the company his first new Mac in purple, green and other neon colors was laughed at by most. Then, all of the "Retail Experts" predicted pending disaster for the Apple Stores, which have turned out to have the highest average sales per square foot of any major retail chain by a huge margin.

Clearly, Jobs was often dismissed or sneered at by other technical companies. His emphasis on simplicity of use was lost on the many who were looking just at faster processor speeds, more ram or more complicated software. His total disdain for the opinions of his peers and maniacal focus on simplicity and elegance of design obviously served him well, as well as all of us who are fans of their products.

Anyway, back to books about Jobs. One of my favorites of the early books was entertainingly titled *Accidental Millionaire*" which was a well-researched and well-written book that was fatally misdirected. His premise was that Jobs was the "accidental millionaire" because he was "just" the marketing guy that rode on Wozniak's coattails. (Steve Wozniak was the technical genius who created the Apple 1 and Apple 2.) The book was a fascinating look at the "take-no-prisoners" side of Steve's management style. The author misread his genius at design and his perfectionism for customer-centered outcomes. Ultimately, anyone who achieves at his level has, at least in the early years, far more detractors than fans, and many more predicting failure than success.

A phrase coined by an early member of the Mac team, Guy Kawasaki, is one that I love. Kawasaki was a "Mac Evangelist." He described his job and that of Steve Job's as being the creation of "Raging Thunder Lizard Evangelists."

There are several large companies that have created cult followings. A great book I read entitled, *The Culting of Brands*, discussed this effect with Harley Davidson, Porsche, BMW and Apple, among others, who have turned their customers into "evangelists" for their products. Steve Jobs' genius was in creating such an emotional connection with his company that customers resembled "Cult Members" It's hard to imagine any customer of Dell, HP or Toshiba computers to be a "Raging Thunderlizard Evangelist."

A final point, and we could go on and on with his accomplishments, is that ultimately Steve Jobs was the greatest salesperson in high tech. A comparable in recent memory might be Lee Iacocca, who ultimately rescued Chrysler on the strength of his ability to sell the product. Or Dave Thomas of Wendy's. By all accounts, Tim Cook is a supremely competent successor to Steve Jobs as CEO. He's an operations genius. But the contrast was evident at his first presentation as CEO. In earlier years Job's charisma was dubbed the "Steve Jobs Reality Distortion Field." For dubbing as "Insanely Great," products with technical specs often not as good as the rival machine from IBM or Compaq. However, they were "Insanely Great" because his genius was in reducing the complicated to the simple, while giving his customers what they wanted and ignoring what they themselves predicted they'd want.

The ultimate key to success for your school is to become a genius at selling your school while providing a product that creates "Raging Thunder Lizard Evangelists."

Rest in peace.

Go Fast, Turn Left

For years now I've been saying that I wanted to attend a racing school. I've always enjoyed driving fast, but I "got the bug" to do it because of two unrelated events. The first was when I bought my first Porsche 911. It was a 1990 C-4 (in Porsche-speak that means all-wheel drive).

When I bought the car, the dealership invited me to a Porsche Club "Day at the Track" the following week. It was a great opportunity to drive your car, with a "coach" as a passenger. The coach showed me the best way to take the curves and when to shift, break, etc. After a few laps, I drove and the coach provided feedback. It was a great time.

It wasn't long afterward that I started hitting the Internet marketing seminar circuit and met Corey Rudl. He was one of the preeminent Internet marketing gurus, and I learned that he was on the race circuit and the rookie of the year. I spoke with him at length, and peppered him with questions — not about Internet marketing, but the racing circuit and the details of participating.

It took me a few months, but I finally found information on the circuit and the race school, and made reservations for the training program. As luck would have it, the date was during the week of my daughter's birth. Obviously, I chose not to attend race school, but the idea remained in the back of my mind; but, several years later, I still hadn't rescheduled to attend the school.

I finally had the opportunity to attend racing school when my wife gave me a certificate for Christmas. The certificate was good for programs held around the county, but upon reviewing its Website, Hampstead Racetrack in Miami had scheduled a school-racing session during the same weekend as a NAPMA seminar scheduled in Miami and only a few days before I was scheduled to travel to NAPMA's offices in Clearwater, Florida. I called Toby to ask if he wanted come with me; halfway through my questions, I received an immediate yes.

I flew into Miami, stopped by the seminar being hosted by Toby Milroy, and then we left— about 90 minutes before we were supposed to arrive at the racetrack.

What happened next probably should have been expected, but we thought we understood the directions, so we left the airport hotel on Friday near rush hour. We immediately missed the highway and were heading south on Highway 1 with bumper-to-bumper traffic.

The drive to the racetrack was frustrating to say the least. I kept turning the map at different angles trying to determine the best way to cut across to the highway. Toby kept screwing around with the GPS on his cell phone trying to find a better way. Anytime we had a break in traffic, I chided Toby to accelerate — explaining that the right pedal is the gas and the middle pedal is the break and that he should make a little more effort to move faster on the way to the racetrack.

We finally decided to enter a Wendy's drive-through lane and ask directions. The woman at the window explained that she lived in Hampstead and that she drove home every day on Highway 1. We asked how to reach the racetrack from the highway, and she patiently explained that she drives Highway 1. Toby tried again, "How would we drive there by the highway?" She patiently explained that she doesn't go that way, while I pounded my head on the dash of Toby's Lexus.

We next asked a cab driver, who very nicely drove us in a complete circle, becoming even more lost. Anyway, after all of that we arrived at the racetrack (after calling its office in South Carolina and the track). That was after about two hours of me chiding Toby about being unable to accelerate properly and playing with his new GPS cell phone toy.

When we arrived, we watched as our racing class left in full-gear to drive the track. We nicely asked the folks in charge if we could reschedule, drive later, stand in for the next idiots who were lost and didn't show up — and heard a very polite, "No, No, No."

Anyway, we bought Mario Andretti racing caps (and "Race Chick" caps for my wife and daughter), took pictures by the cars and talked with the staff. An hour or so later one of the staff asked us if we'd be OK with driving the "Mario Andretti" rather than "Jeff Gordon" cars? Well… yeah! Even though I was told that I couldn't reserve Indy cars when I scheduled the race class, Toby and I were able to drive them instead of the NASCAR-style cars.

By approximately 6:30, we had changed into our race suits, took photos with the cars, and then were taken to a classroom by the track for race school. Racing school was entertaining. We suited up, walked across the track and sat at classroom-style tables for instructions (and I may be embellishing slightly).

"We will push you off. When you reach the orange cone, release the clutch and hit the gas. You will then follow the driver ahead of you and Go Fast — Turn Left. When you've hit your laps, you'll pull into the pit. When you see the cone, hit the brakes (make sure you know where they are when you sit in the cars, since you'll only use them once), and push the shift lever into neutral. You'll do six laps, pull into the pit, and then we'll give you some feedback — you'll then repeat the process."

Now, let me make sure we are clear on this. They were inserting us into 200-mile-per-hour, 600-HP go-carts, with a big brick wall on the right and a grassy center, with buildings, cars, pits, etc. The total instructions were basically "Go Fast — Turn Left."

Anyway, we put big paper "condoms" on our head, and donned helmets. We were "shoehorned into the cars," and then they attached the steering wheel. What happened next was, well, "Go Fast, Turn Left." After six laps, with a death grip on the steering wheel, I was concentrating intently on the car ahead of me trying not to look at the concrete wall. We hit the pits. I received tremendous feedback: "You're doing great; you might think of going a little faster and staying closer to your lead car — OK, go."

While you are in the car you have little or no sense of how fast you are moving. There's no speedometer, only one gear and no tach. You focus on the driver ahead of you and "go fast, turn left." Well, when we were done, we received our track times, with lap speeds and maximum speed on each track.

Now, I had bitched about what a wimp Toby was in his Lexus while we were lost on the way to the track for more than two hours. Anyway, we received our printouts and Toby beat my best time by 30 MPH. My comment…"S***, I've traveled faster than that in my Porsche, with an ice tea in my left hand, cell phone in my right and driving with my left knee up the mountain!!!" Maybe a slight exaggeration, but not far off, as anyone who's ever ridden with me in the Rocky Mountains will attest. (Jhoon Rhee has ridden with me, yelling, "You drive like Bruce Lee!!!")

Toby, for his part, was gracious. Well, actually no. He kept both of our track times, threatening to copy and publish the data on the NAPMA website. He harassed me unmercifully until we drove across

"Alligator Alley" in his Lexus later that night — at 10 MPH LESS THAN the speed limit.

Anyway, is there a moral to my story?

Well, I guess we could analyze personality types. Toby, "the speed demon," was in the relatively safe environment of the track in a high performance racecar. Me, the nut case, was on a mountain curve in the Rocky Mountains in my Porsche. I'm not sure what that means and probably isn't very useful for us anyway.

There is another moral to the story.

There is one crucial difference between the very highest performers and those who sabotage themselves along the way:

"Failure to launch," or thinking they are missing a critical secret, or need to know one more thing to be successful.

Much of being very successful in business is that sometimes "Go Fast, Turn Left" is enough. Don't over-analyze everything. Don't assume that there is a "magic pill." Do gain every slight edge. Do learn everything possible — but go fast, NOW. Implement.

I once heard a motivational speaker (I think it was Zig Ziglar or Denis Waitley) explain that successful people don't wait for every light to be green before driving across town. Successful businesspeople don't wait to know everything before starting. While you must "begin with the end in mind," you must pull the trigger and start, even if you don't know all the answers. You can always tune and tweak along the way.

Now, don't misunderstand me. You can always learn more. You can always make anything you do better. The winners operate on an important principle of "the slight edge." They are always learning and investing in themselves; however, the winners don't wait to know all the answers before they start. They remember that "Go Fast — Turn Left" may be enough to start in a 200-MPH race car — or growing a $1 million-plus business.

A Special Report on Tuition Pricing

Confidential for NAPMA Members Only

After talking with several hundred school owners, it's obvious many still are unclear of true best practices. There are many elements that seem missing from most schools. Additionally, school owners are often timid in their tuition structure.

There are clear commonalities among the schools who are highly profitable. One of these is in creating high value per student. This is true regardless of the target market: Adult Males, Adult Females, "Little Ninjas," Children and Families.

The high value per student factor is demonstrated in just a couple of simple examples:

Inner Circle Member Sean Harvey, Bermuda

Where broke school owners charge $65 to $95 a month for some a "Fitness Class" or Cardio Kickboxing, Sean has taken the principles that I've taught him and truly created a robust personal development program from his "Fitness Kickboxing"® Program. Some even commit financial suicide by selling "punch cards" for 10, 25, or 50 sessions.

Now, in Sean's case, we've worked together to create his "360 program" (watch for the interview with him coming up, and conversations directly with him at our upcoming Peak Performers Meetings). Sean's charging an enrollment of $297 a month for his program. He also now has an "Upgrade Level" at $497 per month. Next up will be his top upgrade, at $997 per month. I'm guessing he'll be a $1,000,000 a year school from that program alone with just a little more efficiency in the next 12-18 months.

Inner Circle Member Robert Blum, Fishkill, New York

Robert's another excellent case study. In about 24 months we've walked him from $6,000 a month, more or less, to the mid $40's. Overall, if you take his active count and divide into his average gross revenue, then he's at about $200 per month average revenue. Now, if you subtract 40–50 "legacy members" and look at members in the past 18 months, then he's closer to an average of $225 average revenue per student.

Some other examples.

In interviews with my old friends Keith Hafner and Buzz Durkin (who I've been pestering for years about their pricing, by the way), both have VERY HIGHLY PROFITABLE schools averaging in the $60,000 to $70,000 a month range with a SMALL number of new enrollments each month. Both are charging $200 a month for new enrollments.

Inner Circle Members Eric Williams and Hai Nguyen of Elite MMA

They've been running a $1,000,000 a year MMA school in Houston. Although that may seem like a big number, to me, they're a work in progress. They have about 650 adult men training mostly in fairly traditional BJJ classes. At 650 active, I'm determined they should be at least at $120,000 a month in tuition only from that program, or $1,400,000-plus — an additional $400,000 ADDITIONAL PURE NET PROFIT. It's one serious point of developmental focus that I have for them as we work directly together to continue developing their very high quality school.

What are Commonalities Among BROKE School Owners?

The thing that I've found by talking with several hundred school owners is that the broke school owners are typically under $125 per month for new enrollments. They use a variety of excuses for their low rates. What excuses? Well, make sure you're not using one of these:

Excuse 1. Everyone else in my area is charging $_____, and I'm already, a.) more expensive than anyone else; b.) nearly the most expensive); or, c.) more than a lot of schools in my area.

As an aside, if you get more than 5% of your prospective students "shopping around," then you have a marketing problem, NOT a pricing or sales problem. We've solved that problem for all of our Inner Circle Members and Peak Performers members. You'll hear some of those solutions with our various interviews with them coming up or at the Peak Performers meetings.

Back to 1983 when I opened my Mile High Karate Schools — opening 5 schools in 18 months and growing to 1,500 students in about 24 months — what's often not discussed is that I was charging at least 50% more than the NEXT HIGHEST school, including some that had been established for 10, 15 or 20 years. I ended up quickly with AT LEAST 10 times more students than the next largest school in the state, charging first 50% more than the next highest school and pretty quickly double then next highest.

Excuse 2. "The Economy."

Another example I'll give is former Peak Performers member and current Mile High Karate Franchisee Sascha Williams about how he's doing in Fresno, California. Now, Fresno is arguably the worst hit city, in the worst hit state in the United States.

Mile High Karate Owner-Operator Sascha and Renee Williams

His results have been for the last 24 months.

He's gone from around $17,000 a month to consistently in the low to mid $40's. I've worked with him to become effective at generating 200 to 250 Intro appointments each and every month this year so far. Now, he's got two problems. One, so much traffic that it's difficult to give personal focus and to handle the volume. His second problem is that he is flooded with a variety of broke people (out of work, migrant farm labor, etc.) and has to sort through a bunch that are a bad fit before finding enough who are a good fit to pay $397 down and $197 per month for lessons.

By the way, I'm determined that Sascha and Renee Williams will be an $1,000,000 school in the next 12 to 18 months. They've got LOTS of volume. They're billings are over $30,000, and as they figure out time management to get their renewal ratios on track then the gross will double almost overnight.

Excuse 3. You can't charge that much in my area because…

1. (Really, I heard this from school owners in Beverly Hills and other rich areas of LA and in Manhattan among other areas): The income in my area is too high and my prospective students are too smart to pay that much. (Yes, I know…I laughed, too.)
2. People in my area are too broke to pay that much.
3. "NO ONE" will pay that much for:
   A. "Little Ninja's"
   B. Krav Maga
   C. Cardio Kickboxing
   D. Add any other style.

See excuse #2 explanation and excuse #1.

I'm reminded also of a seminar/consulting session that I had with West Coast Tae Kwon Do (Ernie Reyes, Sr., Tony Thompson and their dynamic team) years ago. They explained their extremely low tuition rate by patiently explaining that in their area (Silicone Valley) that the cost of living was so high that people couldn't pay more than $75 a month for martial arts lessons.

Another Commonality of Broke School Owners is the absence of a REAL Renewal Process. Now, we use two terms: Renewal and Upgrade.

Let me define them in the following way:

A. "Renewal Process" is a system in the first few months of a new student's enrollment where you educate them about your process and timeline to train to Black Belt and beyond. A process where you make them "Qualify" for the honor of being accepted to train while helping them really make a serious commitment to train to Black Belt and beyond.

B. "Upgrade" is a system to have a higher level program that has higher level of value than the initial enrollment level. That can range from a more robust Black Belt Program and Leadership Program to a variety of Private Lesson packages or, advanced competition team or demonstration team.

Now, after discussing all of the above what are my recommendations?

The first is that all schools should have a "Basic" or "Orientation Program" that's 6 to 12 months. And, then a "National Black Belt Program" and, a "Leadership Program" (aka GOLD Team — Guidance On Leadership Training).

How much should those programs be? Well, at the LOWER end a minimum of:

$200 Enrollment -plus $149 = $349 to get started. Monthly: $149 per month.

As I've mentioned before, we have Inner Circle members who range from $169 to $297 monthly as their basic enrollment. The standard Mile High Karate new enrollment tuition is $249 per month.

How about the "Upgrade" Tuition?

My "Rule of Thumb" is that you can have the lower level upgrade (Black Belt Program) at about a 50% tuition bump. In other words, if you were at $149 you can go to $249 for National Black Belt Program. If you were at $225 then you could go to $335 more or less.

At the higher level upgrade (Leadership or "GOLD TEAM) you can go to double the initial enrollment tuition. In other words from $149 to $297 more or less or, from $225 to $449 more or less.

Again to be clear:

At a FLOOR I'd recommend:

Enrollment: $349 to enroll. $149 per month (X 6 months or X 12 months).

Renewal: National Black Belt Club — $449 to renew. $249 per month (typically X 36 months); Leadership Program (Guidance on Leadership) — $597 to renew. $297 per month.

Clearly, with the examples given above, I believe that REALLY you should go to work on your program and teaching quality and then be at $200 or more for new enrollments and implement renewal programs from $397 up to $997 or more per month.

That's clearly a primary focus in Inner Circle and Peak Performers on creating the highest quality program with HUGE perceived value.

As a final note:

My current project for about 20 of our newest Peak Performers members is a "RENEWAL BLITZ." I'm expecting many of them to do $75,000 to $350,000 in extra revenue in two months by implementing their new upgrade program.

It's a simple process to accomplish that, but difficult to give you a step-by-step. Myself, Toby Milroy, Bob Dunne and Jeff Smith have walked through step by step structuring overlaying a new upgrade program.

With each school it's a little different because we have to personally review what you have already presented to the students. Once we "get in the mind" of your current students and review what you've previously done — then we can create the "Renewal Blitz" strategy. It insures increased commitment from all of your students and a big chunk that enthusiastically move to a higher level tuition and a more robust commitment to your program.

Lessons You Can Learn from Jhoon Rhee

Lesson 1: *An early realization that commercial success was necessary.* Jhoon Rhee (as well as Bruce Lee) was openly reviled by many in the martial arts community, both for their innovation and their commercialism. I recall debates in Black Belt magazine articles in the 1960s: one being "The Case against Commercialism" and another referring to Jhoon Rhee as the Piped Piper of Korean Karate.

Allow me to clarify one point. You might have the idea that Bruce Lee was anti-commercial. Actually, the opposite is true. Bruce Lee was sending Jhoon Rhee advertising from Chuck Norris and others for karate schools and was very interested in the business aspects of martial arts.

Bruce Lee decided, however, that his path to wealth was acting, while Jhoon Rhee decided that his was operating martial arts schools.

Clearly, neither Bruce Lee nor Jhoon Rhee had hang-ups about whether they should be making money from martial arts. Jhoon Rhee said to me, first, it's impossible to accomplish much of anything without financial resources. Second, if you are providing a great service, then you deserve to be well compensated.

Lesson 2: The Mastermind effect. I can tell you from personal experience that Jhoon Rhee's did not associate with schools operators who were failing and making excuses.

Other than Bruce Lee, Rhee was associating with a large group of congressmen and senators and smart and wealthy people, ranging from Jack Anderson to Tony Robbins. He brought Nick Cokinos (EFC founder) into the martial arts business (as well as Jeff Smith, myself and others).

He was constantly seeking those who could contribute to his goals and support his vision.

Think Muhammad Ali, Zig Ziglar, the coach of the Washington Redskins and many others. He affiliated with the VERY top school owners he could find in the country and openly shared ideas with them (Chuck Norris schools among others).

Lesson 3: Immunity from criticism. Jhoon Rhee introduced many innovations. Overlooked may be his early ability to run successful commercial schools, with quality marketing and effective sales processes, while teaching many thousands of students. Next, he associated with rebels, such as Bruce Lee. Grandmaster Rhee surrounded himself with successful Americans (breaking out of the Korean community).

Next, he invented and promoted foam safety equipment. He helped launch full-contact kickboxing, invented musical forms and even had his team wear "color" uniforms (red).

Some portion of the martial arts community considered him a "sell-out" or just a "self-promoter." Safety equipment, rather than being universally embraced, was controversial. Traditionalists proclaimed it would destroy technique. Tournament promoters claimed it would make competition more dangerous. Many refused to use it.

Musical forms, which dominate today, were derided as destroying traditional forms. He managed to persevere, ignore the critics and keep his eyes on his goals.

Lesson 4: Having the resources to produce incredibly high quality students. At the same time that Grandmaster Rhee's school had a huge percentage of the world-ranked kick-boxers on staff and the current and future World Forms Champions (John Chung and then Charlie Lee), other Washington, D.C. areas schools called Jhoon Rhee a "Belt Factory." In reality, Jhoon Rhee's schools had a very high (for the era) graduation rate to Black Belt.

The Black Belts were rigorously screened. Not only were children required to have physical mastery, but also good grades and behavior. The quality of the students across seven, nine and then 12 schools was incredibly HIGH. Far from "selling out," the Jhoon Rhee schools produced many of today's industry leaders.

That would have been impossible unless two full-time instructors per location were able to make good livings (during the 1970s) by running a martial arts school. (I was making a $30,000 base plus commissions, equaling approximately 10% of the gross, while a full-time student at Georgetown University in 1980.)

Lesson 5: Jhoon Rhee relentlessly sought experts to help him grow his business. In the pre-NAPMA days, he sought publicity experts (hiring a full-time PR guy AND Sugar Ray Leonard's publicist). He pulled Nick Cokinos from the dance industry and relentlessly looked for experts in sales, marketing, teaching, management, and even franchising, to help him grow his organization.

Lesson 6: Relentless Promotions. As a staff member of Jhoon Rhee's organization (and a full-time college student), I was annoyed by the constant parade of promotions: A HUGE demo at the 4th of July celebration on the Washington Mall each year; classes taught to the FBI; presentations at elementary schools, high schools and colleges; and a parade of classes taught to everyone from local police officers to Congressmen.

Jhoon Rhee was relentless in finding ways to introduce the public to Tae Kwon Do (and specifically to "Jhoon Rhee Karate"). It was a total, never-ending quest to fill the schools and, there-fore, improve the gross and staff salaries and "spin-off" resources for other purposes. He discusses Muhammad Ali as being a very good promoter — and Jhoon Rhee learned from him and many others how to promote himself. By the way, Grandmaster Rhee was able to convince Muhammad Ali to mention his name in front of 50 million TV viewers and join him in front of millions of fans during their tour of Korea.

Lesson 7: Goals Orientation. Jeff Smith and I were talking with Grandmaster Rhee during a recent late night (12 midnight his time!). He reminded me, "When you were 10 years old, you told me you would go to Denver and open Jhoon Rhee Karate schools." It's interesting that he remembers and was impressed.

Truth is that when I was 10, I said I wanted to open Jhoon Rhee schools. I was about 18 when the idea of doing it in Denver bubbled to the surface; however, the fact that he remembers shows how rarely we set serious goals and follow through. To be successful, you first must make a decision; you can call it setting a target or being goal-oriented. You must decide that there will be no excuses and you will make it happen.

What should you learn from Jhoon Rhee? At the least, you should know that it's okay to make money and grow your school. You should also know that commercialism does not imply "selling out" and that the more resources you have the better you can make your students. Next, you need to spare no expense associating with a quality mastermind team and developing knowledge (and hiring experts) to shorten your own learning curve. Finally, you must be tireless in promoting your school, and make sure that you have the tools and resources to do that effectively.

An Interesting Question from a NAPMA Member

This question is from a Maximum Impact member who should be in Inner Circle. He teaches more than 300 students and grosses more than $50,000 a month after just 4 years in business.

He asks, "How do you charge $300-plus for Leadership Programs? I currently charge $225 per month."

It's an interesting question. I've heard it many times. Among the EFC board members, I used to be asked two questions: "How do you convince someone to write a check for $12,000–$20,000 for karate lessons?" or Jose's question: "How do you charge so much?"

Well, my friend, Keith Hafner, could parrot me now without a moment's hesitation, my answer was always the same, "Ask."

Now I know that's overly simplistic. The first hurdle most school owners must make, whether it's asking for higher down payments, big paid-in-fulls, or higher payments for leadership or other programs, is to "grow a pair." Now, I don't want that to sound overly crude, but really it's mostly a matter of being willing to ask.

Ask expectantly. Ask congruently. Ask sincerely. Ask confidently…practice it in the mirror first, and be willing to hear a few no's before you are good at it.

After that I think the answer is a little more complicated. What I tend to find is that most school owners don't provide great service and have created a curriculum centered on their personal "hobby," rather than truly what students need or want to learn.

When my coaching client, Miko Peled, was with me in Denver for two days during a consulting day and "behind the scenes" tour, his observation, not mine, was that what he most learned (contrary to expectations) was about the depth and quality of the character and personal development curriculum that we've developed.

He observed that EVERYONE: staff, franchise owners, instructors and senior staff were polite, great people, professionally groomed and sincerely happy to be working with students and growing their schools. It's really important to implement your own "No Assholes Rule" (Pick up the book by the same name) — and to make sure that everyone in your environment (including all the senior-ranked students) are walking, talking and breathing "Products of the Product." It's easy for parents or students to justify the tuition if they are surrounded by people "who are what they want to be."

I've had the debate from time to time with Dan Kennedy. He says that selling doesn't have to be "congruent," using the example of not having to do manual labor while traveling around the country doing exactly that. My experience, in our environment, has always been the opposite. I've always been a BIG believer in the "Everything-Counts" philosophy.

Do you want to "sell success?" Well, make sure you and all of your associates and staff are successful. Do you want to sell a high priced leadership program? Make sure you and your staff and associates all exhibit impeccable leadership skills.

Consultation Certificate

This Certificate Entitles the Bearer to a Personal 1-on-1 Martial Arts School Business Analysis With a NAPMA-Certified Business Analyst. This Individual Consultation is Valued at $495.00.

Certificate expires 12 months from the date of purchase.
To schedule your personal business analysis, complete this form and fax to NAPMA at
1-800-795-0853; mail to 1767 Denver West Blvd., Suite A, Golden, CO 80401;
or visit www.PrivateCoachingSession.com

PLEASE FILL OUT COMPLETELY AND WRITE LEGIBLY

Name _____

School Name _____

Address _____

City _____ State/Province _____

Zip _____ Country _____

Phone _____ Fax _____

E-Mail _____

_____
Authorized by Toby Milroy
Chief Operating Officer, NAPMA

3 FREE GIFTS FOR SERIOUS SCHOOL OWNERS

FREE Personal School Evaluation

Two 30-minute Sessions
A sure-fire way action plan to double your results or better.

FREE Two 90-Minute Seminars

with "The Millionaire Maker Grandmaster Stephen Oliver "The 5 Stupid Mistakes All Too Many School Owners Make that Kill Their Growth" and "The Key Step-by-Step Blueprint for Being a Big Winner"

FREE CD-DVD Package and Report

"How Hundreds of Smart School Owners Like You Doubled Their Revenue in the Last 12 Months Even in the Midst of the Greatest Recession since the Great Depresson, and How You Can, Too!"

What's your "Circus Celebrity"?

As may be your situation, now that I have children there are many events and situations that I would have been oblivious to before. For instance, it's a family necessity to hit the circus when it's in town. I had the experience once again last week. Now, my kids are ages 10 and 3. My enjoyment of the circus comes in most part of watching their reactions and involvement — as, I would suspect, is true of most parents.

Now, I'll tell you in the past 10 years I've ended up at the circus a bunch of times, but, at the latest, I was most impressed by Barnum & Bailey's business operations.

First, if you haven't been there, then let me explain that it's an incredible traveling retail operation that also happens to have a show going on with characters that mimic the various stuffed animals and flying men and ejecting cannon. It's a marvel that a toy store more elaborate than found at the local Target or Wal-Mart can be transported from town to town, with at least as much care and feeding as the elephants and tigers.

Second, Jodi was extremely frustrated at this event that we merely had front row seats (at times able to reach out and touch the elephants and other performers), and not, as promised, in the "Circus Celebrity" section (which included a significant boost in the ticket price). Now, what's Circus Celebrity? It's when you are not only in the front row (highest ticket price in the house), but additionally, are included in the show. In the past, that entailed a special gift bag and being loaded at midpoint into a vehicle to be pulled around the floor alongside the performers for a portion of the show while waving to the audience. This time it was merely seated from benches surrounding the rings and being able to watch the horses up close, rather than merely being a spectator from the sidelines.

Third, the staff was extremely well trained. A lovely woman who was selling some sort of Frisbee-like device made a point of stopping and patiently explaining to my daughter that the stuffed elephant she had purchased was, in fact, the newborn elephant of one of the performing animals — and that her name was April. She took the time to tell her a little about the real life baby elephant, including how old it was this week and some interesting details about it.

Next, the guy selling the shaved ice took a few extra moments to let Jodi know that the toy that my 3-year-old was swinging rather wildly was guaranteed for life and gave her a little brochure that explained the policy and included a toll-free telephone number.

Later during the show, several clowns stopped by to do photos with the kids, and the guy throwing Frisbees during intermission took a moment and autographed one and threw it to my daughter, who had been watching with fascination for several minutes.

All of these were "nice touches," none designed to immediately sell anything. All sure to make/help/nudge a return visit next time around and possibly even a few more toys into the bag before the trip home.

In watching the logistics, performances, and interactions, there certainly are many takeaways that could apply to our businesses.

I'll point out a couple and encourage you to be hyper-aware of all well-run businesses for experiences that can give you new ideas or nudge you further towards excellence.

First, let's take the "Circus Celebrity" thing. It's a brilliant idea. Providing an slightly different, and better, experience with a bump in revenue. In a weak economy, many businesses have looked for ways to improve their average customer value and to have a top tier that disproportionately contributes to the bottom line. Look around you for many examples. When I check in at the airline I'm offered a seat with more legroom or a business-class seat that moves me through security more quickly — all for just $50 more. Just about every company now has some sort of expensive ($500–$1,500) VIP experience often including the ability to meet the band or spend some time backstage.

It's certainly true that not everyone will spring for the more expensive experience. However, research shows that a portion of any group will pay more to receive a more interesting or valuable experience (often that's 20% or so).

Another takeaway is in staff training. Now, I don't know how many employees the circus has that travels with them, but I'm always impressed when time and effort has been expended on making sure the lowest rungs of the employees have been trained in how to interact with customers.

For most shows, parts, etc., the person schlepping around selling lemonade, popcorn or whatever, receives training mostly in how to strap on the carrier and keep track of the money. With the circus, they had clearly trained the staff on the history and story behind most — perhaps all — of the toys they sell. Behind the various performing animals. And, behind ways to make customers feel better about their purchases and more comfortable and personal with the various performers and support personnel. That impression was reinforced over and over. While at another toy booth the staff member suggested one of their bigger carrying packs and helped me organize the various stuff I was juggling into one of their bags, and added another smaller bag to help keep some photos dry before we left into the rain. Small touch, but noticeable.

I was reminded of Disney (by the way, that's high compliment to Barnum & Bailey), who require the folks who sweep the parking lot and the sidewalks to take a multi-day course in "Disney Traditions" to understand the significance of the various characters and company history. They then train them thoroughly on everything from bus time schedules and routes and the layout of the park, to be able to give directions. Finally they train them that there's no such thing as "I don't know" when interacting with a guest. They have hidden phones within reach throughout the parks and stern directions to find out the answer when asked just about any question by a guest.

To continue with the Disney example, I remember being in the park and stumbling across a 7- or 8-year old child crying who had obviously misplaced his parents. Jodi walked the child up to the concession stand and mentioned to the kid behind the counter that the child seemed lost.

Now, the staffer was probably 18 or so with 12 or 15 customers in line. He initially looked flustered, perhaps even annoyed. However, he pretty quickly picked up the hidden phone to ask what he should do and immediately become 100% focused on the child. The register was handed off to someone else. He became totally focused on reassuring the lost boy.

Almost immediately four or five other employees descended to both reassure and entertain the child, while immediately launching an all-out "man-hunt" for the lost parents. I'm not sure what specifically the voice on the other end of the magical phone told the 18-year-old "cast member," but it's pretty clear that it included "drop everything," and "your priority without exception is protect and reunite that child with its parents." Again, that's impressive training and even more impressive support systems for the college kid in charge.

Now I ask you, is each of your staff, even your volunteer assistants and your Black Belts, trained to help and support every student and every parent? I've seen examples on both sides. One school where every Black Belt (staff or not) greeted each White Belt and their parent by name. Where any concern was immediately addressed and each point of confusion clarified. Where the school was a family and each new member greeted warmly. Other schools where the owner was the only one who paid attention, and occasionally where he or she preferred adulation over mentorship.

What If There Was A Recession But You Didn't Attend?

An exclusive discussion with Dan Kennedy and Stephen Oliver

For those who don't know, Dan Kennedy is a multi-millionaire serial entrepreneur; author of 11 bestselling business books — including one co-authored by **Stephen Oliver**: *NO BS Wealth for Entrepreneurs* and two new ones we'll discuss here; a popular speaker who has often appeared on programs with a wide variety of legendary entrepreneurs, including Donald Trump, Jim McCann (1-800-Flowers), Debbi Fields (Mrs. Fields Cookies) and even Gene Simmons (KISS) as well as leading business speakers Zig Ziglar, Brian Tracy and Tom Hopkins; and, through his newsletters and networks of consultants and coaches, directly influences more than one million business owners a year — including countless martial arts school owners. I have been relying on Dan for strategic business and marketing advice since 1996; and I have been a member of his most elite Platinum private client group for several years.

While at a Platinum meeting in beautiful Cleveland, Ohio, I sat down with Dan to discuss the economy, business, money and even politics. Here is the result:

Stephen Oliver: Let's start right out with the so-called elephant in the room, the economy, and the dreaded "R" word. Economists are arguing over technicalities. The news media has had us deep in a recession for months. People do seem troubled by gas and grocery prices. What's your take on it all?

Dan Kennedy: First, you always have to temper what people say with objective reality. For example, if you listened to all their weeping and wailing about gas prices, you'd presume everybody had their cars up on blocks, huddled in their homes as if in caves.

But the recent Memorial Day weekend had only a 1% reduction in people driving 50 miles or farther from home according to AAA. There is no doubt that there are segments of the population severely affected … others slightly affected … some unaffected by this very specific inflation of gas and groceries.

In big-ticket spending, the inevitable hitting of the wall with using appreciating home equity as an ATM has whacked big, dumb, slow to adapt companies like Home Depot and Lowe's. Cities and businesses dependent on summer vacation dollars may be hurt this year.

So I am not a "recession denier." However, it's also important to look at all this in full context. For example, as we're doing this, we're in the fourth straight week with declines in jobless claims — less people each week filing for unemployment. The stock market still reflects a fairly optimistic analysis of the overall economy. Real estate is not, as media reports, in an across the board collapse.

In the Cleveland area, where I have one of my homes, foreclosure numbers are roughly 25% to 30% higher than normal, putting the area in the top five markets in the U.S. for foreclosure problems, but luxury home sales are healthy, and even more telling, commercial real estate transactions were up, and there's more new investment in significant development in and around the city than any time in the past seven years. In short, saying "recession" is a big, fat, over-broad, over-simplified generalization. There are plenty of consumers, plenty of investors and plenty of business owners spending plenty of money — and that's one of the things I want to talk about, related to one of my new books.

Further, there's no profit in buying into this concept of a giant black cloud of doom descending over the entire land — and every business owner must constantly be asking himself "where's the PROFIT in that?" — with regard to his own thinking, his own analysis and his own actions.

Stephen Oliver: Before we get to the practical cures, if you will, let's talk a little more about this thought process. How should businesspeople manage their own thinking about the economy?

Dan Kennedy: "We're coming up on a presidential election year, during which well over a half-billion dollars has been spent, and between candidates, parties, and independent groups called 527-c's — for which I write some ad and direct-mail copy — another billion dollars will be spent, most of it aimed at convincing voters that we are in crisis here, there and everywhere.

One side cries "crisis and change." The other side threatens, "Crisis requires steady, experienced hand." Either way, everybody's selling crisis. There's also a profound media bias, even what I call 'media mental illness', a very unbalanced emphasis, excessively reporting bad news, nearly ignoring good news.

On CNN, you get good economic news only in the little type crawl across the bottom of the screen. You actually have to go to Fox Financial News or CNBC or the *Wall Street Journal* to get a fully balanced presentation and, of course, most people don't. So the gloom 'n' doom sales machine is cranked up on high. To quote one of the success authorities I studied very early, Earl Nightingale, "we become what we think about most." So

if you DON'T actually MANAGE your thinking about this … if you let yourself accept the mainstream media's and politicians' selling of crisis, if you think about it, regurgitate it in conversation with others, hang out with others regurgitating it to you … you'll undoubtedly find yourself upside down in it, shit up to your ankles!

It's up to you to seek out better, more complete information. And, incidentally, to turn around and provide that information to your customers (or clients or patients). You'd better be what I call a "good news merchant" yourself, influencing your customers' thinking about this — yours may very well be the only such voice they hear. And being that lone voice of reason and encouragement can be very magnetic.

I'm sure that you, Stephen, have been telling your martial arts school owners this and in the student newsletter and other tools you provide them, doing this for them. There's a thing called the Consumer Confidence Index, a measurement of consumers' attitudes that at least somewhat predicts their near-future spending. Every business owner needs to be actively working at positively influencing his consumers' confidence.

But beyond that, here's how true entrepreneurs think about this: it is a set of circumstances, of changes in the marketplace, to have foreseen and prepared for, now to respond to, in which there is enormous opportunity — and REDUCED competition pursuing that opportunity diminished by fear, indecision, emotional paralysis, resentment toward the need to adapt, and in many cases, lack of agility.

This is a good time to be grabbing market share, acquiring new students, marketing aggressively. There is always a "set of circumstances" and there are always winners and losers. A lot of business owners do well only in a generous economy. But a lot of other business owners get their traction, outpace their competition, and create their greatest wealth during economic times widely regarded by others as "poor." To complain about there being circumstances or changing circumstances is to complain about there being weather.

As an investor, I don't worry a lot over a company's dip in stock price at a time like this, because that reflects the mass public's foolish acceptance of recession as a universal reality, as a completely dark time. I look for companies where insiders are buying up more stock at bargain prices and the company is expanding, growing, and launching new initiatives. In a recession, everything goes on sale. Stock in very good companies. Real estate in very good areas. "Eyeballs" for advertisers and marketers — less people sending out direct-mail means less clutter in my customers' mailboxes means more space and better opportunity to gain their attention and interest for me. Less pages of advertising in the magazines or newspapers my customers read, lower rate negotiated and more attention for me. When others cower, you want to be bold, aggressive, and opportunistic.

Stephen Oliver: Okay, let's talk about being opportunistic. What are the big opportunities you are emphasizing for business owners right now?

Dan Kennedy: There are two big topics I'm spending a lot of time talking about with my clients, coaching members, and readers right now, reflected in my two: *No B.S. Guide to Ruthless Management of People and Profits* and *No B.S. Guide to Marketing to the Affluent* — as they say, available now at a bookstore near you or amazon. com, BN.com and so on. One topic is using this sea-change from generous, indulgent economy to grumpy, demanding one as motivation and mandate to re-assess your business inside out, and get smarter and tougher and more diligent about managing for maximum profit. And it is my contention that most businesses — including those in your industry, martial arts schools, could suffer a 25% drop in gross revenues but simultaneously

enjoy a 25% improvement in net profits, employing the from a-to-z ruthless management strategies in my book.

Also, most businesses could suffer a 25% drop in response to advertising and marketing, a 25% "drying up" if you will of prospective new students coming their way, but simultaneously create a 25% increase in conversions, in converting new prospects to students. In fact, one of the chapters in my management book is titled "How to Profit From The Age Of Mass Incompetence And Coming Monster Recession." As you can see, this is a very timely new book. Second is the grand and glorious, newly developing opportunity to re-direct a business to attracting, serving and securing more affluent students — the subject of my new marketing to the affluent book. So, the hot words are: re-assess, re-tool and re-direct.

Stephen Oliver: Sounds like a lot of unpleasant work — who wants to do all that re-assessing and re-tooling and re-directing?

Dan Kennedy: Hardly anybody!!! — which is why there's such abundant, exciting opportunity for the few who do. You know, I started in business myself during a real recession — that makes where we are now look like a light summer breeze in comparison to Katrina. Thanks to Jimmy Carter, we had the reality of double-digit base interest and unemployment rates and inflation … all more than double the current numbers, high gas prices and gas rationing, a credit crunch … and a widespread emotional malaise as well. It wasn't pretty. For most. But I prospered. And I got to work with quite a few agile entrepreneurs who did. I have absolute understanding that the best time to speed up and gain position is when others are riding the brakes.

But you're 1000% right: most people long for the ability to get their business arranged a certain way and then never have to tinker with it again. But success in business doesn't work that way. I'd love for that to happen with my houses too. One of our homes is just 6 or 7 years old. Re-paint the deck; next replace the deck. Carla wants to put a new floor in the kitchen. Paint this. Change that. Why, oh why, oh why, can't it all just be left alone?

Well, even if you want to, you can't. Style changes, tastes change, furnishings wear out, water tanks wear out, garage doors wear out.

Look, in business, the surest path to mediocrity, to disappointments in income and wealth short-term and long-term, to losing disinterested customers (client/patients) to others' seductions is denial, is resentment or procrastination over the need for constant change. That's why being a part of groups like yours, being coached, being in your Coaching, Inner Circle, Peak Performers teams coming to brain-exchange events like your Extreme Success Academy or Ultimate Martial Arts Marketing Boot Camp is so critically important at all times but treble important in particularly challenging times. You have to see the need for change as exciting opportunity, not as burden. You have to be mentally agile.

With full disclosure, some of the companies I invest in now: Disney, Landry's Restaurants, Amazon, 1-800-Flowers … all of which have been good to me and I expect them to be even better in the future … have creative, agile, innovative, opportunistic leadership and corporate culture. Nothing stays the same. If you are striving for the same, then you'll be slaughtered.

Especially now, but really at any time.

Stephen Oliver: Then let's move on to: change. And let's start with the second topic you raised, marketing to the affluent. Why should my martial arts school owners be eager to learn about and do this?

Dan Kennedy: Without delving into the kind of statistical and in-depth detail that I've assembled and presented in the book, let me paint a broad strokes answer. Domestically, here in the U.S., all the real spending growth is toward the top. The middle class is shrinking, with one-third moving down, but two-thirds moving up. That two-thirds is literally a new class of "middle-class millionaires." These mass-affluents' buying behavior has also served to motivate more status spending by the affluent.

Across the three groups — mass-affluent, affluent, ultra-affluent — there has never been more discretionary income and more spending on a broader and more diverse range of premium, premium-priced goods and services including newly invented categories.

Further, there is convergence and overlap with the biggest part of the boomer population hitting their peak discretionary and non-necessity spending years, spurred on by very different attitudes about both retirement and spending than the previous generation. Anyone who has the sense that money is tight, consumer spending restricted, and prosperity not rampant is simply deluded, paying attention to the wrong information. Essentially, there's a gigantic growth industry, an unprecedented boom underway, getting rich by selling to the rich, near-rich, soon-to-be-rich. Many business owners' knee-jerk reaction to this is either to deny it because it is not their personal experience or to feel it is not what their business is about or that these exceptionally valuable students are somehow beyond their reach.

Well, ignorance is forgivable and fixable, but as comedian Ron White says: you can't fix stupid. *My No B.S. Marketing to the Affluent* book gets all that b.s. out of the way, so you can focus on opportunities instead of excuses. If that sounds harsh, it's supposed to. Earlier I said that THE question is always: where's the profit in that? There's never profit in making the lists of why we can't do something, why we can't capitalize on emerging opportunities. Making such lists is low-grade, low-pay work. Any idiot can do it. If you want high pay — especially at times when a lot of business owners are taking pay cuts — you have to do more high pay work. And certainly, finding ways to follow the money, to appeal to and attract more affluent, willing to spend students is such work. Making excuses, sucking your thumb is not.

So, the basic facts: 22% of the U.S. households own 55% of the earned income. The spending power is concentrated with 1 out of 5. Stephen, your martial arts school owner has three basic choices: one, promote himself to anybody and everybody, taking whatever he gets…statistically ensuring he'll get more of the 4 out of 5's than the 1 out of 5's and risking getting none of the 1 out of 5's. Dumb.

Two, he can — out of ignorance, denial, fear, low self-esteem, sloth — actually focus on the 4 out of 5's. Dumber. Incidentally, the overwhelming majority of the competition is at the bottom, broad base, not toward the top of the economic power pyramid. Wal-Mart does just fine there, and recently has had a renewal of growth, of same store year-to-year growth, and is undoubtedly helped by recession, so I bought Wal-Mart stock in the $40's. And again in the low $50's. And if I can, if it drops there anytime soon, I'll buy more. But do you really want to be butting heads with Wal-Mart and every other large and small competitor vying for customers for whom price is a major factor in buying decisions? Only if you can offer and deliver THE lowest prices while making satisfactory profits. Otherwise, there's no benefit in offering the almost-lowest prices. Or three, re-tooling any and every aspect of your business you must, in order to target market to, appeal to, attract, not just satisfy but thrill, and grow with more affluent customers…for whom price is a non-factor…and who are least and last affected by recession. My two new books, combined, in concert, can help you successfully act on the third option.

Under normal conditions, only 10% of consumers always buy by price, their decisions governed by price — because they have no option. This group is largely made up of "working poor," low-wage working people with more mouths to feed than they can afford food for. Nothing wrong with them as people. A lot to admire — except the choices they make that keep them poor. But no good reason to have them or, worse, seek them out as customers. Yet, strangely, most business owners focus 90% of their energy on price even while only 10% of the customers decide based on price. In recession, this percentage may jump as much as 3 times, to 30%. However, there are 20% who make most buying decisions with little weight given to price or cheapest price and 5% who never consider price. In the middle, people who consider price in context and only buy by price in absence of other persuasive information. That top 5% is admittedly considerably more difficult to get to and satisfy, but infinitely and disproportionately more valuable. The 20% is a little more difficult to get but also considerably more valuable. So, picking up rocks from your driveway is easy and cheap to do but rocks have value only in giant bulk. Mining diamonds actually uses the same skills as picking up rocks applied differently, with admittedly the difficulties of traveling beyond your driveway, investing in mining equipment, etc., but each little diamond you find is worth more than ten tons of rocks. What's important to face up to is that you choose the business you're in. Rocks. Diamonds. Up to you. If you feel you're working too hard to make a living, have no leverage, aren't gaining and may even, now, be losing ground, I'll safely wager you're in the rocks business. Ultimately, all suffering and all prosperity, self-inflicted.

Stephen Oliver: But, Dan, the question that pops, what about the recession? Surely this isn't the best time to be re-directing my martial arts school owners at selling to an emerging affluent market — that's what people will think. That the timing is bad. Better to think about this when "things get better."

Dan Kennedy: 1000% wrong. To be brief, if there is a protracted recession, across a wide swath, or in segments; either way, I'll prefer investing as much of my resources as possible in selling to those least and last affected by recession. And a number of business owners are already quickly finding themselves in deep and worsening financial trouble by not being agile about this, by continuing to waste their resources selling to people with dwindling resources, easily and quickly affected by a rise in the price of gas and Starbucks, and easily and quickly scared silly. There's no better time, and it is arguably an urgent time to move to where the money is in the hands of confident spenders.

I think my N*o B.S. Marketing to the Affluent* book is URGENT reading for most business owners. There is a fundamental path to progress, all progress, that looks like this: Step 1: Awareness, Step 2: Decision, Step 3: Resources, Step 4: Action.

In the *No B.S. Marketing to the Affluent* book, I provide a whole new, thoroughly documented and truly fascinating new awareness of the mass-affluent, middle class millionaires, affluent and ultra-affluent populations, their psyches, their buying criteria and behavior, who they are, what they buy, why they buy, how they buy — plus an even broader awareness of why and how money moves from person to person and place to place.

Step 2 — I guide you in making informed decisions about how you can best connect your business (products/services/practice) to the best segment of this affluent market for you. And I get you convinced, confident and motivated to do so.

Step 3 — I hand you the resources. For example, specific instructions for finding and directly reaching out to the best affluent students for you, in your area. For example, a detailed,

diagrammed, step-by-step "affluent entrapment system" for your marketing.

Step 4 is then up to you. This can quickly change your fortunes. It can rescue you from and immunize you to recession. It can convert an ordinary business providing ordinary income to an extraordinary business providing exceptional income, spinning off extraordinary wealth. Within this context, incidentally, are very specific 'price strategies' that have led to huge income breakthroughs. It's all illustrated with real-life examples. And the book comes with an audio CD inside featuring highlights from my Price/Profit/ Power Seminar, which cost $995.00 to attend, and was recently attended by more than 600 people.

But to zero in: your key to changing your income for the better, even at a time when peers' and competitors' incomes are changing for the worse, is: changing the "who" you are deliberately attracting to do business with.

And further, Stephen, you want your coaching clients to consider equity, not just income. Income is what you make and take home today. Equity is the actual value of your business, represented in a number of ways, including its sustainability; its resistance to ups and downs, even to recession. In its ultimate exit-strategy value. Well, the value of your business is actually the aggregate total of the value of each of your students. Amass low value, financially weak, fickle, easily discouraged customers; own a low value, fragile business.

Stephen Oliver: Seems hard to argue with all that. You make a convincing case. But people are still thinking: sounds great, but deliberately marketing to the affluent must be different and difficult. So, just how different is it, marketing to the affluent?

Dan Kennedy: It IS different. First of all, there are profound — and in most ways, beneficial — psychological differences. These people think differently. That's why they are affluent.

So you have to be in sync, you have to connect with the way they think, with what appeals to them emotionally. You also have to acknowledge different hurdles; they are more thoughtful, critical, and in some ways, skeptical buyers, more demanding customers. Fair, because they are a lot more valuable. So you have to be customer focused, not product focused to an even greater degree. I devote about half the book, about 200 of its 400-plus pages to just who are these people? Where did they come from? How do they buy, why do they buy? Even specific behaviors in different buying categories, such as health, investments, for grandkids, for pets, even business-to-business. Second, there are process differences. While direct marketing fundamentals, systems and system structures don't change, application does.

In the book I diagram and describe a complete marketing system as a template, from lead generation through to the sale and post-sale relationship, and it will be familiar to most of your coaching clients But within the familiar structure, there are significant modifications unique to the buying behavior of the affluent. There are certain known prerequisites before an affluent buyer will act, that must be understood and met. In the book, I support these with considerable research data and actual case histories.

I would quickly point out that ANY and EVERY business can be "tweaked" or, if need be, reinvented to successfully meet these prerequisites so as to appeal to and attract affluent clientele.

Third, and last that I'll mention now, is the issue of finding them, knowing where they are, so you can directly and efficiently reach out to them. The information about that in the book affects both offline and online marketing and media choices. In short, Stephen, your coaching clients can cross-breed everything you provide them with my "Marketing To The Affluent" strategies and systems, and they'll find it all completely compatible. Further, it will open new doors for them, to better and less price (fee) sensitive students, a better business, even a better business life almost immediately. This is a way to take all of your most effective tools and techniques and apply them more profitably, something akin to taking superior farming practices and genetically improved seeds and applying them to more fertile ground. Why wouldn't you want to do that? Now, not later or someday?

Stephen Oliver: Okay, way back when, in this discussion, you said you were working with your clients on two big areas — this one, attracting more affluent customers, but also a second, managing for profit. And in that book title, you use the word "ruthless," which has to rattle some people right off the bat. So, what's that all about?

Dan Kennedy: It connects two ways. First, affluent students are less tolerant of unsatisfactory, even unimpressive sales and service practices. Second, the recently generous, forgiving economy, tolerant, even indulgent of sloppy sales and service practices, has turned grumpy, irritable, intolerant and punishing. Maybe as it should. And very frankly, a lot of business owners have been making their way across the lake every day satisfactorily in very leaky boats. Those days are over. There are going to be a lot of fatalities, large and small, of poorly run businesses. There's also going to be a golden age for those businesses that provide start-to-finish and continuing exceptional experiences. As to the word "ruthless", that's to telegraph that this is NOT a warm 'n' fuzzy book with happy stories about such customer experiences, the equal of a smiley-face sticker. The shelves are full of those books. Fun to read. Maybe inspiring. But now what? Ruthless management is mandated by ruthless times. This is about setting and enforcing standards that yield the best customer (client/patient) experiences and the best attainable profits, by micro-managing the profit impact of every job, every employee and every step in the marketing, sales, delivery and service aspects of the business. It is about creating a winning Program and that having everybody get with The Program — or get gone. I call this book, first of all, the permission slip business owners have been waiting for, to manage their people and their businesses for maximum profit — without anxiety, guilt or squeamishness. It's a liberating and empowering book. Then it has very specific, in-depth how-to strategies. I'm told people laugh out loud reading it, because of its unbelievably blunt and candid, and to some, outrageous and radical revelations. I'm glad people have fun with it. I put some very pointed, original cartoons in it for that very reason. But make no mistake; this is a very serious manifesto for serious business owners in serious times.

Stephen Oliver: I've, of course, read the book — several times, and I was struck by three things I'd like you to talk about, that I would call: process improvement, people improvement and profit improvement. Let's touch on each one.

Dan Kennedy: Stephen, that's a good way of putting it. It all starts with accurate measurement of what's really happening versus having or establishing standards for what's supposed to be happening. For three or four years, I was on a speaking tour, at seminars with 10,000 to as many as 35,000 people in the audiences, and I frequently followed — and got to know — General Norm Schwarzkopf. A line I wrote down from him is: shined shoes save lives. What he means is, being undisciplined, casual, sloppy about seemingly little things inevitably permeates to affect all things, and on the business battlefield where we operate just as on the actual battlefield, it'll get you killed in tough times. So, you need standards for everything. And everybody. Number of rings before phone is answered. Number of referrals per student 90 days, a certain "under" triggering a series of pre-planned actions. Etc. Etc. In other words,

you have to measure to manage, and what you can't or aren't measuring, you can't be managing. Face it. Get real about it. That's foundational to all three opportunities for improvement.

So, as an example, let's take the sales process, which I write about extensively in the Ruthless Management book. I have a client with this process: leads are generated by advertising; leads are moved to the setting of appointments; salespeople make presentations at those appointments; some buy, many don't. There are lots of things to be measured here. Conversions of visitors to the website to requests for information; percentage of those sent info setting appointments; percentage of those setting then keeping appointments; and, of course, percentage buying vs. not buying. And there are many variables that can be worked on, to try and improve each of those results.

If, for example, the percentage of appointments kept is 72% when they speak with Betty when they call in, but only 64% if they speak with Helen, we either find out what Betty's saying or doing differently than Helen and keep training and coaching Helen until she gets her efficacy up to Betty's, or we get Helen off the darn phones. We definitely measure both in real time, day to day; don't keep the results a secret. If there's a script getting Betty the 72%, we insist that it be memorized, practiced and used by Helen … we "mystery shop" and record her calls … and if she won't get with The Program within a reasonable probation period, we fire her.

But here's a big, hidden opportunity found in this business. The non-buyers, left to the salespeople for follow-up, were nearly worthless; fewer than 5% came back and bought within 60 days. Mostly because the salespeople believed them worthless and wouldn't do — and lied about doing — the prescribed follow-up, let alone working earnestly on finding ways to improve the result.

Taking that away from the salespeople and implementing a series of three follow-up letters over six weeks, we got 16% back to buy. That's a gain of 11 buyers per 100 sales presentations. That's big. This company had been doing "just fine" tolerating the 5% when 16% was available during the generous economy. They can't afford it during the turned-grumpy-and-intolerant economy, they shouldn't tolerate it at all.

So, that's process improvement. The Helen-Betty situation might be resolved by process improvement, a better script, training, better supervision. Or it might require people improvement.

Now, given the 5% to 16% improvement created, this business can actually afford a dip in first presentation sales that might be caused by a price increase. Let's play. As example, if their salespeople average 20% sold, plus 5% after the fact, at $1,000.00 each, that's $25,000.00 per 100 people getting presentations…if at a 50% profit: $12,500.00 profit.

If I raise the price to $1,500.00 (thus DOUBLING the profit from $500.00 to $1,000.00) … the percentage buying at presentation drops from 20% to 15%, and that 16% drops to 9%, I'm at 24% vs. the old 25% (down only 1%) … 24 x $1,500.00 gross, $36,000.00 instead of $25,000.00, and more importantly $24,000.00 profit vs. $12,500.00 profit. That's profit improvement.

And, by the way, contrary to common fear, price increases do not necessarily cause significant drops in sales made. Then we can go back around the horn, to try to improve the at-presentation sales with better scripts, new answers to price objections, new financing options, sales training and/or new and better salespeople. And, of course, we could combine all this with deliberately seeking more affluent buyers. That's what my Ruthless Management book is all about. In short, squeezing a lot more good juice out of each orange you have, so even if, temporarily, your tree produces fewer oranges — the recession effect — you still get more juice, not less.

And please don't say: that example doesn't apply to me because — because whatever. I don't use that business model. I don't have salespeople. Yada yada. You just have to be smarter than that. The principles apply everywhere. And ruthless management starts with ruthlessly managing yourself.

Stephen Oliver: We've been plugging your book, but I know you have blatant and crass commercial messages…

Dan Kennedy: I'm willing to sing for my supper — but I want my supper. And I think I've done a lot of singing here, don't you? So. First, the books; they are available at Amazon.com, BN.com, Barnes & Noble and other booksellers and free info about the entire No B.S. book series is perpetually updated at NoBSBooks.com. If you want bulk quantity discounts, if you're buying dozens or hundreds of copies, try 1-800-CEO-BOOKS, or your local Barnes & Noble store has a corporate/business discount program. Both books have audio CDs included right inside, plus online resources at websites provided in the books.

Second, your members (readers/students) can get a terrific free gift collection of other recession-busting resources of mine including three webinars, my Income Explosion Guide, two months of my No B.S. Marketing Letter, and more, all FREE at NAPMA.com/DanKennedy. These are resources that can be of immediate and dramatic help.

It is my firm belief, based not on "positive thinking" but on experience — mine and countless clients, that attending and being adversely affected by the economic storms of the moment, and likely well into or through this year, is OPTIONAL. The antidote is: awareness, decision, resources and bold action. These two books are, I think, the timeliest I've ever written. And, thanks for the opportunity to shamelessly push them on your coaching clients.

Stephen Oliver: Dan, any closing thoughts?
Dan Kennedy: Kate Hepburn said: old age

isn't for sissies. The older I get, the more I appreciate the remark. Business success, especially in difficult economic times, isn't for sissies either. This is a time to ruthlessly hold yourself, your every process, every employee, entire business and its profits accountable. To have a zero tolerance approach to anything or anyone depressing profits.

This is also a time for new thinking, new approaches, new initiatives, and bold action. And this is a time when it is more important than ever to be cautious of toxic influences of relentlessly negative pessimists, cry-babies, complainers as well as media mouths and politicians magnifying crisis and gloom for their own purposes — and to seek out and associate in every way possible with tough-minded, creative, innovative, forward-thinking people in your field, leaders of your field, as well as qualified, credible advisors outside your specific field who keep you focused on opportunity. That's why participating in everything you offer, Stephen, is so important at this time. Frankly, the tendency, the temptation thoughtlessly given into by so many is to cut back on that which should never be cut back on, drop out of what should never be dropped out of, to isolate. Whatever small savings comes of it, the true cost is infinitely higher. Conservation has its place, but never as substitute for investment.

Stephen Oliver: If you missed our Maximum Impact Bonus Teleconference with Dan Kennedy, then you need to make sure you visit your member Web site and listen to it in full. Either download the MP3 or listen to it online.

We are RAPIDLY expanding your Maximum Impact (and Peak Performers) websites. Make sure you visit weekly and take advantages of the growing base of resources located there, including 25 celebrity interviews now available exclusively to Maximum Impact, Peak Performers and Inner Circle members.

Would you rather be the Apple Store or Wal-Mart?

There are those running around the industry teaching you how to be the martial arts school equivalent of Wal-Mart. Now for some that's most comfortable and, I'd never claim that Wal-Mart themselves don't have a profitable business model.

However, I freely admit that I am most interested in developing — and, teaching school owners to develop the equivalent of the Apple Store rather than Wal-Mart or similar. Additionally, we are in a VERY different business from the discounters. They rely on paper-thin margins and the ability to "make it up in volume." I would argue that we rarely have that opportunity. It's either be premium or, broke. There's little in between.

Now, first let me explain. Among all retail chains in the United States Apple is #1 by a wide-margin in revenue per square foot. The Apple Stores are #1 by a wide margin in retail sales per foot at: $5,626, running a distant second is Tiffany's at $2,974 per square feet. On down the list is Best Buy at $831 per square foot.

The other thing to keep in mind is that Apple across all of their products has a MUCH higher gross profit than any of their competitors:

In Mobile Phones:

Obviously there are many reasons for Apple's success. Clearly you can summarize it by having a high end product with pricing far above industry norms.

Let's look at two options for your school. Very real options that I've seen in practice with various schools that I've evaluated.

See Option 1 chart on following page.

Now at first glance which option is easier to achieve. Which option is a better financial outcome for you? Which option is easier to manage and maintain?

Now, often when I talk with schools and recommend a price point they respond "there's no way I could charge that," or "no one would pay that much." The reality is the barrier is mostly in your ability to believe the opportunity and to act upon it. The secondary challenge is that you must create a perception of value from your program.

Let's take a look at how the revenue and expense structure looks like for the Option 2 (see below):

Just to sum up this line of thinking.

First, It's much easier to run a highly profitable martial arts school with "premium pricing" models than with a low price model.

Second, If you are encountering too many prospective students who object to your current tuition price ask yourself two questions:

1. Are you REALLY showing the value of your program to prospective students? Review your advertising, your introductory process, the look and feel of your school, the look and feel of your staff (or, yourself) and the level of "proof" that you are providing for the positive outcomes of your program.

2. Are you "fishing from the wrong pond." Too many schools just accept whoever walks through their door rather than actively seeking their ideal student. You are looking for students that can and will pay the tuition that you are expecting to charge and that will train with you for the long-term.

Another thought, if you currently have a school

full of broke people — focus on sources OTHER THAN REFERRALS (Word of Mouth) to fill your school.

I certainly hope that you will review the value and quality of your martial arts program. Continually improve every element of your student experience and, the increase your tuition rates accordingly.

Option 1. Wal-Mart School

Average Revenue Per Student:
. . . . $75 Per Month
Total Active Students:. 500
Square Feet:. 5,000
Rent: $8,500
Employees: 3 Full-Time, 5 Part-Time

Total Gross: $37,500

Option 2. Apple Store

Average Revenue Per Student: . . . .
. . . . $300 Per Month
Total Active Students:. 300
Square Feet:. 2,500
Rent: $5,000
Employees: 2 Full-Time, 2 Part-Time

Total Gross: $90,000

Ranking to Top 20 U.S. Chains by Highest Retail Sales per Square Foot

Company	Sales (000)	Store	Avg Size	Sales/ Sq Ft
Apple	14,199	327	7,886	5,626
Tiffany & Co.	2,984	232	4,408	2,974
Coach	3,529	723	2,790	1,820
lululemon athletes	632	138	2,877	1,233
Gamestop	9,327	6,582	1,400	1,009
Costco Wholesales	81,352	580	145,000	998
Signet Jewelers	3,417	1,857	1,927	955
Polo Ralph Lauren	2,661	3711	7,6291	904
Whole Foods Market	9,854[1]	308	37,900	867
Best Buy	47,925	4,186	3,899	831
Zale Jewelers	1,654	1,1732[2]	1,7182[2]	742
Walgreens	70,809	7,715	13,778	672
CVS Caremark	58,236	7.266	12,206	666
Limited Brands	8,592	2,951	4,447	653
Sam's Club[3]	51,256	609	33,410	632
Aeropostale	2,211	1,042	3,682	595
J Crew	1,184	337	6,028	593
BJ's Wholesale	11,137	190	108,995	537
Urban Outfitters	1,782	392	8,950	532
Guess?	1,082	484	4,529	510

Results include trailing 4-quarter retail sales (company-operated store, outlets, kiosks and shop-in-sop); excludes e-commerce, catalog, franchise, licensed, wholesale, memberships and financial services revenue.
All store and sales per sq. dt, data is based In "gross" square feet.
1 — Doesn't include 553 concession shop-in-shops which range from 300 to 6,000 sq. ft.
2   Doesn'l Include 673 Piercing Pagoda wgucg aver 188 sq. ft.
3 — Sam's Club is a subsidiary of Wal-Mart Stores, Inc.

Lessons from Top-Performing Schools

I just returned from our fabulous Inner Circle and Peak Performers' meetings at Disney World in Orlando. We have a great team of school owners working on growing their schools and moving the industry ever higher. Between the fabulous content at their quarterly meetings and their monthly one-on-one coaching, many of these school owners are likely to double or better their revenues this year.

The lessons of the top performers, which, frankly, I've discussed many times here and in various NAPMA and coaching materials, include:

The "Parthenon" Principle with your marketing. Have "lots of stuff" going on and focus on results. Most school owners just don't do enough stuff. They miss having enough different things going on to feed enough new students into their school each and every month. (Our Inner Circle members are generating 20-50 new students per month in most cases.)

What are some of the things you should be doing? Well, starting with stuff that's relatively inexpensive:

Rack cards. (300-500) Cost less than $2 per box — possibly even less than $1.

You can get the cards printed through NAPMA's own Print on Demand Systems, and there are various suppliers that we link from your member website.

Lawn Signs, aka "Bandit Signs." Put these low-cost signs out on the major streets in your area — they work. They aren't going to flood your school, but, if you distribute 20-30 every week, they will work. Again, look in our online "Print on Demand" options at your member site: www.NAPMA.com

Door Hangers and Flyers. These work just fine if you distribute A LOT of them. It's got to be thousands distributed each month — preferably directly into prospects hands or, at the minimum, door to door. Big companies, such as Dominos, does great with these, and I've enrolled 100's of students over the years from this by distributing huge numbers.

Flyer/Ad Cards distributed through targeted, high volume retailers in your area.

Community Outreach activities:

Classes taught at Local Day Care facilities with Permission Slips and extensive follow-up.

Classes taught at Summer Camps with Permission Slips and extensive follow-up.

Classes taught at Gym Classes and after-school enrichment programs with Permission Slips.

Booths set up at:

Home and Garden Shows.

Mall Shows

Regional Fairs and Carnivals.

Internal Referral Events and Activities:

Birthday Parties (with permission slips and extensive follow-up)

Pizza Parties.

Obviously, this list is just a start. I haven't touched on media such as television, radio, newspaper. Cold direct mail from targeted lists to "marriage mail," such as Val-Pak or Money Mailer.

The question is, are you doing 10, 15, 20 or more things EVERY month to generate new students? If not, why not? Failures sit at their desk and bemoan their financial situation. Winners get out and hustle.

Continuous Follow-up. Most schools fail to follow up consistently and frequently enough with "leads" — with those individuals who have shown some interest: attended a birthday party or buddy day, registered at a fair or in a lead box, attended an introductory class that didn't enroll, etc. Just because someone doesn't enroll today does not mean that May or August isn't the right time for them. You must follow-up EXTENSIVELY. Certainly, one thing you should do is take the *Kickin' Newsletter* that we provide each month, personalize it a little for your school events, etc., and mail to all prospects and dropouts. This should be just one step each and every month. You should be following up with direct mail, email, telemarketing, text messaging, and broadcast voicemail. We'll teach you each piece and provide the various suppliers. See your member site at NAPMA.com.

High Value per Student. The schools that are doing the best financially look for high average student value. There are many ways to compute that. Two that I like and really pay attention to on a regular basis are these:

Total Active Student Count Divided into Total Revenue:

For example, if a school has 300 active and is grossing $45,000, that would mean that the average value would be $150. The top schools are now averaging $200-$300 average revenue per student. It's really tough to make a living with that average less than $150. You really should be targeting $200 or more.

Total Revenue Divided by Total New Enrollments.

For example, if a school averages $45,000 a month and averages 20 enrollments per month, then the average would be $2,250. This is an important number as well. Top schools can end up in the $5,000 and up range. It dramatically affects your ability to market your school effectively. For instance, if the average student in your school spends $5,000, then you would think nothing of spending $500 to $750 to get a new student. However, if they spend on average $500, then it's tough to spend much, if anything, to generate a new student.

You improve your average student value in a variety of ways. A strong "Upgrade" process into Black Belt Club and Leadership is imperative. Bigger down payments and bigger monthly payments make a difference. Fixing your dropout rate is imperative. The difference between 4% per month dropping out and 2% per month dropping out is huge. Literally it's the difference between needing 10 new students and 20 new students a month to stay even at 500 students.

High Personal Expectations. In part, the difference between the winners and losers is in personal expectations. Your results are to a great extent a self-fulfilling prophesy. You become what your expect to become. If you think that this business is "tough," then you make it that way. If you expect a six-figure or better income, then you rise to that occasion.

Constant Learning. To be a winner you must constantly invest in your own learning and growth. Failures are cheap about this. Winners invest more than anyone else thinks is reasonable on Mastermind events, seminars, books, CDs and DVDs, consultants, etc. Invest in yourself as your first priority.

The 1% or the 99%?

Yesterday I picked my Harley up from the local dealership. It's unfortunately been collecting dust sitting in my garage for most of the past 12 months. After a replaced tire, new brakes, a complete service and, installation of a "trickle charger" much needed I jumped on and was heading to Evergreen.

While sitting at a light I noticed a big oval sticker on a beat-up Suburu. It stated simply "99%." For the next few minutes it caught my attention and with the wind in my hair, well actually the wind on my full-face helmet, eye shield and sun glasses…. But anyway I thought about having that sticker on my car and the mindset that goes with it. Not, don't get offended…I know that many very good people are on salary, earn hourly wages, or pursue careers without really planning on great financial rewards. That certainly includes police, firefighters, school teachers and many others.

However, as I pondered it I was reminded of about 50 school owners that I've talked to in the past six months who have convinced themselves of their own PERMANENT and IRREVERSABLE failure. Many are a negative reflection of the old Henry Ford quote "Whether you think you can, or you think you can't, you're right."

Back to the 1%-99% debate.

Many of the school owner's who have mediocre results — not those who are abject failures — but, those who achieve far less than possible — I find almost universally they suffer from "limited expectations." Expectations of always being in the 99%, expectations of choosing a mediocre income or lifestyle by virtue of pursuing Martial Arts as a career or, in reflection to the incomes of their friends, family, or fellow school owner's.

What's the threshold to be in the 1% of income earners in the United States? Well, it fluctuates a little year to year but it's around $350,000 a year (or, around $30,000 in Net Personal Income per month.)

As an aside, I'll freely admit that I have a different perspective than most any school owner. Since I was 20 I've been fortunate to be surrounded almost exclusively with the top 1% of our industry. Early on my immediate peers didn't necessarily fit that category but, I was in close proximity to Jhoon Rhee, Jeff Smith, and Nick Cokinos. Then with school owners such as Bill Clark. By my early 20's my immediate peers, while usually school owner's financially behind where I was, were in the top 1%. Since I've made a conscious effort to surround myself with friends and peers who only fit in that category. I've also made a conscious effort to work with school owners to move them into the top 20% ($90,000 or $7,500 a month,) then the top 5% ($165,000 or $13,750 a month) then to the top 1% ($350,000 or $30,000 a month.)

What do you need to do to be a top 1% school owner?

Well, with a single school usually it looks something like this:

Monthly Breakdown:

Students:	300
Monthly Revenue Per Student:	$200
Gross: (300 X $200)	$60,000
Rent:	$5,000
Payroll:	$12,000
Marketing:	$9,000
Other:	$4,000
Net Income:	*$30,000*

You could get to $200 Average revenue per student with numbers such as:

Enrollment.

12 months. $279 to Enroll $179 Per month X 11

Renewal:

Black Belt Club:

$479 to Enroll, $279 Per Month X 36 or,

Leadership Program:

$679 to Enroll, $379 Per Month X 36

Average Monthly ATTRITION (Drop-Outs:) 3%

Average New Enrollments to Stay at 300 Active: 10

Now these numbers aren't written in stone. You could have 20 enrollments per month with 6% attrition to be at 300 active. The overall revenue per student will vary with a couple of things. A HUGE variable is your renewal conversion rate the higher — obviously the better.

Next, certainly Pre-Paid enrollments and renewals positively impact your overall gross revenue in reverse proportion to your attrition rate. The higher your dropout rate the more impact pre-paid tuitions have. The exception to that generalization is that fact that obviously a pre-paid program has an advantage of keeping students training at times. If they hit a "road-bump" in their finances. If the program is pre-paid they don't consider dropping out of lessons to make their budge work.

But, back to the overall conversation.

One reason that Americans really don't respond well to the "Tax the Rich" argument is that underneath it all we hope to end up in that category. In fact it's shown that at any time 50% or more of those who fit in that category are NEW to the top 1% moving from lower or MUCH lower income levels. There continues to be tremendous income mobility in the U.S. and in much of the developed world. The current "Buffet Rule" argument really isn't about "taxing the rich" at all. It's misleadingly about "capital gains" tax rates.

If you don't follow the current argument, it's about whether Capital Gains should be taxed as normal income. The reality is that it's about money that was taxed at the personal rate when earned (often a the highest possible rate) then SAVED. Saved either by putting it into savings, into real estate, or more often into private or public investments in companies. That can be through Bonds (loans) or Stocks (Equity.) Then once a gain (or, loss) is realized the gain on that money is then taxed. Historically taxed at a lower rate that "Earned Income" to encourage investment in companies or real estate. Those investments (savings) are necessary to keep the economy growing.

That's an aside from this conversation.

Question 1. How are your expectations about what's possible in the Martial Arts Industry? Is it possible to earn $30,000 or more net through running a single or multi-school martial arts school operation? Yes, absolutely. I've done it for close to 30 years. I've been surrounded by mentors, peers, and friends at that level for 33 years. If you don't believe it, you're missing the evidence and frankly hanging out with the wrong people.

Question 2. Do you REALLY want to be financially successful? Often this is an issue of can you achieve high levels without losing what you love about the art and without working 100 hours per week. It's certainly possible however, it's not possible without personal motivation and a strong work-ethic.

Question 3. Do you set yearly, quarterly, and monthly goals for yourself. Before you hit the next threshold do you set a new higher bar for yourself? If you currently make $5,000 a month personally $30,000 or $50,000 may seem completely out of reach and out of sight.

You always want to set goals that are "just out of reach but not out of sight." Just make sure you don't hit a point where you become "comfortable." Unfortunately, there's no such thing as a "Plateau." It goes back to Ray Kroc's favorite quote: "If you're green you're growing, as soon as you are ripe you start to rot."

Unfortunately I've seen many school owner's who's growth resembles a "Bell-Curve" they grow at a rapid pace. Exceed their personal expectations. Plateau for awhile, then fall apart. It's incredibly easy to "shoot yourself in the foot" by assuming that you've "made it" and not seeing the next peak to climb.

Let's make you VERY successful this year!

Consultation Certificate

This Certificate Entitles the Bearer to a Personal 1-on-1 Martial Arts School Business Analysis With a NAPMA-Certified Business Analyst. This Individual Consultation is Valued at $495.00.

Certificate expires 12 months from the date of purchase.

To schedule your personal business analysis, complete this form and fax to NAPMA at 1-800-795-0853; mail to 1767 Denver West Blvd., Suite A, Golden, CO 80401; or visit www.PrivateCoachingSession.com

PLEASE FILL OUT COMPLETELY AND WRITE LEGIBLY

Name _____

School Name _____

Address _____

City _____ State/Province _____

Zip _____ Country _____

Phone _____ Fax _____

E-Mail _____

_____
Authorized by Toby Milroy
Chief Operating Officer, NAPMA

3 FREE GIFTS FOR SERIOUS SCHOOL OWNERS

FREE Personal School Evaluation

Two 30-minute Sessions A sure-fire way action plan to double your results or better.

FREE Two 90-Minute Seminars

with "The Millionaire Maker Grandmaster Stephen Oliver "The 5 Stupid Mistakes All Too Many School Owners Make that Kill Their Growth" and "The Key Step-by-Step Blueprint for Being a Big Winner"

FREE CD-DVD Package and Report

"How Hundreds of Smart School Owners Like You Doubled Their Revenue in the Last 12 Months Even in the Midst of the Greatest Recession since the Great Depresson, and How You Can, Too!"

The Inner Circle and Peak Performers Invade West Point

I just came back from our incredible Peak Performers and Inner Circle meetings at West Point. Our setting was in the historic Thayer Hotel that sits on the grounds of the United States Military Academy at West Point. We were overlooking the majestic Hudson River. The University is actually located at the point on the Hudson that became a strategic choke-point against the British army during the revolutionary war, our meeting room overlooked that area of the Hudson made famous in part by Benedict Arnold — Hero turned Traitor at that spot in time and place.

Our meetings obviously were inspired not only by the excellence of that institution — but also by the excellence of our many Inner Circle members hitting new personal records (and, in many cases new Industry Records) and the Peak Performers hitting new records in the chase to move to the Inner Circle team ($500,000 and up single schools and Multi-Million Dollar Multi-School Chains.)

Clearly, the lessons of West Point include "Internal Locus of Control," taking 100% personal responsibility for your outcomes with no excuses allowed. One of the early lessons of a Cadet include is that are only three allowable responses to any question: "Yes Sir," "No Sir," "No Excuses, Sir," or, "I Don't Understand."

There's never an opportunity to blame your classmate or teacher for a failure to perform on your part. It's an important lesson that 99% of the world has never learned. The top 1% know that their outcomes are 100% their responsibility, no matter what roadblocks, challenges, or interferences lie in the way.

Another lesson in general terms is just the requirement for EXCELLENCE in everything. Raising your game in everything from timeliness to your personal appearance. On that note, I'd like to point out another recent observation about the world in general and our industry in specific.

Let's talk about this first as "Time Integrity." I've noticed that those struggling the most have the hardest time showing up on time to anything.

There may be notable exceptions visible in our culture. I'm told Bill Clinton, Sean Parker (Napster, Facebook) and Axel Rose were never on time to anything. But, generally, if you can't show up for appointments on time, whether with someone else or with yourself — it's hard to believe that you'll be on top of many other "details" either. In the context of business meetings, or new student introductory classes, being 5 minutes, 10 minutes or more late is a clear sign of disrespect for the other person's time.

For myself, I only do face-to-face meetings or telephone conversations by appointment. I don't use voicemail and don't play phone tag. I have someone else (or, from time to time fax, text or email) set up appointments for me for a fixed length of time. I expect to be prepared and expect the other person to be prepared. For phone appointments, if the other person is more than five minutes late I consider them a no-show and go on to something else.

In the context of "Coaching," our policy is that if you let us know 48 hours or more ahead of time that you're not going to be able to make it, then we'll reschedule. We don't reschedule if you're a no-show without notice.

This may seem to some like a trivial point, however, I guarantee the staff and cadets at West Point would disagree. At West Point, being on-time is always is a VERY Big Deal. Another key to this concept is what I'll call "Moral Authority." The underpinnings are simple, the results stark. We've all heard that children or students do not so much become what they are taught through words, but what they are taught through observation. The same is true of your staff.

If you expect them to start classes on-time and end them on time. To show up for private lessons. To be there for introductory classes and start them on-time. To not leave students standing at a locked door waiting for their perpetually late teacher. Then you accomplish that through first having the moral authority to hold them accountable.

What do I mean by that?

Well, if you schedule meetings with your staff, either one-on-one or as a group, and are perpetually late, then you look like (and are) a hypocrite when complaining about or punishing your staff for being late. No matter what you say or what rewards or punishments you hand out, they'll be no better than you are at any behavior. The boss can't be sloppy and expect and sharp staff. Unfortunately, the converse doesn't always work. You can model the best behavior, but that doesn't insure that your staff will rise to the occasion.

Continuous training, unexpected rewards, occasional punishments and better screening pre-employment are all necessary to have the correct behavior from your staff.

And, with younger staff, unfortunately they've rarely been exposed to a quality work environment, and therefore don't know really what should be expected of them. If anything they've been imbued with laziness and sloppiness. You have to spend extensive time training them to be excellent.

For my own operation for 25 years we had the "drink policy" for meetings.

If you were late for the start of the meeting — and, late included 30 seconds late — a list was waiting for you of what all the participants wanted to drink. Most recently it was the Starbucks list — really added up. Later, we added the Branch Manager and No-Show policy which was, Branch Managers when late, bought lunch. No-Shows, regardless of position, bought lunch (via payroll deduction). I always figured that if they couldn't be on time for a meeting with the boss, how could I possibly be comfortable that they would show up on time for classes or other appointments.

For myself, I was only late once in 25 years. Turned out to be for an Intramural Tournament with about 750 participants. Everything was running like clockwork without me — but, my policy, my responsibility. As owner/head honcho I could easily have ignored the policy or made an excuse. Instead, I spent $500-plus on Pizza Delivery for all staff and volunteers and made a BIG DEAL about falling subject to my own policy.

It bought credibility and compliance for years after that and ensured that no one was going to brand me a 'hypocrite' for exempting myself (something our politicians really should learn).

An article from the *Harvard Business Review* that I just sent to our Peak Performers and Inner Circle members are the "The Real Leadership Lessons of Steve Jobs." A somewhat hippie-ish college dropout and the graduates from West Point may seem at polar opposites — but, I bet there are more internal operational similarities than differences. In fact, the many stories about Apple could be of the Delta Force headquarters or other Top Level military operation. The vigorousness of controls and the excellence expected are no different.

The bullet points from the author are:
- Focus
- Simplify
- Take Responsibility End to End

- When Behind Leapfrog
- Put Product before Profits
- Don't be a slave to Focus Groups
- Bend Reality
- Impute
- Push for Perfection
- Tolerate only "A" Players
- Engage Face to Face
- Know Both the Big Picture and the Details
- Combine the Humanities and the Sciences
- Stay Hungry, Stay Foolish

From the book *Inside Apple*, there's discussion about how at Apple — unlike most big companies — for each task or project there's always a Person In Charge. Someone who ultimately bears the responsibility or the blame for each task and each project. Someone who for all the world to see is in charge of having the outcome tasked with no excuses.

Another article I read and shared with Peak Performers and Inner Circle discussed how Jobs, when CEO, would meet with each and every new Vice President. He'd tell them a story that was more or less this. He'd say that on the way from janitor to CEO there's a point where excuses don't count. Results are all that matter. If the janitor doesn't clean my office for a few days and is asked why, it's okay if he says the locks were changed and no one gave me the new key. Along the way there comes a time when excuses are irrelevant. Where reasons are irrelevant. Where results are all that matter. That point is at your position — at Vice President — you no longer have the option of having anyone care about the reason that our task didn't get accomplished. There's only results.

Sound's an awful lot like "Yes, Sir," "No, Sir", "No Excuses, Sir." Doesn't it?

I'd recommend a quick read — the new book by Colin Powell *It Worked for Me*. In it his checklist

for a new assistant sounds incredibly similar to the Steve Jobs discussion with new Vice Presidents of Apple. He also tells a humorous story about "time integrity" at the White House. About personally being locked out of a Cabinet Meeting when he, as Secretary of State, was running late after taking an emergency phone call. He talked with glee about Karl Rove being occasionally locked out of meetings — having not been present at the designated start time. Sounds a lot like my drink policy.

Something clear from our Inner Circle members (and, my Mile High Karate Franchisees) is that the top schools have now started to Master the Marketing Skills that I've been teaching. Many can open the flow of new students as easily as a water faucet — flooding themselves with new students if they wish, or slowing down the flow to work on sales and operational systems.

One idea is something I did very successfully many years ago was discussed at the AMS Convention as E-Cards (or Enrollment Cards). It's the concept of basically creating a "VIP" pass that can be sold by individuals and organizations. They keep the money, you get an intro. I've used this as what I call our "Children's Hospital" flyers (Tim Kovar used as their "Teen Center" fundraiser). It's a $49 or $29 certificate good for five weeks of lessons, a uniform, a semi-private class and a private personal evaluation with the instructor (or some similar bundle — free CD, DVD, Bag Gloves, Jump Rope, Tee-Shirt, whatever).

In 1999, I used the idea as a $9.97 donation to Chuck Norris's Kick Drugs out of America. With packages of passes bundled like raffle tickets (these can be printed incredibly inexpensively). AMS's version is a $10.70 certificate that students are allowed to sell as a summer job or as a fundraiser for their demo team or other internal group.

The concept WORKS fabulously. One of our Inner Circle Members sold 150 in January and had a 400% increase in one location just from that concept (along with me fixing his tuition structure).

Anyway. Coming up next is the Ultimate Martial Arts Marketing Boot Camp. Having an adequate number of new students is essential to your financial success. At each stage, figuring how to automate. How to move from labor to buying media. Moving from doing it yourself to getting your staff training and capable are all key issues. At the Ultimate Martial Arts Marketing Boot Camp we have ONE Key Objective.

To create the Marketing Plan that will add 100 Active Paying Enrolled Students to each school in September/October.

To have the marketing plan to not only make a huge jump for early fall, but to be able to do that over and over again.

It's a key element of our Peak Performers and Inner Circle Program. If you're a member of Inner Circle or Peak Performers you and your staff attend free. If you are not, you have one choice, which is to qualify for and become a member of Peak Performers now (www.PrivateCoachingSession.com)

Your other choice is to register for the boot camp alone. The registration is $4,997, although there are early registration and member discounts — learn more (www.MartialArtsBootcamp.com) The Boot Camp is a "Can't Miss Experience." I haven't done one for several years — this one will be a complete update with what's working RIGHT NOW.

Dress for Success...

I was on my way to the airport last Thursday. Somehow I had ended up with a "crack of dawn" flight from Denver to D.C. National Airport. I was headed to D.C. to fulfill a promised day of consulting with Carol Middleton at Krav Maga DC.

Anyway, it was an up at 4 a.m. and leave for the airport at 5 a.m. for a 7 a.m. flight type of day — keeping in mind that I'm REALLY not a morning person, and, frankly, had stayed up until 1 or 1:30 a.m. reading, so I was "on fumes."

Along I-70 in my 911 Turbo, I decided to check my rearview mirror, and, there with lights spinning, was one of "Denver's Finest" trying to get my attention.

Sure enough as I checked my speed — I was doing 20 mph-plus over the limit. It was 76 or 77 in a 55.

What happened next?

Well, before I go there, I was reminded of a conversation many years ago. I was on my way to an outdoor concert in Aspen with my friend Howie. We were in my new Mercedes 560 SEC, and somehow ended up in a discussion about cars, clothes, watches and other "social indicators." I was proud of my new car; he was moderately disinterested.

Howie was a good friend who just happened to also be a Kung Fu Master Instructor and student of Chinese Medicine, Lion Dances. He was a non-materialistic type of guy (at least where martial arts were concerned) who taught all of his Kung-Fu classes for free. He was totally not interested in any and all possible martial arts school sales and marketing advice that I might share. Which means at alternative turns he was a great one for me to hang out with recreationally while occasionally exasperating.

Anyway, I was explaining a study that I had seen that drivers of luxury cars were sort of a "dress-for-success" for surviving in traffic. The study said that Mercedes-Benz drivers received deference in traffic. That other drivers were less likely to honk at luxury vehicles. They're more likely to allow the drivers into traffic. And, generally, that luxury car drivers receive deference in many situations.

Howie, argued the opposite point. That either he didn't believe it to be true, or, that if true, shouldn't be true. Rather undiplomatically I argued that "should" doesn't have much to do with the real world. Ultimately, to prove my point, when we arrived I pulled up to the person directing traffic. There was a big sign saying "parking full, do not enter" who was directing all traffic in the opposite direction. I said something to the effect of "we're going up there" pointing past the sign. He quickly moved the sign and said, "yes, sir." While Howie was shaking his head, I pulled up to the front entrance and parked within 15 feet of the entrance rather than a mile a way.

Anyway, back to being pulled over in my Porsche.

The nice police officer knocked on my window and said something to the effect of "nice car, but can you please hold it down a little?" Then waved me on. Now, I have two cars that I drive semi-regularly in addition to my Harley (which I rarely ride.) I have the Volvo XC-90 "Soccer Mom Mobile" that holds five kids and two adults in a pinch and the Porsche 911 Turbo.

Those who know me are clear that I have rather a "Lead Foot." I can share a LONG list of stories about speeding past police officers in the Porsche, only to have them wave, and occasionally suggest with a smile that I should slow down. However, in the Volvo, any time I'm going even a little over the speed limit I get pulled over.

There's a similar story in Chuck Norris's bio. He talks about being broke and being ticketed repeatedly in his beat-up old Chevy. Then, years later, being stopped in his Mercedes and being waved on with only a "slow it down, OK, Chuck?" Sure, it helps to be famous, but, the story likely would be similar for most people.

Really, like it or not, "Social Indicators" are real. What you wear. What you drive. How you carry yourself all have an impact on how people react with you. In most cases you're treated better when you drive up in a Mercedes, wearing

Don't over-do this simple point. It's one thing to look successful and well groomed. Quite another to look like the newest RAP star. In our environment, as I stated in the last newsletter, conservative in appearance is always better (successful, but conservative.)

Anyway, I made my flight and had a great time in Washington, D.C. I spent Thursday night and Friday during the day with Carol and Al and with their staff. I'm sure that we covered enough ground to add $1,000,000 to their school if they implement aggressively. Just in the next 90 days they should do an extra $120,000 or more. Mostly we worked on moving the Krav School from a "fitness center" format to a real education environment. Sincerely, there's little difference in structure between Adult Men training in MMA, BJJ, Muay Thai, or Krav, and Adult Women in Cardio Kickboxing, and typical kid's programs in the macro structure and business opportunities.

Next, I spent some time at our Mile High Karate training center run by Chief Operations Officer Jeff Smith. He and I then attended a Jhoon Rhee Institute 50th Anniversary Celebration. It was a gathering of former World Champions, including Charlie Lee, John Chung, Helen Chung,

Jeff Smith and Gordon Franks, as well as former national champions, including Michael Coles and Larry Carnahan. I started with the Jhoon Rhee Institute 43 years ago.

Jeff was the most senior person in the room (other than Jhoon Rhee himself) who started training with "JRI" 47 years ago. The tables were ordered in a non-too-politically correct way. Old Farts in the front two rows — Charlie Lee and I who both began training in 1969 were in the second row, only preempted by the Rhee Family (none of whom were born when Charlie and I started lessons in 1969).

It was followed by the finals show for Dennis Brown's Capital Classics where Dennis recognized Jhoon Rhee and all of us there for the event. Dennis, as always, ran a fantastic event. I'm continually amazed at the increasing quality of competition. The 14- to 17-year-olds especially are "off the charts" in forms, musical forms, weapons and demonstration teams. I had a friendly argument with Joe Corley: he continually laments the "good old days" of fighting. I reminded him that "The Good Old Days, Never Were." Raymond Daniels and gang would run circles around Chuck Norris, Pat Burleson or Joe Lewis from the 1960's. Now, I'm sure those guys would have "risen to the occasion," but as in anything else the arts have moved forward at light speed.

Joe followed with his usual admonition that I should promote a national tournament again. I followed with my usual: "when hell freezes over." The NASKA Circuit continues to improve, an, the promoters really are unsung heros. They do a heroic job for trivial compensation.

Continue a fine martial arts tradition.… .

Let's see if you can guess?

Porsche 911, Red Mercedes SL, Gold Rolls Royce Corniche. What well-known martial artist drove (in that order) those three cars?

Do you know?

Well, for those "Anti-Materialistic" JKD Community Types — the answer is none other than Bruce Lee. Actually, I misstated a little. While in LA he purchased a Porsche. When he moved to Hong Kong he purchased a used Red Mercedes SL. And, when he signed the contract for "Enter the Dragon," he ordered both a Gold Rolls Royce that didn't get delivered until after his untimely death, and he sent a letter to Steve McQueen gloating that he was paid more for "Enter the Dragon" that McQueen's check for his latest movie. (McQueen responded by sending an autographed photo signed "to my biggest fan.")

There's a great story that I heard on YouTube with Pat Johnson, and I believe also read in the Steve McQueen Biography, of Bruce Lee considering buying a Porsche. One version of the story is that he asked McQueen about buying a Porsche like his, McQueen offered to take Bruce for a "test ride" through Mulholland Drive. Now, for a little back story if you don't know…Steve McQueen studied martial arts seriously with both Bruce Lee and then through referral from Bruce, with Chuck Norris when Bruce moved to Hong Kong. He also had in his background EXTENSIVE experience as a legitimate race car driver.

That having been said, apparently the test drive that McQueen gave Bruce mostly consisted of Bruce curled up in a ball under the dash of the passenger seat threatening to beat McQueen if he didn't stop. McQueen obviously did a full-out high-speed run in the Porsche that Bruce Lee apparently didn't appreciate, although he did turn around and buy a Porsche.

The next part of the story is, I've been delighted to have Jhoon Rhee hanging on for dear life many times screaming "You Drive Like Bruce Lee" in the mountains around Evergreen, Colorado, in my various 911's over the years. Apparently, Bruce had returned the favor from McQueen by terrorizing, among others, Jhoon Rhee, in his Porsche around LA.

Strangely, many martial artists are adamant about not being "Materialistic" and even STILL rail against "Commercialism." I used to have a collection of every *Black Belt Magazine* and *Karate Illustrated* along with some others from around 1960 to 1975. As I look through many of those old magazines it becomes pretty obvious. The martial artists who railed against "commercialism" mostly are names lost in the sands of time. The reviled martial artists gleefully expanding commercial schools or pursuing martial arts as a professional career are the LEGENDS of the industry now. Certainly names such as Chuck Norris, Bruce Lee, Jhoon Rhee, Ed Parker and others fit into that category.

I was recently talking with a Jeet Kune Do Instructor who's worked with me on building his business. He lamented how behind the JKD community seemed to be and even admitted to resisting running his school in a way to earn a substantial income. He was shocked as he read Jhoon Rhee's book *Bruce Lee and I*, which include a series of letters between Jhoon Rhee and Bruce Lee. The conversations often centered around how to get more students, what advertising Chuck Norris or other successful school owners were using, and other ways of marketing the martial arts business.

Clearly, Bruce Lee, that paragon of Martial Arts, (and, the person who still outsells anyone else on the cover of *Black Belt Magazine* 40 years after his death), was very interested in becoming a millionaire through martial arts. As an Instructor he was charging as much a $1,000 an hour (in the 1960's) for teaching privately in his back yard (or, on the set for McQueen and others.)

I've been proud to carry on Bruce Lee's tradition with now, my third 911, but much more importantly, as an avid proponent of spreading the message of martial arts throughout the world. If you focus on that old quote by Zig Ziglar, "You can have anything in life you want, if you help enough other people get what they want," you'll be both rich and wealthy. The satisfaction that I derive by the life-changing impact that we have for your students FAR outweighs any and all financial considerations — but, as the late Steve Covey was fond of saying, "No Margin, No Mission."

The money must follow from numbers of students and quality of service or it's impossible to continue spreading the art and positively impact our communities. You pursue increasingly higher levels of service to your students then expanding your student body — money follows it doesn't lead.

A quick side note, the "Martial Arts Millionaires" will next be gathering in Anaheim, CA, at Disney to learn HIGH LEVEL customer service and to share best practices with each other. If you are serious about growing your student body and your impact on the community then you must be there: www.PrivateCoachingSession.com.

Expect No Gratitude and You'll Never Be Disappointed

I got the latest *MA Success* in the mail today and enjoyed reading the cover story on a former employee of mine who's running a school that he bought from me. He was a student of Don Southerton, and then an employee of Don's. After Don moved to Denver to work with me, he followed and worked directly for me as an instructor, then eventually as a branch manager.

Anyway, back to the article. In the article there's a section entitled "Turn Recruitment Into a Science." In it it's made to sound as if he and his staff searched high and low for a marketing system that would work — trying fairs, carnivals and other things until he had a personal realization that working with local elementary schools was a great feeder program. In reality, when he moved to Denver, I had more introductory traffic than any school that I've seen before or since. I'd personally stepped in to run one of my branches and

relaunch an after-school enrichment program that I had first created back in the late 1980's as a hybrid of something that I had put together merged with an idea that we had put together.

Pretty much the first month that he had moved out to Denver I was literally "Drinking from a Firehose." It was in the first couple of months that I was hitting months where I was doing numbers like 36 enrollments in one day (on regular one-year contracts), and 76 enrollments in a month. That location had exploded from about 100 active to 350-plus in about 9 months. Frankly, I was exhausted, but clearly the new program and process had been proven to work.

In that article it describes his school as $1,500,000 per year, with 600 active and 21,000 square feet.

Let's do a little analysis on those numbers.

Let's say first that it translates into $120,000 gross per month with 600 active. If those numbers are accurate then it means an average of $200 per month per student. That's about right, as he's modeled the pricing structure that I set up many years ago and have continued to tweak. For our Inner Circle and Peak Performers we want a MINIMUM of $200 average revenue per student, per month. Frankly, I'd like to get most of them to $300 per month — I'm still working on that one.

The next part is the 21,000 square feet. Now, I'm not sure exactly what he's paying now for that space, which was formerly a "Sound Track" store. Rents in that area are running around $12-$14 per square foot. The real estate listing says that the NNN's run $4.17 per foot. So, to multiply it out, that's maybe $16 per square foot in rent, times 21,000 square feet. Therefore, around $335,000 per year, or $28,000 per month. Probably add to that $2,000-plus in utility bills and you have a fixed facility overhead of around $30,000 a month. That puts the rent at around 25% of gross.

That's about 10% higher than I'd like to see it — or, $12,000 more than I'd recommend.

Looking at facilities in a different way, Tim Kovar and I came up with a number years ago — actually I think Tim came up with the number, I'm not sure. Anyway, it's seven square feet per active student. With the above numbers that would translate into 4,200 square feet. At the same rental rates that ends up at $5,600 per month plus maybe $400 in utilities. Therefore, $6,000 rather than $30,000. Or, a $24,000 a month or $288,000 per year difference (all of which would go directly to net profit).

Now, my numbers may not be exactly right, but they are pretty close. Some may think that's too little square footage, but I think it's about right 4,500 to 5,000 would be about right. Many years ago one of my schools was about 2,500 square feet with around 600 active. That's definitely "too tight", but any time I've gone much over that seven square foot ratio, the net plummeted. Just remember: "Bigger ISN'T Always Better."

The Kovar's at one time had a 13,000-foot school in Sacramento. I recall Tim referring to their monthly marketing efforts as "Feeding the Beast."

Be careful what you wish for — you may get it!

As a final note. It's been a rough couple of months. Another close friend and Martial Artist passed recently. Terry Bryan, who's been a friend since the early 1980's when I helped him model what I'd accomplished in Denver in Colorado Springs, Colorado. He was a high-ranking leader among Traditional Okinawan Martial Arts, and recently had moved towards coaching and consulting on real estate investments. If you've attended any of our big live events, Terry was often featured as a speaker, and, in reality, was a HUGE support on the behind the scenes operations.

I attended Terry Bryan's funeral in San Antonio. I was happy to see also Shawn Harvey and Penny Pitassi along with many of Terry's former and current students there for the funeral. Terry, as you may know, had been fighting cancer for years. In the past 12 months he'd been fighting diligently a losing battle. He'll be remembered by many. We'll be happy to feature an "Attitude of Gratitude" article in *Mastering the Martial Arts Business* magazine this fall written by adopted student Penny Pitassi.

As a personal note, I used to be someone who avoided any and all funerals with the excuse that my friend/family member was gone. A book that I studied that had an impact was the leadership book by Rudy Guiliani. In it he had a chapter entitled: "Weddings Optional, Funerals Mandatory." That had a positive impact on my thinking, and I'd never trade the opportunity to have been there for Steve and Terry's friends and family in a time of their (and, my) grief.

A call out to you?

We are looking for additional subjects for our "Attitude of Gratitude" columns by students with a personal story to share. If you've experienced a mentorship relationship with one of the key leaders in the industry, living or passed, we'd welcome your contribution. See past features for format and tone.

To Close:

Humbly, I'd suggest that you review a couple of valuable books. One would be my *Everything I Wish I Knew When I Was 22* book, available free on your member website. The other would be the success classic: *Think and Grow Rich*.

"Adding 100 Students in 6 Weeks"?

That was the theme of the Ultimate Martial Arts Marketing Bootcamp just held in Golden, Colorado. Each participant certainly left with a marketing plan good for at least that many new students for Back-to-School.

The Question is not about the plan — I gave them the "Strategy," i.e., Big picture overview and the "Tactics" — specifically what to do first, second, third. There's no question that they all have a plan good for 100 or more new students QUICK. The BIG unanswered question is whether they will be timid, or whether they will EXECUTE. The Ultimate Secret to success is that you must have THREE components: An understanding of Strategy, a clear step-by-step plan (the Tactics), and must JUST GO DO IT. Many don't just "do it" because of a lack of training or the lack of a detailed plan. However, everyone at the Bootcamp left with both completely under control.

Some feedback from the event:

These are MUST attend events. I get to hit a "reset" button. This means: I get to see where I'm at objectively … away from the business, "see" my industry's potential both in service to the students and the bottom line, and get guidance to move in that direction. All this in a fun and exciting environment!!

For those NAPMA members that didn't attend the Marketing Boot Camp, you missed out on 5 things:

1) What marketing works in our industry (and the effectiveness we expect),

2) An AWESOME (overwhelming) explanation on Internet Marketing and the tools available,

3) A Marketing Plan (ACTION STEPS — no excuses) to do in the next 90 days for 100 students,

4) Networking (mastermind principle) with the top tier martial arts school owners (Top 5% — highest grossing), and

5) Learning from Master Oliver (the MASTER at marketing schools — consistently proving his methodology WORKS!). On a side note, we had a chance to meet with all the other school owners at Master Oliver's house.

For those driving your numbers to qualify for the Inner Circle, you missed a chance to problem solve any issues/ challenges and make them OPPORTUNITIES (some topics covered staff training/development, compensation, multiple location issues, software, billing companies, adult introductory…and MORE) with the top performers in the industry (mastermind principle). Then, Master Oliver would give his opinion and recommendation based on his experience. Additional BONUS! Master Milroy and Master Smith also included their wealth of knowledge the last day to make this a truly MEMORABLE EXPERIENCE! P.S. Master Smith's Saturday morning workout gave us a WEALTH of knowledge in the Colorado air!! Don't miss the next one… CUSTOMER SERVICE through the eyes of DISNEY!!

GEOFFREY A. CIELO, KING TIGER MARTIAL ARTS, INC., WWW.KINGTIGERMARTIALARTS. COMM VIRGINIA BEACH, VIRGINIA

I've come to several of Stephen Oliver's Marketing Bootcamps over the years and this one was as valuable as ever. Some people think these are all about how you can pocket tons more money from your school, and there's no question you can do so if that's your aim. But the reason I keep coming back is I always find ways to create more value for my students. I learn new ways to improve the quality of my curriculum and programs, which in turn improves my students' training experience and helps keep them more motivated and successful as martial artists. And when my students are more successful, my school is naturally more successful.

Stephen Oliver is arguably one of the two or three (or one?) most knowledgeable marketing experts in the martial arts industry, but of equal or greater value is meeting and learning from all the other school owners in the room who are also in the top 1-5% of the industry. And Toby Milroy, NAPMA's chief operating officer, brings a wealth of great marketing, internet development, and quality-improvement information to the table, too.

Time and money well spent for any school owner who doesn't mind working hard for the benefit of his or her students, but wants to know how to also work smart.

ERIC SBARGE, PEACEFUL DRAGON, WWW.THEPEACEFULDRAGON.COM

This was an awesome event. It was great to be in a room with the top school owners sharing ideas and expanding my perception of what my school's potential is. I left with a solid marketing plan for my 'Back to School Season', that I am confident will get me 100 new members. I also left with a bunch of new friends that are some of the most successful school owners in the country that I have heard about, but had not had the pleasure of meeting thus far. Thanks for putting together such an awesome event! Cant wait for the next one.

CHRIS BROUGH, ELITE MARTIAL ARTS ACADEMY

Hi! I am very thankful to be here. A lot of things I still knowing but to be surrounded by such highly successful school owners and coaches makes me creative. Made an 10 step implementation process which I will work on and I am sure that will change a lot and solve some problems I have. Master Smith has taken a big part of helping me this morning by taking time to talk to me in a kind of private training. Many many thanks Sir, learned a lot!!!

OLIVER DREXLER, WWW.DREXLER-MA.DE

There's more at:
www.martialartsbootcamp.com/feedback/
We recorded the event (other than, of course, the individual team workshops and "behind closed doors" Inner Circle Conversations. Call the office — talk to Bob Dunne: 1-727-540-0500 Ext. 202 to learn how to get the complete recordings.

The difference between sharing information with people and really seeing HUGE Success mostly comes down to two components. One-On-One Coaching to insure clarity on all the small details and to encourage implementation — and, a regular Class-Room Environment of Peers.

Both elements give "Social Proof" of the achievement of others in similar circumstances. Both elements also include mentorship to encourage action. The success of a martial arts school vs. receiving the "self-defense DVD of the month" comes down to those two elements.

The success of school owners in implementing information shared is the same. What we've done with our Peak Performers team and Inner Circle team is to full form the circumstances for huge success. No amount of dumping CDs and DVDs on someone's desk creates success without implementation.

By the way, during the Bootcamp we spent from 9 a.m. until about 6 p.m. on Thursday and 9 a.m. until about 4 p.m. on Friday working through a series of implementation strategies and tactics for generating a huge flow of new students. The tactics ranted from high-level internet "SEO" to simple grassroots marketing, such as "Bandit Signs" and "Rack Cards." I spent a bunch of time on Direct Mail and Internet. Jeff Smith spent time on simple grass roots marketing implementation. Toby Milroy hit the high level "nerd attack," and Automation ranging from Text Messaging to getting articles and blogs syndicated throughout the internet.

Then we split into small "teams" of 6 to 10 each — led by $1,000,000 school owners. Those teams each came up with their own "100 students in 6 weeks" marketing plans. They came up with budgets ranging from $2,000 to $15,000, and in each case, were instructed to have the "worst case scenario number" equal 100 new students (best case, obviously 150-200 or more).

One of the attendees, an Inner Circle Member (Dave Moss in Northern Virginia), enrolled 50 new students in the week following the Bootcamp — and hasn't implemented the "new marketing plan yet!"

Implementation comes with on-going support from a Mentor and a Peer Group.

Our next big event for Peak Performers and Inner Circle is coming up quickly at Disney Anaheim. We're both going to be exploring High Level Service at Disney and sharing implementation results in the 90 days since the Marketing Bootcamp. It's going to be an exciting event.

Actually, I left directly from the Bootcamp for a Sunday-Sunday marathon Disneyland trip with my 11-year-old daughter and 4-year-old son. I'll talk more about some of the Disney lessons useful for School Owner's next month — needless to say I'm continually amazed about how such a BIG organization can have so many of the details right.

Good Things Come to Those Who Wait — BUT, Only What's Left Behind By Those Who Hustle....

In the same vein I was frustrated in talking one-on-one with one of our Peak Performers. I'd laid out the strategy and tactics for scooping up a HUGE stack of cash and for boosting his monthly revenue by at least 50%, but, five months later he just hadn't IMPLEMENTED. He was lamenting his HUGE amount of debt ($20,000) and his cash-flow strain.

Although I was calm, in reality I wanted to reach through the phone and hit him upside the head. I get emotionally distraught when school owners I'm working with refuse to pick up $100,000 to $1,000,000 or more from failure to TAKE ACTION. Unfortunately I take it personally, makes me physically nauseous.

The Scenario:

He has a nice little school operating at around $20,000 a month. He's a VERY sharp guy who by now should be at $50,000-plus To convert over his school to the new "Upgrade" program I'd walked through implementing a new leadership program. The numbers:

Active Count —
    Eligible to be Upgraded: 135
Likely Number of "Upgrades" with a
Renewal Blitz:
    Low: 65 (50%)

High: 95 (75%)

The financial results would be:

15 Renewals Paid in Full at $7,000 = $105,000.00 CASH

50 Renewals at $100 Bump in Payment = $5,000 additional Payments.

Cash Left over after paying his "huge" personal debt: $85,000

Anyway, for six months now I've just been trying to get him to "LAUNCH." He continues to second guess everything. Another school owner I'm working with literally LEFT $1,000,000 on the table last year just by being "TIMID." Some justify timidity by being "analytic" or, "thinking through all of the steps" or, "waiting until the time is right."

Ultimately though — again it's.

1. Have the Strategy.

2. Know the Tactics.

3. IMPLEMENT.

I'm fond of quoting Patton — who famously said something to the effect of "A good plan violently implemented today is better than a perfect plan next week."

Even better is Arnold in one of his movies: "Do it Now, Think About it Later."

In many cases I'm convinced failure to implement is ultimately a "Self-Esteem" problem. Although in most cases if you told these school owner's that they suffer from low self-esteem they'd laugh and tell you about all of their accomplishments in Martial Arts. However, "Self-Esteem," or better a sense of "Self-Efficacy" is situational. You can personally be the best fighter in the World. You can have taught several "World Champions." And, still not have high esteem about your value as an educator. You can easily project to your students your own sense of your value based upon what you paid for lessons 10 or 20 years ago — or, based upon your "scientific" polling of the "competition" in your city.

I just had to shake my head and laugh when one of our more successful Inner Circle members relayed a story where my principle had finally sunk into him.

Basically, I've railed on everyone to value who they are and what they teach at a higher level. Frequently when it comes to private lessons I've pointed out what the value of YOUR Time has to be.

For instance: If you hope to run a $30,000 a month school, then every hour you personally invest has to be worth at least $187.50. That's $30,000 / 4 Weeks = $7,500 per week. Then $75,000 / 40 = $187.50 per hour.

If you hope to run a $60,000 a month school each hour must be worth $375.00. Anyway you get the idea.

Anyway, back to the story. I'd told everyone in the meeting that all the anti-materialistic stuff is humorous. That I'd come across the story of Bruce Lee teaching privates in his back yard (before he was rich or famous) at $1,000 an hour to the likes of Steve McQueen and James Coburn. My Inner Circle member relayed his story about how it had finally "sunk in" to him. He had been teaching regular privates to a student referred by Chuck Norris who was flying privately from Dallas to Houston to train. The student had mentioned how much it was costing for the plan to wait for him at the airport for the lesson. You might see already that the cost of the commute was probably at least $4,000. Our instructor who was himself running a business doing in excess of $1,500,000 was charging $100 an hour.

So for every private lesson — he was losing a huge amount of money given the value of his personal time. The student was spending at least 40 times that amount just commuting! If he was targeting a $2,000,000 a year business then that means his time must be worth $1,000 an hour. ($2,000,000 / 50 = $40,000. $40,000 / 40 = $1,000.) That's Bruce Lee's number from 1969.

By the way Inflation adjusted $1,000 in 1969 is $6,356 today.

See I shake my head in wonderment.

My parents were paying around $90 a month for me to train back in 1977. The basic tuition at the Jhoon Rhee Institute in 1981 started at $300 for three months. Inflation adjusted again the $90 a month is $348.98 today. The $300 is $748.49 today.

Why many in our industry got their pricing stuck in the 1970's or 1980's is a mystery to me. Probably it goes back to one of two things. It's either "self-esteem," just being afraid to charge what our programs really is worth, or, it's modeling the wrong businesses. Many either look to the big fitness chains to try and figure out what they should charge or they call around to the other schools in their area to be "in the middle" of the competition. The "in the middle" idea is really a mistake. If you're NOT the cheapest then the next position (and, better position) to stake out is be the best. Ultimately what your prospective students want anyway is the best instruction — that they can afford. They don't want cheapest.

Back to another conversation that made me want to smack him upside the head through the phone. A different coaching client many years ago. Said to me when asked about results: "Well, I'm frustrated that I seem to be stuck at $12,000 a month — but, I'm excited that I'm lining up a lot of personal training clients at $80 an hour."

My response?

Hey, pull out a calculator. Have it handy? Do me a favor. Take the $12,000 and divide by 4 weeks then divide by 40 hours a week. What do you come up with?

Obviously the calculation is $75.00. If you are trading your time on an hourly basis for $75 or $80 an hour then it's OBVIOUS why you're stuck.

Now, all this arguably works differently if you have no overhead. If you are running a school with a fixed monthly rent payment, utilities, phones, payroll, and marketing expenses. Then you've got to make sure the hourly rate that you would accept for your time factors in all of those items. It's also why I don't like the 50/50 split with another instructor teaching privates in your school.

Now if you were like Bruce Lee. Teaching in your back yard. Then the cost per hour that you charge could be a direct reflection of what you hoped to earn.

For instance, Bruce's $6,356 (in today's dollars) translates into about $12,000,000 a year (in today's dollars). If you go back to some of the goals statements that he made and his net-worth goals. That's not too far off. Obviously he didn't expect to be able to teach 40 hours per week of privates at that level, and chose to pursue movies as a more likely route to achieve his rather lofty goals.

The Golden Anniversary

The Jhoon Rhee Institute's fiftieth anniversary was recently celebrated in Washington, D.C. I was happy to attend as one of the most senior people there. My associate and instructor (in NAPMA and Mile High Karate) Grandmaster Jeff Smith was the most senior person there (celebrating 47 years-plus) — other than, of course Great Grandmaster Jhoon Rhee himself. Charlie Lee who like myself started with the Jhoon Rhee Institute in 1969 and received his Black Belt in 1978 commented that the room was filled with World Champions.

In opposite areas Jeff Smith was in his opinion (and, mine) the best Kickboxer who ever lived. John Chung was in his opinion (and, mine) the finest traditional Tae Kwon Do competitor who ever lived. Other Champions included Charlie (World & National Forms Champion), Gordon Franks (PKA World Champion), Helen Chung (Forms Champion), along with Larry Carnahan (Fighting Champion and now President of the NASKA Circuit and Michael Coles (PKA U.S. Kick-Boxing Champion).

The Jhoon Rhee Institute was the hub of MANY school operations innovations over the years led by Jhoon Rhee with Jeff Smith, including protective sparring gear (Saf-T-Gear), Musical Forms, Modernized (think kickboxing/MMA) curriculum going back to the 70's, and key innovations in teaching, marketing and high quality school operations. The list of leaders in the industry that came from that hub is endless certainly to include Nick Cokinos, Ned Muffley (EFC), Pat Worley, John Worley, Pat Burleson, Allen Steen, Jeff Smith, myself and MANY others.

Congratulations, Grandmaster Rhee, for your key role in professionalizing the Martial Arts in the 1960's until now, and for the 100's of 1,000's of students that you've impacted over 50 years. Thank you to Francis Pineda for organizing this surprise celebration and to Dennis Brown for hosting it at the 30 year anniversary of his Capital Classics.

Think and Grow Rich

If you haven't read the book *Think and Grow Rich* then you really must pick it up. If you read it years ago, now's the time to pick it back up and really study it. *Think and Grow Rich* teaches the KEY Principles necessary for Your continued growth and I'd like to chat with you about those principles.

I've chatted with a number of top 5% schools and top 10% over the last couple of weeks.

A couple of the one's who I've chatted with this week have said something to the effect of "show me how you can help me. I'm already doing $80,000 a month!?"

Really, it's a great and appropriate question. I was just discussing that with my VERY old friend (we've been friends for a long time now, and frankly, yes, he's older than dirt) Cmdr. Ned.

We were discussing my unique skill in the martial arts industry. My comment was that over the past few years that I've really become outstanding

at taking an $80,000 a month school and showing them how to get to $120,000 and, more importantly how to have it be and ADDITIONAL $35,000 a month pure NET Profit. There's really no one else around who knows how to do that.

He interrupted me and pointed out that in his opinion it was really my strength going back at least to the early 1980's….

I've never really been the ideal person to run a single school. For my own schools for 25 years I was either the "start-up" guy flooding a new school with 250 or 300 new students in the first four or five months, or the "turn-around" guy flooding a poorly-performing school with new students and fixing the underlying systems.

I was uniquely adept at marketing Martial Arts Schools all the way back to 1982 or 1983. Ultimately my combination of academic study, networking with the very top-level people, and practical "rubber meets the road" experience with lots of employees, big marketing budgets and experts of all strips leads me to where I've arrived.

Another old friend, Don Southerton, and I were talking yesterday. He was a founding member of the EFC Board of Directors and a very successful large chain school operator in the 1980's and 1990's. He's more recently moved into high level consulting (with CEO's of Fortune 100 companies in many cases) for companies ranging from Hyundai Motor Company and Kia Motors, number four ranked global carmaker and KIA to Golfsmith International, the world's largest specialty golf retailers, on their International Business Development. While in Denver he often "offices" at my home office — working my deck at 7,800 ft. elevation with a spectacular mountain view.

He had been listening into conversations that I was having with several MAUI members who are preparing to attend the Bootcamp, and, one who was "raking me over the coals" a little.

He pointed out that NOBODY in the Martial Arts Industry is creating the type of HIGH LEVEL developmental process that I've created with my Inner Circle and My Peak Performers.

He joined us during our meetings held on the U.S. Military Academy at West Point campus. He was taking notes and stunned by the quality of the content, but also, The QUALITY of the High Level School Owners in the Room.

Anyway…Back to "Think and Grow Rich."

If you haven't read the book…you really must put it on your list to study and review every 12 to 18 months.

It's basically a project instigated by Andrew Carnegie who opened the doors to all of the millionaires and billionaires of his day to the author, Napoleon Hill. Hill's mission was to talk with Thomas Edison, Rockefeller, Carnegie and others and hone in on the commonalities of success.

The result was ultimately this book which is the book MOST cited by millionaires, billionaires, and Fortune 500 CEO's as the inspiration to their success other than the Bible.

Anyway — touching on three of the Key Elements discussed in the book:

Specialized Knowledge

"Knowledge will not attract money, unless it is organized, and intelligently directed, through practical plans of action, to the definite end of accumulation of money."

Acquiring knowledge, either through the traditional route of formal schooling or from other informal means, is key to making it happen. The more you know, the more you will propel your idea but your education does need to align with your stated goals. After all, how else can you master your craft.

Organized Planning

The title of this chapter says it all. Hill's tips include surrounding oneself with a supportive mentors and people, performing your job to the fullest, stepping up to the plate, and practicing leadership.

Power of the Master Mind

Being able to exchange ideas with other productive individuals and feed off each other's energy is important to shaping or improving your plans. Cultivating a smart network of friends or associates is key.

My mission with the Inner Circle Team and the Peak Performers has been to accomplish each of those KEYS as pointed out by Napolean Hill.

The Key Elements Include:

1. A SERIOUS Master-Mind Team of "Heavy Hitters" who are top 1%

These schools range of formats including adult male focused MMA, BBJ, Muay Thai, Krav Maga — Kids focused Kenpo, Tae Kwon Do, and Kung Fu, Adult focused Kung Fu, and Tai Chi, and Kick-Boxing programs for women and, even Multi-Million dollar transported after-school programs.

These are $500,000 to $1,500,000 single schools and, Multi-Million Dollar Multi-School Owners.

2. Ongoing Coaching on an on-going basis.
No matter how much knowledge you have you've got to have a coach.

Look at ALL top performers, whether it's Tiger Woods or Michael Jordon in sports, or the very top Entrepreneurs and CEOs internationally. Everyone who is extremely successful hires a coach and works with a coach regularly.

You cannot underestimate the value of someone who is not emotionally invested in your day to day issues and problems, who can see your operation objectively on-tap to give you feedback on a regular basis.

My great strength as a coach is to point you in the right direction AND to see minor improvements that you can make that will result in huge increase to your net income.

3. Increasingly "Specialized Knowledge." We're providing an extremely valuable educational process through the avalanche of VERY HIGH LEVEL marketing, management, and student service training that you'll receive.

For a VERY High Performer some of the material will be "Reminding You" of material that you know but aren't implementing well, some will be a review, but MUCH will be completely new concepts for maximizing student quality, automating and accelerating your marketing results, and improving your employee training and development.

You won't show up and repeat the BASICS over and over again.

A clear point that at least 10 high-level school owners that I've talked to who have been involved with someone else's "Mentoring" program have said more or less the following:

> *"I felt comfortable with a wonderful family of school owners working together and, want to replace the missing environment with a team that I'll enjoy spending time with."*

What you will find with the Inner Circle or Peak Performer's in (excuse my language) a "No-Assholes" environment of friendly, smart, successful and goal oriented school owners (just like you?). It's an incredibly supportive team of great people.

> *"The problem was basically everyone training together — so that we always ended up going back to things like "Info-Call" and has a big school I needed more advanced content."*

We're organized in multiple "tiers" of participants.

Really no different that how you'd organize your school with Beginner's, Intermediate, Advanced, Black Belt, etc.

We have the Maximum Impact Level designed for school owners under $200,000 a year. The Peak Performers are school owners who are $200,000 to $500,000 more or less. And the Inner Circle, which is $500,000-plus single schools and Multi-Million Dollar Multi-School Owners. The next addition will be to separate "Inner Circle" single school owners and multi-school owners.

> *"I felt comfortable with the ideas, principles and overall focus — I'm concerned that I associate with high integrity — high quality martial artists."*

Some school owners misunderstand what I focus on in the program.

It's not a "get rich quick", "cash everyone out", "high sales pressure" environment.

Myself, Jeff Smith (former World Kickboxing Champion,) and the rest of my team focus on VERY HIGH QUALITY student service, on championship level martial arts curriculum and achievement and truly "mastering" the martial arts business in all elements. managing cashflows, along with incredibly effective marketing, and high-integrity leadership and persuasion.

The Gross is UP — the EXPENSES are WAY UP — HELP!

A big mistake that you can make is to get sucked into the "Bigger is Better" syndrome. The mission of your business really must be to make your like easier. It must create an income comparable or better (hopefully much better) than your alternatives. It ultimately must serve you — rather than you serving it. Now, don't mistake what I'm saying. Your BUSINESS MISSION should be to have a HUGE Impact on your community. To grow your students to their fullest. To really provide an invaluable service to your everyone you come in contact with.

However, as the business owner. Be careful

about creating a "JOB" for yourself. Realize that your business must be a "money machine" that's designed to "support your lifestyle."

How do your accomplish those things?

First: Run your school through SYSTEMS more so than PERSONALITY. Your school must have a "culture" that reflects who you are, but cannot be dependent upon you personally.

Second: Benchmark your expenses and keep everything in line. I've discussed many times what your rent, payroll, marketing and other key expenses should be relative to your gross. You have to be paying attention to those numbers EVERY Month.

Third: Hold each staff member accountable for measurable results. Know the numbers. Force them to know the numbers each and every week.

Fourth: "Take off the Training Wheels" — force your staff to rise to the occasion and be responsible.

*And, a final reminder...*OK, I know I've already been a little "long-winded" but, there's just so much going on.

1. You've got to "Know Your Numbers."
2. Ultimately your Business hinges only on these key variables:
3. Enrollments
4. Student Value (Revenue Per Student)
5. Student Retention
6. Fix one and your Gross goes up. Fix them all and the Sky's the limit.
7. Take Massive Action — NOW. Most school owners just "don't do enough stuff" when it comes to marketing.

Consultation Certificate

This Certificate Entitles the Bearer to a Personal 1-on-1 Martial Arts School Business Analysis With a NAPMA-Certified Business Analyst. This Individual Consultation is Valued at $495.00.

Certificate expires 12 months from the date of purchase.
To schedule your personal business analysis, complete this form and fax to NAPMA at
1-800-795-0853; mail to 1767 Denver West Blvd., Suite A, Golden, CO 80401;
or visit www.PrivateCoachingSession.com

PLEASE FILL OUT COMPLETELY AND WRITE LEGIBLY

Name _____

School Name _____

Address _____

City _____ State/Province _____

Zip _____ Country _____

Phone _____ Fax _____

E-Mail _____

_____
Authorized by Toby Milroy
Chief Operating Officer, NAPMA

3 FREE GIFTS FOR SERIOUS SCHOOL OWNERS

FREE Personal School Evaluation	FREE Two 90-Minute Seminars	FREE CD-DVD Package and Report
Two 30-minute Sessions A sure-fire way action plan to double your results or better.	with **"The Millionaire Maker Grandmaster Stephen Oliver** "The 5 Stupid Mistakes All Too Many School Owners Make that Kill Their Growth" and "The Key Step-by-Step Blueprint for Being a Big Winner"	**"How Hundreds of Smart School Owners Like You Doubled Their Revenue in the Last 12 Months** Even in the Midst of the Greatest Recession since the Great Depresson, and How You Can, Too!"

Avoid the Tupperware® Convention at All Costs, but Otherwise...

recently came back from a "vacation" with the kids in Disney in Anaheim. The only thing that Disney didn't stage manage at the highest level was the full hot-tube — five Tupperware® women in a hot tub designed for 15. Yeah, there was a Tupperware convention at the Disneyland Hotel, and I'm guessing their target "REP" demographic is mostly low-income women 30-50 years old who are 100 pounds overweight. The elevator conversations were entertaining to say the least. Or, at least that describes a BUNCH of them wondering around and cluttering the pool, complete with about 100 Tupperware ribbons. If I owned Tupperware stock, (I don't) I'd be selling. Anyway, I'm writing this as I prepare to take the flight back to John Wayne Airport and facilitate our Inner Circle and Peak Performers meetings.

We'll be in Anaheim, California, at Disney. The Inner Circle are going to "Disney University." Officially, it's now Disney Institute, but they'll be learning from their trainers all about the Disney approach to staff recruitment, training and support, as well as the Disney approach to customer service. We'll be focusing as a team on dramatically improving student retention and how to finish the year with a MASSIVE renewal blitz to wrap-up commitment to the highest-level training for their students.

Anyway, back to my trip to Disney.

I'm amazed that there's always something to learn. An infinite number of details that they pay close attention to at every turn. And incredible levels of customer service at every turn.

Some people focus on all of the "little details." The hidden Mickey's. All of the little details attended to in construction, look and feel, and structure of the properties.

I am more likely to notice whether the staff maintains the "illusion and magic" or whether they drop the ball. With 30 years of up to 50 employees in my own operation, it's a particular point of focus for me. I'm continually amazed at the combination of culture, screening and training that supports consistently friendly and capable customer service at just about every turn. They work hard to have "the boy or girl next door" who have a smile on their face and consider the experience of the "guest" as highest priority.

Just one simple example: During seven days on Disney Property there was a time or two that my 4-year-old had a bit of a "fit." Both times while on Disney property a "cast member" quickly approached him and worked to cheer him up. Often with stickers, buttons or other trinkets in hand as well.

I had a similar situation at the airport on the way home. The Frontier Airlines customer service representative basically asked if my son had emotional problems and threatened not to let him on the plane. Contrasted with Disney it was a stark and damning difference. Frontier was, for a while, a favorite of mine. They and Southwest had a real customer service focus. Since they were bought out, I've noticed a STEEP decline in the attitude of their people. Southwest is great. Frontier has sadly gone from good to mediocre.

Anyway, one instance on the property was actually in the parking lot behind the hotel. The cast member who worked hard to cheer him up was a gardener. He pulled over his vehicle and told Chase jokes and spent a huge amount of time working to cheer him up. In many organizations, he would probably be in trouble for running late to wherever he was supposed to be headed. There, a gardener knows that cheering up a 4-year-old guest in the parking lot is highest priority. His attitude would have been impressive for a front-line customer service person, but the gardener? We had an equally good experience with a valet attendant at the California Hotel.

Disney knows that anyone who interacts with a "guest" must know their priorities.

Compare that to the "Customer Service" representative with Frontier who insulted me, my 11-year-old and my 4-year-old. Who did nothing to help. Who did a lot to make things worse. Will I fly Frontier again. Probably. Will I be eager to make them first priority if possible? No. They've now sunk to United and Delta levels in my estimation. On both, I was recently in first class and was wondering whether the attendant even knew the passengers were present.

Another instance on property…Chase took off at full-speed. By the time I rounded the corner behind him about 10,000 people in Cars Land were in front of me and he was nowhere to be found. I grabbed a random cast member, who immediately knew his script and process. He calmly asked for a description. Asked me to stay exactly where I was so they could relocate me. Walked across to make a quick call. Within about 45 seconds he was back and walked me to where my son had ended up in the front of a two-hour line for the Cars ride.

Chase had a big smile on his face, a new button and sticker on his shirt, and a happy cast member escorting him back to Daddy while having an animated conversation about Chase's favorite characters from Cars.

On the walk back, the cast member reassured me that it's a common occurrence and noted that Chase obviously really wanted to go on that ride. Rather than a scolding, we received a cheerful

behind-the-scenes description of the ride on the way back to where we started. He then asked how many of us were in our party and then gave me passes to "skip the line" for the ride.

This, by the way, was an early-20's "kid" who was probably new, working there and on to something bigger and better soon.

I could go on and on with stories like that with Disney. It is amazing with the number of staff on their properties and the relatively high turnover of unionized hourly employees that they can consistently instill such high levels of customer service. I've been through the "casting center," and the orientation program at "Disney University." Both are impressive. The primary credit goes to the constant reinforcement of the "service and entertainment" culture of Disney.

Another interesting experience is not actually a part of the Disney organization that I'm aware of, but was an extremely interesting business in "Downtown Disney."

The business: "RideMakerZ." You can check out their website at www.ridemakerz.com. I've been to their locations at Disney World and Disneyland. They're apparently also in Branson, Missouri, and Myrtle Beach, Georgia.

I'm always fascinated with business where there is a "clear comparable," who none the less manage to charge double, triple or quadruple. These guys sell radio-controlled model cars, but in reality. they sell an incredible experience that happens to end up with you being proud owner of a customized radio control toy car.

As an aside, you should note that "toy" retailers have been nearly wiped out by Wal-Mart. Toys-R-Us and similar stores have struggled in the face of low-price competition. I know that just on the west side of Denver several big stores closed in the past couple of years. In the case of RideMakerZ, I was fascinated as I happily dropped $255 on two toy cars (my 11-year-old daughter was at least as enthusiastic as my 4-year-old son). I did my usual "Business Nerd" research by walking about 50 feet across the walkway to the Disney Store.

My kids ended up with between $115 and $135 each for radio-controlled "Character" cars with custom stuff like a special bumper, custom wheels and a "blower" in the front hood (of, "Porsche"?).

Anyway, my quick comparison…

RideMakerZ:

$100-plus-plus

Across the walk-way, Disney Store at Downtown Disney

Lighting McQueen

Radio-Controlled Car with Custom "Glitter" Paint: $69.50

At Wal-Mart:

Lighting McQueen Radio-Controlled Car: $43.66

At the RideMakerZ store you can pick up the Lighting McQueen Body. Then you choose standard or custom wheels. Choose standard or custom tires. Additional accessories such as bumpers, police lights, stickers, etc. Then, you take your wheels and tires to a special "assembly garage" in the middle of the store and a mechanic assembles your car with your help. Asking along the way if you want the upgraded rechargeable battery, the radio controlled chassis, etc.

By the time you're done — even the most conservative of consumer ends up paying at least double the Wal-Mart price. Most likely, triple. Even more telling, paying close to double what a very nice version of the same thing is available for 50 feet away.

Now, before you do some "knee jerk" reaction about it being a rip-off, or about them only "tricking stupid people," keep in mind it's about the experience. They orchestrate everything from the layout of the store to the "assembly garage staff" to make it a cool experience. The "Actual Market Value" of the toy? Well, the lowest price, at

$43.66, is a reasonable starting point. How much more is the "customization" worth? Obviously something. The rest? It's about the experience as much as the actual product.

I'd suggest that you always look for remarkable businesses.

Look for those who are thriving by "bucking" the low price, commodity trends. And, figure out what elements you can borrow to make your school truly memorable and exciting.

Your assignment? Take time to visit if at all possible each of the following businesses:

1. The American Girl Store (http://www.americangirl.com)
2. Build-A-Bear (http://www.buildabear.com)
3. RideMakerZ (http://ridemakerz.com)

All thrive by charging double or triple what comparable would cost at Wal-Mart or Target. Of the three, I believe that American Girl does big numbers as a catalogue/internet business as well. I don't really know, but I doubt if the others do much retail outside of their physical stores. In all cases, it's about the "Experience." Of the three I'd say American Girl does the best in making their customers part of the club. There are American Girl movies, the *American Girl Magazine*, and of course, an incredible experience in the store.

What's the lesson?

Each of these businesses thrive, in great part because it's about the "EXPERIENCE," not the actual product. Notice at many places now "Mini-Build-A-Bear" knock-offs. They mimic the components and have a similar or comparable product at 30–50% less. But not the experience, therefore, are largely ignored.

You should always "Take Note" of any and all experiences you have with businesses.

Does your dentist office stand out as a delightful experience or is it drab and bland. How's service at the restaurants and dry cleaners that you patronize. Look at the difference between "Starbucks" and

"Burger King." Who does a better job? How does their pricing and results reflect that service focus. To take Starbucks again. I heard the founder say in an interview that their pricing was a function of their employee pay and benefits. An interesting perspective, but, certainly, the experience is more about the staff than the actual product.

Take a look at McDonald's. Everyone was worried about "competition" in lattes and mochas from McDonald's. It hasn't made even a small impact on Starbucks. McDonald's is hitting record numbers, but, no one who likes Starbucks because of the ambiance, the quality of the staff, and the overall experience is going to shift to McDonald's to same a couple of dollars. Again, they manage to charge 50% more or double because of the experience, not because of the actual deliverable.

On the same note, having been in and out of hundreds of elementary schools over the years it's always the first thing I notice. Does the staff follow the rules or focus on service? How well do they interact with the kids? Is there artwork from the kids on the walls? Are the teachers engaged? Do they know the kids' and parents' names? The difference between good ones and bad ones is stark. It's in the culture of the organization. It's in the culture of the staff.

By the way, you MUST SEE *Won't Back Down*, based on the true story of a "Parent Take-Over" of a failing school in Pittsburg. Note especially the built-in attitudes and "cultural problems" that represent the failing school.

On a Sadder Note:

I recently returned also from Raleigh, North Carolina. Raleigh's a beautiful city; I hadn't been there in probably 20 years. The occasion was Grandmaster Joe Lewis' funeral and memorial events. Jeff Smith and I were there and attended several events organized by the Joe Lewis Fighting Systems team, including a work-out at a local school/gym along with a dinner banquet that eve-

ning. At the funeral I was happy to catch up with many old friends — too many to list, but I spent much of my time with Jeff Smith, Walter Anderson, Bill and Jane Wallace, Helen Chung, Steve Anderson and Bill Clark. I enjoyed catching up, however briefly, with Pat Burleson, Skipper Mullins, John, Jim, and Mark Graden, Rob Colasanti, Dave Kovar, Tom Callos, Mitch Barbrow, John Corcoran, Steve MaGill and many others.

I was particularly impressed with Mike Allen, Dennis Nackford, Walter Anderson and Walter Lysak, who between them, did a fabulous job of organizing the memorial to this great fighter, friend and teacher to each. I'd be remiss if I didn't mention Bill Wallace and Jeff Smith, who were at Joe's side for the last week of his life and who made frequent trips to Philadelphia to visit and entertain him. And, Chuck Norris, who organized the "Texas Contingent" and filled a plane with old friends to visit Joe at the VA hospital over the summer.

I know through Jeff Smith that the hundreds of cards and photos that he received from friends and fans from throughout the world during his last few months were very appreciated and helped lift his spirits. I'm told the cookies that I sent were enjoyed by the nursing staff.

When I was new in martial arts training (late 60s and early 1970s), I idolized Jeff Smith, Bill Wallace, Bruce Lee and Joe Lewis, along with Chuck Norris, Pat Worley and Skipper Mullins. Joe came to martial arts as an athlete and bodybuilder; that alone set him apart from most. He was a dominant force in the old "blood & guts" point fighting scene of the 1960s, and then an early pioneer in Kickboxing. I don't believe the impact of Joe, along with Bruce Lee, Jeff Smith and Jhoon Rhee can be overstated in the evolution of sport martial arts, whether it's Point Fighting, Kickboxing or Full-Contact Karate. He made a valiant effort to transition that into an acting career which started strong, then sputtered and died.

He was one of the few to turn from being a great fighter to an excellent mentor, coach and thinker about achieving the highest levels of fighting skills. He leaves behind many students who hope to carry on his teaching and principles through the JLFS (Joe Lewis Fighting System). They have my full support, and NAPMA will certainly do anything we can do to help them expand their ranks and keep Joe's principles alive. I know that Jeff Smith and Bill Wallace are happy to help them along the way as well.

Although I started my training in 1969 with a branch of the Jhoon Rhee Institute in Tulsa, Oklahoma, I spent a couple of years training with Roger Greene, who was Joe's first Black Belt and at the time, a part of the Tracy's system. Through Roger I first met Joe in 1976 while attending a small seminar/class held at Roger's school in Tulsa.

I'd first seen Joe fight live in July 1974, during the Top Ten Nationals Professional Karate tournament in St. Louis, Missouri. He lost to Everett "Monster Man" Eddy, 6-4. It was the same night when Jeff Smith lost to Jim Butin.

It was shortly thereafter that I eagerly watched the televised PKA World Championships where three of four of the American fighters won; that of course, was Bill Wallace, Jeff Smith and Joe Lewis. Of the many fighters, the two who were obviously well trained for kickboxing, and in fabulous shape were Jeff Smith and Joe Lewis. Lewis "manhandled" his competitors and won easily.

There can be many arguments in retrospect about who was the best point fighter in the 1960's, 1970's, and who was the best Kickboxer, etc. Regardless of the conclusions in each area, Joe Lewis, Bill Wallace and Jeff Smith have stood the test of time and have gone on to share their knowledge with thousands of students and instructors throughout the world.

Joe will be missed and his influence will be felt for many years to come. Rest in Peace, to a great Champion and Teacher.

In Joe's own words:

60-years from now, when people mention the name Joe Lewis, how would you want to be remembered?

Joe Lewis — I have seriously never given this question any thought. To dignify my efforts and to be able to have been known to live with dignity would be my greatest attribute. I feel that few of us martial artists have ever accomplished that. I have never stated in public that I have beaten anyone by name. I have never misrepresented my real rank nor have I ever claimed to win a title that I had not. Although I failed my first green belt test in Okinawa, a year later, when I was handed a second-degree black belt certificate, I refused to accept it. I am the only martial artist in North America that I know of who has not only trained in every country from Korea southward all the way to Australia, but I am perhaps the only one who received the last rites from the same master priest in Tokyo who administered the last rites to the Kamikaze pilots during World War II. I have tried to make the standard and the status for that which a Black Belt stands to always represent a very noble and worthy accomplishment. I wish others would respect and follow this same rule. I do not expect more than a handful of martial artists to ever be able to duplicate my examples. However, I trust that some will be able to live in the light of dignity, which I have described above.

As a quick side note, genius comes in many forms.

Living in the top 1% or top .00001% of any endeavor is rarely easy. Incredible accomplishment from afar may look natural, but when living it, has many ups and downs, frustration and elation, and often, loneliness, that comes from standing far apart from the masses.

As you study any one truly iconic, whether it's Walt Disney, Steve Jobs, or Joe Lewis, you'll find excellence demands sacrifice. Incredible focus in a single area (or, small range of areas), often demands that many other areas of life suffer. Joe, frankly, had many ups and downs personally and professionally. Some who loved and revered him at times had a hard time liking him. In the end, Walt Lysak made the point at the funeral that Joe, like the few who achieve his status, really didn't internalize or understand how loved and respected he was by thousands.

"It's Lonely at the Top" holds true for those to pursue excellence doggedly. I increasingly understand and try to recognize that reality with anyone who's made a contribution to my life as a martial artist or as a professional. It's a useful lesson for us all. That teacher or mentor who showed human imperfection should be reminded, none-the-less the positive impact they've had. Of the incredible contribution they've made, for they themselves will usually not recognize that reality.

For many martial artists bridges were unnecessarily burned or feelings were hurt in the past. For those who push us to excellence beyond our comfort zone, it's the norm. Work hard to mend those fences and rebuild those relationships. At the very least, have broad shoulders. In reading about Apple and Microsoft in the last couple of decades, or Disney and others in the past, it was often a badge of pride to have "received flame mail" from Bill Gates, or to be called a moron by Steve Jobs. Striving for excellence is messy. Don't take it personally

Sure Ways to "Shoot Yourself in the Foot and Derail your Progress"

Or, Don't Let Your Own Ego Sabotage Your Development

Now, let me take an aside and explain one frustrating phenomenon with any coaching or mastermind program. I've discussed it before, and, a few years ago, was so frustrated that I sat down and wrote a multipage letter with a pretty emotional rant about this that I sent to all of my coaching members at the time. However, the problem persists, and maybe you can separate it into three or four components that includes these elements:

1. Too low expectations. Many people seem to come into something like this with expectations that are too low. In fact, human nature is such that you cannot see the next summit until you've climbed the current one. What I've seen MANY times is that I've worked with a school to go from something like $17,000 gross to $42,000 gross in a short period of time — only to have it BACKFIRE.

Now, what I mean, is when someone goes from, let's say, $4,500 a month in personal income to $12,000 in personal income, is that often their vision of self-worth, lifestyle potential, business and personal opportunities don't keep pace. Many have hit this new level (several were only at $20,000 gross; most were somewhere between $30,000 and $60,000 — double or triple where they started), and suddenly think that's all there is to accomplish. Sometimes, they now think they know "all of the secrets." Other times they think they've maxed out their potential. Others think they have enough ideas for the next four or five years, so why keep learning.

Unfortunately, there's no such thing as a plateau. To quote Ray Kroc of McDonald's, who grew them from one location to close to 9,000 locations before his death in 1984 — who as I recall took this quote from one of our previous presidents (I forget which one):

> *As long as you're green, you're growing.*
> *As soon as you're ripe, you start to rot.*
> RAY KROC

I've seen many who have made HUGE gains pull out — only to CRASH after leaving. The momentum was not about a few ideas but about on-going support. Frankly, in martial arts, it's no different. As you move to higher levels you continue to need a teacher/coach; your skills degrade if you shift to being "self-taught" at any stage. Look no further than Arnold Palmer and Tiger Woods, who constantly look for new coaches to get back in the game.

I URGE YOU to ALWAYS set new goals for yourself that are "out of reach" but not "out of sight."

Suggestions:

A. Improve your Life-Style. Build stable income from your school and then go buy a Rolex, get the Porsche or Mercedes that you've always wanted. Find and set a goal for your dream house. Get over whatever issues that you may have about living too well or about buying expensive things. Ultimately, everything counts. The Rolex Submariner on your wrist is a nice "social indicator" for the higher end clientele that you are hoping to attract. One coaching client that I had REALLY TOOK OFF after getting rid of the house he'd been living in "next to a crack house" and moved into a 5,000-plus square foot home with separate office, five-car garage, and pool. At some level this is about new higher goals, and, at a different level, it's about expanding your sense of "self-worth" and growing into your career.

B. Set Strong "VISUAL" goals about how you want your business to operate and what you hope for it to look like. Really move your expectations up and build the model, or have the blueprint for what you want your school to be like.

C. Build your Net Worth. The real estate and the stock markets have been scary in the past couple of years. However, the long-term path to wealth is either in investing in your own building. Owning your own home, building your investments in rental properties or in the stock market. Frankly, now's the time to buy. It's a great time to build CASH FLOW and invest it towards your future wealth goals.

We'll certainly have several Inner Circle Members — perhaps many — trending towards $500,000 or more in personal income. Don't be satisfied with significant growth in your gross — let's have massive improvements in your personal income and life-style this year.

D. "Too Smart for the Room." Some conclude they are smarter or doing better than most of the others, so why continue to participate (I learned the error of that thinking by watching Ron Le-Grand take ideas from me and a bunch of others doing 10% of what he was. He took ideas that might be worth $100,000 to me — when I shared with him — and he added $1,000,000 or more. Even after flying in on his G5, he was looking for ways to add 1%, 10% or more). Frankly, bigger operations have MUCH HIGHER LEVERAGE from smaller improvements. In the past I benefited more from adding 5% to a $2,000,000 operation than friends did who were running $30,000 or $40,000 a month schools.

I personally experienced this for many years with EFC. I was by far the largest school for many years among the EFC Board of Directors. However, each time I attended I learned something that I would implement and became reenergized, along the way others grew (perhaps, in part from my ideas or example) such as Keith Hafner, Buzz Durkin, Tim and Dave Kovar and others. As others grew their business, it spurred me to stay ahead or keep up, and everyone brought good ideas to the table.

E. The "Consultant Syndrome." A bunch of the folks running around the industry now trying to be a Marketing Consultant came from my Coaching groups (or Franchise). Many fit the syndrome above. One went from $7,000 to $20,000, another from $5,000 to $15,000, another from $12,000 to $35,000; then decided they were the "Guru" of Internet Marketing, Direct Response Marketing, Sales, or some other business function. Some think that since I "charge so much" that they can do the same thing at one-half or a one-quarter of my price and be happy. One was struggling to cover his lifestyle costs of $2,500 a month and decided to steal from me — ideas, customers and content and become a direct marketing consultant. Others just good-naturedly stumble into helping others and decide to be a competitor.

Now, let me tell you a couple of things. First, Y.K. Kim and I discussed this openly at a recent seminar: If I had the "disposition for it," I'd make A LOT more money running one big school or 3 or 5 that I own outright than I've made from all of the coaching and consulting I've done. I do this as the next step of "personal actualization," and, frankly just because the actual day-to-day of school operations, and the people management that goes with it, I find annoying at this point. I was making a strong six-figure income running schools by the time I was 24, and every year since until I decided to morph them into franchises. My teacher/friend Jeff Smith is marvelous at supporting school owners, but also loves the day-to-day of a school and school operations. He operates out of our training center in Virginia. I operate out of my 2,000-sq. ft. home office or Starbucks. Different personalities and different strengths.

The only schools that I have personally owned in the past couple of years were franchisees that failed and I needed to transition the school to a new owner, or gradually close or merge it with a new location (that describes many international franchisors, by the way. Quizno's, as one example, "inherited" a huge number of corporate locations that they are trying to fix and resell. McDonald's flips locations fairly regularly, and on and on). The last time I was paying attention to one of these locations it was netting $120,000 more or less a year with approximately an hour of my time — quarterly.

We do have to recognize and address this issue directly. We are happy to consider a couple of things. First, joint venturing on projects that will truly be "world class." Second, approving and supporting ventures that are non-competitive.

We do frown on and will have a policy of not having members in Peak Performers or Inner Circle who are directly competing with us or using access to our members to replicate our service. Our "Basic" program, i.e., "Maximum Impact," is open to anyone, and we've rarely (if ever) screened who are members as are some of the most successful consultants in the industry, and, frankly, that's unsurprising — I always bought everyone's stuff looking for any "slight edge."

F. *"It's Never a Straight Line" Syndrome.* I discussed in my book *Everything I Wish I Knew When I Was 22* that business success is rarely a straight line to the target. Most successful businesses have had years "in the red." I've personally experienced two major "crashes" in 29 years. I think about it like a boxing match or kickboxing match. If I've won 24 or 25 of 29 rounds I've done pretty good.

Most of those were 10-8 or knock-outs. Look at Donald Trump and Steve Jobs. Jobs was fired from his own company — during which time Microsoft came to dominate his industry — until returning to Apple and again surpassing every other tech company. With Trump I like the Marla quote (remember wife number two?). She said that she and "The Donald" were walking down the sidewalk when he said "Marla, see that bum on the grate, he's worth $280,000,000 more than I am."

I've seen some of our top people suffer some during the "worst recession since the great depression." Now, if we've been working closely together for even a couple of years, the unasked question could be, where would you be otherwise? We're all going to have times that we took the eye off the ball, times when we made some bad choices, and other times when circumstances got the better of us for a time. Staff problems, divorces, illnesses, and recession can knock you off your fast growth trajectory. I've experienced everything under the sun other than personal illness (I've always been pretty healthy). Otherwise, there's no scenario from divorce to staff dating underage students, to every possible staff problem (by the way, the letter I talked about earlier is on the hard-drive of the Mac laptop my former assistant/secretary stole while "disappearing" from the job, never to be heard from again).

The big issue is to make QUICK course corrections and get back on top. Unfortunately, most people hit their first major roadblock and then give up. In my case, being able to lean on a coach and peers who had "been there done that" always got me going again. Whether it was Jeff Smith, Keith Hafner or the "Platinum Group," having someone else who has been there and came roaring back is helpful.

I had that conversation with Dave Kovar a couple of years ago — walking him in confidentially to my conference room with the admonition: "It's never as bad as you think it is." Stay positive and get moving and things will get better and you'll hit new heights.

> *I don't measure a man's success by how high he climbs, but how high he bounces when he hits bottom.*
> GEORGE S. PATTON

An interesting story, by the way. When I first talked about working directly with Chuck Norris on the "Good Housekeeping Seal for Martial Arts Schools," it was an idea to solve his financial crisis. He had $60,000.00 a MONTH in alimony, and no movie prospects on the table. He was scrambling to figure out how to prevent AN-OTHER major financial crisis (remember, he got into acting after going bankrupt with his chain of martial arts schools). Unfortunately for me, he signed the contract for *Walker Texas Ranger* the weekend I was visiting at his ranch. Seemed like things were going to be fine until the production company went out of business (Canon Films) during the first season (and the CEO went to prison, as I recall).

G. *"On to the Next Guru."* It's again natural for people to look for the next guru, however, it's typically pretty unproductive. I've seen some "jumping from lily pad to lily pad," each time disrupting their operation and getting off track. Within our industry it leads to the hodge-podge of unrelated systems that may create revenue but becomes a HUGE headache and cuts deeply into the NET. Several are back in Peak Performers after looking elsewhere for "greener grass." We welcome them back, however a few dropped considerably, or at best, "slid along laterally" during their absence.

Another, even less productive trend, has been doing the opposite of what's really useful. Let me explain. As your career develops you go from "General Information" to increasingly more "Highly-Specialized Information." You go from benefiting from general knowledge to needing VERY specific and specialized information about your particular need, industry or problem. An example would be going from "Generalized" marketing knowledge of the sort taught in a college program on Marketing to more useful and specific something like marketing stuff sold by Nightingale-Conant or one of the variety of "Marketing Gurus," to something like Jay Abraham's $25,000 two-day seminar, to directly hiring a copywriter or consultant (paying Dan Kennedy $12,000 for the day), to finding someone who's distilled that information directly and applied it to our industry and situation with huge success.

That's the natural and correct course of events — going the other direction is not terribly useful. Don't get me wrong. I believe you should read Kennedy's books, pay attention to Halbert, Abraham, Carlson and all of the others. For a comprehensive list of reading recommendations, see my book *Everything I Wish I Knew When I Was 22.*

However, we've had a few who think that going from specific actionable information and strategies to more general information is the way to go.

In JKD, one does not accumulate but eliminate. It is not daily increase but daily decrease. The height of cultivation always runs to simplicity.

> *Before I studied the art, a punch to me was just like a punch, a kick just like a kick. After I learned the art, a punch was no longer a punch, a kick no longer a kick. Now that I've understood the art, a punch is just like a punch, a kick just like a kick. The height of cultivation is really nothing special. It is merely simplicity; the ability to express the utmost with the minimum. It is the halfway cultivation that leads to ornamentation.*
> BRUCE LEE

That ALWAYS BACK-FIRES.

In my own case, I had enrolled over 35,000 students into my own schools through internal events, direct mail, telemarketing, community outreach and broadcast media, ranging from major newspaper budgets to 30-second spots and long-form infomercials before I ever heard of Jay Abraham, John Carlton or Dan Kennedy. Tim Kovar, Keith Hafner and I spent a ton of money and time learning from Jay Abraham, and then a couple of years and nearly $1,000,000 between us getting any of it to work in our specific industry.

I've tracked seven different former coaching clients who become Kennedy-GKIC groupies. One has continued to grow (Lloyd Irvin, who went from $7,000 a month to over $60,000 with my help). The other six are WAY down from then I was actively working with them, and confused and frustrated — blaming the economy for dropping by 50%, while I've coached others to grow by 200% or more. Their material would have been nice support to what we were doing, but it's more general and far less "actionable."

In the case of me working with Kennedy, I've found much of value in building the franchise and in reorganizing NAPMA. I'm not sure if much or any has translated itself directly into martial arts schools. The best concept that I continue to repeat from Abraham is simply the "Parthenon" concept. In other words, "Do a Bunch of Different Stuff" to get new students, and charge a lot more than anyone else — value what you do.

While it's extremely useful to study Tom Hopkins, Zig Ziglar and Brian Tracy on sales — I recommend that you read all of their books and buy all of their CDs and DVDs — it's 1,000 times more valuable to study, script and memorize the Sales Training Bootcamp that we have online at the member site. Going from the "General" to the "Specific" is the way to move from $50,000 a year income to $500,000 a year, then to $1,000,000. Specialized information is always more expensive. Sometimes, much more expensive. But the only finite resource is TIME. Money is infinite and abundant if you believe that and know how to scoop it up.

H. "Sliding Along Laterally." A final concern is perhaps a repeat of "there's no such thing as a plateau." In all of our Coaching Groups (Peak Performers, Inner Circle, Millionaire Wealth) it's essential for us to monitor the thinking that goes on in the room. Please RISE TO THE OCCASION and be on the FAST growth track this year, and have the highest expectations for your professional success. I'm expecting that many of our participants will add $100,000, $250,000 or more to their NET INCOME this year. I'm working hard to make sure YOU ARE ONE OF THEM.

Let's Grow Together and Mutually Support Each Other's Achievements!

Hit the Ground Running for the New Year!

Prepare a Comprehensive Marketing Plan adequate to insure a huge enrollment flow of at least 100 new students January, February, March.

Create a plan for 30-50 Enrollments per month starting in January.

How's your marketing plan for the coming year? If you've paid close attention to our Telecoaching calls, the huge amount of materials on your member website, and especially if you were at the Marketing Bootcamp and the various Peak Performers and Inner Circle Meetings, then you've heard more marketing concepts than anyone needs to add 20-50 new students each and every month. The biggest problem that I see is inaction. You must violently execute an effective plan to grow your school. Below is an action plan in outline form. It's not comprehensive, but we've certainly talked about A LOT of other ideas to market your school. However this list is a good start, especially if you're focusing on the kids market.

1. Children's Hospital Flyers — Distribute this week to:
    a. Every Public and Private Elementary and Middle School in your area
    a. All Day Cares (private, school, church groups, recreation centers)
    a. All Recreation Centers
2. Solidify your relationship with all schools in your area:

Mail to All

This week mail a letter to all schools that explains that we work to support all schools in our community by providing after-school programs and other talks and programs, as well as supporting fund-raising efforts within the schools. We have enclosed one certificate valued at $300 and five valued at $100 that may be used for fundraising, prizes or incentives for students.

Enclose: 1 — Three-Month Free Certificate, and; One-Month Free Certificate to be used for fund-raising efforts to every PTO President, PE Teacher and Principal.

Mail to all Public, Private, Church, and Charter Elementary Schools and Middle Schools.

1. Promote Various Programs that We So In Area Schools to the Student Body:
    Discuss:
    a. Bring your Instructor to "Show and Tell"
    b. Gym Teacher for the Day
    c. Bring your Instructor to "Career Day"
    d. Bring your Instructor to "Foreign Culture Day"
    e. Free Demo Class & Presentations for:
2. Boy Scout Troops
3. Girl Scout Troops
4. Day Cares
5. Church Groups
6. Sports Teams: Baseball; Soccer; Football, Etc.

Reminder: The key to all of these activities is the "Permission Slip." You must always get "LEAD Information," i.e., Name, Address, Mobile Number, Email Address to follow-up via Mail, Telemarketing, Text Messaging, Email and Broadcast Voicemail.

Aggressive Internal Promotions, Including:

1. VIP: Internal Referral push for September. Mail letter with four or more guest passes to every student right now.
2. Promote the GRADUATION DAY big.
    a. Big Demonstration.
    b. All Graduates Bring a Witness.
    c. Invitations to give to friends.
3. Internal Event this month, like a "Movie Night".
4. Internal Event this month, like a "Women's Self Defense" day.
5. Big Family add-pn push for January.

Parent Appreciation Month

1. Parents take class with their kids free all month with free uniform.
2. No Registration Fee and Half-Price Tuition for family add-ons by Jan. 31.
3. Promote birthday parties for anyone with a birthday in the next few months.
4. Promote birthday parties to all prospects.

Day Care Demos:

1. Set up one-day programs at all area day cares: Private, Schools, Churches, Recreation Centers, etc.
    a. Get "Permission Slips."
    a. Follow-up with series of mailings plus follow-up phone call.

Prepare Your Advertising Plan for the Spring

Marriage Mail Options:
    a. Val Pak
    b. Money Mailer
    c. Advo

d. Denver (or your local area) Newspaper Inserts

e. Pocket Coupon

Direct Mail Options:

a. Series of Letters to Prospect Database

b. GetMembers.com (postcard mailings)

c. Local Newspapers
   • Inserts
   • Post-It-Note on Cover

Other Promotional Opportunities:

a. Brochures on counters (Rack Cards; 300-500)

b. Street Signs (Bandit Signs)

c. Banner on your Building

d. Balloon on your Roof

e. Sign (upgrade or add)

f. Signage in your Window

"Shoe Leather" VIPs: Clip Board & Guest Passes:

a. Shopping Mall

b. Grocery Stores

c. In front of Restaurant at Lunch Time

Publicity:

   • Keep on the lookout for interesting stories about students, (exceptional results, special needs or medical, interesting stories, re: their background, occupation, etc.).

   • Work on getting stories about student results in small papers: i.e., church newsletter, high school paper, community paper.

   • Keep on the lookout for students with ANY media ties.

   • Aggressive community service: outreach and document for press releases.

Right away in January. Hit every elementary school within a reasonable distance of your school: five miles, more or less (further away from "city-center")

Gym Teacher for the Day:

Each School: 300 kids — 75% "Permission Slips" = 15-25 Immediate Intros

200 prospects to mail to every month for the year. Many will convert eventually.

Direct Mail Marketing Concept:

Important to Implement — Discuss Farming Out and Automating.

Suspects into Prospects.

"FARMING": Finding extremely targeted lists of "Suspects" and working that list consistently and repetitiously. Example: School Directory — local school with excellent demographics. Or,

Purchased List: Income $75,000-plus, kids 4-12, owns home, geographically targeted.

Step 1. Letter or Postcard #1, #2, #3, #4 (within 6 weeks)

Step 2. "Drip System" Monthly Mailer — Forever.

Prospects into Intros.

Example: Attended a Birthday Party, after-school, demo, etc.

Step 1. Letter or Postcard with telephone follow-up.

Step 2. Mailer #2, #3, #4 within 6 weeks.

Step 3. "Drip System" Monthly Mailer — Forever.

Step 4. January, May, September: Mailer #1, #2, #3 weekly -plus telephone follow-up

Lost Intros into Enrollments.

Example: Came to First Intro — never came back. Cancelled when called.

Step 1. Follow-up letter with lots of testimonials.

Step 2. "Price Drop Offer," i.e., 1 month free, or 3 month $99, or 2 for 1 offer.

Step 3. Telephone call follow-up to "price drop offer"

Step 4. "Drip System" Monthly Mailer — Forever.

Step 5. January, May, September: Mailer #1, #2, #3 weekly -plus telephone follow-up.

Drop Outs into Reactivations

Step 1. Missed you in class call — Week 1

Step 2. Missed you in class call — Week 2.

Step 3. Missed you in class call — Week 3.

Step 4. Week 3. Personal Letter from Instructor — Miss You in Class

Step 5. Week 4. Personal Letter from Program Director.

Step 6. Week 4. Personal Call from Program Director.

Step 7. Monthly "Drip System" Mailer.

Step 8. January, May, August: Mailer #1, #2, #3 weekly.

Reactivation Class, call everyone past 24 months.

"Drip System:" continuing to follow-up on a "suspect," "prospect," "lost intro," or "drop-out" on a very regular basis — monthly or more in peak seasons. Integrate text, email, direct mail, broadcast voicemail, outbound telemarketing.

The Higher You Climb the Ladder, the More of a Target You Become

As I write this the Super Bowl is playing in the background. So far the 49'ers are getting their butts kicked. I pause for the commercials and the occasional Cheerleader Cam. Certainly paused for the Beyoncé show.

I was hoping it would be Manning vs. RG3, and a revenge game of Elway vs. Shanahan to avenge the last time the Broncos met the Redskins in the Super Bowl. Alas, not to happen and no good-natured banter between Jeff Smith and I during the game.

Anyway, I'm not much of a football fan — but I've been watching the "winners" versus the "losers" in Martial Arts school operations for around 40 years now. We're marking the 30-year anniversary of Mile High Karate and my personal 44-year anniversary in Martial Arts.

A couple of recent observations.

"The higher you climb the ladder, the more of a target you become." I've been watching in horror as Lloyd Irvin gets savaged by a group of detractors who have been taking both a "guilty until proven innocent" and a "guilty after proven innocent" approach.

It's a case on one hand of someone without anything productive to add to the conversation about how to be successful as a school operator looking for any excuse to pretend to be the "moral voice" of the industry. The "self-proclaimed green party representative of the Martial Arts" looking to criticize anyone with an ability to share secrets to commercial success. It's sad that he's charismatic enough to lead some people into poverty with misguided insults at the industry's business consultants.

Be clear on a couple of things.

First. Marketing, Sales, Leadership Skills and Speaking Skills are "Values Neutral." Ronald Reagan, Bill Clinton, Adolf Hitler and Chairman Mao were all charismatic, great speakers and persuaded millions. Some for good. Some for evil. In no way am I comparing Reagan and Clinton with the others. Just pointing out that business, leadership and fighting skills can be used for good or evil.

You should always create a WIN/WIN outcome and have a VERY positive influence in your community.

You must learn to be effective at marketing, sales, leadership skills and speaking skills to succeed in our industry. Those tools should be used for the good of your students and of your community. Anyone who tells you not to learn effective marketing or sales is teaching you how to be broke. Anyone who doesn't encourage you to have very high quality student service, long-term student retention, and the highest quality student skills is teaching you to perhaps make money in the short term, but to sacrifice the long-term and to sacrifice the win/win results that you must have to still be strong in 30 years or more.

> *The best way to help the poor is not to become one of them.*
> LAING HANCOCK

On the other side. Someone who, as a student of mine, grew into a powerful voice for marketing MMA schools, who in my opinion mishandled a public relations challenge that was neither of his own making nor one which he had any control over. While I have no direct knowledge over any of the events in question I do know many different friends who have had various publicity problems created by students, employees, even family members. Even those with the most conservative of environments may experience the unexpected negative publicity brought on through no fault of their own.

How do you avoid falling victim yourself?

First: Establish your community reputation in your community under your own terms. Become very active in supporting local charities, local churches, local schools, and community events. Become very public in your community outreach and contribution.

Second: Establish a no tolerance policy for any and all instances of sexual impropriety among staff and students. Have a clearly written no fraternization policy for staff with students. Clearly define what's appropriate for behavior within your school.

Third: There's no such thing as being "too conservative" when you deal with other people's children. Carefully monitor everything from how your staff dresses in and out of the school to their online posts and conversations held in your school and around students.

Fourth: Run background checks and carefully evaluate any and all potential staff members.

Ultimately, if and when a crisis hits….

Consult me before doing anything, or, at the very least, get very high quality advice from someone who's an expert in this field.

Like I said, I've "been there, done that" with just about anything you can imagine in our industry. In 30 years I've managed to never have any significant negative publicity for my schools, but it doesn't mean that staff or students have never behaved stupidly. I've always dealt with it quickly, and yes, brutally. Have always maintained a little or no tolerance policy. And, frankly, have been so actively involved in the community and I had earned the benefit of the doubt ahead of time.

There's a very specific method to be used for handling bad publicity. There are MANY ways to make it worse not better. Be careful if a crisis hits.

Another lesson — about some other high profile "Melt-Downs."

With the General Patraeus affair, there's an important lesson to learn. You can seriously "shoot yourself in the foot" by giving in to impulses and desires that you know at the time you shouldn't give in to. In all things, be "impeccable in your behavior." Ultimately, pause and think about any and all actions that you take — before you do it. The rule of thumb I've heard many times is to never do anything that you wouldn't want to hit the headlines of your daily paper. In the age of the Internet it's an even better admonition since it takes about 30 seconds for negative news — real or imagined about you — to travel worldwide.

Clearly that admonition applies to all areas of your life. Be very careful about what you "tweet," what photos you post on Facebook, and how you treat any and everyone you interact with. While none of us are perfect — pause and think about your actions ahead of time and realize that what seems like a good idea at the time can come back to haunt you and torpedo your career. The higher on the ladder you climb — the more likely any indiscretion will come back to haunt you.

On a Different Subject …

After my last round of coaching calls, and a series of "Heavy Hitters" free consultation calls, something else is obvious.

Those who planned ahead and marketed aggressively to start the year — had a HUGE January.

My advice has been to really market to your existing lead list (anyone who's been in for an introductory class, came to a buddy event, called but never came in, or otherwise expressed an interest in your school but didn't enroll.) That marketing to your existing lead list should include: live outbound telemarketing, text messaging, direct mail, email, and outbound broadcast voice mail. Using each "Sequentially" and "Repetitiously."

The small schools often aren't developing a "lead database." It's an essential skill that you must master. Keep track of everyone who expresses an interest in your school and follow-up relentlessly.

How "relentlessly?"

I'd recommend the minimum frequency for follow-up over a year:

- Email 400-plus times.
- Direct Mail 24-plus times.
- Text Message — 50-plus times.
- Broadcast Voice Mail 24-plus times.
- Live Outbound calls — 12-plus times.

Even the schools who think they are following up pretty well typically do one outbound call and then a bunch of emails.

Keep in mind the hierarchy of effectiveness:

Best to worst:

1. Face-to-Face, belly-to-belly.
2. Live Telephone Call
3. Text Message
4. Direct Mail
5. Email
6. Facebook and other social media

Don't rely on just cheap or easy. Do what works. Do it repetitiously and sequentially.

Keep in mind…

Just because someone comes to a buddy event or meets you at a movie theater or some other live event does not mean that this week, this month is the right time for them to start a new event.

They may meet you in January but be ready to start a new event in August.

If you don't follow-up continuously, when it's time to begin a new activity they are off to something else. Likely it's not off to the martial arts school down the street — likely it's just off to something else.

Another quick review about the follow-up content.

The follow-up series should include a lot of interesting and useful content.

We provide you a HUGE amount of content.

Each month send them the *Kickin' Newsletter* with interesting items about your school included.

Each month send them invitations to all of the events you hold at your school.

Include valuable life-skills lessons in the emails you send (plenty of material provided to you each month on the members site.) You can use this material also for interesting and valuable direct mail. Keep in mind we provide a huge number of pre-done-for-you direct mail items that will support your efforts.

For complete follow-up systems see your member site for recommendations for various software platforms and systems that range from expensive and sophisticated to simple and inexpensive.

Consultation Certificate

This Certificate Entitles the Bearer to a Personal 1-on-1 Martial Arts School Business Analysis With a NAPMA-Certified Business Analyst. This Individual Consultation is Valued at $495.00.

Certificate expires 12 months from the date of purchase.
To schedule your personal business analysis, complete this form and fax to NAPMA at 1-800-795-0853; mail to 1767 Denver West Blvd., Suite A, Golden, CO 80401; or visit www.PrivateCoachingSession.com

PLEASE FILL OUT COMPLETELY AND WRITE LEGIBLY

Name _____

School Name _____

Address _____

City _____ State/Province _____

Zip _____ Country _____

Phone _____ Fax _____

E-Mail _____

_____
Authorized by Toby Milroy
Chief Operating Officer, NAPMA

3 FREE GIFTS FOR SERIOUS SCHOOL OWNERS

FREE Personal School Evaluation	**FREE Two 90-Minute Seminars**	**FREE CD-DVD Package and Report**
Two 30-minute Sessions A sure-fire way action plan to double your results or better.	with **"The Millionaire Maker Grandmaster Stephen Oliver** "The 5 Stupid Mistakes All Too Many School Owners Make that Kill Their Growth" and "The Key Step-by-Step Blueprint for Being a Big Winner"	**"How Hundreds of Smart School Owners Like You Doubled Their Revenue in the Last 12 Months** Even in the Midst of the Greatest Recession since the Great Depresson, and How You Can, Too!"

Be "Impeccable."

L et me start this month for apologizing for a rather intense subject, and not much (if any humor) attached.

I'd like to give you a sampling of headlines that have come through my inbox in the past month (I subscribe to Google Alerts for news regarding Martial Arts, Kung Fu, Karate, Tae Kwon Do, etc.).

Braintree karate instructor faces sexual assault charges
www.metro.us/boston/?p=125385Share

A martial arts instructor is scheduled to be arraigned Monday on charges he sexually assaulted a young female student at his Braintree karate school.

Martial arts instructor to trial for molestation / San Mateo Daily Journal
A San Mateo martial arts instructor accused of inappropriately touching two young female students will stand trial on four felony counts of molestation that could ...

Convicted sex offender arrested / Pensacola News Journal
... three years in prison for sexually molesting two nine-year-old females and a ... May was also reportedly running a martial arts business called ...

Police Arrest Convicted Sex Offender Posing As Model Recruiter / NorthEscambia.com
May teaches martial arts and was reportedly running a business ... for sexually molesting two 9-year old females and a 14-year-old female.

Convicted sex offender Hutton shaves 15 years off 65-year sentence ...
A man who received a 65-year prison term for molesting two girls...from allegations that he molested a 12-year-old karate student.

Spain karate teacher gets 302 years for rape
A Spanish court handed a 302-year jail sentence to a karate champion for raping dozens of pupils at his martial arts school in the country's ...

Minors accuse martial arts trainer of rape / Times of India
3 AHMEDABAD: Two minor girls from Anand have accused a martial arts trainer of rape. The girls registered a complaint with Chandkheda police ...

Maine martial arts teacher accused of sex abuse / WCSH-TV
RANDOLPH, Maine (AP) - Maine State Police say a martial arts instructor has been accused of sexually abusing one of his students. Fifty-three-year-old Brant Perkins of Edgecomb is an instructor at the Maine Isshimryu Karate Academy in Randolph. He was ...
http://www.wcsh6.com/news/article/234201/2/Maine-martial-arts-teacher-accused-of-sex-abuse

Martial arts instructor facing more sex charges / Champaign / Urbana News-Gazette
EAST ST. LOUIS, Ill. (AP) — A southwestern Illinois martial arts instructor is facing more federal felonies alleging that he sexually abused several students, including a 6-year-old. A federal grand jury in East St. Louis has returned a six-count ...

(By publishing ANY of the above I'm not acting

as judge or jury. Some are innocent, some guilty. All innocent until proven guilty — unfortunately, a principle missing in the Internet age. However, all of the above are from news sources — some big, some small. Some print, some online only.)

Now, before you begin to think there's been a "rash of problems" or a huge up tick in rape, molestation or sexual harassment in our small industry, let me share with you a disturbing reality.... This volume is "normal," and perhaps down from a few years ago.

That having been said, and I've watched this for 40-plus years ... it was a HUGE problem in the 1960s, 1970s and 1980s. As I've said before, "The Good Old Days, Never Were."

Why to I make this a subject of conversation this month?

Well. It's been a HUGE concern of mine since watching what I considered inappropriate behavior among various teachers and instructors going all the way back to when I was 15 or 16 years old.

There are THREE important subjects buried in these disturbing news articles for you to pay attention to for your business.

1. How to prevent inappropriate behavior in your school.
2. How to protect yourself against false allegations.
3. How to screen potential staff and volunteers.

And, I should likely add a fourth — for future discussion.

How we as a community protect ourselves from a devastating Public Relations disaster (think, day-care industry a few years ago, or even the Catholic Church.)

This is an extremely important subject.

Recently Facebook has been lit up over some high-profile allegations lodged against some high-profile industry leaders. Much of the conversation becomes "nonsense" in that environment.

Before going any further...

Let me make an observation. Much of our sensitivity as to what's appropriate or inappropriate behavior evolves from the current cultural environment and news reporting, along with high-profile lawsuits and government action.

What was considered okay 10 or 20 years ago may be a lawsuit waiting to happen in our current environment.

For instance:

I was watching a very good interview with Bill Gates recently. When asked how he and his wife met he responded, "We met at work." Then paused, looked a bit embarrassed, and then said "back when that was okay." At Microsoft, a fairly high profile sexual harassment case was in progress over an executive and employee who were dating at Microsoft.

Recently, there have been high profile cases, ranging from Jack Welch to David Patraeus to the CEO of Home Depot and CEO of Best Buy, in various relationship scandals that would likely have been ignored 20 or 30 years ago.

That means in your school, issues such as sexual harassment, what's an appropriate or inappropriate relationship, and appropriate behavior generally, are under a much finer magnifying glass than in years past.

Anyway, some thoughts and suggestions:

I was having this conversation recently with Bill Clark. ATA has done a marvelous job in documenting and overseeing in meticulous detail requirements ranging from background checks to facility layout in an effort to prevent such allegations or actions.

Let's start by dealing with staff and creating the right culture in your school.

First, hiring.

Hiring the right people is an inexact science. For situations like molestation or rape there is always the "first time." for any individual.

How to hire the right person could be a book unto itself. And, in fact, there are several I'd recommend. One is by an acquaintance of mine, Geoff Smart, is called, "Who."

However, the short list of recommendations:

1. Always require a complete list of former employers, and call them. Ask probing questions. If they have a martial arts background (other than with you directly), then call their instructors and ask about their character, attitude and background.

2. Run a background check. It's pretty inexpensive. In Colorado, for instance, we can run a CBI background check for arrest records for about $7. This really should be done with anyone you hire, if nothing else, having it "in the file" can help protect you in the case of a problem, if one should occur.

3. Trust your intuition. I've come to feel that if I have a "bad feeling" about a potential staff member, or one of the others that I have interview the applicant has that "bad feeling," then no matter how strong the resume or references, I'll trust that feeling.

It's rare for a new hire to be a "winner." Most companies have a pretty high failure rate when hiring, especially if hiring from "outside."

4. Have several people interview each applicant. A corporate trend a few years back was "360" evaluations. I'm not sure about that for ongoing evaluations, although it's probably a good idea; however, for hiring it's invaluable. You may "love" a potential applicant, however, someone else with an understanding of your expectations and culture may see elements that you would miss or overlook.

5. Have an INTENSIVE 90-day training program for any new hire along with a probationary period. Observer character, conversation and attitude. If you see a "crack" in the façade, cut your losses quickly.

6. Have a clear understanding up front about appropriate behavior within your school and with and around students (and, their parents) regardless of setting. In fact, have a real chat about how they are expected to behave on "off hours" any where in the vicinity of your school.

Here's a brief excerpt from the Employment Agreement that I've had for many years for Mile High Karate. It includes references to behavior standards, a non-compete agreement, non-solicitation agreement and trade secrets.

Employment agreement excerpt:

EMPLOYEE BEHAVIOR AND IMAGE:

A. Employee agrees to abide by the policies and procedures of Mile High Karate and as developed by the Master Instructor. Employee agrees not to discuss any disagreement or dissatisfaction he/she may have with anyone other than Mile High Karate management. Employee understands that a failure to properly follow policies and procedures, as well as to follow them in a properly supportive spirit, is grounds for termination.

B. Employee understands that he/she must always strive to protect the physical and psychological well being of all Mile High Karate students with whom he/she comes into contact. Failure to take reasonable precautions, exercise proper common sense, and/or follow Mile High Karate policies and procedures may result in Employee's termination and the acceptance of complete and total legal liability for his/her actions. This includes but is not limited to allowing a student to be needlessly injured, embarrassed, or humiliated.

C. Because students, especially young ones, will often develop strong admiration and respect for their instructors, they will often emulate their habits and behavior. The personal appearance and actions of the Employee will reflect directly upon the Employer. It is imperative that Employee reflect the highest possible standards of appearance, professionalism, and ethical and moral behavior both within the work environment and when in public at any time. Employee agrees to carefully monitor his/her dress, personal hygiene, habits, speech and actions whenever in public view. Public drunkenness or any form of illegal drug usage either in public or private is inappropriate.

D. Employer believes that it is inappropriate in almost all cases for an Employee to date or have intimate contact with any student, or parent of a student. No such encounter may occur without prior permission from management, which will rarely be given. Any sexually oriented jokes, advances, gestures, inferences, comments, or inappropriate touching of any student or staff member is strictly against policy and exposes the offending Employee to possible termination was well as any possible legal action.

The next important element is to carefully monitor the culture within your school and among your students and staff.

Ultimately, it all reflects your behavior, attitude and expectations. It's never okay to behave in a way that's less stringent than you expect of your staff. In fact, whether it's in training or behavior, you'll be lucky to get them to 70% of what you model for them. Said another way, "do what I say not what I do," never works.

When it comes to the children's market I've always believed that there's no such thing as "too conservative." Parents, no matter how liberal or relaxed in their personal beliefs, never object to a protective and safe environment for their child.

This again could be a very long and exhaustive conversation. However, I'll tell you that as an owner you must model impeccable behavior and be constantly vigilant. Listen to every conversation going on in your school. I'd recommend that you have audio-video recording in every room (other, than of course, the dressing room/rest rooms.

Listen in on conversations that go on between staff members and between staff and students.

To give you a simple example:

I was in one of my schools a few years ago. One staff member commented to another behind closed doors, that a female member looked good in the splits. I stepped in and immediately pointed out that in public AND behind closed doors that a comment like that was totally inappropriate about any student.

You must make it clear that your school is an environment of total respect and an environment where sexual references, comments, suggestions, and jokes are inappropriate.

Now, don't think that I'm only talking about children's schools. In the 1960s and 1970s the problem was with instructors pursuing students — usually adult students. In some ways the MMA trends and Kickboxing trends have led us back to the '60s and '70s as an industry.

In an adults-only environment, it's certainly okay for students to develop friendships or date one another. It's not okay for your staff to use your clientele as a "dating pool." There's nothing more destructive than having female (or male students) feel uncomfortable coming to your school, afraid of being touched or "hit on." Even a staff member who's courteous can create problems if allowed to date a student. Ultimately, there are two obvious problems. One can be "jealousy" created among other students; the other is obvious: If the relationship doesn't work then you lose a student (or a staff member.)

In the Facebook world, there's the line of discussion that women shouldn't have to learn self-defense, that men should be taught "not to rape."

Frankly, I think that comment is ludicrous.

In the United States and most of the modern western world, pretty much everyone is pretty clear what the rules are at the margins, assuming that they are not suffering from serious mental problems.

No instructor who's raped a student thought that it was acceptable. Rather, they hoped not to get caught. Rarely does an instructor have what they believe to be a consensual relationship with an underage student without knowing that it's legally and morally questionable or inappropriate. No one molests a child thinking that it's going to be okay if discovered.

In fact, it could be argued that generally we've become a little too hypersensitive about workplace dating or other otherwise innocent "male-female" comments or conversations. Again, witness Bill Gates, or the sportscaster who recently got in trouble for commenting that an athlete's wife (a former beauty queen) was beautiful.

Certainly, it's a philosophical argument. As martial arts teachers we certainly must be in the role of teaching boys and men how to behave appropriately, and teaching girls and women how to protect themselves against the VERY SMALL percentage of men who are going to cross the line.

Protecting Yourself Against False Allegations.

Let me begin by saying as a business owner you can be a "pillar of the community" and behave in all instances appropriately. You can be very careful about who you hire and how your train them. You can monitor your culture and every nook and crevice within your school. AND, still have a devastating incident happen by a staff member or student.

There's nothing you can do to be 100% sure that you will never have this type of problem. Several of my friends have had bad publicity problems erupt from the actions of staff, students, or, even in one case, his brother. You still must protect yourself against such bad publicity.

I've been the most diligent, stringent and conservative owner-instructor that I know (and have still had several problems over the years) real or accused problems involving staff and students. None became publicity problems. That was probably due to a combination of solid reputation, quickly addressing the problem, and more than a little luck.

In addition, at any time a disgruntled former employee, frustrated student, or someone else with an "axe to grind," could make an accusation against you or a staff member. Ultimately, once an "Internet feeding frenzy" starts and your local (or, national) newspapers or television stations run the story, it can destroy your business and your credibility in your community. Unfortunately being found to be innocent months or years later doesn't repair the damage that was done.

How do you protect yourself?

We've already discussed many steps. All of the written contracts, pre-screening, monitoring of your culture, and lessons taught to staff and students are all necessary and important.

In addition, you really must start on your reputation in each and every venue now, not later.

At the most basic, be very focused on making sure your ratings and feedback on Google Local, Yelp, Yahoo!, Bing and at the Better Business Bureau are strong. Get lots of positive ratings and evaluations in all of those venues.

Obviously, monitor your Facebook, Twitter, Linked In, and other social media interactions as well as those of your staff. What seems innocent now can cast a different light through the lens of an allegation.

More important is for you to become a "Pillar of your Community."

Become very involved in local charities. Help with fundraising. Help with events and activities. Some of this will directly benefit your school, however, if all that you do are things that are clearly for your own benefit then it won't help that much. Make sure that you, your staff, your Black Belts, and your students are all actively involved in community service.

You need to be known by the area scout leaders, church leaders, teachers and principals, charity leaders and community leaders The more you are recognized for giving selflessly and for encouraging community service among your students, then the more you will be given the benefit of the doubt if an when an incident occurs.

There is also a very important process for handling the publicity after the fact that goes beyond our discussion today. There have been some high profile examples of bungling the PR after the fact. Maybe we'll do a "post mortem on those sometime soon.

To wrap up.

I understand that this is a rather intense subject. It's vital that you be eternally vigilant. There are few things that can kill your school overnight, but an allegation, arrest or lawsuit surrounding one of these issues can easily cripple or kill your school. I'd suggest that you do a little "soul-searching" and have a conversation with yourself and then take action on any problems or missing elements in your school — NOW.

MMA has Killed "Traditional Martial Arts Schools?"

OK, If you've been around awhile then you know that it's a stupid statement on the face of it…However, frankly, a lot of otherwise bright school owners believe the above.

Anyway, to give you a very brief history of your industry, I've got to say that *The Karate Kid* didn't kill martial arts schools, the TV Show *Kung Fu* and the movie *"Enter the Dragon"* didn't kill Tae Kwon Do, Karate and Judo schools. "Ninja Turtles" didn't kill anyone who, well, wasn't a Ninja — or, I guess, a Teenage Turtle. And, Tae Bo didn't kill anyone teaching stuff other than "Cardio or Fitness Kickboxing."

Don't get my statement above, wrong:

A few of these trends HAVE in fact killed off some traditional schools who followed the trend and put themselves out of business.

What's reality?

Right now there is a VERY Healthy market for at least the following groups:

1. Adult Men 18–28 who are interested in MMA.
2. Adult Men 28–40 who are interested in MMA.
3. Adult women interested in Martial Arts as a fitness vehicle.
4. Children 3–12 years of age.
5. Adults 45 & Up looking for Low Impact Activities such as Tai Chi.

This isn't a comprehensive list but, here's a reality: Over the years in the children's market there have been times when just a yellow page add with your phone number would pull a ton of calls. There have been other times when you had to "go hunt for them."

Right now the Adult Market is EASILY accessible in the current version of the Yellow Pages. There is lots of "inventory" of "clicks" for adults looking for what they think of as MMA (typically, actually BJJ or Muay Thai). There is "inventory" of "clicks" for fitness kickboxing and a huge opportunity with Groupon, Living Social and the like.

The kids market right now is a bit different. There's not a flood of searches (or, "Inventory of Clicks") available online right now — however, there are tons of children and family all around you who would be interested is introduced and educated. You just have to know how to find them and how to get their attention and interest.

A big mistake that was made during the initial "Tae Bo" boom was in traditional schools adopting a "fitness center" pricing model. Doing stupid things like selling "punch cards" and, "month-to-month" low price memberships ($39-$99 a month.)

Many school owners didn't learn from that history and are now going back to that idea with Krav Maga, MMA and Kickboxing.

Sadly, many in our industry think that if people are not flooding in their door with little or no effort that their "market has died."

There are MANY kids-oriented schools who are thriving right now. Few are predominantly filling their school with "Search Engine Optimization," "Pay Per Click" Advertising and similar online sources. Most have become very good at community outreach activities, internal "referral" marketing events, and ultimately constant, repetitious, and effective lead follow-up.

Back to the "MMA" market. I recently did a 30 minute video on the "State of the Industry —

MMA" you can access through www.NAPMA. com. In it I point out that right now a properly run adult school can fill their school with effective online marketing. I also point out that having that "one pillar' of advertising is dangerous. It's important to have MANY pillars of marketing for your school even if online search marketing or sources like GroupOn are working well.

Many children's oriented schools closed when the Yellow Pages stopped working years ago. Those (like mine) who had learned MANY different ways to get new students did fine. Many benefitted from the flood but never really learned how to market effectively.

I'll warn the MMA guys that the same is likely to happen in their "niche." At some point you have to get good at a broader base of marketing activities and, I'd suggest that you start now. In addition even if you are doing well online you probably could do much better. Are you tracking your online conversion rate? How's it doing. How's your "squeeze page?" Do you sequentially, and aggressively follow-up all leads with text, voicemail, email, outbound live phone calls, and direct mail? For how long?

I've rarely seen a martial arts school follow-up with their leads aggressively enough or effectively enough. I love times when you can "drink from a fire hose." During those times you want to continue to add to your marketing and continually improve your efficiencies.

81% Upgrade Ratio

Our Inner Circle and Peak Performers focus on Student Retention and the Complete Renewal-Upgrade Process in Washington, D.C. with a special "on-site" at Mile High Karate Training Center with Grandmaster Jeff Smith and Staff.

I just returned from our May Inner Circle and Peak Performers meetings and special "Renewal & Retention" staff Bootcamp. It was spectacular.

Some immediate feedback received included:

> *Carol Middleton: It was better than three of any other conference! We came back Monday and are changing our school for the better in three major ways.*

> *Michael Dietrich: Great to be around my first instructors and to have them continue to be mentors with information that was not only important but inspirational for all of us. Congratulations on an awesome presentation. I will be sure to tell the other Masters I associate with!*

What we covered in specific was the complete "Upgrade" structure and philosophy and the "Educational Institution" approach to running a Martial Arts School as contrasted with the "Health Club" model.

We discussed that our greatest need is in improving the education of our students. Teaching them to plan on long-term follow-through with our schools. Finding ways to really get them to understand the process to get to Black Belt and beyond in martial arts training. Too many schools set their students up for failure from day one by allowing "month-to-month" thinking and by failing to train their new students how to properly think about their school.

One of our Peak Performers members proudly stated that he's DOUBLED his gross revenues since in the past year due to his membership in Peak Performers. Another Inner Circle member proudly stated they've grown 400-plus percent.

Another who had come into Peak Performers at less than $7,000 a month revenue sent me this:

> *So I just wanted to send a note to say thank you. I gave myself 5 years to make this school a 1/2 a million dollar venture - doing our taxes for the year the headquarters school did $519,000 and the new location in only 4 months open netted $10,000 — you have forever changed my life and my business and I am eternally grateful.*

If you were at our May event I welcome your feedback.

Our next Inner Circle and Peak Performers event is the "Ultimate Martial Arts Internet Marketing Bootcamp" to be held in Golden, Colorado in August. Next we'll take the Inner Circle and Peak Performers to the Harvard Business School to really study management at the highest level.

If you're an Inner Circle or Peak Performers member and missed the May event the complete video recordings will soon be available in your member web site.

By the way…you're welcome to view some of the Mile High Karate preparatory steps to the Renewal at www.MileHighBlackBelt.com

One benchmark, by the way, that we were looking at is the ratio of new students to renewal at the Mile High Karate Sterling, VA location:

87% of all new students end up renewing.

Approximately 50% of all new enrollments end

up renewing at White Belt (i.e., first two months.) Approximately 50% of what's left, or 25% of total enrollments, end up renewing by their second Belt (i.e., second Two-Months), and, that leaves about 12% after the fourth month.

Of those renewing, around 90% upgrade into the highest level program — Leadership, at between $325 and $397 per month.

Pretty impressive numbers that we covered thoroughly during the may Inner Circle and Peak Performers meetings.

It is fascinating what happens in our industry… we're MASSIVELY overpopulated with mostly well-meaning "consultants" who are giving advice that either they think is good advice, or that they wish was good.

Recent bad advice:

1. Don't use contracts;
2. Upgrade structures are Evil;
3. Post your complete price-list on your website;
4. Do enough "charity and community service" and your school will magically fill itself.
5. It you are a good enough Instructor then you don't need business or marketing knowledge or systems.
6. Advertising doesn't work.
7. The only advertising your need is a good website.

And, frankly I could go on and on.

There are a bunch of companies making generic or template websites for schools. We've avoided getting into that business mostly but teach the structure and format and recently hosted a series of VERY GOOD Teleconferences on that subject.

We felt the need to do that because between myself, Master Milroy, and Bob Dunne we've looked at well over 1,000 martial arts school websites this spring. Most are beyond horrible. I've seen less than 1% that I could say were good or excellent. Most of those people making websites

for school owners are giving the school owners what they ask for, but not an effective — HIGH CONVERSION site for effective marketing.

Just remember. Unless someone has an excellent track record for both creating excellent results for their own schools in our industry and for reproducing that result in many others that they've worked with then be eternally skeptical of their advice.

Sadly, in coaching we have to spend a huge amount of time fixing things that well meaning owners screwed up by listening to bad advice.

A Quick Follow-up from Last Month:

If you didn't read my discussion about the recent outbreak of scandal in our industry then go back and read the last issue. In your organization behavioral expectations start at the top.

Make a decision to be impeccable. Be above reproach in your dealings with students and staff members. Let's all lead from the top and set an example of respectful behavior and impeccable moral conduct.

An additional reminder is that you must be eternally vigilant. Be aware of the behavior of each and every staff member at your school. Screen diligently and be sure to train thoroughly.

Great Grandmaster Jhoon Rhee

A quick update. Grandmaster Jeff Smith, Grandmaster John Chung, and myself had plans to visit with Great Grandmaster Rhee during my very quick trip to Washington, D.C. for our Peak Performers and Inner Circle meetings. Sadly, he was feeling even worse than has become his norm. As you may know he's been suffering with Shingles over his entire mid-section for over two years. Master Rhee was the most vibrant and fit 80-plus year old man that I had ever met. The last two years have taken a massive toll.

My personal thanks and gratitude go to Jeff Smith, Chun Rhee and the many others who have helped and supported Great Grandmaster Rhee during this trying time. I'd urge any and everyone to drop him a card or send a message via email or facebook of support and solidarity. I pray for him daily and hope for recovery soon from this painful ordeal.

If you haven't read his great book: *TruTopia*, I'd suggest going to www.JhoonRhee.com and picking it up. My teacher — "Father of American Tae Kwon Do" has impacted so many people. From a huge number of U.S. Congressmen to celebrities such as Tony Robbins and Muhammad Ali to Martial Artists like Bruce Lee and Chuck Norris. He's had immeasurable impact in our industry in each decade since the 1960's.

In conclusion, I would remind you that we've spent a huge amount of time on "Summer Success Systems" in recent member calls. I hope that you will ALWAYS Join us live for our Member Coaching Teleconference calls. Be clear that many schools that we are working with have converted Summer from their slowest period of time to the busiest. Implement aggressively and see your summer be incredible.

Hey, First, Some Reminders...

Reminder 1: Each month we do Telecoaching with all of our members. If you aren't on our Maximum Impact live Member call each month, and submitting questions and asking them live, then you are missing a huge opportunity.

ALWAYS book in this time: 12 Noon on the first Wednesday of the month. Submit questions ahead of time to me at StephenOliver@NAPMA.com. If you have a question. Check it on the member Website or, call Bob Dunne at 1-727-540-0500, Ext. 202.

For Inner Circle and Peak Performers we are hosting three Telecoaching calls each month. One is "Owner's Only," two are designed to include your staff, and are fully interactive with myself, Toby Milroy, and often Jeff Smith along, with the rest of the Inner Circle Members.

Reminder 2: Each month I work one-on-one with my Inner Circle Members and the top level of Peak Performers. If you're one of those ($500,000 to multi-million-dollar per month school owners) and Peak Performers members, then PLEASE send me any and everything you want to discuss on our calls a week or more ahead of our call so that I can be prepared.

For Inner Circle and Peak Performers the reminder is, there's no such thing as sending me (or Toby Milroy) too much information about what's currently going on in your school. To maximize what's admittedly, typically big results, then keep me as informed as possible about what's happening with your business.

Reminder 3: The Ultimate Martial Arts Marketing Bootcamp is primarily focused on "Internet Marketing. YOU REALLY NEED to be there. For my Inner Circle and Peak Performers this is an included piece of your membership. For Maximum Impact Members it's a separate fee (see www.MartialArtsBootcamp.com). Frankly, you'd be much better served to qualify for and upgrade to the Peak Performers Team (or, Inner Circle if you qualify.)

The bootcamp is THE MOST IMPORTANT live event of the year — bar none. You've got to be there. It's positioned in August in order to give you the complete plan to add 100-plus students in September and October to finish your year with new records.

FYI: More about Inner Circle and Peak Performers at www.PrivateCoachingSession.com.

For Inner Circle and Peak Performers we're next off to Harvard Business School. It's the Ultimate High-Level Management view of your business. Make sure you have the October dates on your calendar. For all live events we're planning now on a "Staff Training Track," so plan on bringing them all to Colorado and to Cambridge (Boston).

Last year, we held exciting events for Peak Performers and Inner Circle at Disney in Orlando, at Disney in Anaheim, at the United States Military Academy at West Point, NY, and Golden, Colorado for the Marketing Bootcamp.

This year it's been the Hotel Del Coronado in San Diego, Behind the Scenes with Jeff Smith on 87% conversion to upgrades in Washington, D.C., the Marketing Bootcamp in Golden, CO, and then off to Harvard Business School.

By the way...The "Key Ingredient" to success in your school:

1. Personal One-On-One Coaching with someone who's been, there done that...
2. Master-Mind Interaction with other High Performers

A distraction and potential disaster — the new risk, same as the old risk:

A new Peak Performers member discussed several "great ideas" that he'd picked up in some forum on LinkedIn.com. My advice to him was to TOTALLY and COMPLETELY ignore EACH and EVERY Martial Arts school owner forum on LinkedIn, Facebook, and all of the others, EXCEPT for what we create for Inner Circle and Peak Performers members.

Why?

Well, two things happen in those environments. The first thing is that the broke guys tend to shout down the rare successful person. Frankly, most successful school owners are too busy working on their business or enjoying their lives to spend interacting with these random strangers.

The second element of those forums is that you really only have two types of contributors. Those with an agenda and those without a clue. Ideas that get "traction" tend to be those that sound easy, cheap, or altruistic. Rarely do you see real experts sharing in those environments.

I troll from time to time just to keep my finger on the pulse. Actually, one of the bigger ones on Facebook rejected accepting me as a member since they didn't want to hear what I might have to say. I dare you to find a forum where Danny Schulman, Jeff Smith, Bill Clark, myself or anyone with a similar level of "gravitas" hangs out and freely answers any and all questions.

Are you experiencing a "Summer Boom" or are you having a summer slowdown? We've "Beat to Death" the summer success theme in the past couple of months. I'll confidently tell you that many of our top schools are already hitting new records for summer. One of our Peak Performers members just made over 200 Introductory appointments last week (third week of June).

I won't recap this list again here, but there's a nearly unlimited list of what you can be doing in July and August. In some ways, Summer Marketing is different. The same stuff you did in April and October successfully may not work as well (or, at all) in mid-summer. However, there's a bunch of stuff that works even better.

The short reminders would be:

1. Summer is a challenged time for student retention. Make sure you know when students will on vacation and when they will be returning. If they're gone very long, send them a postcard where they're at (Grandma's house for instance). Know when they're supposed to be back in town and make sure you call, text, email, and drop them a note. Get them on a catch-up plan and back on track as soon as possible.

2. Summer is a great time to do two things:
   a. Generate new student enrollments;
   b. Create a HUGE Lead list that's prime for Back-to-School — Fall Marketing.
   c. You've got to always be using the "Parthenon"

Always have a BUNCH of things going to generate new students.

The Pillars:
   a. Multiple Referral Systems;
   b. A lot of "Community Outreach"
   c. Regular "Publicity" and "PR" efforts
   d. Regular Direct Mail (especially targeting your prospect lists)
   e. Charitable efforts to anchor you into the community
   f. Business Co-Promotions
   g. Effective and Targeted "Media" advertising
   h. Effective and Targeted Online efforts including:
      • Search Engine Optimization
      • Pay-Per-Click
      • Facebook Target Marketing
      • Groupon & Living Social

And, much more…

And, now to "Bitch" a bit more…

You don't do enough follow-up on two groups of people:

FIRST: Those who have expressed a "Little bit of Interest" AKA "Leads." What's a lead? Well… they :

1. Attended a birthday party, or;
2. Attended a "pizza party," or;
3. Attended a "buddy day," or they came to a "belt graduation" event, or;
4. They "Opted In" online, or;
5. Entered the drawing at your booth at a fair, home show, movie theater, etc., or;
6. They walked in to your school, or; They called and never came in, or they attended an introductory class and didn't enroll,

or…. Well you get the idea — right?

You are much better served to spend A LOT of time and money following up on any and everyone who's expressed at least a little bit of interest rather than advertising to the general public.

To put in different language, there is a huge chasm between "Suspects" and "Prospects."

A Suspect (for a Kids & Family school) is, for instance, a household within three miles of your school, who earns $100,000-plus per year, owns a home, two-parent household, with kids 4–12 in the household.

A Prospect is someone who fits similar criteria but, add one: They've raised their hand and at least expressed a little bit of interest.

SECOND. Anyone who's "MIA" Missing in action, i.e., Dropouts.

How do you follow-up effectively?

Well, I've discussed many times one-on-one that effectiveness goes in the following descending order:

1. Show up on their doorstep and talk face-to-face;
2. Call and talk to a live person;

3. Mail a big package of information;
4. Mail a postcard or similar;
5. Text Message;
6. Broadcast Voicemail — Live answer connect to Instructor;
7. Broadcast Voicemail — Leave message on Voicemail;
8. Email;
9. Facebook & other Social Media.

In all cases, the key is "Sequential Auto Responder" wherever possible

How many times should you follow-up on them?

Well, Probably take what ever you do now and: Multiply by 100 and extend another 24 months.

Just a quick comparable. A few months ago the *Wall Street Journal* had an article about high-end, big budget retailers. Retailers like Macy's and Neiman. Their email frequency to their customer list ran from a low of 380 times per year to a high of just under 700 times. That's between once and twice a day.

If you watch Groupon and Living Social, how often do they email you?

We're giving you most if not all of the content for your mail, email, and text messages. Frankly, on Voicemail, Email, Text Messages, you can set up 5, 10 or 20 messages, then have your automated system START OVER. Same thing with Direct Mail.

What follow-up should you do with both lists?

1. Invite to EACH and EVERY event that you host at your school. Invite them by calling them, emailing them, texting them, mailing to them, showing up in their "Facebook" feed, and calling them.
2. Send them your school newsletter every month (We do it for you.) Mail it to them, email it to them, put it on your website and text, voicemail them to know that it's there.
3. Send them lots of VALUABLE CON-

TENT (we have all of this for you in your member website). If you just send them your "Introductory Deal" each time pretty quickly they stop paying attention.

4. Send them lots of feedback from your students. Share stories. Share real life turnaround stories.

By the way, as a couple of "tangents"

There's a BUNCH of new stuff on Googleplus and Facebook that has just been released. In fact, with Facebook, it's barely "beta." BOTH Change the game considerably. We'll cover them both A-Z at the Marketing Bootcamp in August. Frankly, two new updates to Facebook have shifted my perspective completely on Facebook. I've gone from very skeptical to really enthusiastic about Facebook just in the last couple of months.

Google, on the other hand, continues to "piss me off." However, in "Search," they're the 800 pound gorilla. You've got to master Google. And, Google Places just changed the game dramatically, and, they are getting ready to "rock the boat" again. We'll teach you what's new and what you must make sure you're doing right now. We'll cover it extensively at the Bootcamp.

Anyway…let me challenge you to think for a second about a friend, peer, perhaps instructor who's failing to make a living running a martial arts school. What's likely the common element?

Well I guarantee that it includes the following:

1. They are lazy about marketing and selling their lessons to their community;

2. They have many "preconceived" ideas about what will and won't work and therefore automatically discount a lot of what would work for them since they believe it won't work in their city, state, for their style, or their students, or some similar excuse.

3. They've concluded that it's just not possible to make a good living without "compromising" their art.

Two key elements of success?

Willing to invest time, energy, and money in their own education. A nearly unlimited budget for that component of their business. And, they implement quickly and aggressively.

My challenge to you…

Really dig in deeper. Never miss an Inner Circle or Peak Performers meeting. Make sure you're live on all telecoaching calls. Fully utilize personal coaching and really make sure your expectations continue to expand.

Consultation Certificate

This Certificate Entitles the Bearer to a Personal 1-on-1 Martial Arts School Business Analysis With a NAPMA-Certified Business Analyst. This Individual Consultation is Valued at $495.00.

Certificate expires 12 months from the date of purchase.
To schedule your personal business analysis, complete this form and fax to NAPMA at 1-800-795-0853; mail to 1767 Denver West Blvd., Suite A, Golden, CO 80401; or visit www.PrivateCoachingSession.com

PLEASE FILL OUT COMPLETELY AND WRITE LEGIBLY

Name _____

School Name _____

Address _____

City _____ State/Province _____

Zip _____ Country _____

Phone _____ Fax _____

E-Mail _____

_____
Authorized by Toby Milroy
Chief Operating Officer, NAPMA

3 FREE GIFTS FOR SERIOUS SCHOOL OWNERS

FREE Personal School Evaluation

Two 30-minute Sessions A sure-fire way action plan to double your results or better.

FREE Two 90-Minute Seminars

with "The Millionaire Maker Grandmaster Stephen Oliver "The 5 Stupid Mistakes All Too Many School Owners Make that Kill Their Growth" and "The Key Step-by-Step Blueprint for Being a Big Winner"

FREE CD-DVD Package and Report

"How Hundreds of Smart School Owners Like You Doubled Their Revenue in the Last 12 Months Even in the Midst of the Greatest Recession since the Great Depresson, and How You Can, Too!"

NAPMA MEMBER CASE STUDIES

RESULTS IN THEIR OWN WORDS

Still Not Convinced?

Here are Just a Few of the THOUSANDS of School Owners JUST LIKE YOU That Have Had Amazing Results from Our Program…

"Added $250,000.00 to school revenue in 12 months…!"

Dear Master Oliver,

A quick note of thanks for another excellent Boot Camp. You provided the most impressive representation of Martial Arts success I have ever seen in one place. I counted eight individuals who represented more than 60 locations. I toyed with trying to estimate their collective net worth but clearly each one of them had easily exceeded the million dollar mark.

I originally attended your Boot Camp because you are one of the rare individuals who has experienced the fortunes and pitfalls of being a multiple school operator. Now, thanks to this year's Boot Camp I was privileged in hearing, meeting, and conversing with many more. Thanks again for a truly invaluable experience.

MASTER DAVID SHIRLEY
8TH—DEGREE BLACK BELT
VILLARI'S MARTIAL ARTS CENTERS

"…from $16,000/month to $55,000/ month and still climbing!"

"My name is John Cantu. I'm an instructor out of Houston, Texas. Just outside of Houston, Texas, I have a school named Southeast Texas Martial Arts.

For the first nine months, I really just kind of relied on the program, but as soon as I settled on the program, the first three months just took off. It has created a totally different environment for me and my staff. We've now become a professional school. Our monthly was probably around the 16,000 to 18,000.

Now, we're about $50,000.00, $55,000.00 and we're still climbing. The student value or should I say the student quality has increased. Now, we really have high quality students.

Being with Master Oliver and being surrounded with so professional individuals that are heading the same direction, it's not hard to actually just move forward. Basically, just do what they say. They coach all the way through the teleconferences and everything. It's just been more than wonderful. My staff has now — has more vision of what we're going through now and we are looking to expand and all this is basically 'cause of Master Oliver's program."

MASTER JOHN CANTU, SOUTH EAST TEXAS
MARTIAL ARTS, HOUSTON, TX

"...recently went from $18,000 to $110,000+ per month in the last 12 months..."

"First of all I would like to give you my compliments on once again an outstanding Extreme Success Academy just last October in San Antonio Texas.

I couldn't think of a better two words than Extreme Success....

When we joined NAPMA about a year and a half ago we were struggling to make a turnover of about $18,000 (eighteen thousand usd) a month.

Since joining your organization, receiving your marketing packages (as maximum impact members) attending your seminars and most importantly; implementing your business systems and ideas, we are now doing well over $110,000.00 (one hundred thousand usd) turnover a month, with less effort and labour!!

This is going to be our best month ever!! Just as important, the quality of our instructors has also drastically improved as well as our student satisfaction. It is a win-win situation!! Of course you need dedicated people who believe in the value of what they are teaching. People who believe they can contribute in a positive way to people's life and have a life changing impact on their students life. However, without the proper marketing and business systems in place you will fail. It is as simple as that.

Why reinvent the wheel while so many dedicated martial artist have already learned (through trial and error) what works and what doesn't So for us, if you believe in your martial art, if you believe in the positive impact you can make on your students life, if you believe in yourself, then the only right thing to do in my opinion is to do it professionally, to do it right!

That means putting the same amount of time, effort and dedication to the business side of your martial arts school as you have done (and still do) to your martial art. That way your students benefit from a professional organization with well paid, high quality, well educated and extremely motivated instructor's.

We have therefore made the only right choice and have upgraded to inner—circle members so we can continue to improve and grow and share our experiences and learn from others. For us the core value of NAPMA and its employees and members is the vast amount of knowledge and experience they have accumulated over the years and most importantly the willingness to share it. Furthermore they are always on top of all new marketing systems that are out there and are extremely innovative.

For any martial arts school who is now struggling, there is something out there besides mere hope... It is called NAPMA! For schools doing well and would like to improve; NAPMA.!

Without NAPMA's vast contribution I would not be working full time as a Program Director at my school involved in martial art I love, making a very good income so I can provide for my family while also making a larger positive impact on more people's life.

So I thank my sifu, GM Sergio P. Iadarola for introducing our organization here in Holland to NAPMA and I wish to thank Master Oliver, Master Smith, Toby Milroy and all other staff members for your never-ending pursuit of high quality education and dedication to make all instructors, all schools and all students more successful! Can't wait till the next seminar!"

PAUL RESNICK
PROGRAM DIRECTOR/INSTRUCTOR
IWKA BV AMSTERDAM
THE NETHERLANDS

"Stephen Oliver Literally, made me a millionaire in 24 months!"

"I was at the Air Force Academy teaching karate, and I had my own commercial school, getting ready to expand and, go for it. And I heard there's this young kid up in Denver.

So I went up to Denver and they had something called a black belt graduation. Well, this is the mid age. I mean, I had no idea what a black belt graduation is. I went into a high school and there must have been 2000 people sitting there, and he was graduating maybe 20 or 25 people with black belt. And I was like wow! You know, I had never seen anything like that.

So I followed his lead and I did what he told me to. In 18 months I had 4 schools, 1200 students, and was grossing $1,000,000.00 a year in an industry where nobody in traditional karate had ever done that. It was simply because I listened to him. And after I started making a lot of money, I went back to Steve and I said, "Steve, why would you share this to me?" It was because he wanted to edify the industry. He wanted to build an industry.

And so, how do you repay a man that made you a millionaire in two years? You edify him and his teachers, and say, What can I do to help?"

Kyoshi Terry Bryan
Built 4 Schools and 1200 Students
Traditional Okinawan Karate

"...from $19,000 to $47,000.00 in 9 months."

"My name is Duane Brumitt. I own Tri—Star Martial Arts Academy in Bradley, Illinois, about 60 miles south of Chicago, and I've been a coaching client of Master Oliver's for about nine months now. And what was kind of funny was

I went to the regional boot camp earlier this year and learned a whole bunch of material, and unfortunately, I'm the type of individual that wants to have everything in place prior to actually implementing it. And being on the coaching calls with Master Oliver, he definitely helped me to take that leap of faith and to, you know, just to go for it.

And the very first month that I actually put into the practice the things that he was teaching me, my normal gross was about 19,000 on those months, and that June, that month that I actually implemented everything, I did 47,000 that month, and so the investment is peanuts compared to the money that you're going to make and the things that he's going to teach you. And so, it's absolutely and really worth it, and you'd be stupid not to do it in my opinion."

Duane Brumit
Tri—Star Martial Arts, Bradley, IL

"Instead of getting 20 leads from this activity, now I get 200 plus..."

"Mr. Oliver gave me about 4 sentences of advice which changed one of my lead strategies tremendously. Instead of getting 20 leads from this activity, now I get 200 plus. By listening to his advice, I received more leads in a week's time than I have in 4 months."

Brad Fantle, President
Tallahassee Taekwondo Academy
Martial Art Educator and Success
Coach, Tallahassee, FL 32308

"...from 40 students to now, over 1000 students..."

"We have been members of NAPMA since August of 1999 and we have made major progress since the addition of NAPMA's materials. We have been able to implement messages of the week among our three locations, with consistency, thanks to the NAPMA Words of the Week. We are able to plan events using our monthly packages. I read it as soon as it comes in the mail and I don't put it down until I have finished reading it!

The video workshops have allowed us to expand our Master's Training curriculum and we always have more exciting information to provide to our students. I enjoy the Black Belt Leadership support and use it in my team meetings.

I feel that we owe much of our continued growth to the support we receive from NAPMA and I would love to give back to the organization. I feel that the networking with other schools will be invaluable and I will never forget that we started with only 40 students on a month—to—month basis.

We would never be where we are now without the help we have received from NAPMA. We now have approximately 1000 students over our three locations in North Alabama, we teach the martial arts and Kardio Kickbox classes for the University of Huntsville in Alabama, we are currently building a 10,000 sq. foot strip mall to house my location. I would be thrilled to support other people on a similar path and keep the martial arts community thriving! If you have any questions for me or would like to discuss anything, please don't hesitate to contact me!"

KRISTEN ALEXANDER
USA FAMILY KARATE, HUNTSVILLE, AL

"I was able to grow my school to over 600 active students..."

"Over the past thirty years, I've studied with some of the best martial arts masters in the world, thinking this would help my school grow, but this was not the case. It was only after I enrolled with NAPMA eight years ago, studied their material, then applied their material each month, that I was able to grow my school to over 600 active students. I've been with NAPMA from the very beginning and I can't thank them enough. A raving fan!"

LAMON KERSEY
MR. KERSEY'S KARATE SCHOOL

"...go out and pursue our passion full time..."

"Thanks to NAPMA and the Little Ninjas program we have been able to go out and pursue our passion full time now. We have just opened a 4,000 square foot dojo and have new students enrolling daily.

Thanks for the great marketing tools."

CHRIS & TAMI SPRAGUE
PERSONAL DEVELOPMENT
INSTITUTE, INC., LINCOLN, IL

"...from 70 students to 321 and holding STRONG!"

"Hi guys, My time with you has been nothing short of great the info packs that you send out every month have been excellent, I gotten so many great ideas from you and implementing them has put my schools in the lead here my competition have not got a chance with the way the currently are doing things.

I have gone from a school of approximately 70 and I say approximately because we did not have good statistics, to a school of 321 and holding strong and expanding to larder facility I doing all this out of 1,000 sq. feet dojo, I use to charge $35 per month now, after dramatically raising my prices, I have people charging a lot less for classes a half a mile away and we are still 4 time bigger. So thank you NAPMA. Could you please send me role and duties that you think a Program director should have. We are looking to put on a Program director."

FRANK MONEA
CHIEF INSTRUCTOR KEMPO KARATE
AUSTRALIA

"1,500 Students, 1.5 Million Gross, net $400,000.00 the folks at NAPMA have helped me quite a bit!"

"My days seem to run together lately as we continue our growth. I would like to write the piece for you, but I have to see if I can budget the time to get it done.

The schools are running great and I'm busier than ever. Honestly, I'm not 100% sure how many students we have, maybe it's 1,500? My primary focus is on the dollars generated and the bottom line, which keeps getting better. Final numbers aren't in from my CPA just yet, but it looks like we'll gross around $1.5 million and net about 30%. It's truly unbelievable how awesome it is to be in this business. I could have never imagined the kind of success I've experienced over the last ten years…and the folks at NAPMA have helped me quite a bit."

JOHN BUSSARD
BUSSARD KARATE

"My student base went from 83 to more than 450 students in less than 9 months!"

"NAPMA has set me free from headaches. Each month its new ideas and marketing materials takes away all the guesswork.

With NAPMA, my student base went from 83 students to more than 450 students in less than 9 months. NAPMA showed me the way.

It's simple: follow the NAPMA guidelines, do a little cut and paste and you're on your way. Now I spend my time doing what I like to do, and do best…Teach. Experience the difference… NAPMA (speaks the truth)."

BRUCE DRAGO, MASTER DRAGO'S KARATE, READING PA

"We grew over 100 students from scratch over the first summer we opened and are now approaching 300 active martial arts students (284 today)."

"I left a very lucrative position as a Microsoft Executive to dedicate myself to martial arts. This is a career I hope to enjoy the rest of my life.

As for my commitment to NAPMA, I think we've been very dedicated for many years. As a previous co-owner of Mid—Cities Martial Arts in Bedford, Texas, I had been a member since around 1997. As I started my new school, signing up for a NAPMA membership was as fundamental as having a mat on the floor. NAPMA has been invaluable to our success.

We opened our doors here in April 2002 with 1600 square feet. By January 1, 2003 we had to double our space. We grew over 100 students from scratch over the first summer we opened and are now approaching 300 active martial arts students

(284 today). With the number of calls and walk—ins we're having today I should hit 300 this week. I'm also exploring demographics for additional school locations and even building my own facility.

We have implemented several NAPMA programs over time, i.e., Cardio Karate, UBC, EZ—Defense, FAST Defense, and are launching our Tai Chiclass this week. I took 3 employees to the World Conference. Based on our success I now have 5 paid Instructors and took 10 people to the next Conference.

Although I think I'm a pretty sharp guy, NAPMA membership has contributed significantly to our success here by showing us things that work, things that don't work, and generally stimulating our thought processes with all the articles, letters, flyers, tips and tricks about how to run a successful business. I get lots of information regarding martial arts from several other affiliations too but NAPMA is my primary source for business management issues."

Joe Turner,
Chief Instructor & President Turners Martial Arts Studios

"NAPMA was the reason why my school grew to 300 students"

My name is Korbett Miller and I own Miller's Martial Arts Academy in Kirkland, WA I recently got back with NAPMA after a couple year break. I really like what you bring to the table. NAPMA was the reason why my school grew to 300 students. The new format is great for giving really solid advice. I am interested in the Kingdom promotion that you folks are doing. I don't know if I ever got a log in for the website. Could you point me in the right direction.

Korbett Miller, Miller's Martial Arts Academy, Kirkland, WA

"We have gone from 250 students to 330 and our income went from $23,000 to $30,000 every month and this last month Jan. $41,000."

"Just wanted to let you know that since the summer convention and our many discussions things have been going much better. Jason and I applied the concept of clear and precise instructions on a daily bases.

As a result the positive aspects of marketing, retention, and good will has resulted in an increase in every area including attitude and excitement.

We have gone from 250 students to 330 and our income went from 23k to 30k every month and this last month Jan. 41k. The moral to this story for other owners is keep it simple — apply the simple rules of management each and everyday and allow the laws of compensation to work for you. Again, thank you for being there when I needed you — and I am sure it will be an ongoing relationship."

Sensei Brad Wenneberg
Fullerton Martial Arts Academy
Fullerton, California

"Added $180,000 to his school's revenue in 12 months..."

"Master Oliver,

I want to share with you a few thoughts regarding the Extraordinary Marketing Bootcamp last week. As I told you, last year I was literally blown away with the tried—and—true information you shared with us to increase our student base, our gross, our net and our market share.

Because of last years Bootcamp, my company had a major jump in quality, gross and net from last year. This year's Bootcamp was even better. I loved the way you brought in THE MASTERS of this industry so they could share their wisdom and understanding of the industry.

I also appreciated your insight in splitting the groups into Marketing and Management. So the strong schools could get stronger and the owners who wanted to have multiple schools could learn from those who have 10 to 20 successful schools. Brilliant.

Also I wanted to thank you for inviting me to your Black Belt Extravaganza in December. That gave me a completely different view of you. The only Master Oliver I knew was the one that was extraordinary in Marketing. The Black Belt Extravaganza showed me a completely different Master Oliver.

One who was truly interested in his students, his Black Belts and their success as Martial Artists. Not only do you give out great business information that has high levels of success, you are the "real deal" with your students. That's important to me, because I am in the classroom with my students as well, and I want to learn from those who can relate to me.

This industry has grown so slow and has been fragmented for so long. I believe it is because most Black Belts in Martial Arts are White Belts in business. I am glad you are sharing this information with those who really want to advance their Martial Arts business.

Ever since I returned, I have spoken to several school owners who want the low down on what the seminar was about. Are you offering the full seminar on audio and/or video format? If so, should they call you or can they purchase it from your website? I also want to purchase a set. My staff will greatly benefit.

TERRY W. BRUMLEY
PRESIDENT, TAEKWONDO UNIVERSITY

"I've gone from my daytime job, to Martial Arts FULL TIME!!"

"I have been a NAPMA member for three years (and love the material). My job as president for the NTFA involves me in trying to help our other 16 affiliate schools grow to a professional level. I have actively been helping them reach new levels for the past two years and really enjoy sharing the knowledge that I have gained through NAPMA with them.

We recently "officially" started the NAPMA Little Ninjas program. It has been fantastic. I went from five "ninjas" to currently 40 in just three months of running the program according to the manual.

Over the past three years I have slowly made the transition from working a full-time sales job while running two clubs to just doing Martial Arts full-time. With the help of NAPMA I have been able to do this.

Thank you for all of your guidance."

JOEY PERRY, JOEY PERRY'S MARTIAL ARTS ACADEMY, JONESBORO, AR

"...also reached our goal of 350 active students."

"I would be remised if I did not send a BIG thank you to the NAPMA organization.

I have been a NAPMA member for ten years and have not regretted one moment of it. NAPMA has been the industry leader when comes to innovation and change.

The program that your fine organization offers has allowed me to become a true professional martial artist. Ten years ago we implemented the Cardio Karate/Fitness Kickboxing program, which is still going strong today.

We also redesigned our preschool program to encompass the Little Ninjas curriculum. As for staff training, we use the "Way Of", ACMA Instructor Manuals and the NAPMA Staff Development programs. The audio and video/ multimedia package that I receive as a member each month has been without a doubt the greatest benefit of being a NAPMA member. The contents of this package keeps me up on the latest trends in our industry and provide excellent content for my staff meetings.

Through our membership with NAPMA we have not only achieved 15 years in the industry, but we also reached our goal of 350 active students! Thank you, NAPMA!

CHICK GAVITT
ICHIBAN KARATE STUDIO
WAKEFIELD, RI

"I am so glad I found NAPMA."

"I have just joined NAPMA in Australia and received my start up kit and I have watched your video and thoroughly enjoyed myself, it is so refreshing to find an organization with the blinkers off !!! I am so glad I found NAPMA and I just wanted to touch base and say well done!"

HUGH BURNS
SUCCESS SELF DEFENSE
BRISBANE, AUSTRALIA

"9–1/2 years as a NAPMA member and I still get excited with my packages!"

"I want to congratulate and thank NAPMA for an awesome monthly package in April and May. I know that you have to vary the content since NAPMA members come from different styles and backgrounds yet you guys catered directly to my interest these last two months with Kathy Longs reality based self de-fense and Danny Driggs functional training.

Oh and let's not forget the champions reunion.

I was amazed to see the similarities between Kathy's techniques and attitude towards a street situation and the way I was taught kung fu. I have taken Kathy's class at the NAPMA conference before yet I had never seen her self defense. I am showing the video in all my teen and adults classes to my students to show them how a aggressive a women should be when encountered in a street altercation.

I also loved Danny Driggs MMA fitness drills. That is what I've been doing for approximately 4 years in my XFT class when my kickboxing class started to die off. I'm a student for life and truly appreciate what NAPMA is doing. I know that some people enjoy the traditional one step self defense and the old fitness kickboxing and you will continue to satisfy all your members yet I wanted you guys to know how much I learned, enjoyed and used the packages in the last two months. Keep up the great work and give us more on this. 9 1/2 years as a NAPMA member and I still get excited with my packages."

JULIO ANTA (CPT/KBC)
HUNG GAR KUNG FU MASTER
ANTA'S FITNESS AND SELF DEFENSE

"You and your organization have revolutionized the martial arts industry."

"Dear NAPMA, I personally feel that you and your organization have revolutionized the martial arts industry, and I think being a member of NAPMA is a wonderful value for all school owners. You guys are good. Once again, I just wanted to share my thoughts. No need to respond. Keep up the good work."

LANCE FARRELL, FARRELLS USA MARTIAL ARTS AND FITNESS

"...from less than 50 students, to today I have close to 250."

"Dear NAPMA,

I've been a member for several years now. When I first joined NAPMA I had less than 50 students, today I have close to 250! I think NAPMA is a great organization and is a great window into the professional martial arts industry for those of us who live far from the US.

The style of martial arts I teach is called Zen—Do Kickboxing. Zen—Do Bahrain is probably the largest school in the Middle East. I teach children from as young as three years. Our oldest student is a 57—year—old grandmother!

My membership has been worth every penny. Thank you for making it such a great success."

SUHAIL G. ALGOSAIBI
HEAD INSTRUCTOR AND FOUNDING
DIRECTOR, ZEN—DO BAHRAIN

"He's helped double our gross. It's really been paying off."

"I've been a coaching member with Stephen Oliver for about one year now and the biggest thing I'd like to mention was my fear of getting into the coaching program and thinking, "My gosh, it's not cheap. Am I going to see my return?"

His key is retention, just like in his schools. If he's going to want to keep his coaching clients, he's got to make sure that he's making you earn some money. And he's been doing that for us. That's obvious. He's helped double our gross. It's really been paying off."

DUNCAN RICHARDSON
ACADEMY OF WORLD TAE KWAN DO BOISE,
ID

"I would not have been able to go full—time without the many ideas and motivation I have received from NAPMA."

"I am a full—time martial arts instructor and have been teaching on my own for 12 years. I would not have been able to go full—time without the many ideas and motivation I have received from NAPMA. I owe it all to your organization. By contributing to the monthly package, I truly feel I have given something back to the organization I owe so much to."

RAFFI A. DEDERIAN, DEDERIAN ACADEMY
OF MARTIAL ARTS

"The Little Ninjas Program has probably been the biggest benefit to our school."

"I would have to say that the Little Ninjas Program has probably been the biggest benefit to our school. This is our third year in our area and we have parents begging to get into our program. We always have a waiting list for this. The next biggest benefit would have to be the Random Acts of Kindness program. I have implemented this into the karate kids aged students as part of their Black Belt Training and they have to have at least four journal entries per month. Mandatory.

If they do participate doing their part to make kindness effortless then they lose their hard earned stripes. I am determined to do my part in making this a better world. I also have to say another huge benefit are the brochures and cards to choose from I use them every day in some way. The posters are awesome too.

Our biggest developmental need at our school is probably the lack of excitement in our students learning katas. I try to make it interesting having competitions in class etc. I think they still don't totally understand the importance even though I tell them quite often!! I would also like to develop excitement for a demonstration team.

Thank you in your interest in my opinions you all are awesome and have helped me to get where I am today.

GEER PATRICK
2ND—DEGREE BLACK BELT
LOW COUNTRY KARATE, LLC

"If you are not yet a member of NAPMA (National Association of Professional Martial Artists) I highly recommend you become one."

"If you are not yet a member of NAPMA (National Association of Professional Martial Artists) I highly recommend you become one. They were kind enough to bless me with a sample package of what they have to offer and it's already been a tremendous help to me. I'm currently organizing a martial arts program for the local community college with hope that it will be offered this January, NAPMA will be the first tool I obtain to help me maintain the program once it's operational."

JASON HUNT, SHINJA MARTIAL ARTS

"From 0 to over 300 students in our first year"

"We moved to Santa Barbara where we knew one person and opened up a studio. We decided that it would be a good idea to go to the NAPMA convention and pick up a few ideas. What we found were programs that we could use to build and manage our business, an experienced, professional, helpful NAPMA staff, and other successful martial arts business owners that were happy to share their ideas on how to make a business grow.

We've been in business now for a little over a year, have over 300 students and we're still growing. For over 30 years I've kept my martial arts "sword" sharp by daily training, now I keep my business "sword" sharp with NAPMA. Thank you NAPMA. We couldn't have done it without you.

DAVE WHEATON, PRESIDENT
HAPKIDO INTERNATIONAL

"I briefly cancelled my membership to NAPMA but soon realized how big a mistake I had made."

"Dear NAPMA Team,

I briefly cancelled my membership to NAPMA but soon realized how big a mistake I had made by canceling. I am now a member once again, I reactivated my membership yesterday.

NAPMA helps me to not only increase my profits each time without fail, but also serves as a monthly motivational tool for all areas of my life. I would like to thank the NAPMA team and take this opportunity to congratuladte you on a truly excellent service."

DANILO DUSOSWA
KERRY REGION KARATE SCHOOLS IRELAND

"We doubled our tuition on a monthly basis and more than tripled our cash flow and gross revenue."

"I own three Tae Kwon Do—based schools and I've been working with Master Oliver for about three months. My initial hesitation was not so much whether or not the investment would be worth it, but whether or not I could fit it into our cash flow because our schools always had a really strapped budget.

But I gathered my courage, took the leap and

the first three months went like this: the 1st month I got all of the information, the second month I learned about it, and the third month I implemented it. That third month, we doubled our tuition on a monthly basis and more than tripled our cash flow and gross revenue. Just in December of 2004, I've tripled the amount of money that I'll pay to Master Oliver in the whole year of 2005, just in one month."

SCOTT MANNING
S J MANNING'S FAMILY TAE KWON DO
TERRE HAUTE, IN

"Don't sign up for this program unless you're ready to achieve phenomenal success!"

"WOW, what is Master Stephen Oliver's Mastermind & Coaching program worth? Well with ideas and help of Master Oliver and his unlimited knowledge we will likely quadruple our gross at each of four locations. The mastermind work, the personalized help have made such an amazing difference for us! I would recommend this program to anyone wishing to do the martial arts business right! It is truly the difference between feast and famine!"

MASTER ART MASON
6TH—DAN BLACK BELT HON SANG MU
SA HAPKIDO, FOUNDER, THE PEACEFUL
WARRIORS' MARTIAL ARTS INSTITUTE

"Your monthly support materials are worth 10 times what you charge (maybe I shouldn't say that)."

"First of all, I would like to thank you and NAPMA for your help. When my wife and I decided to open a martial arts school, we had practically no business experience. With your monthly business tips, eye—catching ad material, and video support, we've grown by leaps and bounds.

When we first joined NAPMA, we had approximately 25 students and were teaching in an old television repair shop out of the city limits. Both my wife and myself were working full—time jobs plus running our school full time.

We were years ahead in offering any type of cardio karate in this area, because we took NAPMA's advice. This was one of the things that allowed us to more than double our enrollment and be able to move to a better location. I was also in the first group who was ACMA certified. Not only did this give me local publicity, but it also enhanced my teaching techniques.

At the NAPMA World Conference, I was introduced to Krav Maga. My wife and myself traveled to California and went through the Krav Maga instructor program. I go to CA several times a year now to train. Krav Maga has not only enriched our training, but it has enabled us to double adult student enrollment by adding an exciting, to—the—point style of self—defense.

We cannot begin to thank you enough for helping build the backbone of our dojo. We now have a student base of 130, and have recently expanded our school to double the size with a bigger lobby, smoothie bar, and a second classroom currently under construction. This is now our full—time job. Our plan is to be at 200 students within this year.

Your monthly support materials are worth 10 times what you charge (maybe I shouldn't say that). Not only would they help a school just starting out, but also help existing schools by adding new ideas and maintaining retention."

MARK MYERS, MYERS FAMILY KARATE
CENTER, LLC, HAMMOND, LA

"I joined NAPMA because their advice made sense and didn't compromise the integrity of my art."

"I teach traditional karate—do. I joined the National Association of Professional Martial Artists because their advice made sense and didn't compromise the integrity of my art or my position as a teacher.

NAPMA is about education and raising the standards of professionalism in the martial arts. For a few dollars a day, I've hired a prolific team of graphic artists, marketing experts, martial arts business consultants and researchers that have helped me become financially independent and have allowed me to pursue the essence of karate without selling out. If you're passionate about teaching the martial arts,

NAPMA membership is an absolute must."

BRAD JONES
TRADITIONAL SHOTOKAN KARATE
TRAINING, BRAD JONES KARATE DO AND
FITNESS TRAINING CENTRE
NEWMARKET, ON, CANADA

"I did the best thing in my life:"

"I became a NAPMA member. Before I become a NAPMA member, my wife and I struggled every month and had a lot of problems. I did the best thing in my Life: became a NAPMA Member. Things changed fast since I've been a member (I think I am now in year 4), and in the first month I had over $2,000 more income, and in these bad times it was coming in the right moment.

Now after these years and two Conventions — I cannot believe why I was not a member of NAPMA earlier. I opened my first school in 1990, bought a bigger one to impress others (my greatest failure) in 1994. But in the past four years I am growing constantly. My active student count is 281 in my first school (population in my town 3700). In October 2003, I opened my second location five miles away with 90 active students.

My wife Claudia and I manage the schools. We have three full—timers and have, after starting the G.O.L.D. Team (thanks to NAPMA), 14 part—timers (everyone is doing his job for free).

Last week I received this month package and it's one of the best I ever held in my hand. From the great bonus ad to the DVD. There is so much material inside. Awesome job!"

OLIVER DREXLER, 5TH—EGREE BLACK
BELT, TAE KWON DO, GERMANY

"You have helped me grow into a successful business with two studios, five recreations centers, over 450 students and 11 instructors."

"I wanted to express my satisfaction with the NAPMA product and what it has done for my business. For ten years I worked out of recreation centers and sports clubs. NAPMA helped me transition from a part time karate teacher to a full time karate school owner.

The programs that I currently use in my school, from self—defense to business software, have come to me through ideas from NAPMA conventions or from articles in MAPRO.

I have been in business for 17 years and a NAPMA member for the past nine years I can proudly report that you have helped me grow into a successful business with two studios, five recreations centers, over 450 students and 11 instructors.

I appreciate all that you have done and continue to do to help me with my growing business."

KEN KLOTZ
KLOTZ INSTITUTE OF KARATE

"We have over 550 active members and 7 satellite locations. Thank you NAPMA!"

"Since 1997 NAPMA has had a tremendous impact on how we run our martial arts business. They have given us many tools to implement. In turn, this has helped us to elevate the professionalism of our staff, the amount of students we teach, and the quality of the programs we offer. Now in our 10th year of operation we have over 550 active members and seven satellite locations. Thank you NAPMA!"

STEVE STEWART, SSMMA FAMILY FITNESS CENTER, CANADA

"...have been to many seminars and meetings over the years and I must say this one tops them all!!!"

"Hi Toby,

I think the meeting was fantastic also. I have been to many seminars and meetings over the years and I must say this one tops them all!!!

I received lots of information from the group and feel I walked away with a group of new friends. I think we have a great group that will work very well together.

I am very Impressed with your wealth of knowledge. It would be great to have someone with your knowledge hang out at my school for awhile...

I am already driving Kathy (my partner) crazy with the aggressive changes. I can see this year being our best in terms of organizing the office, profit increases and improving the student service. I am looking forward to working with the group.

I think I walked away with ton questions and ideas. Now I just have to prioritize all of them and put a plan together to implement. I am looking forward to talking with you in the one on one.

Thank you for the upcoming successful year,"

CHUCK CRONE — MASTER INSTRUCTOR — CRONE'S TAE KWON DO SCHOOL

..."gained 100 students in 100 days — I now have 400 students!"

"My NAPMA membership has influenced my business enough that it changed my standard of living. Seven years ago I received my NAPMA package announcing a new program — Fitness Kickboxing. I followed the video, instructions and marketing ideas.

I launched my program and gained 100 students in 100 days. My program grew to 400 students and is at that level today! I currently have a NAPMA after—school program, a Little Ninjas program and a Padded Weapons program; and I am looking forward to starting a Tai Chi program. It just takes one monthly package, one idea…!

I would like to thank NAPMA for providing me with the information, marketing tools, education and programs that took my school from 150 students 600 students. I attribute my success to the content and service of NAPMA and lots of hard work. I have looked at many so— called "marketing packages" throughout the years and none compare with the content of the NAPMA package. I've reviewed all the "me, too" and slick—looking packages but none contained the professionalism and information that helped me grow my business to what it is today. Beware of the wolves in sheep's clothing!"

CHARLIE FOXMAN
MIDWEST MARTIAL ARTS

..."from 3 students to 123 paying students."

"I would like to thank you for all the support that NAPMA has gave me and is still giving me. I brought my school from three students to 123 paying students in less than a year, without a sign in the out side of the school, with no advertising, and no money to do so.

I couldn't have done it without the coaching of your great organization. I am really grateful and happy that there is an entity that is worry about bringing your school to the next level. I was a National Champion, but I didn't know how to pass my knowledge to the students and thanks to NAPMA and its stuff I learned how to be an effective instructor."

HENDER ALVARADO
GOLD HENDER MARTIAL ARTS

"...grew to over 300 students."

"The best thing about NAPMA is that it has helped me realize the value of martial arts training. It was over 10 years ago that I quit my full time job in nursing to open my school. I'm glad I was insightful enough to join NAPMA six months before I even opened the doors! NAPMA has been there with me from the beginning — from how to choose a location, to systems for tracing enrollments and retention, to special events, and really effective "NON—BLACK BELT EYES" ads.

NAPMA has been there with me, every step of the way, as I completed an expansion literally doubling my mat space.

But best of all, NAPMA encouraged me to truly value the character development skills I teach and to price the training accordingly. Without that encouragement, I'm sure I couldn't be where I am today. NAPMA is great at helping school owners to do their best because NAPMA is the BEST!"

DIANE REEVE, OWNE
VISION MARTIAL ARTS CENTER
PLANO, TEXAS

"...become so excited, that I "kick" myself for having ever left."

"Dear NAPMA,
After belonging to NAPMA for several years, I decided that I no longer needed the tips, advice, and sounding board that offered me more training, teaching, and administrative ideas that I thought I could ever use. After ending my membership, NAPMA could have simply went on its way and left me to my own devices.

Fortunately, I continued to receive NAPMA's Martial Arts Professional Magazine month after month even though I had ended my monthly membership. I continued to read and ingest what was presented in this martial arts trade journal, and finally came to the realization that I needed to get "back on the saddle" and continue to push hard for my students and instructors by keeping the lines of communication and education open.

In short, we recently signed up again and have become so excited, that I "kick" myself for having ever left.

If it wasn't for the continued mailings, ever increasing quality, and true spirit of martial arts that NAPMA has emulated, I might still be struggling to find the answers, new goals, and increasing questions that any school owner has. I feel that, in a way, we have gotten back on the horse and are ready to ride to future successes with the ever—present education and leadership that NAPMA seems to stand for. Thanks, NAPMA for being there for us! We will be at the NAPMA World Conference and any Regional Seminar we can get our hands (and feet) on. I sincerely believe that NAPMA affects more school owners then it is aware of."

JIM SAUTEL
MOO SUL KWAN MARTIAL ARTS
INSTITUTE, COLORADO

"NAPMA has been the single most beneficial organization I have joined ever."

"NAPMA has been the single most beneficial organization I have joined ever and through my association with you I've learned what I was doing wrong in the "early years" that kept me at such a small number of students, and with addition of NAPMA, two things have just exploded for us this year. We're at 200 active and growing by leaps and bounds. We project to be well over 225 by year's end.

My strong points are leadership and curriculum development as well as copywriting and advertising. Thank you for everything and I await your response,

JAMES THEROS, LEVEL 10 MARTIAL ART

"We were up $10,000 in November and are already up $7,000 in December.

"I am a diehard NAPMA fan. In the last 12 months, NAPMA has given me and my school ideas and plans that really cannot be fully equated to $$. Just to list a few things that we have done:

We have begun the NAPMA padded weapons program with unbelievable success. We have begun the NAPMA Little Ninja's program and it has been excellent as well. In November we had our first one—day holiday sale ever and grossed over $4,000.00 in retail sales. We did more retail sales in November and December than the previous year. So the one—day sale was just a bonus!

In December we had our first ever Holiday Party/Dinner featuring the demo team and awards for everything I could think of under the sun. This party alone fired up the entire school so much that we picked up 11 students from referrals in the week following the party.

In my 9 community education schools I implemented portions of the theme—based curriculum

with phenomenal success. We have already signed 26 kids from the program (out of 171 possible) to 1—year or 3—year programs. The best I have ever converted with these programs is 17 kids last year.

We were up $10,000.00 in November and are already up $7,000.00 in December for month end and I have 2 weeks left! If only my stock portfolio was doing this well <grin>."

JEFF DUNCAN
FARMINGTON MARTIAL ARTS

"I know that joining NAPMA is one of the best investments I have ever made."

"I just want to say thanks for contacting me about NAPMA and its benefits. I've started applying the marketing ideas and improving some of my programs to benefit better the students and the center. The book is a great source of information and has given me a better understanding of the martial arts industry. I know that joining NAPMA is one of the best investments I have ever made."

JAMES ISLER, CHIEF INSTRUCTOR
AMERICAN MARTIAL ARTS TRAINING
CENTER, EUFAULA, AL

"...my personal income is well over $100,000.00 per yea, I look forward to coming to work each day/"

"Hats off to NAPMA! Plan your work and work your plan! Starting with 60 students and most of their tuition already cashed out, bartered, or late the school had a gross income of a whopping $6,000 per month!

As an immediate call to action I pulled a secret weapon out from under my sleeve...my action plan. I got to work right away by applying all that I learned from my mentors at NAPMA. In martial arts we generally learn stances first to establish a strong foundation to build up to learning the basics. The first six months was stance training!

The curriculum was burned and revamped to suit the needs of a modern martial art student from children to adults and no I did not sell out or comprise the integrity of my style! I got to work on getting my rear in gear with personal development such as goal setting and time management. The belt ranking system was enhanced to keep students motivated. I could not even afford to pay myself yet I hired my program director, now my lovely fiancé. I didn't know where the money would come from I just figured her work would generate cash flow which it did, by the way did I mention that I was living out of a spare locker room in the school! The basics where added on with a renewed pro shop, Christmas sales, movie nights, belt award ceremonies, low cost marketing strategies, leadership team, picnics, black belt club, masters club.

A lot of these things we had in place already but there is an enormous difference in doing things and doing things right. Six months later the school was generating cash flow and it was time to keep statistics. The monthly total gross now up to double digits before the comma $13,284.89! Growing to 182 students later that year I moved the school to a new location, $12,922.19 then $16,498.64 monthly gross, I built a monster and it was growing. Year two the monthly gross peaked to $25,760.44 and I was drawing a paycheck and had long moved out of my locker room sleeping days. Each year I attended the NAPMA World Conference and return for the next round of rolling up my sleeves and getting busy.

Long story short my school grosses on average $23,651.24, my personal income is well over $100,000.00 per year and I look forward to coming to work each day, I love what I do! I now have disability insurance, life insurance, health insurance, IRA's, an increasing net worth, $0 Debt and it has

only been 3 ½ years later. I enjoy my involvement in our community, I get to train 2 hours per day in my martial arts just in my personal practice before classes start in the morning, not to mention positively impacting the lives of others all day long. I continue to utilize my NAPMA knowledge applying as much as I can from each package.

Most importantly, and here is where I shed a tear, is that NAPMA has elevated my life to a higher level of growth, development and personal achievement. My success personally and professionally is a direct result my NAPMA membership. This has been a nice stroll down memory lane and I thank you NAPMA for making it all possible. Oh, sure. I could have perhaps done it without them but I am positive it would have been a heck of a lot longer and harder, a heck of a lot!

Daniel Rominski,
Olympic Karate Institute

"Before NAPMA I averaged around $150,000 per year, after I joined my sales went thru the roof to over $1,000,000 a year."

"I first joined NAPMA a few years after I opened my school in Houston Tx. Bear Creek Tae Kwon Do & Kid Fit Sports Camps. Before NAPMA I averaged around 150k per year, after I joined my sales went thru the roof to over 1,000,000 a year, in only a few years. Without NAPMA I would have never reached such a huge goal.

Not only did it teach me how to grow, but how to grow it correctly and retain what I had. I have also been able to take a lot of what I learned into other businesses. When I got out of the martial arts business after almost 2 decades I had realized that NAPMA was one of the biggest reasons for my success and will always remind myself that. So thank you .

Thank you for your time feel free to contact me at anytime."

MASTER JAMES T. STOVAL

"You provide an invaluable service."

"A great big thank you to the staff at NAPMA for your willingness to help and answer the questions that I might have. Finding new students has been challenging during the first 6 months of 2005 so I called NAPMA with questions about ideas that I might use to bring new people in the door.

After being in business for 26 years we had tried many things over the years to bring in new students but for one reason or other some of those things weren't working for us so we need to find the little thing that we are not doing right to turn these efforts into successes or be reminded of the things that we are no longer using that we should try again.

The staff have always been helpful in helping me find the little thing that I might be missing. You provide an invaluable service. Keep up the wonderful work!"

FRED NICKLAUS
MARTIAL ARTS AMERICA, LA CROSSE WI

"...our enrollment increased by 200 students."

"I became aware of NAPMA many years ago when I was training at B.C. Yu Martial Arts Center in Ann Arbor, MI. I owned and operated my own ad agency at the time. I was also helping Grandmaster Yu run his school, acting as Program Manager, but without the formal title. I was enrolling students, teaching, cleaning the school and training. I have been a loyal student with B.C. Yu for 24 years — and still training.

Soon after that, Master Yu joined NAPMA. He was so excited about the organization and how professional they were. He knew his school could benefit by having such a great organization to help martial arts school owners run the business end – efficiently, and effectively. And it worked! By following NAPMA's lead, our enrollment increased by 200 students that year.

We received monthly tapes, used the newsletter materials, and followed the lead of the NAPMA tutorials. It was a big step. The marketing materials were professional and easy to use. They made a big impact on our marketing efforts. Even with my many years of graphic design and advertising background, I realized the benefit of using the NAPMA materials by not having to start from scratch. It saved a lot of time, work and money.

While at the conference, I spoke to a school owner who told me "When you open your own school, just treat the students as you would guests in your home. Treat people with respect, teach them, be pleasant and courteous, and give them your best. You will be successful."

I joined NAPMA immediately and used their flyers to get new students. My first 2,000 flyers went out, and by January of 2000, I had enrolled 150 more kickboxing and TKD students. It was working!

The next three years I attended the world conferences and became more inspired each year, bringing back at least one new idea that I incorporated. There was so much to learn and so many new ideas to implement, it was too much for one person to do. So if I incorporated one new idea, and did it the right way, it made a difference. Whether it was new sparring drills, new children's programs, or a new seminar guest to invite to our school, I wanted it to be a success.

Through NAPMA, I learned how to teach exciting classes, how to motivate, inspire and teach with a sincere smile and warm heart — but with strength and discipline. I learned about the true value of martial arts instructors and how we make such a positive impact on people's lives. I learned that we need to believe in the value of our work by charging accordingly. I learned how to enroll and keep students. I learned to improve the kickboxing classes. I learned about and incorporated UBC into my curriculum. I learned that little kids are great students and how to teach them with the Little Ninjas program.

Anything worth having takes extremely hard work and effort. Every goal we set takes planning, timing, help and support from experts in the field we are in. And that's what NAPMA gave me; the knowledge, experience, support and encouragement to continue to reach success in my school.

My goal is to teach people to be their personal best — physically, mentally and spiritually through martial arts fitness. I had to be the role model and see aid believe in the value I was bringing to the students. NAPMA helped me to see that — and helped me to continue and reach out to others in the same position. To learn from others successes – and failures. Thank you, to all the wonderful martial arts professionals who make up NAPMA, for helping me to reach the goal of having my own school. You ROCK!!"

> PAT COLE
> OWNER AND MASTER INSTRUCTOR
> COLE MARTIAL ARTS CENTER, LLC

"...because I was honored as BUSINESS MAN OF THE YEAR in a very influential newspaper in our region."

"I have been a member of NAPMA for a long time, and I have learned a great deal thanks to NAPMA and its core leaders, such as you! And I just wanted to let you know a couple of things. First this past summer I co-organized a fund raiser for St. Jude Children's Research Hospital with a student and friend, through the martial arts and our family based school we were able to raise over 8,000 dollars.

I never dreamed of reaching such a number, but we all forged on and the numbers kept rising. It was truly a magical undertaking with an amazing result. Our even brought people together, families together, which ultimately brought the community together for one day! WOW! We also, as a school, pulled together and raised clothes, toys, and other essential necessities. We filled over 100 Leaf bags and boxes. Not to mention the combined efforts of our school and the local Chamber of Commerce, we had developed an adopt—a—soldier program that we ran for six months sending various necessities over seas to help our courageous soldiers to show them that we care and to say we are thinking of them. They were very honored and offered many letters of thanks.

The reason I am telling you all of this is because I was honored as BUSINESS MAN OF THE YEAR in a very influential newspaper in our region. I was totally shocked and surprised myself, but my phones are ringing from others commending me on this prestigious award. And I want to thank NAPMA for giving me the tools to succeed in my school and in the ways of business.

> ANDREW STIGLIANO
> OWNER/CHIEF INSTRUCTOR
> UNITED MARTIAL ARTS CENTER

"For the wealth of information you get from NAPMA, makes it well worth the money."

"My name is Henry Hyde; I am a 5th—Degree Black Belt in Tae Kwon Do, and owner of Hyde Tae Kwon Do Inc. I have been a NAPMA member since 1999. When I first heard of NAPMA, I wasn't interested in joining. I felt I didn't need someone to tell me how to run my school. Boy, was I wrong. I was a very traditional instructor and just wanted to teach Tae Kwon Do. Long story short, I joined NAPMA.

Since being with NAPMA, I now teach Grappling, Judo and Kickboxing. I have also been certified in CDT (Control Direction Takedown). I currently have 16 Black Belts under me and every month I share the NAPMA information with my instructors. My retention rate is very high, which I am very proud of. For the wealth of information you get from NAPMA, makes it well worth the money. I would encourage any school owner to join. It would be the best business decision you ever make. In today's martial art world, one must have business savvy, in addition to extensive techniques to teach in order to thrive and not just survive. NAPMA puts you in that arena.

I would like to thank NAPMA for putting together a great organization for all Martial Artists,"
MASTER HENRY D. HYDE

"Not only have I been able to QUIT my Security Job of more than 12 years to teach full time, but I have also found that people understand that you get what you pay for."

"When I opened my school a year ago, my family and I had a dream. We knew it would be hard but with work and determination anything is possible. A year later, we have 90 students and are grossing over $5,500 a month. Some people said that a Martial Arts School would never be anything but a Part Time Hobby. That if you charge more than $45.00 a month, students will find somewhere cheaper to train. Not only have I been able to QUIT my Security Job of more than 12 years to teach full time, but I have also found that people understand that you get what you pay for. I am proud to say that because of NAPMA, I can finally live my dream. Because of NAPMA I have time to spend with my children and wife(something I could not do before, because I worked at night). I had sustained a severe Knee injury 10 years ago. Ever since than I have had a constant battle with my weight. I am now on the road to complete recovery. With the time that I have extra, I am able to focus on my training everyday. I have lost 25 pounds and have 55 to go. If it wasn't for NAPMA, I would only have the time to go to seminars and training camps. Now I can TAKE BACK my life and become a

ROBERT STAPLES
STAPLES MARTIAL ARTS

""I doubled the size of my school in two months...from 123 to 254 active."

"On January 1, 2002 our active enrollment was 123 students. With the help of NAPMA's Little Ninjas preschool program and the Ultimate Body Shaping Course, I grew my school to 254 students by the end of February 2002. The momentum continued with 35 new students that March. My school leaped to the next level and the momentum has driven us to even greater successes."

Not only does it give each Little Ninja something to focus on every day, but it also gives him a reward each day. It also causes the instructor to focus on each child individually each day instead of looking at them as just a sea of eyes and bodies. They focus on individuals. The Little Ninjas program creates a special moment for each student every day.

Comments: I have tried the business of martial arts and with a management company. I must say that my livelihood is much better with the company helping me out. I have been a NAPMA member and have attended all their seminars and conventions. I went from a 200—student school to a 400—student school since joining with them. I must say I sleep better at night not having to worry about every little detail that goes on.

My classes are better now that I am constantly motivated. I don't need to pick my own brain now that I have professional consultants and people to network from. The entire NAPMA staff is the most professional in this field. But don't take my word on it ask any NAPMA member and I'm sure they would say the same!

Our summer slowdown (if you can call it that) lasted exactly 1 month. September is going to be a wild one as well. We should be at 300 students at the very latest by the end of October and are on track for 350 — 400 by the end of the year....

I've gotten such a response for Ninjas that I've added a second evening group that is already filled (I split them into low and high belts) and am starting morning Ninjas and Pre—Ninjas in two weeks. We're still working on improvements and additions to the system and it's showing. Let the games begin.

If I hadn't started Fitness Kickboxing I'd still be working a job. If I hadn't started Little Ninjas and the UBC I'd still be just getting by. I became a member before I even opened the doors to my school and I'm thankful that I did. Without the great new ideas and help from NAPMA I know all this wouldn't have happened! Thank you NAPMA!"

KEITH WILKES
FEAR KNOT MARTIAL ARTS

"We've become one of the most respected schools in our community... thanks NAPMA."

"Thanks to our membership in NAPMA, we are exposed to the techniques of the most successful businesses in our industry, allowing us to be the beneficiaries of what they have learned both artistically and financially. I am proud to be surrounded by such elite, professional teachers and businessmen in a very exciting period in our field and to be a part of this growing and evolving industry that is earning the prestige it deserves.

I also want to extend my gratitude to NAPMA for helping Perfect Balance Martial Arts and Fitness to become one of the most respected schools in our community and allowing us to be able to coach, teach Martial Arts and transform lives while living our dreams.

The medical profession has the AMA, the legal profession the ABA, and the Martial Artist has NAPMA. It certifies our quality as professional teachers and helps us realize our value and worth to an ever—expanding client base."

MASTER AL AGON
PERFECT BALANCE MARTIAL ARTS AND FITNESS, CORAL GABLES, FL

ELIZABETHTOWN, PA

"...from having approximately 60 active students to now over 200 active students, and still growing!"

"NAPMA has been a great source of strength for my school and myself. The Annual World Conference has always left my wife and myself hungering for more of what NAPMA has to offer us. The monthly package is something that we look forward to eagerly! Why? Because we both know how much NAPMA has done to improve our business.

We became NAPMA members after being members of another organization for many years. During the time with this other organization, our school would climb a little and then sink back down. Needless to say, we were growing very frustrated. No one was helping us. Then we heard about NAPMA. We left that other organization, found a new billing company and became NAPMA members. Since joining NAPMA we have left our old location, which was approximately 1,000 sq. feet and opened up in a prime new location with 3,000 sq. feet and have been there for over 2 years now. Our numbers have also increased! We went from having approximately 60 active students to now over 200 active students, and still growing!

We have also enjoyed belonging to the NAPMA listserv, which is a great resource! And we have learned so much from all the wonderful people we have been able to network with through this medium. Because of this, we have even started doing our own in—house billing which has been great, thanks to all the help and advice we have received through this list.

From almost Day 1 with NAPMA we have always felt like we were part of a family! People with NAPMA are REAL people who are always there to help us.

We cannot say enough about NAPMA and the wonderful things NAPMA has done for our school. "

ROBERT M. CHESTER
EAST COAST MARTIAL ARTS CENTER
GROTON, CT

"...my school has brought in more than a million dollars because of NAPMA

"NAPMA has had a very positive influence on my school. It has provided my school with resources for good advertising and marketing strategies. In particular, it has helped both our children's and Cardio—Kickboxing programs to grow tremendously. I also received audio and video resources that sharpened my staff's management and Martial Arts skills.

I would say that my school has brought in more than a million dollars because of NAPMA's supplements. NAPMA has taught me that you do not have to have a big school or chain of school to be successful. In fact, I am very confident that my school in the basement was the one of the most profitable schools in the nation for that size. I think all of this happened because NAPMA has provided my school with the advantages I need to be a successful and professional martial artist.

As a former NAPMA regional director, I have had a unique perspective on the martial arts world. I have witnessed that the majority of martial arts schools go out of business within only a few short years of being open. If they survive those first few years, many of them barely make enough to pay for their living expense. This is not necessarily because the instructors are not good at their art. In fact, most of these schools fail because of a lack of necessary management skills.

NAPMA helps schools to form a strong management foundation. It supplements your school with advertising information, training videos, audiotapes, and essential articles to learn to manage correctly. These supplements, if used properly, increase your chances of becoming a highly successful school."

SAM AN, ROCKFORD ACADEMY OF
TAE KWON DO , ROCKFORD, IL

"...from 60 students to 180, and my DREAM House thanks to NAPMA."

"Two years ago, I decided to start teaching karate on my own and I joined NAPMA. I started with 60 students, teaching for the Stratford Recreation Dept. Since then, I started two more programs at the town of Orange and the Valley YMCA in Ansonia.

I now have my own business teaching full—time and have 180 quality students! I bought my dream house six months ago and I'm the happiest I've ever been. Joining NAPMA helped me a lot! I have 3 huge Little Ninjas programs

I received my ACMA certification, and I have started a GOLD team to start creating future instructors. I use NAPMA's ads in my fliers, which are sent out to schools in the towns that I teach. I use many of the drills and business/marketing ideas that I get from my NAPMA packages every month. I currently have 5 instructors working for me. My business is growing faster than I ever imagined! Thanks NAPMA for helping me become a professional martial arts instructor."

Chris Sansonetti
Stratford Rec. Karate
Milford, CT

"The NAPMA kits you send out monthly are a godsend to schools both small and large."

"I wanted to drop you a line to tell you what a fantastic job you and your staff have done so far to renew my faith and interest in NAPMA. I as well as many of the martial artists I know agree that you have taken what I consider to be a cancerous organism and have not only cured it, but have literally breathed new life and excitement into it.

The NAPMA kits you send out monthly are a godsend to schools both small and large. I am a direct response marketer and dojo owner and have for the last eight years helped to produce a perennial top ten infomercial, which is an industry leader and top performer.

Having said that — I have never held much faith in print. But to be honest, your creative staff have, month in and month out, created emotive copy and striking graphics that has changed my whole perspective on print advertising. The functionality of your print interface is very good and easy to navigate.

Your audio CD series is innovative and informative and the rest of the package is top notch as well. All of these kudos point to the kind of visionary leadership backed by a strong support team that was needed to honorably rekindle my faith and TRUST in NAPMA.

I thank you all for the hard work you have done to reach this point and look with interest to the future of marketing and networking in the martial arts — NAPMA."

Grandmaster Kevin Huunjin Cullen

"My NAPMA membership has changed my vision..."

"I opened my first studio at the age of 21. My vision was to teach martial arts as a hobby while I pursued a career in law enforcement. I never realized that martial arts could be a serious profession (let alone a profitable one).

When I connected with the people at NAPMA, I learned that becoming a professional martial arts studio owner was more than just a daydream. They taught me how to run a professional studio, integrate new and exciting programs and turn my vision into reality.

I currently have a dedicated program that includes grappling and kickboxing with alternative upgrade programs such Black Belt Club, Masters Class and Leadership training.

My vision has changed, my studio has grown and my way of life has improved dramatically...I went from part time hobby, to full time enjoyment!

Shane G. Weaver
Senior Instructor/Owner
Red Griffin Martial Arts Studio
Canada

"...from running a school part time to become a full time martial artist!"

"My name is Mike Fillmore and I was one of NAPMA's original members in '95. At that time I was a part—time martial artist with lots of talent and no business sense.

Since then I have learned so much from my relationship with NAPMA that I have gone from running a school part time to become a full time martial artist! It was difficult at first because I got all of this information but I had a mentor that was steeped in the "Old Way" of doing things and as a result it stunted my growth..

As the years went by NAPMA gave me a vision and even more than that through the seminars of Joe Lewis and Ernie Reyes and others I developed the confidence to go out and "JUST DO IT". At this point and time I am doing better than I ever have before and I am only a few inches away from the brass ring

I have taken this knowledge and have mentored many of my students in their own efforts and as a result five schools have spawned from this inspiration.

I am fired up and fearless at this point and I look forward to working with others to bring the martial arts to the next level. I want to see martial artists have the same if not even more prestige than doctors, lawyers and politicians in the community. It is my wish that I could be a representative of NAPMA on the state level because I am one of those people who went from nothing to something in this business as a direct result of NAPMA. I run Ultimate Force Martial Arts in Stafford, Texas and I would be Proud to represent the NSSN."

MIKE FILLMORE
ULTIMATE CHALLENGE TAEKWONDO

"…help myself promote my school more effectively, better and to be able to get more students and up my student body…"

"Hi my name is Mark McGee and I'm from Unlimited Success in Allen, Texas and the reason I joined the Inner Circle group was to help myself promote my school more effectively, better and to be able to get more students and up my student body. What I've taken away from this weekend is to better market my school.

That is my main goal. I have poor marketing so I want to make sure that I get into more magazines of different levels, not just penny magazines, but also higher level magazines. Make sure that I get more lead generation and therefore get the numbers of people coming into my school to make it better. We have a decent conversion ratio now, that's another section that I'm going to work on the next time. So over the next 90 days better marketing, better lead generation, double, triple my efforts for that.

MARK MCGEE
UNLIMITED SUCCESS MARTIAL ARTS

""Just wanted to say "thank you" for all you do for the industry and what I gain from it personally."

"Just wanted to say "thank you" for all you do for the industry and what I gain from it personally.

I know I'm not the most vocal NAPMA member but I still listen to as much as I can and implement as many ideas as I can. The audio from your special Quantum Leap presentation was very inspiring and prompted this message. I LOVED it!

You described my former approach to the "art" of JKD to a tee!

I also wanted to commend you for the Brass Balls Factor you displayed in your recent "anti—MMA" cover story. As usual you're correct and it was the best expression of my own thoughts I've seen.

Down here in Miami (65% Hispanic) you can imagine how MMA "dominates". So I'm strategically working on attracting the contrarian remainder in our community who think differently through our websites and direct mail reactivation efforts.

DWIGHT WOODS

"NAPMA stands at the forefront of the industry, forging new ways of looking at things and developing new ideas."

"I have always been motivated more by ethics than by money and NAPMA has, for the five years in which I have been a member, been honest, forthright, direct and ethical in all its actions.

You have never been afraid to speak out where necessary and to break established paradigms in favor of a better way of doing things for the students.

NAPMA stands at the forefront of the industry, forging new ways of looking at things and developing new ideas concerning all aspects of running a professional martial arts school. My experiences tell me that NAPMA has always been motivated by what is best for the industry and has consistently provided excellent service to its customers.

Dr. Chris Dewey
Starkville Martial Arts Academy

"...proof, however, that it's possible to run a successful Martial Arts business, especially in the remotely populated Highlands of Scotland."

"I joined NAPMA in April 2006 when my organization's billing company: NEST Management, became the NAPMA UK representative.

As you no doubt know, unlike the US, the vast majority of Martial Arts schools here in the UK are conducted in sports and community centres

Again, unlike the US, there are few Professional (self-employed) Martial Arts instructors in the UK, sadly many Martial Artists don't agree with making a living from Martial Arts. This attitude stems from the Martial Arts 'amateur club' mentality.

I am proof, however, that it's possible to run a successful Martial Arts business, especially in the remotely populated Highlands of Scotland. It wasn't easy in the early days since I had to change our organization from an amateur club and make many other syllabus, structure, and billing changes such as having students pay a small fee per class to a much larger monthly fee via Direct Debit (EFT).

I would like to take this opportunity to publicly thank NAPMA for their assistance in enabling me to make a living from teaching Martial Arts! Keep up the great work I thoroughly enjoy my monthly NAPMA business boosts!

Kyoshi Neil Hourston,
Scottish Kempo Academy
Tain, Scotland

"...you surround yourself with a group of people who are committed to making a difference..."

"I'm Michael Mertens, from Buffalo, New York. You know, this weekend has been a great opportunity for me. You know, I always look forward to the opportunity to network with other people in the industry. You know, it's a good reminder to keep your head on straight.

A lot of stuff going on in the economy right now on recession, but you surround yourself with a group of other people who are committed to making a difference to still growing their business, to overcoming any kind of challenges in front of you, and then of course, a lot of resources for new information, which is always helpful.

I think the main thing that I want to bring back to our staff and all of our schools is just the concept that okay, during the recession, maybe the print ads, maybe the media stuff, that's not working as well as it used to. But the one thing that's going to always work well is going to be that belly-to-belly, face-to-face contact, and that's something that we have resources for in our schools. But, you know, to really go back and get fired up about it. Hey, we know we've got great services. We know we've got great classes. We just need to get in front of people, show them what we do, connect with them about how beneficial our service can be, and they're going to still get involved. I mean, that was a good message to hear and a good reminder to take back to my team."

MICHAEL MERTENS
MASTER CHONGS TAEKWONDO
BUFFALO NEW YORK
5 LOCATIONS, 2,000 STUDENTS

"NAPMA has allowed me to compete and be successful in the modern martial arts industry without sacrificing the integrity of my traditional martial arts."

"Since joining NAPMA in 1996, my schools have risen to the next level. Running a multi—school operation can be hectic, but fresh ideas and quality support from the entire NAPMA staff has allowed my organization to experience continuous growth. NAPMA has allowed me to compete and be successful in the modern martial arts industry without sacrificing the integrity of my traditional martial arts."

ROGER A. JARRETT
PRESIDENT AND CHIEF INSTRUCTOR
USA MARTIAL ARTS FEDERATION

"...not just educational, but motivational as well..."

"Oh, it was a great experience. You get to rub elbows with some of the top business leaders in the industry and open your mind to new ways of thinking. And Master Oliver brought up a great point. In today's economy, your knowledge is going to be very important and I like to gain as much knowledge about the industry as I can. I came away with a lot of great ideas so it was a fantastic experience. Just the ideals of marketing, retention, staff training, all the vital areas to be successful, and I got great ideals from each speaker.

It was also motivational as well, not just educational, but it was also motivational as well.

I think the thing that separates the people that do real well to the people that just get by or the people that are struggling is that people that do well is they find out everything they can about the industry. They know the industry inside and out of their knowledge and putting that knowledge to use has been their key to success. So you get here to see it. They've been there, done it, and that's the best way to learn."

HILARY SANDOVAL
AMERICAS BEST KARATE CENTER
EL PASO, TX
22 YEAR VETERAN MARTIAL ARTS
SCHOOL OWNER

"...you know they say, if you keep doing the same things and expect different results, it's not working..."

"I'm Troy Dorsey. Well, I really wanted to be a part of a group of people, a group of students and business owners that will take me to the next level. I've been kind of stuck at the same level for a couple of years now, just kind of being what I call on the karate treadmill, just been doing a — I'll have some great months then I'll have some not so good months and just kind of jumping up and down anywhere between 8 and $10,000 and this seemed like a fit for me to help me reach some new levels.

And I've not done anything in quite some time

and not really committed to anything I guess is what I should say, but I've committed to this both financially and every other way too to really make a change.

At my school, I teach most of all the classes. I'm open six days a week and I teach five days a week, and I'm interested in doing that, but it's just taking so much time away from my family and I really want to do something that will be able to change what I'm doing in my school. I've been doing the same thing for 20 years and I want to stay keep doing the same thing and expecting different results, and that's just — it's not working. So I want to make a change."

TROY DORSEY
8-TIME WORLD CHAMPION KICKBOXER

"I am already seeing the results of the Peak Performers group."

"I just wanted to thank you for a copy of "Think and Grow Rich". It was a pleasant surprise receiving it in the mail yesterday. I think it's a great time to re—read it. I am already seeing the results of the Peak Performers group.

May was our best month ever and I am hoping to see even better results in the following months. The information I got off the forum has helped greatly and I am learning from everyone on it. I am starting to allocate time each day to write or respond on the forum. The future is looking great!"

SENSEI TIM ROSANELLI
MAXIMUM IMPACT KARATE

"UP 40%!"

"I AM ON TRACK! My enrollment hit 310 yesterday, which was my June 1st goal! I set income and enrollment goals last year for this year. I have been blowing past my financial goals (which were based on about 33% growth, even though I was steady between.

I have had a very strong financial year. My YTD goal was $215,887; but, in fact, I hit $261,584! That's 20% over goal! Last year (for the first 5 months), I had made only $185,899, which is 40% growth!!!

Thank you guys so much for your help! For the first time I can remember, students asked to upgrade. Very empowering.

I've learned—that despite the unexpected—Stephen Oliver and Dan Kennedy were right in their predictions I raised my prices, increased my volume and closing rates, decreased complaints about money and students are upgrading into even more expensive programs, even when consumer confidence is supposedly low.

WOW! This is cool! Thanks again, guys. You have been a support and inspiration."

JONATHAN METCALF
ENFIELD, CT

"I am projecting $1.15 Million..."

"My number is still growing, and I am projecting 1.15 M for this year. I will let you know exact number early next year. I have seen that NAPMA has been doing lots of changing and improving.

NAPMA is always helpful to improve my Martial arts school in business and my teaching skills since the first day of joining. Inner Circle Meeting has been extremely helpful, and all members are very open minded and eager to work together.

Again thank you for your help and all the great work in NAPMA, and I wish you and NAPMA continuously grow in the future. I will see you in July at the Inner Circle meeting."

JASON YI
NAPMA INNER CIRCLE MEMBER
WOODBRIDGE, VA

Consultation Certificate

This Certificate Entitles the Bearer to a Personal 1-on-1 Martial Arts School Business Analysis With a NAPMA-Certified Business Analyst. This Individual Consultation is Valued at $495.00.

Certificate expires 12 months from the date of purchase.
To schedule your personal business analysis, complete this form and fax to NAPMA at 1-800-795-0853; mail to 1767 Denver West Blvd., Suite A, Golden, CO 80401; or visit www.PrivateCoachingSession.com

PLEASE FILL OUT COMPLETELY AND WRITE LEGIBLY

Name _____

School Name _____

Address _____

City _____ State/Province _____

Zip _____ Country _____

Phone _____ Fax _____

E-Mail _____

_____
Authorized by Toby Milroy
Chief Operating Officer, NAPMA

3 FREE GIFTS FOR SERIOUS SCHOOL OWNERS

FREE Personal School Evaluation	**FREE** Two 90-Minute Seminars	**FREE** CD-DVD Package and Report
Two 30-minute Sessions A sure-fire way action plan to double your results or better.	with **"The Millionaire Maker Grandmaster Stephen Oliver** "The 5 Stupid Mistakes All Too Many School Owners Make that Kill Their Growth" and "The Key Step-by-Step Blueprint for Being a Big Winner"	**"How Hundreds of Smart School Owners Like You Doubled Their Revenue in the Last 12 Months** Even in the Midst of the Greatest Recession since the Great Depresson, and How You Can, Too!"

Critique Certificate

This certificate entitles the bearer to submit a single printed marketing piece, brochure, post card, flyer, direct-mail piece, advertisement or similar promotional material, by mail, for critique by Stephen Oliver.

Send Certificate and Material to:
Stephen Oliver, NAPMA—Marketing Critique
1767 Denver West Blvd., Suite A, Golden, CO 80401

(Please include your FULL contact information, including E-Mail address)

Terms and Conditions:
Certificate expires 12 months from date of purchase. Allow 2 to 4 weeks for Mr. Oliver's response. Consultation materials accepted by mail only. Actual finished materials or planned copy or designs may be submitted. Only 1 critique per client per product purchased is allowed. Certificate redeemable for only listed services. Additional consulting may be contracted for, subject to Mr. Oliver's schedule; fees available on request.

Please be advised that any materials submitted for review, included those submitted with this certificate, may be published as examples of publications authored or edited by NAPMA or Stephen Oliver. Submitted materials will NOT be returned. Do NOT submit materials you are concerned about keeping private.

NAPMA
NATIONAL ASSOCIATION OF PROFESSIONAL MARTIAL ARTISTS

$1297.00 VALUE

$1297.00 VALUE

87944514R00161

Made in the USA
Columbia, SC
31 January 2018